COLLECTING MYSELF
A Writer's Retrospective

SCHOLARS PRESS
Studies in the Humanities

COLLECTING MYSELF
A Writer's Retrospective

by

A. Roy Eckardt

edited by
Alice L. Eckardt
with Norman J. Girardot
and Harriet L. Parmet

Scholars Press
Atlanta, Georgia

COLLECTING MYSELF
A Writer's Retrospective

by

A. Roy Eckardt

Cover design by A. Roy Eckardt

Library of Congress Cataloging in Publication Data
Eckardt, A. Roy (Arthur Roy), 1918–
  Collecting myself: a writer's retrospective/ by A. Roy Eckardt;
edited by Alice L. Eckardt with Norman Girardot and Harriet Parmet.
    p. cm. — (Scholars Press studies in the humanities; no. 19)
  Papers originally published 1936–1992.
  Includes bibliographical references and index.
  ISBN 1–55540–898–2 (alk. paper)
  1. Philosophical theology. 2. Christian life—Methodist authors.
I. Eckardt, Alice.   II. Girardot, N. J.   III. Parmet, Harriet.
IV. Title.   V. Series.
BT55.E35   1993
230'.76—dc20   93–28414
                                            CIP

Printed in the United States of America
on acid-free paper

In Memory of

JUSTUS BUCHLER (1914-1991)

and

For Members of

THE AMERICAN ACADEMY OF RELIGION

I think if you write long enough you will be a healthy person.

—Alice Walker

This God, who is an idea only, can perhaps persuade and inspire; but He surely cannot succor, love, and forgive...

If the decision of faith is on the same level as other possible decisions, man makes God's sovereignty or even His existence depend on his belief in, or acceptance of, Him. This is the final heresy. The distinctive nature of the decision of faith is that it is at the same time no decision at all, because in accepting God's sovereignty man realizes that he accepts that to which he is subject regardless of his decision.

—Emil L. Fackenheim

Every writer is engaged in ontology—the nature of being, why we are here, what is the meaning of life. And in that sense every writer is a rabbi.

—Cynthia Ozick

Artists cannot be choosers; they have to do the work that wants to be done by them, not the work that sensible people think they ought to do.

—Edward L. Galligan

Contents

Editor's Foreword

Alice L. Eckardt

My husband Roy Eckardt believes that the critical analysis of words and ideas is decisive within a scholar's literary and teaching contribution. He attributes much of this concern to his training in philosophy. In the course of chapter nine of this book he says, "I write—that's who I am—or that's what I *do* (the two are *one* are they not?)." Accordingly, the volume essentially involves a critical survey and reconsideration of Eckardt's thought and written work over a period approaching fifty years. He barely touches on his private life, even though these areas mean a great deal to him. I am present by virtue of our collaborative effort through the years. Nor are all of Eckardt's ideas fully represented in the present collection, with special reference to his more recent thinking.[1] (For a full listing, see "Author Writings" at the end of this work.)

I have been part of Roy Eckardt's life during all the time of his writing, and have read and evaluated early drafts of all his work, at least until later years when my own teaching, lecturing, and writing have rather precluded this.[2] On the present occasion of studying this book in manuscript form, I am particularly struck by the measure of my husband's self-criticisms and by his readiness still to revise and even repudiate some of his earlier thinking—in some instances I disagree with the criticisms and new affirmations (for example, of Jesus' resurrection)—as well as to acknowledge what he calls "nagging incoherences" respecting the competing norms of intellectuality, spirituality, and ethics.[3]

During our life together we have shared a deep concern about how Christian society (including the church) has used its intellectual ascendancy and theological dominance, stemming from and in conjunction with its political

---

[1]   Among the excluded materials are a number of articles and editorials directed to colleagues in the university teaching of religion, together with an essay on the animals, a particular interest and concern of his.

[2]   A major exception is the rewriting of *Long Night's Journey Into Day* with its new subtitle: *A Revised Retrospective on the Holocaust*, an effort that was primarily mine.

[3]   For author's comments at this last point, see the end of chapter eight.

power, to demean, castigate, and persecute the Jewish minority within its province.[4] Involved here is an entrenched ideology and theology about Jews and Judaism that is passed on from generation to generation (sometimes quite unthinkingly) and from one part of the Christian world to distant outreaches where, even though the church itself is only a minority community, it is yet capable of disseminating anti-Judaic and even antisemitic teachings. However, I must not lead readers to conclude that Eckardt's work is either entirely, or even primarily, about Christian-Jewish relations. This is said or implied about him all too frequently, in ways perhaps not free of an intention to dismiss his work as marginal or even irrelevant. What is primary in so much of his writing is his criticism of Christianity for its absolutist claims, bound up as these are with theological anti-Judaism. Thus his own self-image is simply one of a writer who believes that the question of right and wrong is crucial to responsible Christian literary effort. I would reenforce that evaluation: Eckardt is incensed by injustice. Consequently a more accurate assessment would identify him as (a) an original thinker who has never abandoned his own Christian faith, although he has consistently criticized Christian thought where it has, in his view, gone astray by attempting to encapsulate God in human dogma and thus restrict God's love and concern to its own community; (b) an individual who is primarily concerned with (at times even obsessed with) issues or morality/immorality,[5] including the possible immorality or irresponsibility of God;[6] and (c) a philosopher-theologian who is ready to fault the most salient doctrine should it

---

[4]   To be sure, not only Jews have suffered from Christian absolutist thinking and restrictive policies; Africans, Native Americans, Orientals, and Muslims have all had their own experiences of Christian imperialism and intolerance. Yet Jews have been the primary victims of Christendom.

[5]   See Eckardt's reference to this element with respect to antisemitism in chapter one. This same moral concern and outrage led him to deal early on (chapter three) and in later years more extensively with the evils of racism, i.e., hostility to Blacks, and also anti-womanism. (Examples from this later period are found in chapters seven and eight, and more extensively in a few of his later books.)

[6]   An early reference to the question of God's faithfulness to Israel versus a "trial of God" over the divine unfaithfulness is to be found in chapter three, section II. Eckardt was to continue to wrestle with this question over the years.

lead to human suffering and injustice. In this sense he is a child of the Social Gospel movement in its more mature and openminded stage (as I am also).[7]

It was Eckardt's prior concern for truth and justice that brought him to acknowledge and attempt to deal with Christian anti-Judaism and antisemitism in his doctoral research and first book (see chapter two, sections I-V) and repeatedly brought him back to these same issues through much—though by no means all—of his later writings. Yet, ironically, Eckardt comments at the start of chapter two that he finds himself more critical of or dissatisfied with this aspect of his work than with others. His overall contribution is much broader than a concern with Christian-Jewish issues, as shown by a thorough reading of this book. (But note that only one of the three afterwords focuses on the wider and deeper dimensions of Eckardt's writings.)

My husband's later turn to the theme of comedy/humor (broadly conceived) and its relationship to moral and religious questions (particularly the issue of radical evil) has, in fact, been a long time in coming. This subject has in recent years captured the interest of an ever-growing group of scholars beyond those who practice the vocation of being humorous. Eckardt prefaces one of his earlier books, *The Theologian at Work*, with the statement, "theology must stay open to the longings and ponderings of new generations. It has to come to grips with options entirely different from its own, particularly the contentions of those many human beings for whom theological affirmation is nonsense." Eckardt is now beginning to explore the possibility of creative links between nonsense and theology, theology and nonsense.

While the present volume set out to be a final retrospective upon the author's work as he concluded that endeavor, it has already been made incomplete by his new and continuing efforts.

Few persons can be a John or Robert Kennedy, or a Martin Luther King, Jr., with their verbal power and dynamic presence to inspire individuals and crowds. Others are given the power of the written word, the effects of which are always difficult to gauge. My husband has been granted this second kind of gift.

---

[7]   The American teaching of equality of and for all regardless of race, creed, or nationality was certainly so imbedded in each of us that we saw it as entirely consistent with Roy's and my religious upbringing in the Methodist Churches. Hence our shock when we discovered that this affirmation was anything but crucial during most of the history of the churches.

Foreword

Norman Girardot and Harriet Parmet

We dedicate this foreword to A. Roy Eckardt on the 75th anniversary of his birth, August 8, 1918. Eckardt has said that he wishes to be known primarily and simply as a "writer." These collected essays eloquently testify to his success in that calling. Indeed one suspects that he would largely ratify Samuel Beckett's observation that "writing is not something: it is the thing itself." For other writers, such a simple self-identification says all that needs to be said and all that can be said about the art and agony of anyone dedicated to the scribbler's life. But a ritual occasion such as this requires that we remember and honor Eckardt by writing what a true writer often chooses not to write. We therefore acknowledge Roy Eckardt the Writer, the Leader, the Professor, the Theologian, the Philosopher, the Scholar, whose passion and fierce dedication to justice have given birth (as author, editor, or collaborator) to some fifteen books and many dozens of articles.

The Roy Eckardt we knew at Lehigh University was, in addition, a dedicated and spirited teacher who influenced several generations of students and colleagues, a successful academic administrator who developed the Department of Religion Studies at an institution known more for engineers than ethicists, a visionary co-founder and past president of an organization's brand new version, the American Academy of Religion, and the innovative first editor of the Journal of that body. The task of a leader is to translate his loyalties and commitments into viable programs and to orchestrate them into unified, concrete and cohesive courses of action. Thus our colleague was the pioneering figure along with his wife and intellectual partner, Alice Eckardt, in the creation of Christian-Jewish studies and Holocaust studies as vital new fields of scholarly interest and humane concerns. All this, we hasten to note, is but a partial litany of Roy Eckardt's accomplishments at Lehigh University and within the worldwide academic study of religion.

We would be remiss if we did not draw attention as well to Eckardt's deceptively mild-mannered demeanor—that is, his quietly unabashed—and at times (in a writerly and deadpan way) mischievous—wit and humor. For those of us who have known and worked with Roy at his home institution, we take special pride and pleasure then in memorializing this book of his collected writings in the name of our distinguished colleague, treasured friend, wise author, and theologically provocative humorist. At the end of this ritual inscription, let it be said—as Job and Voltaire knew so well—that God is mostly "a comedian playing to an audience that is afraid to laugh." As Eckardt himself has written, God may be, after all is said and written, "a comic who is free to do the best she can." Happy is the institution, happy the generations who have been fortunate to have known this man for all these years. And we his colleagues smile along with him in this his 75th year.

Norman Girardot
Professor, Department of Religion Studies,
Lehigh University

Harriet Parmet
Senior Lecturer, Department of Modern Foreign Languages
Lehigh University

September 19, 1993

Author's Preface

The name of this book, *Collecting Myself*, is half mine and half someone else's. In assigning the title *Collecting Himself* to a compilation of James Thurber's writings, the editor Michael J. Rosen says that he intends something akin to "composing himself," in other words, Thurber's idiosyncratic genre of literary composition. But I rather have in mind positioning myself—trying to apprehend a little better what I have been doing over a professional lifetime. However, I should wish to go beyond Elie Wiesel's assigning of but a single motivation to the (hasidic) storyteller: "to tell of himself while telling of others" (*Souls on Fire*). I hope that the present exercise won't be all that self-centered. For it is my aim to tell a story that does not finally depend upon a single person. I am merely trying to add a few passages to one of the lively and significant chapters of recent and contemporary American intellectual-religious history.

A. ROY ECKARDT

Lehigh University
Bethlehem, Pennsylvania,
United States
    and
Centre for Postgraduate Hebrew Studies,
University of Oxford,
United Kingdom

1
Originations, Pre-1944

Human life is the gathering of memories.

As we grow old, a complication develops: The more recent past becomes blurred and distant, while the further past stays relatively clear and close.

Death is when we run out of memories.

Alice Walker supplies the first of this book's four epigraphs: "I think if you write long enough you will be a healthy person." The notion "long enough" is conveniently ambiguous. It may point to the considerable time needed to develop the healthiness Walker describes. But it may also be saying that the available or proper time is coming to an end. I have the second meaning particularly in mind.

I

The volume before the reader comprises an encounter with certain ideas that are contained in a discrete body of writings, an *oeuvre*. This particular work may perhaps be treated as a kind of literary memoir or, alternately, a historiographic memoir. I construe my books and occasional publications as together falling under the rubric of *haute vulgarisation,* in the strictly French connotation of that phrase. And I should like to characterize my literary/life experience in its entirety as a kind of journey toward humanization. (But I seek always to keep in my consciousness, if not my conscience, that "university professors of religion" are not exactly an endangered, much less indispensable, species.)

I venture here to provide a descriptive and evaluative retrospective upon my publications, viewing them (with a measure of objectivity) in the context of particular recent and current ideas and ideologies. I reckon historically, critically, and systematically with (sympathetically put) the development of my thinking and (more negatively put) the vagaries of that thought from early years through the present, the whole set against the background of certain philosophic and theologic trends. The period covered is somewhat over fifty-five years— from 1936, when I started in college and began, without knowing it, to prepare for my life's work, through the early 1990s.

To the end of readying the present volume I undertook the task—not always pleasurable, sometimes tedious, at places a bit confusing—of re-studying all my published writings. I endeavor to support and fill out this new effort by reproducing representative essays of mine (and two small pieces of verse) over the years. Some of the essays are slightly emended from the originals but only for purposes of clarity. I have let stand for the reader's own assessment various judgments and data within the essays that I should myself now question and even reject (including recurrently sexist language, particularly in connection with the earlier years). Again, certain passages in the essays are clearly dated. By no means are all my writings separately commented upon or covered. Some duplication of figure and content creeps into the whole. I have not weeded out all such; the pedagogic people tell us that repetition, so often a vice, can have its virtuous side.

The book is thus not an autobiography in the exact or dictionary sense. In traditional autobiography a subject's ideas are treated as just one facet of his or her life-experience as a whole. In this volume the opposite is the case: Experiences and life events are subordinated to thinking. Chapter one and passages elsewhere of a more or less personal sort are given a place only in order to set various intellectual or literary stages, or for explanation's sake. It would be hard to compose a responsible account of an individual's intellectual fortunes while excluding all personal details or variables.

Self-assurance has never been a strong suit of mine—or, perhaps more accurately, whatever self-assurance I have managed to garner through the years, aided by manifold good fortune, has been counteracted by continuing and nagging self-doubt. This condition may help account for the fact that I have always felt a little awkward in talking about myself as a person. I also have a certain *Tendenz* toward intermittent depression—evidently, in my case, an inherited proclivity. I mention all this for its bearing upon my tendency toward self-criticism but also upon the partially polemical and sardonic emphases within my outlook and contribution, especially in earlier and less mellow years—not that the polemics and the sardonicism are thereby emptied of all legitimacy.

Withal, there are major objective reasons for being critical of one's own ideas as of everything else about oneself: (1) Ideas and belief-systems can have and do have destructive consequences. (2) No one is God—other than God (granted that God is God). None of us is a very good God—or even a very good god. Needless to say, self-criticism never attains onto fully objective truth; no human individual can reach the latter goal. Self-criticism is not disinterested criticism. And it is not necessarily free of dubious motives. Nor need it be devoid of self-approbation. Readers will quickly note that some of my own self-evaluations have a way of emerging as self-praise or at least as self-justification. I suppose the only legitimation of this is that self-criticism become self-denunciation is not an authentic assessment of the self but is instead its destruction.

A great deal in my thought and writing does not belong only to me; my wife Alice Eliza (nee Lyons) shares in it. We have together composed and published many pieces, including two books. I am not able to state categorically where either person's point of view takes up or leaves off. I am only assured of two things: My wife is largely responsible for whatever good there is in the things we have done together; and she cannot be held responsible for any of her husband's errors, shortcomings, or sins. Nor are the two of us always in agreement. One major ongoing difference between us has to do with the resurrection of Jesus.

All in all, that a human being should, in a sense, reveal himself by camouflaging himself behind his thinking and the critique of that thinking is not without psychological, perhaps psychoanalytic, import.

II

I was born and raised in Brooklyn. Brooklyn is the American Gentile's Israel. True, many Jews live in Brooklyn, but they don't *need* Brooklyn the way the rest of us do. Why not? They already have the *real* Israel, what might be called Israel's Israel. We who are no more than poor Gentiles at least have an American Israel. That place is Brooklyn. To live outside Brooklyn is to live in *galut*, exile. This explains why when the Brooklyn Dodgers left for Los Angeles, they did not simply "leave" Brooklyn. They *betrayed* Brooklyn. And Brooklyn has never been the same since. It has never really recovered from that act of apostasy.

In the Autumn of 1936 I enrolled in the Brooklyn College evening session. In exchange for fifty cents a year (a semester?) library fee and a pittance for second-hand textbooks, and as a resident of Brooklyn, I was presented with a first-class liberal education—and, as things were to turn out, an eminently practical one—with a major in philosophy. (I had first considered mathematics, then political science.) As part of the City University of New York, Brooklyn College today charges tuition; this old graduate naturally finds that practice lamentable. For the only reason I ever entered Brooklyn College was that, as a friend had informed me, it didn't cost anything. You may not believe this, but it is literally true. I had no other reason or justification to go to college. If the Great Depression had hammered one thing into our heads it was: Always take advantage of something if it's free. (From 1929 to 1941 my father could not find steady work.) I had absolutely no notion of what college was to be about or what it would mean to my future; in my family it was unheard of for anyone even to *think* of going to college. I was to be led into a wholly new and wondrous dimension of life, discovering along the way that while I was not a genius, I had been blessed with a fairly good ability to think critically and even sometimes constructively.

With the exception of my final year I attended college at night, working full time for seven years as a clerk and outside salesperson at a manufacturer and wholesaler of surgical instruments, Fred Haslam & Company, now defunct. (The advertisement in the *Brooklyn Eagle* had read, "Young man wanted in Christian establishment." Little did I realize the actual intent of these words: "If you are Jewish, don't bother to apply." For that matter, young women were not to apply either. In those days the wording that Haslam used was entirely legal.)

As an undergraduate I was most influenced by Justus Buchler and philosophic positivism and empiricism. Buchler's courses in general philosophy and in logic opened for me a whole universe of critical intellectuality. I would say to myself, Wouldn't it be great to be like Buchler and to do what he does! I was also influenced by other teachers: H. Van Rensselaer Wilson and his Spinozist persuasions; Edward Fenlon and his Thomism; and John Pickett Turner and his Santayanist convictions. (An obituary of Justus Buchler from *The New York Times* is found at the end of this chapter.)

Next I worked my way through a graduate theological degree at the Divinity School of Yale University (with additional aid from funds that my late brother had left). Among teachers who had an impact upon me at this stage were H. Richard Niebuhr, Roland H. Bainton, Liston Pope, and Robert L. Calhoun. Finally, with the goal of university teaching now firmly in mind, I pursued a doctorate in the general field of philosophy at Columbia University, in conjunction with Union Theological Seminary. (This last extended beyond the period of the present chapter, involving as it did the years 1944-1947.) At this juncture, beyond half-time work of my own, my wife became my primary support, financially as in every other way. Upon graduation from Oberlin College she joined the staff of TIME-LIFE, and would later have surely been running much of their show had not such events intervened as our move to Minnesota and points Midwest, where I was to begin teaching. At Columbia/Union I was most influenced by Reinhold Niebuhr. Of lesser but important effect were Paul J. Tillich, John Herman Randall, Horace L. Friess, and Herbert W. Schneider.

I have never really abandoned or been able to surmount a considerably philosophic stance or *modus operandi*. Save for one year, professional philosophy has not been the primary way I have earned a living. But I do tend to think in philosophic ways. I construe philosophy as the general existential-critical effort to make sense of things, the critical element entailing, indeed demanding, rational-moral self-criticism along with other levels of criticism. To me, philosophy stands basically for existential coherence, for structure —although our sorties toward structure do not have to pretend onto complete systems. During the time I was to serve as editor of *The Journal of the American Academy of Religion*,[1] we listed on our style sheet a watchword for would-be contributors: "The god we serve is consistency." Of course, the watchword had only to do with literary construction and usage. But ought not the same standard apply to all thought? However, this does not have to mean a

---

[1]   This journal was founded in 1933 as *The Journal of Bible and Religion*. In 1967 we changed the name to the present one.

failure to allow for or to honor the prodigiously paradoxical and ambiguous elements in the human world. In a word, I see philosophy as the general, existential quest for truth and meaning, a quest that does its best to be coherent yet cannot help but concede or work with the great incoherences of life, and a quest that is, accordingly, tempered and balanced by historical experience.

This overall philosophic outlook has served a special predisposition of mine: a desire for order or, more psychologically put, a penchant for methodicalness. Also, one advantage, so to speak, a philosopher has over a theologian is that the philosopher is not liable to a religious body or power that may subject the thinker to heteronomous pressures. I rather like Emil L. Fackenheim's judgment that philosophy entails a "search for truth in which all remnants of apologetics are cast aside."[2] The philosopher is, of course, responsible to an intellectual community, which primarily means (in my particular situation) the university. However, I have always done theological work along with philosophic work —which brings up the fat question of whether I have actually managed to hang on to my fondness for the norms of consistency and coherence. As will be evident in subsequent pages, I continue to think of myself as a member of the Christian community, though perforce a critical one. I do not pretend to have overcome in my work all the conflicts that may obtain between philosophy and theology.

III

My reference to membership in the Christian community points to influences upon me other than intellectualist ones. Coincident with the foregoing educational whirl have been experiences of a moral and religious sort.

A prevailing influence upon me was my mother. She was constitutionally and regularly incensed by all instances of human injustice and unfairness. She was to me growing up what Amos, Hosea, and Jeremiah have been to many, including me in my youth and ever since.

In my teens I became involved in young people's activities in the local Methodist Episcopal church (as Methodist churches then identified themselves) and also in the national Methodist youth movement. As heirs and practitioners

---

[2]   Emil L. Fackenheim, Preface to Michael L. Morgan, ed., *The Jewish Thought of Emil Fackenheim: A Reader* (Detroit: Wayne State University Press, 1987), p. 7.

of the Christian Social Gospel, we young people of the 1930s saw fit to busy ourselves with "building the Kingdom of God" right here on earth. We never did make it—for reasons made plain to me only later. Yet certain facets of liberal Christianity have always stayed with me, such as distaste for the dogma according to which only Christians are or can be "saved." For us in those times, the issue of "salvation" was pretty much assimilated and subjected to Christian moral, social, and political obligation. This explains why while at Brooklyn College I was anything but enthusiastic with the program of an undergraduate Christian Bible club, which operated under the assumption that it had to "save" all the Jewish students (and by implication all other non-Christians). By contrast, I was being taught in my own local congregation that the religious problems that count are those that involve human problems—such things as world hunger, war, racism, and the rights of those who labor. The liberal Methodism I knew was simply devoid of the supersessionism vis-à-vis Jews and Judaism that has through the centuries plagued Christianity as a whole. Believe it or not, it was only after I started working upon my doctoral dissertation that I learned there was such a reality as Christian antisemitism. This was after leaving the Yale Divinity School armed with a graduate theological degree! Ignorance can sometimes be genuinely blissful. But my mentors at Yale and elsewhere had surely been deficient in not making plain the anti-Jewish aspects of the Christian tradition. The only excuse I can think of for them is that they may not have been educated in the facts either, or had somehow repressed the facts.

I have remained in the Methodist Church (today the United Methodist Church, so named by virtue of having devoured the much smaller Evangelical United Brethren Church in 1968).[3] I was ordained into the Methodist ministry, becoming a member of the Minnesota Conference, transferring to the Wisconsin Conference, and then moving to the New York East Conference, now the New York Conference.

To bring this introductory chapter together, my interests and contribution were to come to focus within the trialectic of philosophic, theological, and

---

[3]   The least we could have done was to take some such name as Methodist Brethren. The way matters stand, all that is left of the E.U.B. name is the generic and inconsequential word "United." Church mergers, like industrial takeovers, often smack of imperialism much more than of Christian compassion or even equality. Of course, today the name "Brethren" would be dismissed as sexist.

political ethics—more simply, in the dialectic of reason (especially the moral reason) and faith.[4] I ended up a kind of theological ethicist or political theologian, but one who is ever open to and subject to philosophic criteria and effort. The major professional influences upon me have been of two kinds, and as such they are anything but unusual or spectacular: the demands of critical thinking, and the demands of moral judgment and responsibility. These injunctions constitute, of course, the two pillars of any *moral philosophy*. They were to play equal roles in my life.

Unanswered here but yet begging for an answer is the question, What is the difference, if there is one, between moral philosophy as such and Christian moral philosophy? All my work has centered and continues to center upon a singular issue: Is there a way to be religious—Christian, in my case—and still be *unqualifiedly* a morally responsible human being?

----

[4]   In a review of Richard Kroner's 1959 volume, *Speculation and Revelation in the Age of Christian Philosophy*, I was to ask whether it is possible to be a Christian philosopher without being a theologian in disguise, and whether Christian philosophy possesses independent significance within the domain of faith. I suggested that whoever takes seriously Kroner's argumentation may very well answer yes to these questions.

Justus Buchler, 76, Ex-Professor
of Philosophy at SUNY, Is Dead
By Alfonso A. Narvaez

(*The New York Times* 22 March 1991)

Justus Buchler, distinguished professor emeritus of philosophy at the State University of New York at Stony Brook and former chairman of the philosophy department at Columbia University, died on Tuesday at a nursing home in Chambersburg, Pa. He was 76 years old and lived in Garden City, L.I.

He died of a stroke, his sister, Beatrice Gotthold, said.

Dr. Buchler, who specialized in metaphysics, was the editor, author or co-author of more than a dozen books. Among them were "Toward a General Theory of Human Judgment," "Nature and Judgment," "The Concept of Method," and "Metaphysics of Natural Complexes," all published by Columbia University Press in 1951, 1955, 1961, and 1966, respectively.

He also wrote "Introduction to Contemporary Civilization in the West," and "Chapters in Western Civilization," both published in two volumes by Columbia University Press in 1946 and 1948, respectively.

Dr. Buchler, who was born in New York City, earned a Ph.D. from Columbia in 1939. He played a major role in developing the graduate program in philosophy at Stony Brook after joining the faculty in 1971 as a distinguished professor. He retired in 1981.

Previously he was Johnsonian Professor of Philosophy at Columbia from 1959 to 1971 and chairman of the department from 1964 to 1967. He joined the Columbia faculty in 1937 as a lecturer and from 1938 to 1943 was also an instructor at Brooklyn College.

While at Columbia, he helped develop the core curriculum and, from 1950 to 1956, he was chairman of the contemporary civilization program.

He was a member of several professional organizations, including the American Philosophical Association, and was an official of the American Civil Liberties Union.

He is survived by his wife, the former Evelyn Urban Shirk, a daughter, Katherine Tessen of Lititz, Pa., and his sister, who lives in Saddle River, N.J.

2

Early Times, 1945-1950

To the end of a review and assessment of my writings I am dividing the exposition into workable time periods. The dates "1945-1950" together with those that accompany subsequent chapter titles refer primarily to years of publication.

I

Right at the outset a fundamental literary anomaly manifests itself. I am today more critical of or dissatisfied with my work and experience within the Jewish-Christian dialogue—a condition aided and abetted by the obdurateness that continues within that relation, particularly on the Christian side—than of my efforts in other fields. That I have become known primarily for my endeavors within the Jewish-Christian relation thus gives an ironic cast to my work as a whole.

Upon occasion I am asked how I came to be caught up in the Christian-Jewish encounter. The question is salutary because during my student days no such encounter had as yet developed in any weighty fashion within the public theological-moral and philosophic scene in North America and Europe.

Most of the students in the high school and college I attended in Brooklyn were Jews, and I knew a number of Jewish people throughout my youth. One day in late 1944 or early 1945 Harold A. Durfee and I were mulling over possible subjects for our doctoral dissertations. We had been at the Yale

Divinity School together and were now in New York City. It was my good friend Durfee (to become professor of philosophy at American University) who suggested that I might wish to consider for my own research the general topic of Christianity's relation to the Jewish people and Judaism. The subject would be entirely new for me with respect to scholarly study yet not at all strange from the standpoint of my personal experience and background. Durfee's suggestion struck a responsive chord.

I had already come to venerate Reinhold Niebuhr. One day I mustered the courage to go to him and inquire concerning the tenability of the above subject. He was most accepting of the idea and gave me every encouragement. (On this matter and for more on Niebuhr's influence upon me, please consult in chapter 5A, "A Tribute to Reinhold Niebuhr, 1892-1971.") For worse or better—I sometimes think for worse, as I shall make plain—I was enabled to join my teacher and with him become among the pioneers in this country in the contemporary Christian-Jewish *Auseinandersetzung*. James Parkes, the great British historian and churchman, was already pioneering upon this subject in Great Britain, and I was later to work with him as well (see below, under chapter 6A, "In Memoriam James Parkes, 1896-1981").

In those days the Fellowship of Socialist Christians,[1] under Reinhold Niebuhr's leadership, published a quarterly, *Christianity and Society*, "devoted to Christianity and social reconstruction." The first article I ever wrote, based upon the earlier phases of my doctoral research, appeared in that journal (1946). Incredibly, I titled my meager exploratory piece "A Theology for the Jewish Question." Beyond typifying the brazenness of the young graduate student, the title reflected the haughty Christian presumption that there is such a reality as "the Jewish question" upon which Christians presumably have a right to pass judgment. The real question in the Jewish-Christian relation, as I was soon to learn, is the Christian question. However, in this first essay I did emphasize that antisemitism is a serious and continuing temptation in Christianity, especially within absolutist forms of Christian faith that claim to possess the one and only truth. I pointed to the moral and theological dilemmas that beset any Christian missionary approach to Jews, and I referred briefly to the question of Zionism.

---

[1]   In 1948 the group changed its name to Frontier Fellowship: Christians for Social Reconstruction.

II

The above article outlined some of the ideas subsequently contained and expanded in the book composed in my late twenties, *Christianity and the Children of Israel* (1948), which pretty much reproduced my doctoral dissertation.[2] (Having read the dissertation draft, one of my doctoral committee members wrote to me that the analysis rather reminded him of two morticians arguing over whose commission it was to dispatch a particular corpse—"a question of great moment to the undertakers but of supreme indifference to the corpse." I never did quite figure out what my critic was trying to prove, especially since I can report that, oddly enough, he was eventually to become rather sympathetic to what I was seeking to do.)

Christianity and the Children of Israel was my initial full-length study in Christian-Jewish relations, treating "the Jewish question" from the point of view of "neo-Reformation theology" in contradistinction to both "religious absolutism" and "religious relativism." The book was heavily historical and phenomenological.

In the course of my graduate studies I was exposed to more conservative or traditionalist Christian expositors than I had known in earlier days. Karl Barth, Emil Brunner, and company were all the rage. I was considerably influenced by neo-Reformation theology (often and erroneously called neo-Orthodoxy; it was not fundamentalist[3]). What I sought to do for some time—*Christianity and the Children of Israel* is an early expression of this—was to take the resources of neo-Reformation anthropology (its teaching on the pervasiveness and power of human sin) and bring them to bear upon the understanding of and attack on antisemitism. This kind of application, in light of the evil character of Christian antisemitism itself, seemed fully to justify and even to vindicate such a Christian stance. I have never entirely abandoned the view that Christian thinking, particularly major genres within Protestant thinking, has developed a rather more profound apprehension of the depths of human depravity than has Jewish

---

[2]   In addition to Reinhold Niebuhr as supervising chairman, my Columbia-Union doctoral committee included Salo W. Baron, Joseph L. Blau, Horace L. Friess, H. Richard Niebuhr (of Yale University), Herbert W. Schneider, and Paul J. Tillich.

[3]   Some interpreters typed Paul Tillich (and Reinhold Niebuhr) as "neo-Orthodox," a quite inaccurate label.

thinking.[4] (Paradoxically, Jewish *experience* knows infinitely more about the ravages of sin, especially the sins of Christians, than does Christian experience, granted such an exception as Black Christian experience.) Yet within neo-Reformation thinking/praxis, there was present a malignancy, one that was not identified by me, or not grasped by me, for a long time. That thinking/praxis was absolutist in its Christology (not excluding, ironically, even my preeminent teachers, Reinhold Niebuhr, H. Richard Niebuhr, and Paul Tillich): Christ is *the* way, *the* truth, *the* life. It took me many years to recognize and confess that preponderant Christian faith can help to guarantee antisemitism. This fateful condition and consequence have bedeviled the church's entire Christology, its Christology-as-such, and this despite whatever profound or saving help the Christian faith may render via its anthropology, with the latter's recognition of human sinfulness and its advocacy of humility and self-abnegation. Thus was I entrapped by my own theological and educational conditioning. The very theological structure that was boasting and reflecting the highest moral intentions and epistemological resources, and was demonstrating the profoundest insight into the human predicament, proved as well to be open to immorality and untruth.

In this early period, my personal and professional life and the specter of antisemitism came to converge upon each other, and a wondering and baffled concern with antisemitism gained a crucial place in my apperceptive and scholarly world. *Christianity and the Children of Israel* reflected, sometimes helplessly, sometimes helpfully, sometimes despondently, sometimes hopefully,

---

[4]   In a 1951 review of Morris Goldstein's *Jesus in the Jewish Tradition* I was to comment upon the author's reference to the enlightened spirit present in modern civilization: "How statements like this...can be made by Jews in the very century when over one-third their number have been slaughtered perplexes the Christian imagination...[The] interpretation of human sinfulness remains a chief difference between Judaism and Christianity." Parallel comments were to be offered in a 1952 review of Alfred J. Marrow's *Living Without Hate*, wherein I contrasted the Marrow volume with Will Herberg's *Judaism and Modern Man*, and also in a 1953 review of Henry Enoch Kagan's *Changing the Attitude of Christian Toward Jew*. Will Herberg was greatly influenced by Christian anthropology, i.e., by, primarily, Reinhold Niebuhr. I was in turn much taken with Herberg's theology (cf. Eckardt reviews of Herberg's *Judaism and Modern Man* and *Protestant-Catholic-Jew* [the latter with Alexander Miller]). The judgment that Christian thought is more profoundly aware than Judaism of the depths of human depravity is a relative generalization that must of course admit of many exceptions (cf., e.g., Emil L. Fackenheim, *Quest for Past and Future* [Bloomington: Indiana University Press, 1968], pp. 27-51). Yet Judaism and Christianity are united in the assurance that humankind the sinner remains part of a good creation.

upon what I denominated "the Jewish plight" before the dread fact of the German Nazi war upon the Jews of Europe. The opening passage of that volume reported a Rumanian Jew's testimony to a British military court about the killing and burning of 80,000 Jews, the entire remaining population of the ghetto of Lodz, Poland, in a single night at the death camp of Oswiecim (Auschwitz). I followed the report with this response: "The Christian church is confronted today with 'the Jewish question,' as epitomized in such figures, and the church must try to give an answer. Christian theology seeks for the meaning of the Jewish plight, if there is any such meaning, not simply in order that the church may understand but that understanding will lead to Christian action." I found myself convinced, with Scholem Asch, that the whole Christian world carried accessory guilt, if not all-decisive guilt, for the Nazi slaughter of the Jewish people. The Jewish plight was, in truth, the Christian plight.[5]

Here was *Shoah* (Holocaust) theology groping in the night, before there actually was any such thing as *Shoah* theology, and finding itself disturbed and uncertain—not that theological effort necessarily reduces human disturbance and uncertainty (theology may only compound them). However, it is not the case that the *Shoah* was *the* inspiration in my attack upon antisemitism. That struggle has always been independently based. Robert A. Everett points out that James Parkes did not "need" the *Shoah*. It was well before the Holocaust that Parkes saw "the whole demonic dimension of Christian antisemitism."[6] I did not "need" the *Shoah* either. A fundamental dialectic appears inescapable: On the one hand, the moral requirement of a revolution in Christian dogma long antedated the *Shoah*. For that dogma helped produce the *Shoah*. On the other hand, as Alice Eckardt has pointed out, while we Christians ought not to have needed the Holocaust to change our reprehensible ways, if *now* we do not make the morally demanded changes, the Holocaust thereby makes us culpable to an irremediable degree. It is in this latter sense that the *Shoah* must remain decisive within any ongoing Christian moral revolution.

Antisemitism kills Jews, as it kills the killers of Jews. But it ensnares as well multitudes of other people, with destructive consequences yet also with

---

[5] *Christianity and the Children of Israel*, pp. 1 (slightly emended), 47 (hereinafter referred to as CCI).

[6] Robert A. Everett, "Christian Theology After the Holocaust (2)," *Christian Attitudes on Jews and Judaism* (London) 51 (Dec. 1976): 11.

potentially constructive consequences should such people be moved to fight the evil. If in my initial writings I already identified Christians and Christianity as blameworthy for the hell of Jewish suffering, the question stayed terribly open (and does still today) of whether such public identifications help extinguish the fires or instead just add fuel to them. Here I think of the splendid young creatures who in this moment fill the halls of our colleges and universities. Most of them come to us as walking incarnations of the blissful proposition that ignorance is virtue. The many nominal Christians among them simply do not know enough about traditional Christian faith to be themselves anti-Jewish. (They may well be anti-Jewish anyway, yet without any comprehension of the specific nature and power of their social conditioning.) They come to us never having been told the unending tale of Christian contempt for Jews. And what do we do? Confidently and responsibly, we proceed to move into their lives and apprise them of the truth about Christian history and teaching—thereby driving them out of the Garden of Eden forever. I sometimes wonder whether what we do in *raking up the muck* of historic and continuing Christian antisemitism differs practically from what today's media do for terrorists: give them a powerful hearing.

As I shall be recounting, at different periods I have managed to climb out of the morass of antisemitism and devote my attention to other questions. Yet ever and again I have been driven back to that question. How is this? Why is this? I am not sure. I do not really know. One thing I think I know is that whenever we stop to ask how it is that a particular individual has come to occupy a given time/place, we are at once confronted by, conservatively speaking, hundreds and hundreds of reasons. One problem, or fact, about the universe into which we have been thrust is not merely that it is determined, but that it is overdetermined. I call to witness an observation from *The New Yorker*: The world is simply bursting with "interconnections, interrelationships, consequences, and consequences of consequences...[The] web of all these interrelationships is dense to the point of saturation."[7] On the other hand—to speak in Whiteheadian categories—life proceeds by simplification, even by oversimplification. For the Christian of today, simplification may entail lifting out morally a solitary cause from an infinity of causes, and zeroing in upon that one cause. The English word "cause" is challengingly ambiguous: *producer of an effect* is

---

7   "Notes and Comment," *The New Yorker*, 26 Aug. 1985, p. 19.

matched, or even excelled, by *a value or enterprise to which one becomes dedicated*. On this second meaning, from within a massively overdetermined flux one may *simply choose* to engage in the war against antisemitism—as in some other calling. The fact that from out of an infinity of causative reasons the choice is in a real sense made for us does not diminish in any way the integrity and the potential significance of our own personal decision-making. Spinozist determinism and Kierkegaardian choice are simultaneously and equally present.

III

The theological-moral question of the Covenant is not explicitly analyzed in *Christianity and the Children of Israel*. Nevertheless, that question lies at the foundation of the study and is brought to the fore therein by means of other terminology.

At this early time I was insisting that the Christian's acceptance of Jesus as the Christ does not insinuate any exclusion of Jews from salvation[8]—this, in harmony with a point made in chapter one of the present retrospective. If such an affirmation implied that the Covenant of the Jewish people was not to be impugned, I was also impelled to raise a question that may be spoken of as the ineluctable covenantal misery of Jews (though it does not have to be construed only in that way[9]): "What other people has been made to suffer over so long a period of time and to such a horrible degree?"[10]

The dialectic that ties together the Covenant and antisemitism thus suggests morally dubious, even ghastly, possibilities. Yet Will Herberg maintains: "Bringing God to the world, Israel must suffer the hatred and resentment of the world against God and his Law."[11] What kind of talk is this? Is antisemitism the inevitable and destined, even predestined, consequence of the Covenant? If so, how can the teaching of the Covenant continue to be humanly tolerated? This entire dialectical condition has assailed the Jewish community from early

---

[8] CCI, p. xiii.

[9] The reason for this qualifying parenthesis is the plain fact that antisemitism is a human fabrication.

[10] CCI, p. 4.

[11] Will Herberg, unpublished ms., as cited in ibid., p. 4.

in its history, and it manifests itself as well within the Christian church. How, if at all, may the conflict that is implied here between religious assertions on the one side and human rightfulness and dignity on the other side ever be resolved?

In *Christianity and the Children of Israel* I nevertheless saw fit to concentrate upon the "transcendent mystery" of the Jews as the continuing people of God, adducing in support of this idea the biblical, and more especially the Pauline, witness (cf. Rom. 11:25-36). At the same time, the plain effrontery and arrogance in my discoursing upon the meaning of Jewishness totally eluded me, a non-Jew. In retrospect, the one excuse I had or have—"excuse" may indeed be an inexcusable notion in this frame of reference—is that I was at least advocating a moral struggle against the kind of Christian theological antisemitism that rejects original Israel's Covenant with God. I interpreted the apostle Paul to mean that the Jews did not lose their chosen people status despite their nonacceptance of Jesus as the Christ.[12] (I was later to find objectively/ historically incorrect this way of rendering Paul. I was also to disagree with the apostle's position as I finally came to understand it.)

The concept of the "mystery" of the Jewish people was applied by me to their genesis, present life, and destiny. I apprehended these several stages in fundamentally theological terms. Under the influence of my teacher Paul Tillich, I set the "Lord of time," the God of universal justice, in opposition to the "gods of space." "Jews are divinely preserved to represent the justice of the one God and to bring the Messiah to the world." Thus, it is simply not true that the Christian church has replaced the Jewish people in the intention of God. Hatred of Jews is to be seen as "a tragically accurate barometer by which to measure the spiritual idolatry of Western culture." However, if justice is truly universal it can perforce turn upon the Jewish nation itself (cf. Amos 3:2). "The prophets threaten the elected nation as well; that it too will be rejected by God because of injustice is the final victory over the gods of space." On the other hand, "the elected nation is not called upon to sacrifice its existence. A soil, a holy land, an elected nation are never holy by their very being, but they may become holy if and when they realize truth and justice...The Jewish people could justifiably become a nation in a given space after they had become a nation of time. The 'side by side of space' becomes insignificant before the historical process which

---

12 CCI, p. 40.

moves in the direction of the divinely-established Kingdom of God."[13] (Following upon the Second Great War, Tillich confessed that his earlier view that Israel was wholly a people of time beyond attachment to space had been mistaken. Jews had to have their own national place where they could protect themselves.[14])

The theological absolutizing of Jesus Christ by the Christian church could undoubtedly serve to actualize latent Christian antisemitism. From my study of the Nazi period I learned how the Faith Movement of German Christians (*Glaubensbewegung Deutsche Christen*) would repeat ad nauseam charges of the apostasy of the Jews, of their "condemnation" by God for "their crucifixion" of Jesus, and of their inferiority as a "race." On the other hand, I equally learned how the Confessing Church in Germany (*Bekennende Kirche*) fought antisemitism in the church on the very ground of an unqualified commitment to God's revelation in Jesus Christ, all this in opposition to the German Christian Movement with the latter's effectual prostituting of the Christian faith to the service of the State and the Aryan "race."[15]

I became much impressed by the paradoxically self-sacrificing Christian absolutism of the Reformed Church in Holland, many of whose members put themselves in mortal danger through standing up to the Nazis with such declarations as, "How can we expect justice before the judgment seat of Christ if we have not sought justice here on earth?," and, "The fact that the Jewish people is declared to be inferior contradicts the Word of God, for it has pleased God, in his marvelous and unfathomable mercy, to give redemption to all peoples and races through Jesus Christ, who came from the midst of the Jewish people."[16]

The Christian praxis of such groups as the Confessing Church in Germany and the Dutch Christians may very well have helped me or prompted me to imply agreement with the neo-Reformation avowal of Jesus Christ as "man's

---

[13]   Ibid., pp. 40n, 38, 39. These passages rely heavily upon an unpublished ms. of Paul Tillich.

[14]   Ronald Stone, "The Zionism of Paul Tillich and Reinhold Niebuhr," *Christian Jewish Relations* (London) 15 (Sept. 1982): 41.

[15]   CCI, pp. 88, 98, 100, 101.

[16]   Cited in ibid., pp. 98, 99.

only Savior and Lord"[17]—or at least such witnesses as these served to keep me from realizing the grave moral-theological troubles in such an avowal. I do remember being made uneasy when I read a pastoral letter of the General Synod of the Dutch Reformed Church (dated September 1941), which asserted that Israel's rejection of Christ led to a "judgment of blindness" and that "the true destiny of the Jewish people lies in its conversion to Christ, by joining the Christian church."[18] Yet I myself spoke of the national pride that Jews may exhibit, as this is made possible by the affirmation that they are the people of God. I added: "The invectives of the biblical prophets would never have been necessary had the Jews fully comprehended the meaning of their election by the God of universal justice. The prophets themselves were never entirely devoid of nationalistic bias."[19] That I could have spoken in such adverse fashion, and right in the middle of the terrible post-*Shoah* agonies of the Jewish people, remains a formidable and grievous transgression. However, I then turned around the foregoing kind of argumentation and applied the category of human sinfulness to the very interpretation of antisemitism. Seeking to grapple with the historical singularity of antisemitism, I proposed the following hypotheses: (1) Generically speaking, the hatred and the persecution of Jews incarnate the pagan-human war against the God whom the Jewish people uniquely represent. (2) Within a discretely Christian frame of reference, antisemitism perpetuates the war that Christians wage against the apodictic and eschatological demands made upon them by Jesus the Jew. We project upon the Jews our own rejection of the Christ. It is hardly a mere coincidence that Jesus was a Jew, that Christianity is a Jewish religion, and that no people on earth has ever been hated or hounded the way Jews have—especially in the Christian world. We are not able to dispose of Jesus directly but we may seek to get rid of him obliquely by defaming and destroying Jesus' own people.[20]

---

[17] Ibid., p. 132.

[18] Cited in ibid., p. 101.

[19] Ibid., pp. 38-43. My use of "nationalistic" here is inadvertently anachronistic, since nationalism is a modern phenomenon. I think I must have picked up this judgment upon the prophets from Reinhold Niebuhr.

[20] Ibid., pp. 50-65.

According to the second of the two hypotheses, Christian antisemitism is at base anti-Christianity, or a form of Christian self-hatred. The two hypotheses are explicated much more fully in the book than is necessary here. I also develop in those pages a number of criticisms of my own argumentation. (One reviewer of *Christianity and the Children of Israel* responded that the hypotheses do not take into consideration that the New Testament already has antisemitic aspects.) However, I have never had reason to abandon the hypotheses. Subsequent reflection upon the dread tale of antisemitism has sometimes even reinforced the interpretation in my mind. As I now look at the hypotheses, perhaps the major substantive difficulty with them is that, even granted the possible evidence for them that is afforded by one or another case study of individuals, the interpretation is nevertheless not amenable to proof. If the view cannot be disproved, the problem of scientific verification yet remains a formidable one.

An alternative and perhaps more convincing and unalloyed explanation of historical and contemporary antisemitism in the Western world is the dissemination and success of the Christian "teaching of contempt" (Jules Isaac) for Jews over the centuries. Yet I think that there is no necessary conflict between this rather pristine and even truistic view and my own more depth-psychological hypotheses with their recognition of the power of the collective unconscious.

IV

I further paid considerable attention to the Christian missionary dilemma.[21] According to the traditional missionary apologia, the obligation to "bring all human beings to Christ" can hardly exclude the people from whom he came "as of the flesh." Indeed, any such exclusion is held to be an instance of antisemitism. But in that first book I adduced factors that call into question an out-and-out missionary policy. With indebtedness to Paul Tillich, I referred to a peculiar place that Judaism and Jewish people occupy in the divine economy: to testify, for the sake of the God of universal justice, against the demonic forces of paganism.[22] In Tillich's formulation, by their very existence the people of

---

[21]   Ibid., pp. 145-151.

[22]   Ibid., pp. 146, 147.

time, the Jews, "break the infinite claim of the gods of space that expresses itself in will-to-power, imperialism, injustice, demonic enthusiasm, and tragic self-destruction." The Christian church is unable or unwilling to take this function upon itself; the church remains a peculiar prey of pagan distortions. The church is ever in danger "of adoring the gods of space in which she is ruling...[The] prophetic spirit included in the traditions of the synagogue is needed as long as the gods of space are in power, and this means up to the end of history, as Paul seems to assume in Romans 9-11, the first Christian interpretation of the historical fate of Judaism." Indispensably, Judaism and the Jewish people serve as a corrective against the paganism that forever corrupts Christianity.[23] In alternate terminology, Adolf Hitler and his cohorts had to seek to kill all Jews simply because they were Jews, whereas the churches and any Christians (though not of course Jewish Christians) could escape the Nazi wrath through proper obeisance or just by not "making trouble."

I was led to insist that the integrity of the church's missionary vocation in the world is in no way subverted by a non-missionary stance vis-à-vis Jews.[24] "Synagogue and church should be united in our period in the struggle for the Lord of time, a period in which more than ever...the gods of space show their power in men's souls and in nations."[25] To argue that the exclusion of Jews from Christian missionary endeavor compromises the church's evangelical task is to violate the distinctive relationship between Judaism and the church.[26]

On the other hand, I went on to place the missionary question within the context of a claim that Judaism is part of the "latent" Christian church. Here too Tillich influenced me. (In later years I would turn this contention upon its head, now locating the very integrity of the Christian dispensation within Jewish reality.) While acknowledging that Judaism must reject any Christian effort to subsume the synagogue under the church, I stipulated that "neo-Reformation theology is absolute at the point of affirming that Jesus is the Christ" and that

---

[23] Paul Tillich, unpublished ms. (slightly emended).

[24] CCI, p. 148.

[25] Tillich, unpublished ms.

[26] CCI, p. 148. I qualified this judgment with a recognition that "conversion of individual Jews to the Christian faith is to be distinguished from the destruction of Judaism" (p. 148n).

"to surrender this affirmation is to surrender the whole Christian faith." Once the Christ appears, the covenanted assembly of God becomes the assembly of Christ (*ecclesia*); before his appearance, that covenanted reality is the assembly that awaits him.[27] As Tillich expressed the matter, "in Judaism the church is latent in a national theocracy and its representatives. It becomes manifest fragmentarily in individuals and groups who struggle against the national limitations of Judaism without being able to overcome them. This refers to the prophetic and universalistic attitude toward Jewish nationalism." Before the coming of Jesus as the Christ the church is manifest only by anticipation; after his appearance it is also manifest by reception. "The latent church always engages in the quest to become manifest, while the manifest church is continually exposed to criticism by the latent church. The latent church within Christian civilization is a negative as well as positive challenge to the manifest church. The acknowledgment of the latent church undercuts ecclesiastical and hierarchical arrogance without rejecting the claim of the church to be the community in which the New Being in Christ is actual."[28]

The foregoing paragraphs point up a baffling moral and intellectual problem: The Christian church—together with the Jewish community—is beset by the paradox of making universal claims while yet living in a condition of fragmentariness and sin. In *Christianity and the Children of Israel* I strove to sustain the assertions of both Christian absolutism and Christian relativism. I did my best to distinguish between "loyalty to Christ as the transcendent Truth who stands above the relativities of history," and Christianity, a religion that sinfully participates in those very relativities and has in truth "placed itself in the forefront among forces persecuting the Jewish people." And yet, in declaring that reconciliation to God ultimately takes place through Jesus Christ, for Jew as for Gentile, I was hardly being consistent with any categorical rejection of the missionizing stance toward Jews. I nevertheless concluded that a radical rethinking of the missionizing view is demanded, with special attention to the welfare of Jews as human beings. And within one salient moral context—the struggle against antisemitism—I persisted in the paradoxical judgment that Christian absolutism excels Christian relativism. That is to say, in behalf of

---

27 Ibid., p. 148.

28 From lecture mss. of Paul Tillich (slightly emended).

"orthodoxy" I engaged in a polemic against the latitudinarian kind of "liberalism" that subverts the commitments of a distinctively Christian social action. One virtue of Christian orthodoxy, I argued, is its avowal "that in the purely pragmatic question of an effective Christian ethic, the conviction that the Cross means the suffering of the only Son of God (John 3:16) and hence that in gratefulness for God's gift we must remedy the sufferings of other sons of God incarnate in our Jewish neighbors affords the basis for true Christian love." (Note the sexist language here.) I subscribed to the affirmation of Reinhold Niebuhr that the claim that Christ reconciles humankind to God is authenticated whenever Christ shows the power to overcome human idolatry. Christ becomes the final truth about human life insofar as he is able to negate our egoistic corruptions of life, particularly those that involve hostility to and derogation of other persons.[29]

In later pages of the present retrospective, elements of self-refutation within the above Christological viewpoint will be brought out.

V

A final question considered in *Christianity and the Children of Israel* is one I at the time referred to as the ethnic quality of Jews. "Ethnic" is, in fact, much too narrow a concept; Jewishness encompasses numerous ethnic groupings. Jews are a *laos*, a people, even a people of peoples, a much broader and deeper reality than is allowed for in connotations of ethnicity.

Is there any legitimacy in calling upon the universal, anti-pagan role of Jews in a way that raises questions about their particularity as a people? I adhered to Reinhold Niebuhr's unqualifiedly negative answer to this query, and I have done so ever since. Absolutist religious and moral demands, together with an embodied commitment to these demands by Jews or others, must never be permitted to threaten human life and human rights. We are obligated to foster a creative tension between high moral demands and historical possibilities and necessities. To ignore or underestimate Jewish particularity is to violate that aspect of the prophetic tradition which understands the earthly foundation of human existence. Because it is entered into with a particular people, the Covenant can never be reduced to a purely "religious" dimension. The

---

[29]   CCI, pp. 149-151, 152-155, 177.

Covenant is impliedly political and social in character. There is simply no way for a covenanted people to fulfill a divine mission apart from maintaining its individual integrity. Again, justice for human beings extends to aggregate rights as much as to personal ones. The religious teaching of the goodness and legitimacy of the "orders of creation" validates the collective will-to-live of any people (which is not to exempt this survival impulse from its liability to human corruption or unrightful will-to-power). Accordingly, Christians have no right whatever to prescribe that the Jewish nation be a church, for this is, in Reinhold Niebuhr's words, to require "the highest idealism of a people which is least secure in its survival." "How can the 'particular' be a servant of the universal, if the life of the particular has no security?" In sum, there has to be a political solution to the problem of Jewish survival "without reference to the final religious problem." Any denial of historical particularities is a species of utopianism and imperialism. The fact is that Jews have even been obliged morally to utilize their religious faith in behalf of survival in a hostile world.[30]

The right of collective existence is undermined whenever it is deprived of a political base. Such a state of affairs is especially threatening when the group involved has been perennially subjected to persecution or mere "toleration." I concluded that the Arab-Jewish conflict of the time together with decisions respecting Jewish sovereignty would have to be approached from the perspective of moral relativism (relationism or situationism) rather than that of religious claims. For every principled argument in behalf of an independent state for one people (such as the Jews) is an implicit argument for that same kind of state for another people (such as the Palestinian Arabs). But in the 1940s the Arabs were not in the same plight as the Jews and were not deprived of a place of their own. While I was prepared to ask "why the Arabs must be made to suffer for the Jews' lack of a homeland," and although I cautioned that the church must not act to further "the welfare of Jews at the expense of other peoples" (a caution that was hardly coherent with an existential appropriation of the *Shoah* on my part), I proposed that a workable decision respecting Palestine ought to be made, at least in part, on the basis of the relatively "greater need of one people over another, recognizing that it is impossible to find a completely just solution for one or the other party." But I contended that since absolute claims in human affairs are at variance with the Christian faith, neither Jews nor Arabs

---

[30]   Ibid., pp. 166-170.

nor anyone else possess an exclusive or ultimate (divine) right to any particular land. (My introduction of "Christian" criteria as supposedly applying to Jews and Arabs was quite imperious.) There is, I continued, a point at which prophetism comes into conflict with nationalist messianism; the Jewish prophetic spirit must always be alert against the special idolatries of nationalism and the nation-state. Finally, I opposed any assumption that the Zionist solution could resolve the problem of antisemitism.

The foregoing reasoning underlay my support of Zionism. Among the elements I failed to deal with or include was the historical right of the Jewish people in Palestine. This was, in any case, where I stood shortly before the re-creation of the State of Israel in 1948. My thinking on Zionism and the potential reestablishment of Israel was quite rudimentary and superficial. As Will Herberg wrote in a review, the section on Zionism is the weakest part of *Christianity and the Children of Israel.*

All in all, that book was, on the one hand, unwarrantedly defensive and commendatory of neo-Reformation thinking and, on the other hand, overly nonsympathetic and critical of Christian liberalism. Today I reject my apologia for the one and my polemic against the other.

VI

During the latter part of the 1945-1950 period I explored several areas other than the Christian-Jewish relation. Included were articles upon the conflict between Roman Catholic and Protestant Christianity; an advocated societal synthesis beyond both medieval corporateness and modern individualism; an attack upon the idolatrous religions of humankind; and the relating of a given theological orientation to the study of religion in the university.

From the standpoint of the changed spirit in Catholic-Protestant relations during the period from the late 1960s through the 1980s, my strictures against the Roman Catholic Church for its absolutist claims may have come to appear somewhat unseemly or at least anachronistic. But in light of today's Vatican and papal moves back to the theological and social right, and particularly their attempt to quash Catholic "dissent" in the United States as elsewhere, my writing against Rome may not now seem quite so illicit or dated.[31] On his visit

---

[31] "The Real Catholic-Protestant Conflict."

to the United States in September 1987 Pope John Paul II made his view clear that "dissenting" Catholics cannot be good Catholics. A year earlier, Joseph Cardinal Ratzinger, head of the Vatican's Congregation for the Doctrine of the Faith, pointed out that Vatican Council II maintained that any doctrine taught by pope and bishops together in a definitive way is to be considered infallible. Said Ratzinger: "The Church does not build its life upon its infallible magisterium alone but on the teaching of its authentic, ordinary magisterium as well."[32] There is a move on the part of Rome in recent years to apply the concept of infallibility to its teaching authority upon moral issues. However, my Protestant outlook of the 1940s likewise involved its own species of religious absolutism and imperialism: "The church must make it known that man, both individually and collectively, is subject to God through Christ and yet that this fact is precisely the proper foundation for true [human] freedom."[33]

My piece "Attack Upon Religion," republished herewith, applied Tillich's observation that the greatest crimes in the story of humankind are invariably committed in the name of some kind of faith. Yet in that very essay I sought to exempt the essential "Christian revelation" from this kind of judgment. And my attempt in that same year to supply a theological rationale behind introductory religion study in a church-related college, while grounding the presentation in "the Protestant principle of self-criticism" (Tillich), nevertheless assumed that positive Protestant Christian faith stands at the apogee of humankind's religions. For example, I supported the norm of reading the entire Bible "from a Christo-centric perspective."[34]

All in all, as I now reread such materials as these, they together exhibit varied forms of Protestant arrogance, however enlightened their appearance.

At the end of this period I came back to the Christian-Jewish encounter —first, through a long, critical review (reprinted below) of Jean-Paul Sartre's tour de force, *Anti-Semite and Jew*, with the latter's unsurpassed description of the Jew-hater's psychological state; and second, through an article in *The*

---

[32]   TIME, 1 Sept. 1986, p. 65.

[33]   "The End of a World and the Beginning of a New One." For the view that today's top Roman Catholic ecclesiastical authority is seeking to obliterate the liberal advances of Vatican Council II, see Hans Küng and Leonard Swidler, eds., *The Church in Anguish* (New York: Harper & Row, 1987).

[34]   "Theological Presuppositions for an Introductory Course in Religion."

Journal of Religion upon the role of Judaism in relation to Christianity (applying the argument of Paul Tillich's *The Protestant Era*). The second article involved a fresh presentation of historical relativism, with help from H. Richard Niebuhr, Karl Mannheim, and Arnold Nash, and it adumbrated peculiarly Christian resources in the struggle against intolerance. The Protestant Christian imperialism referred to above was somewhat meliorated in this latter piece—in part through a critique of the divorce between "the Jesus of history" and "the Christ of faith" (with aid from Donald M. Baillie), and in part through an attack upon the liberal Christian-optimist rejection of the traditional Christian doctrines of humanity as sinner and God as judge.[35]

---

[35]   "Christian Faith and the Jews." However, I wrote there that "Jesus Christ is judge over every aspect of our lives, including our religion." Today I should reject the idolatrous quality of this statement and instead say, "God is judge..."

2A

Selected Essays

(1945-1950)

Jean-Paul Sartre on Antisemitism[1]

(Review-Article on Sartre, *Anti-Semite and Jew* in *The Review of Religion* 14 [1950]: 311-318)

It is probably not necessary to recommend Sartre's writings; he is being read. This particular work is intriguing as an attempt to wrestle with a pressing social issue from within a framework of atheistic humanism and a pessimistic metaphysics. Can such a philosophy avoid ethical nihilism? Sartre believes it can, and *Anti-Semite and Jew* is a brave rendering of that conviction.

For, if nothing else, Sartre's brand of existentialism seeks to force responsibility upon man. "It is *by my agency* that everything must happen"—so the hero of *The Age of Reason* sums up the point of view. We can dispense with the hypothesis of God all right, but Sartre would ally himself with the religious prophet who castigates the conservative believer for complacently waiting upon God to accomplish the miracle of social regeneration. The author tells us that merit, like truth, must be sought. But "the anti-Semite flees responsibility as he flees his own consciousness"; his is the "fear of being free." The Jew-hater consequently "finds the existence of the Jew absolutely necessary. Otherwise to whom would he be superior?" (pp. 27, 28). As a Manichee he sees his enemy as the incarnation of evil; hence "he is under no necessity to look for his personality within himself" (p. 21).

The antisemite is a pathological being, a victim of passion. Sartre's description of how the antisemitic mind operates is brilliant for its psychological insight. Jew-hatred "is an involvement of the mind, but one so deep-seated and complete that it extends to the physiological realm, as happens in cases of

---

[1] For simplicity's sake I retain in this review the wording employed in the translation of Sartre, "anti-Semite" and "anti-Semitism." Such expressions are unfortunate. James Parkes used to call that usage "pseudo-scientific mumbo jumbo," a usage implying that the phenomenon in question is somehow a movement against a real quality called "Semitism" or for that matter against people called "Semites" (in contrast to Jews). The word "antisemitism" is "not a scientific word, and it is entitled to neither a hyphen nor a capital" (James Parkes, personal conversation). The correct forms are "antisemitism" and "antisemite."

hysteria" (p. 11). For example, some men suddenly become impotent when they discover that the woman with whom they are having an affair is a Jewess. The reader may be tempted to ask whether there is an empirical basis for many of Sartre's contentions. One cannot always be sure that some of the author's stories and striking illustrations stand for objective events rather than being simply parables or images intended to drive home the point. This is particularly true in his later characterization of the Jew. It should be noted that, with one or two minor exceptions, the book limits itself to the French scene. Hence Sartre cannot be held accountable for a correct interpretation of, say, the situation in America. *Anti-Semite and Jew* serves to remind us that America is not alone in its Jewish "problem."

From this reviewer's own investigations and experience, Sartre's portrait of the antisemite is accurate, at least in the sense of being true to the situation in this country. We are told that the writer "questioned a hundred people on the reasons for their anti-Semitism" (the milieu of a Left Bank cafe might not exactly reproduce the controlled conditions of a public opinion poll, but, conceivably, it might be more human) and how the Jew-hater's attitude toward the Jews was never based on experience but on the prejudgments which he always brought to particular situations. "Far from experience producing his idea of the Jew, it was the latter which explained his experience" (p. 13). A classmate of Sartre at the lycée was failed in his *agrégation* the same year a Jew passed. "You can't make me believe that that fellow, whose father came from Cracow or Lemberg, understood a poem by Ronsard or an eclogue by Virgil better than I." On closer questioning, Sartre discovered that his associate looked at the examination as a worthless academic enterprise and had not prepared for it. We have an example here of an individual resembling "those madmen who, when they are far gone in their madness, pretend to be the King of Hungary but, if questioned sharply, admit to being shoemakers" (p. 12).

In addition to moral cowardice and fantasy, antisemitism involves "impenetrability" and "mediocrity" (pp. 18-32). Some people want to be impenetrable; they have a fear of themselves and of the tentativeness which is implied in the seeking of truth. They prefer passion to reason and research. A strong emotional bias is the only thing that can give them certainty. Antisemitism is also an attempt to "create an elite of the ordinary," to merge with the herd and its morality. As an antisemite, a man does not have to act or think on his own.

Although Jew-hatred is fundamentally irrational, it nevertheless proceeds from out of a certain intellectual framework (pp. 33-50). As against the "spirit of analysis" in which bourgeois democracy was born, antisemitism has fallen back on a "spirit of synthesis," which means the conviction that a whole is more than, and determines the meaning of, its parts. For example, courage is not an *analyzable*, autonomous element which preserves itself indifferently when it enters either a Christian or a Jew. There is a Jewish *character* which, upon contact, alters courage. Jewishness is a "metaphysical essence." This gives us a key to understanding how the enemies of the Jews can talk of contradictories like "Jewish capitalism" and "Jewish Bolshevism" in the same breath. The Jew cannot be expected to act rationally; he may even choose his own destruction. Furthermore, in order that the antisemite may really hate him, the Jew must possess freedom; we do not hate natural phenomena. But, of course, such freedom is not freedom for good. Like Augustine's man after the Fall, the Jew is free only to do evil. Sartre writes, "there is only one creature, to my knowledge, who is thus totally free and yet chained to evil; that is the Spirit of Evil himself, Satan."

This brings us to the essence of antisemitism. Sartre combines the note of responsibility as a goal (from which man often tries to escape) with a philosophy of metaphysical hopelessness, the latter of which is reminiscent of Bertrand Russell's conviction that life is ultimately meaningless, but that man should struggle against fate with all his might.

The anti-Semite is afraid of discovering that the world is ill-contrived, for then it would be necessary for him to invent and modify, with the result that man would be found to be the master of his own destinies, burdened with an agonizing and infinite responsibility. Thus he localizes all the evil of the universe in the Jew. If nations war with each other, the conflict does not arise from the fact that the idea of nationality, in its present form, implies imperialism and the clash of interests. No, it is because the Jew is there, behind the governments, breathing discord. If there is a class struggle, it is not because the economic organization leaves something to be desired. It is because Jewish demagogues, hard-nosed agitators, have seduced the workers (p. 40).

This is the Sartrian explanation of antisemitism. Man attempts to escape from the agony of being free. Another must be responsible for evil: the Jew. The Jew *is* Evil. We are told "that the anti-Semite does not have recourse to Manichaeism as a secondary principle of explanation. It is the original choice he makes of Manichaeism which explains and conditions anti-Semitism."

It is interesting to reflect that the atheist Sartre and the Christian theologian join in presenting freedom as the occasion for human sin. The difficulty with Sartre's interpretation is that, while it may help to explain hatred, it does not explain Jew-hatred. It is too general. Why do we select the Jew? A possible way out might be that a particular historical and experiential situation has potentialized the Jew as a scapegoat. But Sartre cuts off this possibility. In the opening pages of the book it is denied that the antisemite is inspired by such external causation. Not only does antisemitism develop apart from experience in general; more specifically it is not explainable by historical data, e.g., how many Jewish soldiers there may have been in 1914 (pp. 13-16), or by "social facts," e.g., that there may seem to be too many Jewish doctors (pp. 16f.). Even if every Breton were a physician, we would merely remark that Brittany provides doctors for all of France. Further along, the author admits that "if the anti-Semite has chosen the Jew as the object of his hate, it is because of the religious horror that the latter has always inspired," but he denies that this explains modern antisemitism (pp. 67f.). Sartre underestimates the religious element in hatred of the Jews.

Our author is in the nebulous state of explaining an empirical situation with no empirical data to buttress his hypothesis. Why not express our Manichaeism in the form of hatred of red-heads? If the Jew is selected as Satan it must be that he either performs a unique function or represents a particular challenge. Where, for example, the Jew is looked upon as the representative of a God of justice (which opinion has actually been historically expressed) and where men are seeking to escape blame for their own refusal to further justice, then, by means of an unconscious psychological process, the Jew can conceivably become the real instigator of injustice. We project upon the Jews our own guilt, having already become incensed at these people for giving Amos and Isaiah to the world. The present reviewer has no desire to campaign for such a theory at the moment; he is simply presenting a sample way of filling in what is to him a fatal gap in Sartre's otherwise provocative analysis. We should add, on the author's side, that Sartre does not look at antisemitism as unique. "The Jew only serves [the anti-Semite] as a pretext; elsewhere his counterpart will make use of the Negro or the man of yellow skin" (p. 54). But Sartre would then seem to be forced into the admission that the choice of the Jew is simply an accident. Can this explain the tragic fury and universality of antisemitism?

Space prohibits more than a mention of two additional and more ultimate queries. Why is man afraid of freedom? And why does he have a sadistic longing for Evil? (pp.45-50)

The remainder of the book is an attempt to analyze who and what the Jew really is and to present "a basis for stating the conditions on which a solution [to the Jewish problem] might be envisaged" (p. 143).

To return to the problem of an analytic versus a synthetic anthropology, the Jews' one friend, the democrat, made a wrong choice of analysis back in the eighteenth century (pp. 55ff.). The democrat is no real protector of the Jews for "he resolves all collectivities into individual elements." Consequently, he has no deep feeling for the Jew or the Negro. He wishes to destroy the Jew as a Jew and to leave nothing in him but the man; the antisemite wants to destroy the Jew as a man and leave nothing in him but the Jew, the untouchable. Sartre agrees with the antisemite in denying that there is a "human nature" made up of wholly isolated elements. But the Jew-hater goes astray in his application of the spirit of synthesis; he comes out with an evil Jewish principle. Sartre's own constructive interpretation (pp. 59ff.) involves the conviction that man is a being in a particular situation and

forms a synthetic whole with his situation—biological, economic, political, cultural, etc. He cannot be distinguished from his situation, for it forms him and decides his possibilities; but, inversely, it is he who gives it meaning by making his choices within it and by it. To be in a situation...is to *choose oneself* in a situation...

Sartre does not deny that the Jews are a race, but not in the sense of an "indefinable complex" of physical, intellectual and moral traits. The Jews do have common ethnic characteristics, but these are limited to various "inherited physical conformations" found more frequently among Jews than among Gentiles. It may be better to say Jewish *races*. We cannot claim that all Jews show the same character traits. A particular Israelite is an "inseparable ensemble in which the psychical and the physical, the social, the religious, and the individual are closely mingled..." He can be adequately defined neither by his religion nor by his existence in a strictly Israelite national community. The one thing that all Jews have in common is their common situation, but—and this is important—non-Jews have placed them in this situation. In principle, the Jews are assimilable; Gentiles won't let them assimilate. *We have created the Jew.* "The Jew is one whom other men consider a Jew: that is the simple truth from which we must start." Sartre is right that Jewishness is largely a gentile decision, something that makes considerably irrelevant discussions among Jews over whether they are a people or simply representatives of a religion as the Protestants are. But there are some people, among both non-Jews and Jews, who will deny that the Jews have had nothing to do with an autonomous choice of their own national and/or religious character, antisemitism or no antisemitism. In any event, the Israelite's plight is tragic:

> Whatever he does, his course has been set for him. He can choose to be courageous or cowardly, sad or gay; he can choose to kill Christians or to love them; but he cannot choose not to be a Jew...if he does so choose, if he declares that Jews do not exist, if he denies with violence and desperation the Jewish character in himself, it is precisely in this that he is a Jew (p. 89).

Within this fateful context there yet remains a choice. A man can decide whether to be an "authentic" Jew (pp. 90-91, 136-41) or an "inauthentic" Jew. Briefly, authenticity means accepting one's condition as a Jew, with all the incumbent responsibilities and even martyrdom that this entails, while the inauthentic Jew tries to flee his situation. We as Gentiles can never *blame* the Jew if he takes the latter course. Such a choice "does not concern us"—by which Sartre, magnificently, implies the dignity of the person.

There follows a long description of inauthenticity (pp. 91-136). A sufficiently clear distinction between Sartre's own interpretation of the Jewish outlook and the antisemitic mythology is not always evident here. We are told of the Jew's inferiority, his pathetic search for security, the perpetual tensions in which he lives, his own antisemitism, his masochism, his undue rationalism, his attitude to his own body and to property, his "uncultivated spontaneity," his uneasiness. The description is shrewd, but some of Sartre's generalizations may be questioned (something which likewise holds in his analysis of the "democrat"). The tension remains between those who, in hesitating to present a conclusion without exact scientific data, are led to perfectionism and silence and those who proclaim the essence of human relationships through intuition and poetic insight, thereby running the risk of arbitrariness.

The authentic Jew accepts his place as a proscribed and untouchable being—but he asserts his being on that very basis. Sartre appears naïve in holding that authenticity "takes away all power and all virulence from anti-Semitism." Then the antisemite "must be content to yelp at the Jew as he goes by, and can no longer touch him." But the author is quick to add that the authentic response only makes its contribution on the level of ethics and integrity; it does not solve the social or political problem, even among Jews themselves.

It is in Sartre's solution to the Jewish problem, or his "basis for stating the conditions for that solution," that this reader experienced a distinct letdown. In contrast to the author's superb analysis of the psychopathic character of Jew-hatred, we are told that deliverance will come through an alteration in the pattern of social organization! Sartre admits that education may not accomplish much and that laws "will never embarrass the anti-Semite, who conceives of himself as belonging to a mystical society outside the bounds of legality." And the practice of "good will" easily plays into the hands of the Jew-hater (pp. 70, 72). But then Sartre presents his trump card:

...anti-Semitism would have no existence in a society without classes and founded on collective ownership of the instruments of labor, one in which man, freed of his hallucinations inherited from an older world, would at long last throw himself wholeheartedly into *his* enterprise —which is to create the kingdom of man. Anti-Semitism would then be cut at its roots (p. 150).

Thus there appears an underlying conflict in the author's understanding. The Jewish problem is initially placed on the level of personal responsibility and freedom. But Sartre ends up in objectivication: the environment, the social situation must be transformed. We will change people by changing the social structure. This sentimental outcome hardly accords with Sartre's genius at other points. He contradicts his earlier insight that social evil is traceable to an internal, personal flight from freedom. At best Sartre ends up with a half-truth. If "to be in a situation...is *to choose oneself* in a situation," social reorganization may fulfill a positive function, but what about the *self* and its psychopathic tendency and irresponsibility? Why won't these latter exert themselves in a classless society?

Sartre's intellectual contribution is matched by his compassion for the Jews. His is a keen and empathic understanding of how difficult it must be to be a Jew. But he never loses sight of the Jew as an individual, as an autonomous being, with the image of his true self by no means destroyed. Sartre confesses the guilt of Christians and gentiles and recognizes that the Jews can be delivered from their plight only by non-Jews, who bear the ultimate responsibility. We have in this study a matchless description of the diabolism of the antisemite and of how contemporary antisemitism manifests itself. It is a pity that this is unaccompanied by any real contribution either in a comprehension of the ultimate *why* of antisemitism, of how it is that the *Jews* are selected for perpetual and universal crucifixion, or towards a solution of this dreadful social malady.

Attack Upon Religion

(*Christianity and Crisis* 10 [1950]: 20-22)

One need not be a disciple of Karl Marx, to be in agreement with his statement: "A critique of religion is the beginning of all criticism." The function of Christian thought is to criticize—to criticize everything that is human in the light of everything that is really divine. And a basic point at which to initiate a critique of the human is with religion; for religion is one of the biggest sources of man's troubles. It is not *the* biggest source—man is his own greatest difficulty—but a very great source nonetheless. A critique of religion is the beginning of all criticism because religion is the place where human tragedy and conflict come to their sharpest focus.

Some people today feel assured that our world is headed for destruction. Let us consider a more modest proposition. *If* our world is headed for destruction, religion is and will be a major cause of such a state of affairs. As the term is used here, religion means the assumption of, and commitment to, a being or principle held worthy of devotion.

II

Let us look into the question of why our deities cause so much trouble and tragedy and why, therefore, they should be attacked. One reason we cannot approve of mankind's various religions is that there are so many of them that it is confusing, and we do not like being confused. There is abroad in our world a whole bevy of gods and it is terribly hard for anyone to decide which he should follow. Some people choose to devote themselves to their nation or race while others give themselves in obedience to an economic or social class. Some men seek solace in the laboratory while others find refuge in a political system. And of course if none of such faiths seems too attractive at the moment, a man always has himself to worship, or some part of himself like sex.

But the whole picture is quite bewildering. One god many of us have found particularly tantalizing is Reason, whose followers bid us join the cult of objectivity. Their creed is, "Be objective and thou shalt inherit eternal life." Reason has his competitors, however. Aphrodite, goddess of love and passion, is not dead. Even in this age of science she calls to us, "Come unto me and I will give you rest. I will be music unto your ears and beauty unto your eyes and peace unto your soul." The spiritual and emotional barrenness of a world given to technology bolsters Aphrodite's cause. Thus the temptation comes to join the cult of subjectivity, to substitute a religion of feeling and will for a religion of the intellect. But on what basis are we going to make our choice? Those who assume that the one way to reach Truth is to be objective have forgotten that their assumption is a subjective one, and that they themselves are never really objective when their own reputation and interest are at stake. Yet if we ignore them and go in the other direction we soon see that subjectivity, when it is not chastened by objective consultation with one's fellows very easily becomes arbitrariness. However unsatisfactory a god Reason may be, we must not contend that the flouting of reason is prerequisite to salvation.

III

Another thing perplexing about religion, something that makes man's deities seem rather like devils, is the fact that our gods are very exclusive, and thereby they further injustice. Arnold Nash recently told a group of how the son of an African chieftain who was studying abroad once asked him whether it was true that two out of three doctors actually endorsed a certain product. Dr. Nash tried his best to explain. (I am quoting from memory.)

"Well, no, it's not *literally* true. That's just advertising. That's what you have to expect in this country."

"You mean the manufacturers tell untruths ?"

"I don't know that you could put it that way. The people here believe that business is business. They would tell you that somehow or other a man has to sell his product."

The young man thought for a moment, remembering how he had recently been told by a sculptress that she believed in art for art's sake. "I'm beginning to understand the religion of you white men," was his slow and startling comment. "Business is business. Art for art's sake. It's the same as in my tribe where the rain god has exclusive care of the rain and no one else dares to interfere with him." The young African had been officially introduced to the polytheism of Western culture.

Not long ago an official of the Metropolitan Life Insurance Company defended the policy of racial segregation in his company's New York City housing projects by affirming that no social issue was involved and that it was merely a matter of business and economics. Look out for the rain god! Or is it the god known to us as Mammon?

In a recent article a professor of psychiatry was quoted as saying that the best way to make one's marriage last is to accept conventional patterns of life. The happily married couple is one that submits to group standards, since that is the best way to adjust to society. One of our newfangled exclusive gods is Adjustment. There is a principle worthy of our devotion! What could be more vital than getting oneself adjusted? Whether group standards are worth adjusting to is something that could never occur to the devotee of this god, and the mere suggestion that injustice and the status quo are frequent bedfellows appears as blasphemous. The suggestion could come only from a Communist.

Our gods are almost always exclusive gods and an exclusive deity is invariably a threat to universal justice.

IV

Not only are we bewildered in the presence of a great host of competing gods, and not only are man's gods so often ethically questionable, but they are also always battling with one another. What happens when the religious loyalties of one group of men conflict with the religious loyalties of other men? There is bound to be a struggle, and the outcome is often bloodshed and suffering. In our contemporary scene the most aggressive world religion is communism, although probably secularism runs it a close second. Communism, as *The Christian Century* once summarized it, "has its sacred scriptures, its inspired revelators, its inerrant dogma, its saints, its martyrs, its hagiology, its demonology, its heresy trials, its inquisition, its excommununications, its pope, its ruling hierarchy, its initiatory vows, its consecrated priesthood, its missionaries, its sacred shrines, its proselyting passion, its apocalyptic future to make up for a grim present." But there are other religions and other gods readily available. The story is told of how L. P. Jacks, when he returned to

England one time from a visit to America, was asked his opinion of American democracy. "I didn't investigate it," he replied, "I don't like to disturb people at their devotional exercises."

Listen to these words: "Every German must rededicate himself to the principles of Germanism and pledge himself to fight this Jewish monster and its propaganda wherever it rears its head. Our government must be purged of traitors. Our schools must be purged of those professors who have only scorn for our German institutions and praise for the Jewish international. German youth must be educated in the German way of life, dedicated to German ideals and all foreignisms must be purged from our public life; there is no room for them here." The Nazi god of blood and soil was defeated not long ago but he has his counterpart in America today. For the words just quoted were uttered on August 18, 1949, by the head of a benevolent and protective order meeting in Appleton, Wisconsin—except that I have substituted the word "German" where he used "American" and "Jewish" where he used "Communist." The speaker also referred to his own order as the "greatest organization on earth."

We in America have our gods all right, and many of them have their sleeves rolled up. It is always well to have a god (as well as a devil to serve as a scapegoat) because if you can once cloak your designs with expressions of divine favor, then, when you set out to show your strength against your fellows, you can never be legitimately accused of doing wrong. You are simply being faithful to your god. You are not sinful; you are merely sacrificial. Soviet Russia has tortured and annihilated untold numbers of people and said, in effect, "Why these were hopeless heretics. They offended against the Most High, and in the name of Economic Determinism and Its only begotten Son, Josef Stalin, these depraved ones had to perish." We Americans can in good conscience prepare for our part in the slaughter because after all we are not thinking of our interests. It is the "American way of life" we are concerned about. It must be preserved at all costs, for it is truly divine, and any sacrifice we can perform in its honor is less than our real duty.

I personally feel that this particular god of ours is somewhat more respectable than one or another of the Russian deities, but I wonder sometimes whether this is simply because I am an American. In any event, man's gods are always getting into fights, and we cannot really approve of that, any more than we can approve of either the confusion they cause or their exclusiveness. How often one hears, "Now if only more people were religious, maybe there would be more harmony in the human family." We may wish to laugh at that, for the greatest crimes in the history of mankind are always committed in the name of some kind of religion.

V

Where does Christian faith fit into the attack upon religion? Religion is of course inescapable and all-pervasive. No man can live without something to give his life meaning. To be or not to be religious; that is definitely not the question. The only question is whether you and I are going to have an uncritical faith or one which serves as a critique of all our religious loyalties. In the Letter to the Romans the apostle Paul describes man as one who worships and serves "the creature rather than the Creator" (1:25). Man, in his present state, is fundamentally an idol worshipper. We set up deities of our own choosing and bow down and adore them, fancying that they are God Himself. We subscribe to particular truths and make them synonymous with universal Truth. We give our allegiance to particular beings and equate them with universal Being. We kneel in devotion before finite powers and principles and imagine they can give us infinite security. We employ our gods as excuses for exerting will-to-power over other men.

But then the Christian revelation appears, to remind us, as Reinhold Niebuhr puts it, that "religion is not simply, as is generally supposed, an inherently virtuous human quest for God. It is merely a final battleground between God and man's self-esteem." The Christian revelation comes to us in the name of One who is not an idol, but the deadly foe of idols, the God of Jesus Christ, the only One who is justified in destroying other gods because He is the beginning and the end of all existence. The Christian revelation is, among other things, an attack upon religion, upon man's perennial attempt, by means of idolatry, to escape from the real God who is not *a* god or *a* being or *a* principle but the infinite Source of all things and therefore the Judge of *all* gods and *all* beings and *all* principles. The Christian revelation is a Word from the Creator of the universe, who is also universal Truth and Justice, and who calls upon men to give up their worship of the creature, to cease their servitude to partial truths, and to surrender their allegiance to unjust gods. The God who is the end of man's religious confusion, whose righteous anger is aroused in the face of exclusiveness and injustice, and who embodies that peace which the world can neither give nor take away, is the only real God and is alone worthy of our devotion. In other words and paradoxically, the Christian revelation means the end of religion.

3

Intellectual/Moral Concerns, 1951-1962

Over the ensuing twelve years the centers of my work lay elsewhere than in the Christian-Jewish relation. During this time, most of my articles, reviews, editorials, sermons, and pieces of verse were on other subjects. I did not publish a second volume upon the Christian-Jewish meeting until nineteen years after the first one. The single book I wrote between 1951 and 1962 dealt with a different topic. The two occasional pieces I did upon the Christian-Jewish encounter came toward the end of the twelve-year span.

In the course of this period my efforts extended to the following areas:

1. Faith and the world.
2. The race question.
3. The critique of religion.
4. The university study of religion.
5. The nature of scientific method.
6. The quality of Christian ethical motivation.

I

"Faith and the world" is shorthand for such consanguine themes as interfaith relations, the interpretation of history, the dialectic of individual freedom and social order, and the vocational role of the Christian scholar. I pursued these themes in several essays.

In "The Catholic Dilemma" and "The Christ Child and Bishop Sheen" I came back to the Protestant-Catholic encounter. These pieces expressed two paradoxical concerns: the regrettable uncharitableness of some Protestants vis-à-vis Catholics, and elements within Catholic dogma that nevertheless make difficult Christian charitableness toward Catholics, or at least toward the Catholic Church. Fulton J. Sheen was an enormously popular figure in the 1950s. I wrote that "the bishop's moving reflections on the Babe and the cross...remind us tellingly that beyond the many differences between Roman Catholics and Protestants, the gift of God's only begotten Son as Savior is the one powerful, uniting fact." I then proceeded to fault the bishop for subordinating faith to reason and to history at the point of Christological claims; for misapprehending the content and thrust of biblical-messianic prophecy; for obscuring the decisiveness of Jesus' resurrection; for perpetuating elements of Docetism; and for, contradictorily, overstressing reason and history within the realm of faith. In the life of faith, reason and history remain "part of the problem rather than of the answer."

The critique of Catholic teachings and dogma—as of Protestant teachings and dogma—continues as one of the ongoing and enduring obligations of Protestantism.

In "Two Marginal Notes on the Prophetic View of History" I argued that the conviction of some of the biblical prophets "that spiritual and moral regeneration, as against 'entangling alliances,' is what saves a nation from destruction cannot be followed as the unilateral foundation of political policy." This was straight Reinhold Niebuhr. Furthermore, relations between nations and between humankind and God are much too complicated for any historical event or series of events to be able to "prove" affirmations of faith. Historical data cannot in themselves serve to interpret the meaning of history or to discern meaning in history—this in partial divergence from Reinhold Niebuhr. A philosophy of history cannot furnish a theology of history; the latter can only derive from a particular faith.[1] Many years later, in *For Righteousness' Sake*, I was to reapply much of the argument of "Two Marginal Notes"[2] but at this

---

[1]   See also A. Roy Eckardt review of Roger L. Shinn, *Christianity and the Problem of History*.

[2]   *For Righteousness' Sake*, pp. 252-258.

early stage I had by no means worked out a comprehensive view, or even a tolerable one, upon the relation between history and faith.

A subsequent essay, "The Christian and Secular Answer to the Dilemma of Freedom and Order" (1953), again followed Reinhold Niebuhr, this time in grounding American democracy upon the insight of the "founding fathers" that the individual possesses certain inalienable rights but that no individual or group is good enough to have final control over others. Here is the moral rationale for the political instrumentality of checks and balances. But the validation of human equality can never be purely experiential or secularist. Universal equality may be affirmed only "from the vantage point of the One who puts down the mighty from their thrones and exalts those of low degree." However, I was still immured in a theology that, in effect, failed to build a wholly monotheist or wholly theocentric foundation for human dignity and equality: "The Son of God laid down his life as a ransom for many. This is the freedom that defies enslavement and yet creates [a social] order where license is folly. Already it is given us to share in that death and that resurrection." True, I was at that time seeking to formulate a political anthropology (the social interpretation of what it means to be human) that would be at once true to living experience and validated by Christian faith. Yet the stubborn question remained, as I now grasp it: Wherein lies, if anywhere, the *needfulness* of a Christocentric genre of faith in establishing the principles of human equality and political responsibility? Why is not, say, Jewish faith or, for that matter, Islamic faith sufficient? And may not an absolutist Christology act to subvert a universalist anthropology and a universalist politics?

A second piece upon the Christian interpretation of history, "Land of Promise and City of God" (appearing in the tenth anniversary number of *Theology Today*), mirrored the (Reinhold) Niebuhrian and biblical dialectic of a responsible thisworldliness (= affirmation of the meaningfulness of human history) coupled with eschatological awareness and commitment (= affirmation of the meaningfulness of eternity). Humankind is capable of "indeterminate possibilities" of goodness and justice in this world; humankind is equally capable of infinite destructiveness and injustice. Yet in this essay I was once again giving voice to a form of Christian absolutism: "The center of Christianity is the faith that the eternal world has broken into time in Jesus as the Christ. Things are different now." The difficulty with my position here is that in

Judaism, as also in Islam, this world is already granted eternal significance because of having been created by its Lord. Why is not the latter kind of attestation sufficient? But alternatively, may such attestation be sufficient theologically but perhaps not sufficient anthropologically? (cf. the Christian teaching upon "the Fall"). And what is the relation—granted we are capable of fabricating one—between the theological question and the anthropological question?

"Christian Scholarship and Christian Hope" saw little possibility of the establishment or reestablishment of "a Christian society grounded in Christian intellectual and theological assertion." Yet what appeared to be saddening then would not have quite the same effect upon me today, for since that time I have come to comprehend much more the evils of "Christian nations." The moral threat inherent in the Christian claim had not yet impressed itself upon me—otherwise I should not have written that people "who have known 'the power of Christ's resurrection' are granted a hope and a joy that by contrast make sad the heartiest laughter of their atheist associates."[3] I exhibited some fear of a Christian future, but not at all with reference to Christology: "An explicitly Christian social structure would not be the greatest blessing... Christians are not Christ...[The] most Christian culture is always judged and found wanting by the God of absolute love and absolute justice...In the Cross God makes foolish the wisdom of this world." In addition, I supported the Tillichian claim that the principle of justification through faith may be applied not only to the religio-moral domain but also to the religio-intellectual domain. From Tillich's point of view, even those who must live "in doubt" may nevertheless be justified through faith. And it may be, I proposed, that the justification principle "as applied to the intellect can establish the most meaningful contact between Christian evangelism and the secular mind in the university of today." As I now write, the latter hope impresses me as rather excessive and as deficient in realism.

---

[3]   I was to end a published sermon, "The Conquest of Futility," with the words, "it is Christ Jesus who, as the innocent servant suffering in our place, conquers the fatefulness of nature; who, as the Lord of history, conquers the fatefulness of time."

II

A longstanding interest in problems of racism was exemplified in an essay, "Racial Prejudice and Discrimination: Civil and Christian Approaches." The subtitle was intended to reflect continuities and discontinuities between secular and Christian understandings and remedies. Among other arguments, I contended that the melioration of racist bias is achievable through such praxises as legislation, strategic utilizations of or invitations to a given race's self-interest, and the struggle against segregation.[4]

A word of self-criticism is in order with respect to the area last-mentioned. Representatives of black power and rights in recent decades often espouse a separatism that contrasts not only with immoral segregationism but with a highly problematic integrationism. While opposition to segregation as such may be all right and good, the opposite stance, integration, does not in itself guarantee any end to oppressive white structures of power or unjust power distribution.

In the late 1980s I was to return to the subject of race and racism in a volume dealing with several areas of liberative thinking/praxis, *Black-Woman-Jew*. The separatist line of attack is given voice in that study.

III

A critical stance toward religion and the religious life was grounded in liberal Social Gospel influences upon me. That outlook was further supported and developed by such mentors as Liston Pope, the Niebuhr brothers, and Paul Tillich. My wariness respecting religion was oriented particularly toward religion's ideological proclivity to sanctify questionable or evil human causes through equating them with the will or purposes of God. There is no business like religion business, because there is no idolatry like religious idolatry.

"The New Look in American Piety," an occasional piece that appeared in *The Christian Century* and reappears below, created something of a national

---

[4]   Cf. my sermon of 1959 entitled "Brotherhood."

stir.[5] The article sought to assess—not unsympathetically but from a traditionalist Christian perspective—the so-called religious revival of the 1950s.

How would a collateral assessment today of movements and/or cults such as have been represented by Jim and Tammy Bakker, Pat Robertson, Jerry Falwell, Oral Roberts, Robert H. Schuller, et al. be received? My hunch is that the considerable splash my essay made would not be repeated. The socio-religious picture in the late twentieth century is exceedingly complex and amorphous, as against the scene forty and more years ago. In the earlier case, I managed with relative ease to get an analytical and evaluative handle upon the overall situation. I don't think that would be possible today. Of fundamental importance here is the fact that competing religious and quasi-religious causes have themselves greatly multiplied. There is a sense in which the religiosity that is associated, correctly or incorrectly, with the California scene has expanded into the entire country—with massive help from television. For example, the number of Americans who pursue one or another variation upon Eastern mysticism are now in the hundreds of thousands. But, in general, Americans today would appear to be either a little too baffled, or perhaps too busy with other things, to pay great or sustained attention to a particular religious critique such as mine of the 1950s.[6]

I have just recovered from old files an item marvelously exculpatory of Norman Vincent Peale, one of the butts of my "New Look." It is from 1961. In a sermon Peale faulted Bishop James A. Pike for opposing racism on the latter's ground that it must lose the United States the support of uncommitted nations: "I am fed up with hearing preachers say that we must practice non-discrimination because of its effect upon the so-called colored peoples of the world...Christians should oppose discrimination for only one reason—because it is wrong."[7]

---

[5] See editorial, "'God and the Juke Box,'" *The Christian Century* 71 (1954): 1543-1544. A recast version of "The New Look in American Piety," directed to students and titled "Down With the New Religion," appeared in *Youth* and *The Baptist Student*.

[6] However, a survey taken by Gordon S. Black for *USA Today* found that the most important thing 21 percent of Americans continued to derive from religion was peace of mind and spiritual well-being (*The Christian Century* 104 [1987]: 817).

[7] TIME, 10 Mar. 1961.

The essay in *The Christian Century* led eventually to my second book, *The Surge of Piety in America* (1958). Together with the essay, the book reflected a prophetic-Christian viewpoint but it was somewhat more irenic than the short piece.[8] Today, i.e., from a post-Holocaust perspective, I should look at things somewhat differently. Is there not a compelling, even frightening, sense in which the lot of humankind and the lot of God are in our time interchanged? Perhaps it is not so much human beings, for all their foibles and idolatries, but rather God who appears to be standing trial. Which is better and which is worse: a God who would never hurt anyone—in the *Century* article I referred to the treatment of God as "a childish projection of granddaddy"—or a God who seems to enjoy a view from the sidelines as millions of human beings are murdered? May it not be precisely our narcissisms in all their pitiableness, our trivialities in all their laughableness, our fealties in all their foolishness that cry out for—and deserve—all the compassion that can possibly be mustered? As one pastor wrote to *The Christian Century*, "Is it any more blasphemous to use God for human ends than it is to state, as Eckardt does, that 'the Bible tells us that God uses us for his ends'?" The post-*Shoah* critique of God raises shattering questions concerning God's abuse of human dignity and values.

A partially redeeming note in *The Surge of Piety* may be singled out, something that was not present in the article. In the book I subscribed to Reinhold Niebuhr's claim that there is a worse sin than human idolatry: moral irresponsibility. As Niebuhr wrote, "the Christian faith enables men, not to escape idolatry absolutely, but to accept responsibilities, knowing that those responsibilities will involve us in idolatries from which no form of human

---

8   At the beginning of *The Surge of Piety in America* I pointed out that we could hardly discern a great "religious revival" underway in the country; the most to be said was that there was definitely an upsurge of *interest* in religion—a matter of religiosity. I conceived "piety" in terms of what I called "folk religion," meaning popular religion in alliance with human interests and human ideals—quite the antithesis of George Santayana's presentment of piety as "reverence for the sources of one's being." The book discerned the roots of the "surge" within certain distinctive and ongoing socio-psychological processes in American life. Much of the assessment was made from the standpoint of the concept of irony. Unlike *The Christian Century* piece, the study paid a lot of attention to the neo-fundamentalist, revivalist enterprise of Billy Graham. *The Surge* became a Religious Book Club Selection. My excuse for getting this in is to point out that religious-institutional publishing interests in our country can easily give voice to the *critique* of religion—on the odd but enabling basis that their commitment is, after all, to some form of financial solvency rather than to a given faith. (Cf. Luke 16:9: "Make friends for yourselves by means of unrighteous mammon.")

perfection will redeem us."[9] Much of the entire problematic in the retrospective before the reader centers in the struggle between two massively competing forms of sin: idolatry, and moral irresponsibility—with special reference to the vocation of writing. For even if we agree with Niebuhr that (at least in some instances) the Christian faith empowers people to accept moral responsibilities, this hardly meets the fateful question of whether the idolatries that accompany the church's Christological claims may themselves be contributors to moral irresponsibility. In *Judaism and Modern Man* Will Herberg identifies idolatry as the root source of all wrongdoing and all moral evil; presumably, that root extends to human irresponsibility.

Through several later essays I carried forward the critique of religion as discussed thus far. "The Pulsation of Religion" addressed itself to the social, psychological, and theological dialectic of the sacred and the profane, or the relationship between religion and culture. The article grappled with the question, How far can we go in expanding religion into every phase of life without diluting spiritual vitality? A prevailingly "spiritual" faith is deficient in responsibility for the "world," but a prevailingly "secular" faith loses its peculiar calling.

"The Rise and Fall of Popular Religion" was a kind of epilogue to *The Surge of Piety in America.* Differing forms of religion function as important means of social-psychological identity and location for the American people. American religiousness can thus be highly secular in character and yet retain its religious visage and intention.

The question of the essay "When Is Faith Not Faith?" was answered: when "faith" is "among other things, religion-in-general, American style. It is then that sociological and psychological analysis has the right to be heard." The article applied the sociological and social-psychological theory of the Americanization and secularization of religious faith (the triumph of religious pluralism—a pluralism that is itself *not* religious—plus the dominance of religion-in-general) to the question of the Catholic identity of Senator John F. Kennedy and his "chances" of election to the presidency in 1960.[10]

---

[9]   *The Surge of Piety in America,* p. 167.

[10]   A final piece that bore upon the critique of religion was "Ventures of the Post-Freudian Conscience," a review-article that dealt with the encounter between religion and psychology, particularly psychiatry. Three volumes were analyzed, O. Hobart Mowrer, *The*

IV

The previous section upon the critique of religion has introduced some foundation elements for this next section upon the study and place of religion in higher education.

"The Strangeness of Religion in the University Curriculum"[11] (reproduced below) addressed itself to the ambiguity of meaning and the tension in substance that religion manifests within the secular university. As I today review that exposition, I am unable to find any overruling incoherence within it. But I am disconcerted by my inclusion in the course of the analysis of a couple of Christological protestations: "University education, in common with all areas of life, stands under the judgment of Jesus Christ, the only begotten of the Father...If without Christ 'not anything was made that was made,' we should expect Him to be the invisible Logos of every university, as He is of every community and of every nation." To raise a question close to one I hazarded near the beginning of the present chapter, Wherein lies the *necessity* for this sort of Christian avowal? Here was analytical gratuitousness in almost pure form.

There may be some use in placing the interpretation of the study of religion contained in "The Strangeness" into the context of the aims of a university, as I at present think of these. The goals of any university education issue forth from anthropological and moral understanding: What is humankind? What are humankind's needs and obligations? In observing that most of the characteristics that traditionally and reputedly describe the human essence can be applied to destructive as well as creative purposes (and hence are insufficient), John E. Smith argues to the alternative and synoptic conclusion that "man" is that being "who can be called to account for himself and his deeds."[12] Accordingly, university education ought to be fundamentally practical in character. Its task is one of vocational (*vocatio*, calling) training. (*Training*: "the education,

---

Crisis in Psychiatry and Religion; Simon Doniger, ed., *The Nature of Man in Theological and Psychological Perspective*; and W. Earl Biddle, *Integration of Religion and Psychiatry*.

[11] This was the presidential address before the 1956 annual meeting of the American Academy of Religion (founded in 1909; name changed in 1964 from the National Association of Biblical Instructors).

[12] John E. Smith, "A Responsible Animal," *Yale Alumni Magazine and Journal*, Nov. 1976, p. 12.

instruction, or discipline of one who or that which trains"; *train*: "to develop or form the habits, thoughts or behavior of a person by discipline and instruction."[13]) In the university we seek ways to think better and to be more responsible (*verantwortlich*, answerable). "Scholarship is not very compatible with absolutistic exclusivism and uncritical authoritarianism."[14] Amidst and throughout our effort the individual (student, professor, administrator) endeavors, and is enabled, to develop her/his peculiar gifts. In a word, the university is a place where historic and analytic intelligence is brought to bear upon human decision-making.[15]

V

The nature of scientific method (in the human and social sciences) was brought home to me through day-to-day experience during 1955-1956. The one major stipulation in a grant from the Ford Foundation's Fund for the Advancement of Education was that the recipient work in a field or fields outside her or his own. I chose the psychological and social sciences, and spent the year as a faculty fellow in the Department of Social Relations at Harvard University, concentrating upon recent research and methods in psychology, sociology, and anthropology. I was much aided by such worthies as Gordon W. Allport, Jerome S. Bruner, Clyde Kluckhohn, Henry A. Murray, and Talcott Parsons. A tangible outcome of this effort was a somewhat technical philosophic and methodological piece in *American Scientist*, "The Contribution of *Nomothesis* in the Science of Man." As I now reread the argument there, I am not sure I still grasp it all, but the thrust of the exposition was the eminent worthwhileness of nomothetic, i.e., abstractive or generalizing, techniques within the scientific

---

[13] *The Random House Dictionary of the English Language.*

[14] John C. Bennett, "Two Christianities," in Paul T. Jersild and Dale A. Johnson, eds., *Moral Issues and Christian Response*, 2d ed. (New York: Holt, Rinehart and Winston, 1976), p. 29.

[15] For the Committee on Pre-Theological Studies of the National Association of Biblical Instructors (American Academy of Religion; see n. 11 above) I prepared a report, "Pre-Seminary Preparation and Study in Religion" (adopted by the organization as an official statement of policy in December 1958). The report, upon which I was greatly aided by an active committee, dealt with the relation between undergraduate religion study and graduate theological school work, from the perspective of liberal education.

enterprise. Wilhelm Windelband was the first to apply the terms *nomothetic* and *idiographic* to point to two modes of activity of the human mind. In the former case the search is for general laws. In the latter case there is "fidelity to the unique occurrence" (M. Brewster Smith), meaning that the emphasis is historical, for history, whether taken microcosmically or in larger configurations, is always the parturition of *this* time and *this* place, and is hence kept from exactly repeating itself. The two procedures are not strictly dichotomous, since they share many elements (such as the drawing of inferences).

The genius of *nomothesis* is precisely its origin within the human being as a unique being. *Nomothesis* is a singular, even momentous attainment on the part of humankind, the cultural animal. For how could generalization or abstraction be achieved by other than a peculiarly symbol-fabricating being? I went on to apply this orientation to certain problems and challenges within logical and scientific causation, law (pattern), explanation, and prediction. Generalizations, even profound ones, do not, of course, convey universal truth; scientific generalizations are most often or normatively modest in their claims (cf. the fitting truism, "other things being equal"). Nevertheless, the creativity that suffuses the process of generalization testifies well to the historic peculiarities that are present in humankind. To engage in the work of abstraction is to manifest human singularity in one of its distinctive forms or incarnations.

My efforts within the human sciences, as expressed in the *American Scientist* piece, realized a combination of philosophic concern and everyday applicability. This combination was further applied in "A Note on Theological Procedure" (see below), which sought to reckon with the relations among science, history, and theology—each of these interpreted as a different and equally legitimate way of looking at the one world.[16] Much later, my wife and I were to utilize the nomothesis/idiography dialectic in an essay upon the philosophic understanding of the Holocaust. I was further to apply the two concepts within a volume upon contemporary moral philosophies.[17]

---

[16] Further to the science-religion encounter, see two of my editorials, "Science and Man's Uniqueness" and "The End of the Science-Religion Dialogue." The latter was perhaps pretentious or at least premature in its suggestion that our age is turning postscientific, but I stand by its judgment that the science-religion controversy is at a nadir.

[17] "The Holocaust and the Enigma of Uniqueness: A Philosophical Effort at Practical Clarification," by Alice L. Eckardt and A. Roy Eckardt (1980); *For Righteousness' Sake* (1987), pp. 276-283.

VI

My current misgivings with certain traditionalist foundations that are customarily adduced for Christian morality have been hinted at in this chapter. These misgivings are an outcome of rather long and hard experience and thought. The essay, "The Ethical Motivation of the Christian," represented the traditionalist Christian outlook almost with a vengeance. I argued in behalf of the human need for a continuing moral transformation through the grace of God in Jesus Christ. To recast an earlier question: Wherein lies the *necessity*, morally speaking and therefore theologically speaking, for the final three words in the previous sentence? To be sure, the nascent and succeeding Christian community's entry into the Covenant with Israel as the people of God was made possible by the event of Jesus—the statement is but a truism—and perhaps the entry would not have taken place otherwise. But just how does this authorize (= make needful) my affirmation in the article that "human life and history are finally made meaningful through their center in Jesus Christ"? Is not a subtle deviation involved, *from* an essentially historical observation concerning Christianity's inception *to* an absolutist theological conclusion? This shift is revealed in further passages from the essay:

> Christian faith maintains a concreteness concerning the divine answer
> to the human plight that is not found in Judaism. It is in Christ and
> through Christ that men may stand beyond the power of fate...Through
> the forgiveness and the power of Christ, the very being of man may be
> transformed and emancipated...The Word the Christian church offers is
> the one made flesh in the Lord Jesus Christ, through whose life,
> crucifixion, and resurrection the meaning of this life is disclosed and
> eternal life becomes a present reality...[18] [The] incarnation of Christ

---

[18]   For a similar affirmation, cf. the poem "Between Christmas and Good Friday." This verse was not bad but it was illustrative of traditionalist Christian piety. (When I say the poem was not bad I imply that I know how to judge poetry, a condition that may well be contrary to fact. My consolation is that I am not sure that today's professionals in the field can themselves agree upon the criteria of poesy.)

is qualitatively different from other events. It is a final event that transcends the usual history of this world.[19]

The above attestation is open to severe moral questioning that may serve to meet the position upon its own ground: Does not traditionalist Christocentrism —e.g., "no one comes to the Father, but by me" (John 14:6)—impugn itself morally by means of its very imperialism and absolutism? May it not simply create barriers between people rather than break the barriers down? May not its "we versus them" mentality comprise a threat to morality rather than a contribution to morality? Is not its mentality functionally and hence substantively (historically) idolatrous?

Lineaments of my present theological position will become somewhat more evident in subsequent chapters. Yet even in my older years I cannot offer a viewpoint that fully satisfies me. I have not been able to achieve a final "system." But I have not become completely assured that this condition is bad. To prepare the way for later discussion, I here add one comment and include one story. The comment is that I should today affirm a theonomous and theocentric imperative as a possible resource for us, in a negative sense and in a positive sense—negatively, as a means of struggling against the exclusivism and immorality of traditionalist Christology; positively, as a means of implementing moral obligation. Later in this retrospective I endeavor to recapture the Christian teaching of the Incarnation, but upon a confessional, rather than apologetic, foundation.

The story is that of Rabbi Marshall T. Meyer, who during the worst days of the junta in Argentina searched the jails for people who had "disappeared" and consoled the families whose children had been taken from them. Subsequently, in his synagogue, B'nai Jeshurun in New York, the rabbi established a shelter for the homeless.

---

[19] The central emphasis in the essay was upon Christian moral action as a loving and obedient response to the love, mercy, and righteousness of God. I do not pursue that emphasis in the present context because it can be readily argued that identical affirmations may be made respecting Jewish or other non-Christian moral action. The deciding interfaith issue remains the alleged fact of the Incarnation—hence my present concentration upon that question.

What is certain is the strength the rabbi draws from his faith. Before the plaintive, shattering cry of the ram's horn ends Yom Kippur tonight, Rabbi Meyer will again read the words of Isaiah, preparing himself and his flock for year 5748.

"Share your bread with the hungry, take the homeless into your home," goes the scripture. "Clothe the naked when you see him, do not turn away people in need."[20]

VII

I mentioned at the start of this chapter that the time span surveyed herein includes toward its end two pieces of mine that appertained directly to the Christian-Jewish encounter. I am rather ashamed of the one but not substantively dissatisfied with the other.

The very title of the first of these, "The Mystery of the Jews' Rejection of Christ" (here excluded), mirrors a Christian presumption and bias not unreminiscent of the old saw utilized in the teaching of logic, "Have you left off beating your wife?" However, I did include the point that the categorical proposition, "the rejection of Christ by the Jews," is historically misleading and irresponsible. But, wrongly, I made Jesus' interpretation of his messianic role conflict with the dominant view of Messiah among first-century Jews; this error was not to be corrected until later writings.[21]

This first article was heavily (and lamentably) Pauline. I now think of the practice of applying (from the Christian side) the category of "mystery" to the Jewish people and Jewish existence as troublemaking. It bolsters the habit of treating Jews in ways different from the treatment of other people. But the worst aspect of the essay "The Mystery," partly under the recreant enticements of Edmund Perry, was my flirting with Christian triumphalism in the guise of a supposedly obligational Christian mission to the Jews (*Judenmission*). Thus, I spoke of "the promises to Israel" as having been "fulfilled in the new people of God, the church." I perpetuated the unfortunate Tillichian notion of treating

---

[20] Douglas Martin, "In His Despair, Rabbi's Strength Revives Temple," *The New York Times*, 3 Oct. 1987.

[21] Consult, e.g., *For Righteousness' Sake*, chap. 4.

Judaism as part of the "latent church"; thus was I violating the dialogic norm that the identifying of a group's or faith's being or role is solely the business of that group or faith. Today I should reverse Tillich's argument and speak of the church as in a sense a latent part of Judaism, at least when the church is not wholly betraying Judaism.

The second article was "The Theology of Antisemitism," which appears below. Among other things, it sought to apply in broader and deeper terms than I had grappled with before the phenomenon of the Jewishness of Jesus as being integral to Christian antisemitism. The piece did retain the unfortunate concept of "mystery" respecting the Jewish people. Behind the essay lay a presupposition, sustained by historical and psychological findings: The life of Christians and the Christian community is assailed by self-contradictory and even self-destructive forces. But the exposition itself sought to give full credence to those facets of traditional Christian faith, centering in the transcendent mercy and judgment of God, that have constituted powerful deterrents to antisemitism.

We earlier noted the hypothesis of antisemitism as a displacement upon Jews of the Christian's repudiation of Jesus because of his demands. In this 1962 exposition the hypothesis was enlarged to cover the Christian repudiation of Jesus, not just for his demands, but for the very fact of his integral Jewishness.

So here I was back with antisemitism. Who wanted to be in that condition? Yet could I escape it?[22]

---

[22] Book reviews by me of relevance to the final section of this chapter were these: Will Herberg, *Judaism and Modern Man*; Mary Jeanine Gruesser, *Categorical Valuations of Jews Among Catholic Parochial School Children*; James Parkes, *End of an Exile*; and Jakob Jocz, *A Theology of Election*.

3A

Selected Writings

(1951-1962)

The New Look in American Piety

(*The Christian Century* 71 [1954]: 1395-1397)

When the Apostle Paul visited the Athenians he perceived that in every way they were very religious. Paul would probably make a similar observation about this country at mid-20th century. "Religion," Ralph Sockman recently pointed out, "seems to have become the vogue in America."

Piety is more and more diffusing itself among our people, particularly in ways that supplement the regular ministry of the churches. A nationally circulated "slick" magazine carries a page on which a well-known clergyman dispenses "peace-of-mind" religion to people writing in with spiritual problems. Religious books continue to lead best-seller lists. Popular song writers profitably emphasize religious themes. Radio stations pause not simply for the usual station breaks but for recommended moments of meditation. The movie makers know that few productions can out-box-office religious extravaganzas. The new piety has successfully invaded the halls of government. Attendance at prayer breakfasts is quite the thing for politicians these days. Ostensibly, even cabinet meetings can function better after a "word of prayer." And the pledge of allegiance is given the new religious look by the addition of the words "under God."

Elements of American "Culture Religion"

John C. Bennett has pointed out that today's religious revival is largely a matter of American "culture religion," involving the following elements:

1. The tendency to reduce Christianity to a gospel of happiness and success with no place for...the biblical warning against idolatry, judgment, repentance on the cross.

2. The loss of any basis of criticism on our culture as a whole and the close alliance of religion with the forces of nationalism.

3. The capitalizing on the fact that communism is atheistic and the strong suggestion that because we are against communism, God must be on our side.

4. The close cooperation between many of the leaders of this religious movement and the forces of social reaction. ["Billy Graham at Union," *Union Seminary Quarterly Review*, May 1954.][1]

The divergent voices of American culture religion are one in the faith that God is an exceedingly handy fellow to have around.

It is hardly fair to condemn out of hand revivals of religion. There is doubtless sincerity of motive in much of the new piety. Besides, God is able to use not alone the wrath but also the foibles of men to praise him. For St. Paul the thing that counted was that Christ was preached, whether in pretense or in truth. The extent to which a reawakening religion may be born of the Spirit and may indicate genuine religious devotion is immeasurable.

It hardly follows that the new piety is to be accepted uncritically. There is nothing in the Bible to support the view that religion is necessarily a good thing. Scripture has no ax to grind for religion; on the contrary, it is highly suspicious of much that passes for religion. The lamentable thing about the current revival is the failure of many people to make discriminating judgments of differing religious outlooks. The truth is that a given brand of piety may represent nothing more than nice, virile idol worship.

Peace of Mind

Consider three aspects of the new piety which should cause Christians concern.

1. The cult of "peace of mind." The Christian church speaks in the name of the Great Physician who makes whole minds, souls and bodies. Were we to turn away those who hunger and thirst for spiritual peace, we would betray part of our pastoral function. That this cult has spread so phenomenally may well represent a divine judgment upon our ministry.

---

[1]   Even Billy Graham, whose evangelism does not fit this description of "culture religion," has praised quite indiscriminately those very aspects of the religious revival (peace-of-mind piety, the back-to-God movement of the American Legion, etc.) that hardly accord with his own Fundamentalism. For documentation of John Bennett's fourth point, see George Younger, "Protestant Piety and the Right Wing," *Social Action* (15 May 1951): 5-35.

The fact remains that the peace-of-mind cult readily turns into religious narcissism. The individual and his psycho-spiritual state occupy the center of the religious stage. Here is piety concentrating on its own navel. The Christian gospel, we must object, is in its redemptive wholeness a challenge to men to surrender themselves for the sake of Christ with the result that their hearts will go out to their brethren. The New Testament forcibly reminds them that in this world they have tribulation. They are to be of good cheer, but only because Christ has overcome the world. The shadow of his cross may indeed fall across their own lives.

The peace-of-mind movement is deficient morally and empirically. It has no grasp of the deep paradox that "whoever would save his life will lose it, and whoever loses his life for [Christ's] sake will find it." Lasting peace of mind is impossible apart from peace with God; yet enduring peace with God comes only when a man is ready to surrender his own peace of mind.

Personal Adjustment

This new cult counsels "personal adjustment." But adjustment to what? New Testament Christianity is hardly adjusted to its environment. It makes us seriously wonder, in fact, how much the social order is worth adjusting to. The gospel urges us to nonconformity: "Do not be conformed to this world but be transformed."

An evil aspect of peace-of-mind religion is its acceptance, by default, of the social status quo. An unannounced assumption is that the present condition of the social order is irrelevant to one's true needs and outside the scope of one's obligations. In truth, to limit religion to "spiritual" concerns is to abdicate responsibility in the struggle against man's inhumanity to man. The tragedy is that the peace-of-mind cult unwittingly furthers the rise of radical politico-economic movements which step in to fill the void left by the absence of a social gospel.

A final irony is that peace-of-mind religion fails to address itself to the very cultural crisis which helps produce more distraught souls than the practitioners could ever handle. But its greatest sin lies in using God as a means for human ends. This is blasphemous. The Bible tells us that God uses us for his ends.

"Woe to those who are at ease in Zion, and to those who feel secure on the mountain of Samaria."

The Man Upstairs

2. The cult of the "Man Upstairs." A rhapsodic inquiry greets us from the TV screen and the radio: "Have you talked to the Man Upstairs?" God is a friendly neighbor who dwells in the apartment just above. Call on him anytime, especially if you are feeling a little blue. He does not get upset over your little faults. He understands. We have been assured by no less a theologian than Jane Russell that the Lord is a "livin' Doll," a right nice guy. Thus is the citizenry guided to divine-human chumminess.

This view of religion is not wholly unlike the one just considered. However —to borrow William James's terminology—the peace-of-mind cult makes more of an appeal to the "sick soul" religionist, while the cult of the Man Upstairs attracts more the "healthy-minded" type. The latter individual is not so much weighed down by fears and complexes. On the surface at least he is well adjusted. The appeal of religion is that it can make him get even more pleasure out of life. Fellowship with the Lord is, so to say, an extra emotional jag that keeps him happy. The "gospel" makes him "feel real good."

In this cult, religion verges on entertainment, perhaps merges with it. Thus "gospel boogie," replete with masters of ceremonies, gospel quartets, popcorn and soda pop, is able to play to jam-packed audiences in many cities. The financial take from the paid admissions is considerable.

Those whose God is the Friendly Neighbor would not dream of hearing him say,

For three transgressions of America, yea for four, I will not turn my wrath away.

Our new culture religion is helping to mold us into a people possessed of the certainty that the Lord is squarely on our side. Whatever we think and do can be carried on in good conscience.

Buried in Triviality

The stern fact remains that to behave as if man *as man* were not anxious with himself in the presence of his fellows and, especially, of God, is to dull the moral sense. It is to destroy man's dignity as a free being. He is dehumanized. His life is reduced, as Will Herberg says, "to the level of subhuman creation which knows neither sin nor guilt." The moral and spiritual life is buried in triviality.

The Christian whose norm is Scripture must always have a particularly uneasy conscience. He recognizes the gulf between the quality of his life and the sacrifice of God's only Son on the cross. He knows the love that came down on Calvary. He knows the judgment too. And he knows that the love cannot be separated from the judgment.

The Man Upstairs is a foolish idol fabricated from out of the proud imaginations of the human spirit, a childish projection of granddaddy. The real God is the relentless One who pursues us and gives us no peace until our religiosity is transformed by repentance. In the very hour that the gospel quartet soothes with the universalist-hedonist refrain, "Everybody's gonna have a wonderful time up there," the sheep and the goats are being sorted out. "It is a fearful thing to fall into the hands of the *living* God." Old Testament scary stuff? No, the Epistle to the Hebrews. The adjective in the phrase "livin' Doll" is precisely what causes us so much trouble. The real God is the Hound of Heaven. We wish he would go and live somewhere else. But the Lord refuses to move, no matter how we try to take the threat out of him by reducing him to a friendly neighbor. The cult of the Man Upstairs meets its nemesis before the Holy Presence.

Chosen People

3. The cult of "we" versus "they." This cult is more tangibly sinister than the other two. It is just a short step from a god who is the Great Adjuster and/or the Friendly Neighbor to the god who fights on the side of his chosen people, supporting their racial, economic or national interests. The crucial point is that the first two cults have already stimulated and endorsed powerful human

emotions. The obvious outcome is that it is un-American to be unreligious. We are the good spiritual people. The God of judgment has died.

In a searching analysis Joseph E. Cunneen describes our third cult as follows:

> At present there seems to be a wave of enthusiasm for a rather undefined "religion" in America. What is its origin? There is fear in the atmosphere: fear of the unknown forces in man, fear of the natural forces he has learned to release without yet knowing how to control. But the fear emphasized by the new religionists is chiefly fear of "the others" as "we" feel it. Well publicized and shrewdly aware of our general uncertainty, the movement appears to give calculated encouragement to an attitude which at its mildest is the vague, almost unconscious resentment against the neighbor who always crosses our lawn to get to his back door; at its worst, it is that of a lynching mob. [*Cross Currents*, Fall 1954.]

Only the ethically blind will, for example, equate the moral health of world communism and the United States when it comes down to how "they" should be treated. Yet it is perverse to conclude that our cause is God's cause. To equate the two is to be in for a shock before the transcendent justice of God.

The dangers in the "we" versus "they" cult are especially evident today in relations between this country and the rest of the world. The nation that best fulfills its God-given responsibilities is not necessarily the nation that displays the most religiosity. A country possessed of the might of the United States might do better to go into its closet and pray to its Father in secret rather than standing on the street corners parading its piety before men. The piety of individuals stands a relatively better chance of inducing repentance than does the public piety of nations. The temptation is just about irresistible for a powerful nation to rely on its religiosity as proof of its own virtue. Thus is threatened the possibility of sober and responsible political action.

Against all human idolatries we may set the peace of Christ which passes all understanding. We have not earned his peace. It is a gift we have received. It does not center in the self or the group. It centers in the cross and the empty tomb. It provides an ultimate vantage point from which the whole drama of life may be viewed. It is the peace of a disturbing forgiveness. God ceases to be fashioned in our image; we are made over into his. We are granted not a short-cut or trivial solution to our anxieties but the grace to laugh and to know that our anxieties are of no ultimate consequence. The peace of Christ comes, mysteriously, when we forget all about our peace, when we prostrate ourselves before the holiness of God, and when we discern the source of evil not in "them" but in our own hearts. What is more humiliating than to be forgiven by the Lord of heaven and earth, to be accepted just as we are—petty and full of pride?

The peace of Christ issues in the nonchalance of faith and service. The gospel meets the desperate human need of which the cults are an ominous symptom. It does so in the very act of defeating idolatry.

The Strangeness of Religion in the University Curriculum

(The Journal of Bible and Religion 25 [1957]: 3-12)

In a recent monograph Daniel Jenkins employs the seemingly strange title, *The Strangeness of the Church*. To most people in the West, we are reminded, the church is an extremely ordinary and obvious institution. But whatever the state of popular opinion, there is a strangeness about the church "in that while it stands in the midst of the everyday life of the world, it yet makes unusual claims for itself and displays unusual qualities in justification for them."[1]

I hope it will not be presumed from my title, in the context of the quotation, that I intend to assign the role of the church in the university to departments of religion. I am, however, attracted by Dr. Jenkins's phrasing and I am prompted to say that the concept of strangeness is not inapplicable to a discussion of the place of religion in the university curriculum. Religion is found in the everyday life of many university curricula and yet, as I propose to show, it embodies an ambiguity of meaning and a tension in substance which reflect strangeness. On the side of one possible link between religion and the church, the relation between religion and the university manifests, as we shall see, an analogy to the relation of church and state.

The double thesis underlying the discussion as a whole is, on the one hand, that it is necessary to be aware of the unique character of the problem of religion if we are to attain a defensible educational policy, and, on the other hand, that it is possible to affirm a positive relation between religion and university education.

I

Let us approach our problem by inquiring whether religion should have a discrete place in the academic pursuits of the university. Expressed in terms of

---

[1]   Daniel Jenkins, *The Strangeness of the Church* (Garden City: Doubleday, 1955), pp. 9-11.

a specific issue, ought the university include an identifiable department of religion?[2]

I do not display great wisdom in saying that the answer will turn on two questions. What is the nature and purpose of the university? How are we to understand the term religion?

If a university views its purpose as itself "religious," one series of answers may be forthcoming. My remarks fall in the context of the more influential —although not for that reason more happy—assumption that education has a secular goal, something that is interpretable, of course, in a variety of ways. We are all familiar with variations within a secular purpose—the advancement of learning, aid in successful living, the integration of personality, the search for truth, etc. If the representative of religion agrees to work along with a generally secular point of view, then, however great that view's distance from his own convictions of faith, he cannot very properly turn to such a norm as "religious nurture" as a basis for discussing university education. He is better advised to take an empiricist stance. This need not imply the total exclusion of auto-biographical elements. Some of these latter are in the background of my exposition.

What is there about religion that raises an issue for curricular policy? As a point of departure we may refer to a multiple ambiguity within the term religion. Four possible dimensions of religion are most relevant. All of them overlap and tend to converge at one or another point. Beyond the fact that they do not pose the same existential problems, the four dimensions are not on the same conceptual level. My intention is not to provide definitions of religion or to classify religion into types. The categories I suggest are simply instruments for analyzing the educational problem of religion.

---

[2]   I am not directly concerned here with the rationale for maintaining a divinity school along with a medical school, law school, etc. That fairly prevalent practice presents problems of its own, associated in large measure with the fact that divinity schools are usually considered primarily professional in character. The relation of the divinity school to the university as a whole does, however, present a problem somewhat analogous to the one I raise. Divinity schools usually think of themselves as explicitly Christian in outlook, while many of the universities of which they are a part do not officially or publicly espouse a Christian philosophy of education. Since the relation between departments of religion and the universities is analogous to the situation just mentioned, the suggestions in parts III and IV of the present essay may have a bearing upon the problem of the divinity school.

1. *Inevitable (Implicit) Religion.* Unavoidably, man is *homo religiosus.* By nature he is a religious being in that he seeks something in which the meaning of his existence may be grounded.[3] Without this "something," the way is opened to basic anxiety. Religion is a fundamental psychological and anthropological fact. Thus considered, it may manifest itself behaviorally, but lack of such manifestation does not mean that inevitable religion is absent. The question of whether there should be religion in this first sense within the university is gratuitous, since wherever there are human beings there is religion.

2. *Behavioral (Explicit) Religion.* Religion makes itself pervasively evident as an integral facet of human life. It is practiced very widely, talked about incessantly, continually studied. Religion is a basic historical and cultural fact.

3. *Finite Religion.* In much inevitable and behavioral religion the "divine" power or reality that may arouse ultimate concern is not itself ultimate. That is to say, it is a being beside other beings.

4. *Ultimate Religion.* This dimension is opposed to the third, although from one point of view it resembles the latter in being more restricted conceptually than the first two. There is religion in which an individual's or group's ultimate concern rests in the "unconditional." Here the power or reality that gives meaning to life is not a conditioned being beside other beings. It is instead the creative source of all things. The skeptic may think of ultimate religion as nonsense but he can hardly insist logically that the God of Judeo-Christian faith is in fact no more than a human idol or illusion. For, as a matter of fact, the biblical view not only interprets the divine as other than one more being but also embraces within itself the very legitimate insistence that no man can himself grasp ultimate truth. (The mystery remains of how men can engage in such insistence all by themselves.)

II

How does this brief exercise in logomachy bear upon a decision for or against the inclusion of a department of religion in the university?

An affirmative decision is often met by the objection that the teacher of religion is usually a "committed" person who does not view his—or any—

---

[3] Will Herberg, *Protestant-Catholic-Jew: An Essay in American Religious Sociology* (Garden City: Doubleday, 1955), p. 270.

subject matter impartially. (This characteristic can become associated with the whole department.) Huston Smith, in *The Purposes of Higher Education*, makes a strong case for holding that, in point of fact, genuine commitment and real objectivity bolster each other.[4] Objectivity is a chief mark of the genuineness of one's convictions.[5] Professor Smith maintains that the man who is convinced of the validity of his beliefs can afford to be open-minded. I interpret this to imply, with respect to the teacher of religion, a confidence not unlike that of the Pharisee, Gamaliel (ignoring for the present the fact that the council of Israel was confronted by apostles of the Christian faith). In the spirit of Gamaliel—a teacher by trade—if this positivist theory of history or this behaviorist form of psychological experimentation is of men, it will fail; but if it is of God, we will not be able to overthrow them. And even if the latter, so much the better for the cause. It would be a distinct existential embarrassment for the teacher of religion to "be found opposing God."[6] From this point of view, the scholarly freedom to which the teacher of religion gives his allegiance should excel that academic freedom which lacks an ontological and/or theological foundation. Much representation of academic freedom is hard put at the point of supplying ultimate intellectual justification. However, both sides can agree with Huston Smith that objectivity as a positive virtue means fairness to evidence, respect for reasonable differences in point of view, and avoidance of an attempt to proselytize.[7] And clearly the work of a teacher of religion is to be judged by the same standards of competence as the work of any other teacher.

Once all this is said, there is an important element of truth in the objection concerning partiality. The allusion to Gamaliel has already suggested this. The truth in the objection arises out of the convergence of ultimate religion and inevitable religion and the convergence of ultimate religion and behavioral religion. Even if all professors face the problem of personal commitment, are they all committed in a way that has the same direct implications for their work? True, religion is not the only area that manifests an unavoidable dimension.

---

[4]   Huston Smith, *The Purposes of Higher Education* (New York: Harper & Bros., 1955), chap. 3 - "Objectivity Versus Commitment."

[5]   Ibid., p. 44.

[6]   Acts 5:33-39.

[7]   Smith, *Purposes*, pp. 42-43, 129.

According to the concept of "economic man," for example, human beings inevitably work out some way of exchanging goods and services. Yet a real difference is involved here which may prove to be a difference in kind. The commitment of the professor of economics—at the point where personal commitment and professional activity bear crucially upon each other—is not usually or potentially as intense as that of the professor of religion. One does not normally "bet his life" on, say, Keynesian economics. Other loyalties may demand allegiance. Only in ultimate religion is the commitment able, in principle, to stand in judgment upon all other commitments. Yet is this not precisely where the teacher of religion may readily take his stand? In prosaic terms, he usually "believes in God," often in the biblical sense of allegiance to the transcendent creator and judge of all things. In his own faith, he is at least a Gamaliel and, more often, he is some kind of apostle—sometimes, indeed, an ordained clergyman. To be sure, the professor of economics may be possessed of the same ultimate commitment that the teacher of religion professes. The former may be a convinced Christian. But the significant difference is that in the case of the economist personal religious conviction is not intertwined so intimately and dialectically with teaching, writing, research, personal associations, and other professional responsibilities as are the activities of the religion teacher. In short, professional work in religion and ultimate commitment simply cannot be kept apart. And yet, we can hardly demand that the teacher of religion not be a religious man (in the dimension of commitment to the source of all things). The alternatives are to have a "disinterested" analyst teach religion—which raises its own problems—or to entertain adherence to some form of finite religion as a credential for employment.

One methodological dilemma, not wholly lacking in other academic disciplines, is whether religion is to be taught from "inside" or from "outside." We are often reminded that a classroom is not a church. To summon students to get down on their knees to pray in order to learn about prayer is quite illicit (even apart from the potential blasphemy in such a pedagogical technique). I have heard the claim that provision for "religious opportunities" on the campus can help offset limitations in course offerings in religion. From the standpoint of an academic-intellectual treatment of religion, this claim does not seem to make much more sense than an assertion that we can go easy on courses in marketing if a number of stores catering to students are located near the campus. There is, nevertheless, a measure of truth here. It is not only as a Christian that a religion professor will support student participation in religious activities. As a teacher of religion he knows that the bystander approach to religion must be supplemented by participating knowledge or insight. The professor concerned to advance learning in religion can scarcely rest content with external, descriptive analysis. Religion is in essence an affair of extreme intimacy. Education in religion remains superficial until phenomenological analysis is reinforced by sympathetic knowledge related to the presuppositions of the faith or faiths under study. Yet this necessity poses its own difficulties. "Commitment" for the sake of study is hardly genuine commitment. On the other hand, the phenomenological examination of a religious faith can be dissociated neither from inevitable religion nor from whatever the professor —and often the student—may regard as normative religion, i.e., ultimate and sometimes even finite religion. Presence of these other dimensions will assuredly color the analysis made.

The human tendency even among erstwhile advocates of ultimate religion to find the meaning of existence in some finite reality poses an added dilemma. To the extent that people many times become ultimately concerned over something which is not ultimate (family, political party, nation, etc.), a significant complication appears. The distinction between religion and non-religion tends to break down.[8] This situation helps keep open the perplexing question of the extent to which religion is in essence a separate category of life justifying a separate academic department in the university. In this connection, it cannot be emphasized too much that the exponent of a biblical world view and the secular educator may be in accord at a very significant point. In the biblical tradition the separation of religion from life as a whole is indefensible.[9] From the Christian standpoint, religion has no ultimately justifiable place as a discrete category of human existence. The secularist who is opposed to a separate department of religion may be unconsciously testifying to a view from which he

---

[8]   A course in contemporary religious trends in at least one university other than the writer's examines the Communist Manifesto as a "scriptural" document. An all-inclusive treatment of religion has become rather widespread in recent years.

[9]   For Alexander Miller, provision for a department of religion is not the proper rationale in the relation of religion and higher education. A proper rationale "requires the positive presentation of the [Christian] tradition in its historic and systematic relation to *every* academic discipline" ("Religion and Higher Education: Some Theological Considerations," unpublished).

fancies he has long since emancipated himself. In truth, there are many respects in which prophetic Christian faith has always been at serious odds with religion.

This aspect of the discussion points to an important analytical problem with existential import. Distinctions between religion and something other than religion are soon driven into the normative question of how to distinguish "true" from "false," "good" from "bad" religion. The latter question is highly decisive in the matter of where, if anywhere, religion should come into the academic curriculum. A university which is not itself committed to ultimate religion could hardly justify the apportioning of study in ultimate religion to a department of religion and study in finite religion to other departments! Christian faith, for all its idolatrous distortions through the years, is primarily a matter of ultimate religion. And yet, again and again in the curricula of ostensibly secular universities we find that the majority of religion courses are devoted to some aspect of Christian faith. It almost seems that the right hand of the university does not know what its left hand is doing. Here is modern education at the height of ambiguity—ambiguity of meaning by no means unrelated to tension in substance.

III

Lest the exposition thus far lead us to favor the exclusion of religion as an autonomous department in the university, we must look at the other side of the matter. Exclusion creates its own perplexing problems.

From one point of view, inevitable religion as a general state of affairs might at first appear to support exclusion. Do not university departments require specific, as against diffuse, subject matter? Inevitable religion is a highly diffuse thing. However, under the assumption that the inevitable dimension of religion is potentially subject in some way to meaningful discourse, could not that dimension be analyzed sufficiently within such disciplines as psychology, anthropology, and sociology? In addition, could not religion in its behavioral or historical manifestations be treated satisfactorily within these disciplines? Unfortunately certain serious issues arise.

If, as we have noted, ultimate religion and inevitable religion tend to converge, so do inevitable religion and any world view. By a world view I mean a principle (or set of principles) which is not subjected to any other principle or area of life but instead provides a framework of meaning for all of one's life. The university professor is possessed of a world view—not because he is a professor but because he is a human being. His world view cannot remain entirely hidden.

It is evident that religion cannot be taught at all apart from decisive presuppositions about the nature and meaning of religion. The question of the inevitable character or non-inevitable character of religion is a question not merely for scientific and philosophical analysis; it is in itself a religious question. Further, how is the professor of psychology, anthropology, etc., to deal with two or more competing forms of religion, whether implicit or explicit? If he seeks to limit himself to description, he cannot wholly avoid conveying the impression that the views involved are in some sense alike valid (or invalid). But if he makes relative value judgments between the faiths he cannot wholly escape associating himself with that evaluative action which is intrinsic to religion as a phenomenon of human life. And, no matter which approach he takes, he must know that all teaching, like all communication, has to resort to symbolic language, which precludes any sure coincidence between thought and reality. No teaching in any field totally eludes the problem of objectivity and commitment.

A number of representatives of the other fields I have mentioned hold that religion as a whole belongs to the childhood of the race and will be gradually outgrown as man progresses and becomes more rational. In other words, the assumption is that religion is not inevitable, much less tenable in some abiding way. Under the influence of figures like E. B. Tylor and Sigmund Freud, many teachers have made precisely this assumption, although it is true that the picture seems to have changed somewhat for the better in recent years. We would never tolerate the teaching of physics by someone who believed that the principles of physics are ultimately an illusion—unless by some miracle this belief were not permitted to color the teaching.

Inevitable religion cannot be dismissed either by an evolutionary theory introduced *a priori* or by any other rationalistic *tour de force*. The criticism I am making applies also in the study of behavioral or explicit religion, but the problem remains more delicate with respect to implicit religion. Most scholars who scoff at religion have sufficient integrity to be willing to describe religious phenomena with some degree of impartiality when occasion demands. At the same time they are often careful to imply that they regard themselves as having been successfully emancipated from the immaturity of religion.

Yet the "religious" teacher of religion faces correspondingly delicate ethical difficulties. If he protests against a "scientific" treatment of religion, what happens to his erstwhile support of freedom of thought? Willingness to have religion in all its forms subjected to the most thoroughgoing criticism must be contingent upon provision in the university for instruction which will counteract a negative or even neutral treatment. This qualification suggests the necessity of a department of religion or its equivalent. Freedom for the challengers of Gamaliel's faith but not for Gamaliel himself is not genuine freedom.

If the professor of psychology or anthropology or sociology is tempted to pre-judge the total religious situation, the representative of ultimate religion has a parallel moral problem. He is tempted to devaluate finite religion in a way that lacks charitable understanding of the psychological, historical, and social factors helping to produce finite religion. One contribution of a religion department may be to make apparent, through proper attention to historical testimony and through "case studies" of real human beings, how there is a persistency in religion in all its dimensions. There is nothing inherently impossible in this aspect of our work. Where discussion is sufficiently intensive and honest, the varied ways in which people are religiously concerned disclose themselves with fair readiness.[10]

The goals of secular education imply thorough knowledge of religion at least as a phenomenon of human life and culture. Even where prior provision has been made in other departments for courses in history of religion, sociology of religion, psychology of religion, and the like, in none of these cases is explicit religion viewed synoptically and in its own right. Without a department specifically charged with instruction in religion, there will probably remain a certain omission of subject matter together with a lack of adequate administrative supervision and specialized study in religion. Exclusion of a religion department hinders comprehension of the significance of religion in human affairs. Courses of the types just mentioned usually, and with a certain

---

[10] Some slight mitigation of the problem posed by the different dimensions of religion, and particularly by inevitable religion, may be possible through alteration in departmental names. For example, at the University of Pennsylvania the title, Department of Religious Thought, is used. In some small measure this may tend to shift attention away from inevitable religion toward the other three dimensions.

propriety, consider religion from an external standpoint rather than from inside. I have already maintained that both perspectives are needed.

Not alone in its unavoidable and explicit dimensions as such but also in and through the other, more discrete dimensions, religion influences human life and destiny. Where but in a department that specifically addresses itself to religious concerns can the decisive issue of ultimate versus finite religion be wrestled with in the depth it requires? Academic representatives of religion tend to be much more aware of the third, or finite, and fourth, or ultimate, dimensions of religion than other academicians. (The same can probably still be said for our day with reference to the first, or inevitable, dimension.) Elucidation of this awareness is itself a contribution to the understanding of religion in its totality.

IV

If it is agreed that religion taken in its several dimensions stands in a peculiarly problematic relation with university education, can we rationalize that relation positively? Much of what I have said thus far has already carried us beyond the multiple ambiguity of meaning within the concept of religion to the problem of existential tension within the substance of religion. Paul Tillich has formulated this latter problem in general terms as one of, on the one hand, the resistance by religion of any attempt to subsume it under the category of culture through putting it alongside other cultural realms and, on the other hand, the presence of religion within and throughout all cultural realms. This tension creates an important question in applied theology (and educators either have to become theologians in the presence of the question or turn their backs on a practical issue of great import). That question is, what is the relation between man's ultimate concern(s) and university education?

Perhaps we can live a little more wisely with the strangeness of religion if we set the whole problem within the context of our common national life. I should be the last to say that our religio-cultural arrangements are finally normative. Yet, if we are to be our brother's keeper in a fallen, untidy world, we must ever seek some form of relatively creative compromise. Do I go too far in hypothesizing that, within the general ratio and proportion of American culture, from one point of view religion is to the university as church is to state?[11] This is no more than an analogy, but let us see where it leads.

In the American tradition the churches do not call upon the state as such to be explicitly or positively Christian, any more than they want, in principle, to attack the structure of the state. The democratic state in a pluralistic society does not identify itself overtly in terms of biblical faith. This arrangement obtains despite the fact that—or, to make the paradox more transparent, because of the fact that—our national life already rests upon innumerable supports of faith. Evidently a serious desire continues and even grows that our nation retain its biblical foundations, which means support of the churches as explicit spokesmen for the foundations. The churches are openly permitted, indeed expected, to speak for the divine Law and the divine Love. Were a political threat to arise against freedom of this form of religion, few would be surprised if the churches rose to meet the threat. More significantly, in such an eventuality the churches would call out very great popular loyalty and support. This underlying attitude would not be present if Christian convictions had not already been deeply rooted in our national conscience. That we do not have an explicitly Christian state may be providential for the Christian cause. It helps preclude the ultimate sin to which the churches can fall prey, that of calling upon ultimate truth to justify what prove to be policies of self-glorification.

To pursue the analogy, it would not do for religion to call upon the university to be explicitly or positively Christian, any more than religion would want, in principle, to attack the structure of university education. The university does not identify itself overtly in terms of biblical faith. This arrangement obtains despite the fact that—or, indeed, because of the fact that—the life of the university rests upon innumerable supports of faith. The foundation is revealed to the extent that in the university history is taken seriously, human dominion is fostered over nature, and young men and women are guided to a fulfillment of their social responsibilities. It is quite true that the most spacious platforms in the modern university are provided for the proclamation of, or at least information about, various finite deities. However unnecessary these opportun-

---

[11] Religion here must refer to a primarily intellectual (including a theological) treatment of religion in its various dimensions. Otherwise we could as readily say that the university chaplaincy is to the university as church is to state. The latter figure may indeed hold, but the frame of reference is then different from the present one.

ities in a kingdom of God, they are required in a free society. Whether they are not simply necessary but in addition morally and theologically defensible turns on the question of whether ultimate religion is also present as a live intellectual alternative.

It is the case at present that academic representatives of religion are increasingly permitted, and perhaps even expected, to speak for the divine Law and the divine Love. If an academic threat were to arise to freedom of this form of religion, we should hope that these representatives would rise to meet the threat. More significantly, I believe there would be considerable professorial and student support of the resistance—other things being equal. If there were not such support, we should have to stand our ground anyway and continue to assert through all available means that university education, in common with all areas of life, stands under the judgment of Jesus Christ, the only begotten of the Father. Meanwhile, the lack—with some notable exceptions—of an explicitly Christian university may be providential. Potentially, religion is the most idolatrous area of human life, for so often in religion ultimate sanction is sought for dubious ideas and reprehensible policies.

I referred earlier to the problem of a commitment which exercises a judgment upon all other human commitments. I have intimated that within the context of the categorization of human life and of a potential conflict of commitments, a certain plausibility appears for questioning the place of religion as a separate division in the curriculum. If the university, through the instrumentality of openness to truth, may come unwittingly to implement a divine judgment upon the idolatries of, say, a department of religion, what is to check manifestations of idolatry within the persuasion that there is saving power in "openness to truth"? A department of religion may serve as critical guardian against the easy habit of idolatrizing particular human insights into the nature of truth (including philosophic insights founded in the claims of reason). It is the case that, by its very structure, the university may embody something of the Protestant principle of self-criticism. Very often an intellectually defensible vantage point that is not dissolved by the criticism but makes the criticism possible lies buried in the unconscious of the university. Yet we must go beyond this. The required vantage point can become at least pre-conscious and perhaps tangibly forceful in and through a department of religion, itself as much an integral part of the university as any other part. The relation of religion and the university, like that of church and state, may embody a built-in check upon the idolatries of either of the two sides.

This is not to ignore the possibility of more positive relationships. As the sociologist Howard Becker suggests, it may well have been the close relation of theological studies with general university training in German-speaking countries, in contrast to some others, that kept the battle over biological evolutionism from involving more than a few skirmishes.[12] We may note too that the tension between religion and the university is itself a matter for study within the religion curriculum.

Is there not a growing apprehension in the universities that there ought to be provision somewhere in higher education for a word from the God beyond the gods? If silence testifies to the glory of the real God—a sobering thought for any professor—yet a genuine word from the Lord is sometimes heard through human speech and action (unless I misapply the human meaning of Jesus). A colleague of mine in philosophy has, not atypically, long since exchanged his Jewish birthright for the gospel of naturalism. I do not think I am starting a false rumor when I say that I get the impression he is secretly glad there is a Department of Religion at our university. However self-idolatrous that department, in company with sister departments elsewhere, there remains a widespread yearning among thinking men not merely for the realization of partial truths but for the Truth that, in judging us all, redeems us. My friend is repelled again and again by various forms of idolatry. But why? Many of our most secular educators are heirs of the Prophets and even of the Christ. They comprise an unknowing remnant of faith, testifying in a halting but unmistakable way, "Thou shalt worship the Lord thy God, and him only shalt thou serve." Our trembling times make plain the source of the disquiet everyone shares. Wearisome repetition, oral and written, does not change the fact that nuclear weapons have huddled us all into a dark corner where, some as believers, and some as non-believers, we reach out and feel the cold sweat of original sin on one another's bodies.

A qualification is that the word from beyond all finite words is not permitted to create too formidable a stumbling block to the autonomy of the human mind. To afford academic respectability in the form of a department may be to keep

---

12   Howard Becker, in John Gillin, ed., *For A Science of Social Man* (New York: Macmillan, 1954), p. 122.

the barbs of faith from inflicting too much pain. Holy zeal is appropriately diverted to the practical business of self-preservation and self-advancement. It is true that, in comparison with the grand estate of medieval theology, our domain is humble. Yet there is an important sense in which we should be grateful for this. Theology as queen of the sciences descends into a worse despotism than sciences that lack theology's exalted message. Perhaps a voice that is small is peculiarly qualified both to question the notion that the pursuits of an ostensibly emancipated scholarship will automatically add up to the greater unity of truth and also to proclaim that theonomy is not the heteronomous foe of autonomy but instead its fulfillment. At the very least, in the court of learning there is always need for a court jester, practitioner of a most serious art. The court jester can do much to prevent professors and educators from taking themselves with undue seriousness and from assuming that, by the exercise of thought, they can add cubits to the stature of existence. On the other hand, the court jester is immediately driven to the essential paradox that speaks of the saving and losing of one's life. Ideally, the jester in the court of learning is one who would rather be a doorkeeper in the house of the Lord than dwell in the tents of the self-assured. He is, in fact, somewhat unconscious of his role. He does not take himself too seriously. His vocation, in pale but positive reflection of the kingdom of God, is a gift and not an achievement. Otherwise we witness the terrible state of affairs referred to by John Dillenberger: "A self-conscious concern on the part of religious individuals for the exposing of the premises of others falsifies the human in reducing men to the level of manipulable ideas and displays a form of intellectual tyranny rather than an encounter in charity."[13]

Never quite consciously affirmed by either nation or secular university, there remains the exceedingly more positive power of the Christian *kerygma*, numbering among its fruits love, joy, and peace. Yet the seed of the kingdom of God is never entirely missing from the hardest soil of academic life. If without Christ "not anything was made that was made," we should expect Him to be the invisible Logos of every university, as He is of every community and

---

[13] John Dillenberger, "Teaching Religion: Problems and Requirements," *Union Seminary Quarterly Review* 9 (March 1954): 5. Dillenberger holds that the idea of a Christian university tends to foster a temptation to outright domination on the part of Christians. "Since no individual can claim to have all the truth, the search is safest when it is in the hands of diverse individuals, and best even for the welfare of Christians, when it is not exclusively in their own hands" (p. 4).

of every nation. This is one Christian application of the view that the powers that be are ordained of God. The opposite demand of obedience to God rather than man maintains the tension. The option of protest lives for all professors whenever, for example, a threat appears to academic freedom. In the very name of the God who judges finite claims, ultimate religion is, logically, the first to oppose such a threat. Academic freedom is grounded in the Truth by which religion too is judged.

V

In some such way as the foregoing we may live with and support the strangeness of religion in the university. Our most significant conclusion is that the question of religion within the contemporary curriculum involves certain issues of a *sui generis* kind. We do not get very far when we assume that problems in the teaching of religion no more than reproduce problems in teaching other subjects.[14] The uniqueness of the problem of religion overshadows superficial similarities. One temptation is to try to solve the whole problem through making higher education "religious"; another is to imagine that the establishment of a religion department takes care of the problem of "religion in education." In truth, neither solution provides a final or creative answer, for the simple reason that when religion is deprived of its strangeness, it is reduced to either spirituality or secularity. We have tended to proceed as though one or the other of the two elements comprising the strangeness of religion can be safely ignored—either the cultural element or the transcendent element. In truth, religion remains in the world yet not of the world, in the university yet not of the university.

Daniel Jenkins's word on the relation of church and state is relevant. The relation between the two sides constantly changes and hence is always in need

---

[14] The professor of religion is a kind of walking embodiment of the strangeness of religion. He cannot grant that religion is just one more separable aspect of human life, and yet he has to teach religion as though it were precisely this. It is interesting to note that, in a recent symposium devoted to the problem of religious perspectives in the teaching of various disciplines, almost every major area of the university curriculum is given a chapter save religion itself (H. N. Fairchild, ed., *Religious Perspectives in College Teaching* [New York: Ronald Press, 1952]). Is it assumed that religion is automatically taught from a "religious" perspective? I do not necessarily criticize the omission. Yet it may well reflect the impossibility of putting religion on the same conceptual level as other disciplines.

of redefinition. There is no ideal Christian attitude to the state, for the realities involved are living rather than static.[15] So too with religion and the university. Our primary task is to act from our side to keep the tension creative.

George A. Buttrick of Harvard has remarked that the presence of religion in the new curriculum implies the confession that all is not well in the camp of the exponents of humanism and naturalism. He would agree, I am sure, that the presence of religion in the university, as in the world at large, points to the fact that all is not well anywhere, including the relation of man and God. Only in a pedagogical kingdom of God could a society of religion professors be all in all. In the true kingdom of God, the separation of religion and the university comes to an end, just as does the separation of church and state, for it is the Christ who is then all in all. In the interim the tension remains. In the final resort, the strangeness of religion, like religion itself, is inevitable. For it lies deep within all of us, "strangers and exiles on the earth."

---

[15]   Jenkins, *Strangeness*, pp. 131, 136.

Between Christmas and Good Friday, a poem

(The Christian Century 74 [1957]: 128)

For a little while we have lived back in
The enchanted world of childhood. But now
Someone has taken down the wonderful
Christmas tree, put all the bright toys away.
The children are back in school, robbing us
Of their annoying, glorious laughter.
It seems as though all the furniture has
Been moved out of the house. We have nothing
To do but sit on the bare floor looking
Out of the window at the dead Winter.
Tomorrow is the old age that lies like
The charred tree next to the rubbish barrel.
The three long months of Winter are the three
Days that begin with Good Friday. By then
Another tree will be taken down with
A Man stretched across it. On the third day
He will melt the January ice in
Our souls and make us children forever.

A Note on Theological Procedure

(*The Journal of Bible and Religion* 29 [1961]: 313-316)

That the pursuits of science, history, and Christian theology are related is a truism. There are "historical sciences," and, conversely, it is possible to think of history as in certain respects a science. "Historical theology" is an accredited subject. Theology itself has sometimes been construed as in some sense a science. And there have been attempts to provide theologies of history and of science.

It is equally obvious that these disciplines maintain distinctive emphases. The present note comments upon the nature of theological procedure relative to the procedures of science and history.

I

The sciences, according to Ernest Nagel,

seek to discover and to formulate in general terms the conditions under which events of various sorts occur, the statements of such determining conditions being the explanations of the corresponding happenings. This goal can be achieved only by distinguishing or isolating certain properties in the subject matter studied and by ascertaining the repeatable patterns of dependence in which these properties stand to one another...To explain, to establish some relation of dependence between propositions superficially unrelated, to exhibit systematically connections between apparently miscellaneous items of information are distinctive marks of scientific inquiry.[1]

---

[1] Ernest Nagel, *The Structure of Science* (New York-Burlingame: Harcourt, Brace & World, 1961), pp. 4, 5. See also A. Roy Eckardt, "The Contribution of *Nomothesis* in the Science of Man," *American Scientist* 49 (March 1961): 76-87.

History is frequently interpreted as differing from science through a concentration upon events or states of affairs which are unique. As Joynt and Rescher have shown, this view must be severely criticized.[2] The simple truth is that all events are unique; they "are rendered non-unique *in thought only*, by choosing to use them as examples of a type or class." Further, the discipline of history "conforms fully to the standard hypothetico-deductive paradigm of scientific inquiry..." Accordingly, the distinguishing marks of history lie neither in its subject matter nor in its methods.[3]

What, then, is the peculiarity of history? It is found in a practical reversal of the means-end relationship between fact and theory that obtains in science as such. The sciences seek to provide generalizations and, ideally, universal laws governing the range of phenomena constituting various factual domains.

In the sciences, the particular events that comprise the facts studied play an indispensable but nonetheless strictly subordinate role: the focus of interest is the general law, and the particular fact is simply a means to this end.

In history, on the other hand, this means-end relationship is, in effect, reversed. Unlike the scientist, the historian's interest lies, first and fore-most, in the particular facts of his domain...[However,] the historian is not simply interested in dating events and describing them, but in *understanding them*. And "understanding" calls for interpretation, classification, and assessment, which can only be attained by grasping the relationship of causal and conceptual interrelation among the chronological particulars...

...[For the historian] the role of generalizations is strictly instrumental: they provide aids towards understanding particular events. The scientist's means-end relation of facts to laws is thus inverted by the historian.[4]

---

[2]   Carey B. Joynt and Nicholas Rescher, "The Problem of Uniqueness in History," *History and Theory* 1 (1961): 150-162.

[3]   Ibid., pp. 150, 151, 152.

[4]   Ibid., pp. 153, 154.

There is a sense in which history deals with the "unique": through its concern with temporally limited patterns. History takes its own unique character from the connection between "the temporal process and the existence of the limited generalizations which give a specific character to a particular historical epoch or set of historical conditions."[5] The historian exposes his interpretations to the scrutiny of others and trusts that his version of the materials at hand will gain public assent, at least among his peers. All disciplines have to come to terms with unique realities and relationships. Science is able to attenuate to a certain degree the confusions of the spatio-temporal flux through the device of abstracting (choosing out) hopefully common elements displayed by disparate phenomena. The public character of scientific findings is widely celebrated; we seem to hear less of the heavy price so often exacted by such sharing: a surrender of the individuality of things.

II

Where does Christian theology stand with reference to the procedural schemes just outlined? If the historian seeks to understand the past for its own sake and does not view facts in their instrumental role as data for laws,[6] the theologian concentrates upon certain facts of the past not only because they possess intrinsic value but also for instrumental purposes. In this last-mentioned respect, the theologian's intention parallels to some degree that of the scientist. However, instead of seeking to formulate general laws as such, the theologian approaches his facts as the partly instrumental source and inspiration of the life of faith. The "public" to whom he relates himself is, in the first instance, the community of faith, although this does not mean that he will not himself sometimes call upon purely scientific and purely historical resources.

It follows that the theologian's procedures are in part like the historian's and in part like the scientist's, without being the same as either of the other methods. The happenings to which the theologian directs his hearers are believed to be revelatory, in some positive and decisive way, of ultimate truth or reality. As everyone knows, Christian thought is heir to Jewish prophetic

---

5   Ibid., p. 160.

6   Ibid., p. 154.

"explanations" of events. Thus, the conviction that Israel had violated the terms of the original Covenant act became a crucial means of accounting for the varied sufferings of the nation. (The historian is wary of "explanations" as "high-level" as this one; when he does venture upon them, he has actually assumed the mantle of prophet or of theologian of history.)

The peculiarly Christian "explanation" is summarized in H. Richard Niebuhr's words:

> The special occasion to which we appeal in the Christian church is called Jesus Christ, in whom we see the righteousness of God, his power and wisdom. But from that special occasion we also derive the concepts which make possible the elucidation of all the events in our history. Revelation means this intelligible event which makes all other events intelligible.[7]

The event of Jesus Christ is, needless to say, not at all to be associated with a "universal law." Yet its recital does bear one important resemblance to any recourse to scientific law: *It offers a decisive key to general understanding.* (One could argue that modern scientific explanation carries forward in this one respect the traditional role of theology and Christian philosophy within Western culture.) From the standpoint of Christian commitment at least, in Jesus Christ the meaning of the entire course of human life is shown. Theology joins with common sense in agreeing with the historical judgment that all temporal events are unique, but it goes beyond pure history through its assertion that Jesus Christ is uniquely unique. That is to say, if within the sciences, as Joynt and Rescher indicate, particular events are subordinate to concern with general laws, in Christian theology the various events of history before and since Jesus Christ are subordinate to—i.e., they derive their ultimate significance and value from—the one event of Christ. If history reverses, in effect, the scientific means-end relationship of fact and law, theology unites with history in a concentration upon particularities. However, where historical understanding is

---

[7]   H. Richard Niebuhr, *The Meaning of Revelation* (New York: Macmillan, 1941), p. 93.

content with "limited generalizations" rooted in "transitory regularities,"[8] the Christian theologian hazards an "unlimited" or "eternal" affirmation: that Jesus Christ is the "center of history."

As Ernest Nagel reminds us, the peculiar business of science is explanation. But, as he makes plain, on the one hand explanations are defined in science as statements of the conditions that determine the occurrences of various sorts of happenings, and on the other hand scientific explanation entails the process of abstraction amidst "repeatable patterns of dependence." It is, of course, meaningless to seek after scientific conditions for God's acts of self-disclosure; the most we can do here is to ponder with great care such expressions as "the fullness of time" and to speak of the "condition" of man and his world (sin, freedom, finitude, etc.). Further, Christian theology dares to offer an "explanation" not alone of the alleged patterns of all human events but also of their seeming chaos, an "explanation" which is therefore in a sense universal but one that nevertheless rests upon radical uniqueness. Theology is involved in and founded upon an event rather than upon a set of abstractions. In the Christian view, an ultimate "explanation" may be applied to pattern and patternlessness alike—"behind the dim unknown, standeth God within the shadow"—yet without the necessity of paying the price (alluded to above) that accompanies so much scientific explanation: a loss of reality in its concreteness. Theology takes its uniquely unique happening and proceeds, with much boldness, to relate it to an understanding of all events: this martyrdom and that betrayal, this sunshine and that rainfall, this success and that failure, this deed of friendship and that act of hostility.

Such ultimate accounting must not lead us to equate faith and knowledge as such or to preempt alternate methods of understanding (including that of philosophy). Roger Hazelton is quite right in warning against "claims for theology which cannot be made good." Hazelton points out that "there is something decidedly presumptuous in the implication that theology is a sort of master perspective by which any sort of event or meaning can be reckoned with and put in its proper intellectual place."[9] The truth is that *any* event or series

---

8   Joynt and Rescher, "Problem," p. 156.

9   Roger Hazelton, *New Accents in Contemporary Theology* (New York: Harper & Bros., 1960), p. 18.

of events can be subjected, in principle, to purely scientific procedures. The same is true with respect to historical procedures. And theology hardly qualifies as an intellectual *deus ex machina* that can be hurried to the aid of philosophers in trouble. Each of the disciplines under discussion here is internally unlimited. To hold that one discipline possesses a monopoly upon one area of life or, conversely, that it must not trespass upon reserved ground is to misconstrue the nature of all these pursuits. Essentially, they represent *different* ways of dealing with the *same* world. Accordingly, all that we need insist upon in the present context is equality of opportunity among the several disciplines. But this means that peculiarly theological "explanation" must not be discriminated against. From the perspective of faith, Jesus Christ remains the "intelligible event which makes all other events intelligible."

III

I should not deny that, from another point of view than the one here stressed, the disciplines under consideration stand in an alternative relationship. We may all agree that, since Christian thought is grounded in a uniquely unique event and is thus committed to "the scandal of particularity," theology may be said to lie at the opposite pole from science:

Science   History   Theology

In this respect, theology is, so to speak, even more "historical" than history. It has found—or has been found by—an event of incomparable price. But the fact remains that a second continuum is equally in order:

Science   Theology   History

For, as we have noted, Christian theology limits itself neither to concentration upon the event that inspires it nor to the limited generalizations proper to the discipline of history. Theology applies its event to the work of universal understanding. Its one "explanation" is, accordingly, either out-and-out falsehood—all general "theories" are subject to this fateful eventuality—or a finally valid and objective key to the life-and-death meaning of things. If it is the latter, those who subscribe to it are in fact afforded the most rational and universal "theory" that is achievable, a "theory" which is able *ad extremum* to "exhibit systematically connections between apparently miscellaneous items of information." The outcome is ultimate wholeness:

    Theology   Science   History

Generically described, Christian theology moves about among the places allotted in the sets of terms listed. It moves from event to application, from a concrete and fundamental epistemological assertion ("I know who it is in whom I have trusted") to practical liberation ("you shall know the truth, and the truth will set you free"), and then it reverses its course. In these late years we have been nurtured upon the necessity of attending to the original event and of maintaining its qualitative integrity. Must we not remember as well that when the ecstasy of faith is isolated from any "explanatory" function, it is made irrelevant to life?

The primary motivation of this note is the persuasion that the relationship suggested by the second set of terms found above cannot be ignored. We have seen that there is at least one fundamental point at which theology is closer to science than history is. From the perspective of the considerations here advanced—and only from that perspective—we are justified in sometimes assigning the procedures of Christian theology to a place somewhere between the procedures of science and those of history.

IV

I have no more than opened the question of ways in which a given theological venture may emphasize historical method, or generalizing (systematic) method, or both methods together. Nor have I, save in passing, entered the critical area of inquiring just what it means to assert that the event of Jesus Christ affords intelligibility to all other events. The specific fashion in which Christian theology operates through the work of theologians is a matter for discussion elsewhere. However, two general considerations may be advanced:

1. It must be emphasized that the "betweenness" of theology vis-à-vis science and history is not a mere synthetic compromise. If it were, theology in its totality would simply be scientific where it was not historical and historical where it was not scientific. We have to say, on the contrary, that the "betweenness" of theology derives ultimately from its claim to "beyondness": Particularity and explanation are wedded in the event of Jesus Christ.[10]

2. Both science and history, for all their differences, at once refer to objectively occurring events and seek to interpret and understand them. The latter attempt entails subjective or ideal achievement. To the degree that contemporary theology ignores the objective side, it falls into existentialist docetism; to the degree that it ignores the subjective side, it falls into historicism.[11]

---

[10]   A basic resemblance will be noted here and above to the claim within Christian philosophy that in Jesus Christ is found an answer to the ancient enigma of "the one and the many."   .

[11]   In actuality, there is nothing terribly profound in recognizing the stubborn duality of events and our reactions to them. This duality helps to characterize the human situation, and most people seem aware of it. Science, history, and-ideally-Christian theology are merely responsible professional and intellectual attempts to come to grips with the duality. The theologian may here unite with the scientist and the historian simply because they are all human beings.

The Theology of Antisemitism

(*Religion in Life* 31 [1962]: 552-562)

Antisemitism has been in the news again—is it ever out for long?—through such diverse stimuli as the Soviet government's recently initiated restrictions against Jews and a resolution adopted by the Third Assembly of the World Council of Churches. At New Delhi it was found necessary to recall the Amsterdam Assembly's denunciation of antisemitism thirteen years before, for the reason that "situations continue to exist in which Jews are subject to discrimination and even persecution."

The well-known truth that Christian theology has itself fostered antisemitism is actually hinted at in the ambiguous title of the present article. Although my concern here is with theological understanding of the nature of antisemitism, and secondarily with theological resources for alleviating it, I know that in this realm as elsewhere theology has more than once proven to be "mere ideology."

I

If one fate—or temptation—for theology is its association with immorality, another temptation involves the surrender of theology's peculiar form of understanding. This latter temptation may be fostered in either of two ways: One of these is the transformation of theology into a different form of understanding—historical or religious or scientific or whatever. Against this temptation, we must insist that a Jewish or Christian theological understanding of antisemitism is meaningfully distinctive only in the measure that it derives from elements in Jewish or Christian faith. From the standpoint of faith, attention is focused upon the ways of God and his revelation. This perspective stands in substantial contrast both to religion in the generalized sense of that term (where stress falls upon the spiritual experiences of mankind) and to religion in the investigative sense (where emphasis is placed upon the philosophy of religion, psychology of religion, sociology of religion, etc.). However contiguous to one another faith and religion may be, the fact remains that the preeminent subject of the former is God while that of the latter is man.

The other way in which the distinctive character of theological understanding may be lost is through a tacit denial of the unique theological character of antisemitism. In this second eventuality the phenomenon could still be talked about by theologians, but as no more than an embodiment of such wider and basic wrongs as religious bigotry and ethnic bias. The present essay maintains an opposite point of view. It is assumed that not only the theological approach but also antisemitism are *sui generis*. This is not to insinuate any derogation of non-theological approaches or any allegation that theology has all the answers.

It must be granted that the distinctive elements in antisemitism can be apprehended to some extent by historical analysis. However, the ultimate nature and roots of antisemitism are not so readily accessible. Like science, theology seeks patterns of explanation; like metaphysics, it searches out ultimate levels of reality; but unlike other endeavors, it probes existentially and faithfully the mysteries of God, the world, and man. (Here is theology's immanent tragedy; the very grandeur of its effort makes its failures grotesque.) Are we able to retain the integrity of a theological conception of the peculiar phenomenon of antisemitism without giving unwitting aid or comfort to those who sanction the evil? Within the Jewish and Christian theological traditions we encounter such ideas as the people of God, the war of God against the gods, and man as sinner. Can these ideas help us comprehend the defamation of Jews in a way that resists both the temptation to nurture ideology and immorality and the temptation to lose the distinctive quality of theological understanding?

At least two difficulties in such an approach must be freely admitted: For one thing, we face the limitation that few theological analyses are addressed primarily or exclusively to antisemitism. Most of the available studies bearing on our subject are concerned primarily with various facets of past and present relations between the church and the synagogue, and between Christians and Jews. This means that if we are to ferret out the implicit bearing of such discussions upon antisemitism, we must resort to implication and application. Secondly, there are serious obstacles to the squaring of theological assertions with data offered in behalf of historical, psychological, and sociological theory; and even to the squaring of such assertions with other theological affirmations, such as the conviction that divine election and the struggle against idolatry are meaningful only among people touched by the biblical tradition.

II

Unlike the philosophy of religion, theology assumes the reality of God, and Jewish-Christian theology further assumes that God is active in human history. The two sides of the question before us are brought together in the concept of the people of God and the oppression of them which is antisemitism. The idea of the people of God may be quite false—here is the boundary-condition of every human presupposition—yet I am at a loss to know how, within a Christian frame of reference at least, the theological approach can start anywhere else or proceed on any other basis. There is something disingenuous in a Christian referring Jews to their divine election. He is, in many ways, an outsider. Yet the election of Israel is fundamental to Christian doctrine.[1] In the presence of Jews who are committed to the conviction, there is no need to remind them; with those who are emancipated from it, there is not much point in trying to reinstate the idea. Perhaps a little saving justification is found in Jewish uncertainty on this matter.

Testimony that persecution of Jews may be understood in theological terms has been forthcoming from thinkers representing a variety of backgrounds and persuasions. A prevailing concept here is the *mystery of Israel*, with antisemitism interpreted as a concomitant betrayal of God. Among Jewish thinkers Franz Rosenzweig and Will Herberg are representative of this point of view. To Herberg, antisemitism "is the other side of the election and vocation of Israel,...the revolt of the pagan against the God of Israel and his absolute demand...as 'mysterious' as Israel itself." This general orientation is found in such interpreters as the Russian Christian Nicolas Berdyaev, the French Catholic Charles Journet, and the German-American Protestant theologian Paul Tillich. For Tillich, the Jewish people as "the nation of time" are persecuted "because by their very existence, they break the claims" of the pagan gods of space. And according to Karl Barth, the world, by being hostile to the Jews, proves itself

---

[1]   There are, of course, marked differences within Christian thought on the issue of Jewish election. For some interpreters, the election of Israel ceased with the advent of the church; for others, notably Paul (see Romans 11), Jewish election is unending.

"blind, deaf, and stupid to the ways of God." Thus, antisemitism is seen as a perverse method of getting back at God for daring, through Israel, to interfere with human autonomy, with the desire of man to be his own God. Needless to say, the category of the "mystery of Israel" transcends any distinction between the "religious" and the "secular," and we cannot come to grips with it in purely empirical or scientific terms.

Theological understanding may carry us even further—to a more particularized thesis abetted by historical and logical considerations. The abiding seriousness of the persecution of Jews is closely associated with a particular historic condition: Jewish life within a so-called Christian civilization. Although more than anti-Judaism is involved, we must consider antisemitism primarily as a problem for a reputedly Christian society.

Are Christians antisemitic because of their faith or in spite of it? Both. The second alternative needs no documentation; followers of Christ are supposed to bring forth love, not hate. The first alternative obtains as well, but on somewhat different reasoning than is found in the usual interpretation. How are we to make sense of the fact that Christians, representatives of a universalist faith of charity and forgiveness, are not only almost morbidly fascinated by the "Jewish question," but so easily fall prey to antisemitism? Traditional historical views emphasize the elements of anti-Judaism and religious antisemitism in Christianity going back to the formative early centuries, the Middle Ages, and the Reformation, and issuing in a condition of deep, continuing prejudice. The reasoning behind an assertion that Christians are antisemitic because of something in their faith itself may be rather different from, though not necessarily opposed to, this traditional, or religious, view.

Jesus was a Jew. The four words seem to comprise a most unpretentious historical truism. But say them over no more than twice and the infinite qualitative difference from their counterparts—Napoleon was a Frenchman, Lincoln was an American—is at once revealed, in excruciating clarity. Then paint the words on a sign and nail it up over the entrance to a medieval ghetto or to Auschwitz or to the local yacht club. Discrepancies in locale and horror quickly contract. Now add to this the fact that the words "Jesus was a Jew" are, to the Christian, much more than a bare temporal assertion. Neither "Jesus" nor "Jew" is a neutral term. Christians are natively ambivalent toward both. At the very moment when the nascent Christian learns to assign the predicate to the subject he has already been conditioned to a derogatory understanding of "Jew." As for Jesus, while ostensibly embodying the divine forgiveness, he also brings to Christians the divine imperative, insisting that "no man is worthy of me who does not take up his cross and walk in my footsteps."

But how are Christians to go about refusing the imperative and denying Jesus? They cannot very well get their hands on him. Yet they *can* get their hands on his people, the Jews. That the mechanisms involved are of a below-conscious sort does not annul their force; it probably compounds it. And, convenience of conveniences, are not the Jews, in the Christian primordial image the ones who did Jesus to death? The Christian is beset with ineluctable guilt for his rejection of Jesus; what better way to assuage it than to displace it upon the "*really* guilty ones," the ones who to this day not only refuse to "accept" Jesus but willfully continue to dub themselves the "chosen people," flouting the truth that the *church* is the New Israel? Christians have their own ways of turning on the people of God. Few defense mechanisms are more pervasive or deadly than the one which says, "*I* am not the guilty party. *You* are." Antisemitism is the reenactment of the "murder of God." It is also, in Maria Fuerth Sulzbach's words, "the expression of Christian unconscious self-hatred and self-disgust." Maurice Samuel's characterization of more than twenty years ago is still most telling: Christian antisemites "must spit on the Jews as 'the Christ-killers' because they long to spit on the Jews as the Christ-givers."[2]

If ever such psychological categories as ambivalence, displacement, and transference possessed compelling application, surely it is in connection with the specter of Christian persecution of Jews. Theological understanding joins social psychopathology in emphasizing the essentially irrational character of antisemitism in its origins and nature, and, accordingly, the great obstacles to overcoming it. Associated as it is with powerful below-conscious mechanisms, antisemitism cannot be dispelled by purely rational or superficially educational means. As a way of combatting hostility to Jews, the current educational literature of various Christian bodies often stresses that Jesus, who suffered for

---

2   In *The Great Hatred* Samuel speaks from a liberal Jewish point of view and it is understandable, therefore, that he should identify the term "Christ" with Jewish-Christian morality. The Christian version of this general position holds that "the rejection of the Jews is for the purpose of rejecting the Christ in whom God is uniquely confronted" (A. Roy Eckardt, *Christianity and the Children of Israel* [New York: Kings Crown Press, 1948], p. 60).

the sake of men, was himself a Jew. Without depreciating the good that this might do under generally favorable moral and spiritual conditions, we must not underestimate its opposite effect. We have to take into account the psychospiritual syndrome in accordance with which it is unconsciously insisted that because Jesus was a Jew, he really "had it coming." If the Christian's salvation "depends on the cross" (*Catechism of the Council of Trent*, Art. IV), this means that in a significant sense it depends upon the death of a Jew. But may this not open the way to a malicious logic, promulgated by sinful men and by distorted minds, that if this one Jew suffered to save us, other Jews can do the same? The line from Calvary to Auschwitz and the other death camps is in this respect one of simple geometrical progression: One Jew, six million.[3]

It must be admitted that the interpretation I have outlined can have no validity with reference to pre-Christian or non-Christian antisemitism. At the very most, the theological understandings here represented and reported are relevant only to Western Christendom. Nevertheless, should we be tempted to shrug off the interpretation offered, its relentless empiricism ought to call us back. Theology is not history, yet in the Jewish and Christian traditions any theological claim that does not take history seriously is open to a charge of empty speculation. Jesus *was* a Jew. The Christian faith *has* come out of Judaism. No other people *has* been treated so horribly, both in duration and in intensity, as have the Jews. At the very least, any attempt to account for antisemitism in Western culture cannot gainsay the momentous fact that the one who is to Christians the Son of God has come from among the people whom so many Christians have learned to despise and oppress. Intellectually speaking, this is a place, where, as is already recognized to some extent, history, depth psychology, and theology crucially converge, and suggest a direction for basic research. (The question remains of whether those psychological investigations according to which antisemitism is not really possessed of uniqueness but is linked with certain personality patterns and social pressures, can actually be reconciled with a theological emphasis upon the sacred mystery of Israel and

---

[3]   This is why there is an important respect in which a Jew is able to claim Jesus of Nazareth with much less guile than the gentile Christian is able to do. When Martin Buber testifies, "From my youth onwards, I have found in Jesus my great brother," he need not be embarrassed. Buber speaks as one Jew of another. When the Christian speaks this way, the sound of his testimony is muffled by the unstilled voices of the tormented Jews of Christian history.

with the historical particularities of faith discussed thus far. The research suggested must come to grips with this basic theoretical issue.)[4]

III

What are some of the implications of theological understanding for the other two ways of reading our subject—the aggravation of antisemitism and the alleviation of it?

The fashion these days is dialogue. As with fashion in dress, dialogue may help make life somewhat bearable, or it may, without meaning to do so, foster dehumanization. And if Bishop Stephen Neill is right that genuine dialogue between faiths is possible "only when each makes some claim to universality," the persistent majority-minority relation between Christians and Jews helps the sentiment revive harsh memories. Some notation of the developing interfaith conversation in the United States and in Europe ought, nonetheless, to be made. Here is a noteworthy contrast to both the dreary medieval monologue of Christian self-defense and the latter-day "nonalogue" of liberal sincerity serving to repress the issue of conflicting truth claims. Unhappily, the dialogue in this country has as yet assumed little theological proportion. Taking the long view, we may be heartened by contemporary theological and liturgical trends away from the religious notion of the Jews as a condemned people, trends accompanied by efforts to rectify misrepresentations of Jews in religious educational literature. There is an identifiable, though not prevailing, movement in Christian circles to affirm the unending Covenant between God and Israel, and there is continuing and considerable recourse to the elemental religious and moral principles of love and justice for all men, and particularly for the

---

[4]   The reader will have noted a possibly serious inconsistency in the analysis to this point. I began with the claim that a truly theological interpretation is *sui generis*; I have now suggested a hypothesis which, whatever its tenability, can be translated into depth-psychological and social-psychological terms. Of some relevance is the fact that no interpretation of the origins and nature of antisemitism can be divorced from what the interpreter brings personally to the comprehension of this horrendous phenomenon. Disparities in viewpoint and conclusion are largely the result of individual presuppositions. However, because the data considered have, objectively speaking, certain shared characteristics, it is entirely possible that different *dimensions of understanding*, such as theology and depth psychology, will tend to converge at one or another point, especially where the presuppositions involved are in some ways parallel. See also A. Roy Eckardt, "A Note on Theological Procedure," *The Journal of Bible and Religion* 29 (1961): 313-316.

persecuted. Among churchmen, Protestant and Catholic, concern over antisemitism and concern with justice for Jews, and particularly with Christian culpability for antisemitism, have continued since Nazism and World War II. Whether a hidden impulse here is simply the salving of conscience is a moot question, and the same may be said for a possible felt need for any and all allies in an essentially post-Christian time. If a genuine spirit of repentance for the sin of antisemitism is actually stirring in Christian quarters, it would be a supreme tragedy for us to react to recent developments by insisting that they are merely novel incarnations of hypocrisy and ulterior motivation. We should probably be thankful for goodness whenever it appears, and then seek to appropriate it in the ongoing struggle against bigotry and discrimination.

The most general but highly relevant dichotomy in the present context involves the alternatives of *self-criticism* and *self-defense*, or in theological terms, group repentance versus group idolatry. James Parkes, the noted English authority on Christian-Jewish relations, describes the contemporary state of affairs as follows:

> As I see it there is at present a very clear issue on this matter—an issue brought to the fore by the entry of the Roman Catholic theologian and historian into a field which has up to now been largely occupied by Jewish and Protestant scholars with the exception of a few isolated Catholics such as the Scottish layman Malcolm Hay. The issue is this: Are the recurrent persecutions of Jews merely manifestations of something which predates Christianity and which can only occur where there is no genuine Christian influence or do they have a direct connection with the life of the Christian church, even though the church never intended its teaching to have so terrible an issue? Roman Catholics are increasingly insisting on the former view. On that view, antisemitism is a dreadful thing, but it is rooted in human nature, not in *homo Christianus*.[5]

Some Christian interpreters, and notably Dr. Parkes, assert that it is the Christian movement which has been most to blame for the propagation of

---

[5]   From a letter to the author, 27 June 1961, reproduced by permission.

antisemitism. Wherever there is Christianity, the oppression of Jews lurks in the near shadows. The fact that Nazism, for example, was a foe of Christian faith does not negate the truth that the soil for the Nazi slaughter of the Jews had been largely cultivated by the church, and that by their silence and inaction Christians became virtual co-conspirators with Hitler. The life of Christians and the Christian community is ridden with self-contradictory and even self-destructive forces; this is really the thesis behind the present essay.

It is, of course, clearly immoral to demand group repentance beyond the bounds of identifiable group responsibility. Further, we simply cannot ignore such recent expositions as that of Gregory Baum. Those who have found little of self-criticism among Roman Catholic apologists are advised to take seriously Father Baum's study of the New Testament gospel and the Jews.[6] Baum has harsh words for many a pope and many a bishop. Thus, for example, in speaking of the denial of justice to the Jews by Bishop Ambrose in 388, he quickly grants that in "the person of her bishop, the Church had taken a stand against the natural law of human society"—and his book bears the *Nihil obstat* and *Imprimatur* of the ecclesiastical authorities. On the other hand, in addition to wanting "to defend the Jews against the calumnies contained in the theological legends of past centuries," Baum seeks "to defend the gospel against those who accuse it of anti-Jewish bias...and to defend the Catholic doctrine on the Church against the generous belittlement found in some modern writings" by Christians. If it is unfair and inaccurate to lump the New Testament indiscriminately under antisemitic literature, we must nevertheless admit that some of the seeds of antisemitism are therein contained. The theological question for Christians here is the old but persistent one of what it means to affirm that the New Testament is the Word of God—a major unresolved problem in the Christian community. With full acknowledgment of the contribution of Father Baum and others, I believe that James Parkes puts the matter fairly: Although antisemitism today contains aspects which have nothing to do with Christianity, we who are Christians cannot deny our responsibility "for the creation of the instrument" which antisemites "now use without us."[7]

---

[6] Gregory Baum, *The Jews and the Gospel: A Re-Examination Of the New Testament* (Westminster, Md.: Newman Press, 1961).

[7] From an address to the London Society of Jews and Christians entitled "The History of Jewish-Christian Relations," March 1961, unpublished.

Will a continuing insistence that the Jews are the people of God contribute
to antisemitism? In and of itself, no. True, the notion that there could be no
antisemitism if there were no Jews is, logically speaking, unassailable. A
complication is that the issue of social assimilation versus social differentiation
is not the same question as that of the end of the chosen people versus their
continuation, even though the two questions are related. Here is a place where
theology, sociology, and ethics converge—only to diverge and perhaps conflict.
The collective will-to-survive of any people cannot be denied without flouting
human freedom and individual dignity. The theological conviction of the chosen
people builds upon and then transcends such ethical considerations through its
emphasis upon the place of the Jews in the ultimate salvation of humankind.
From this broader perspective we see that, in principle, the chosen-people
persuasion cannot of itself be correlated with the aggravating of antisemitism.

And yet, when all is said and done, and the theologians have composed their
balanced, judicious statements, there is only one empirically absolute certainty:
Any and every idea, any and every conviction, is tragically subject to the
machinations of antisemitic depravity. To reflect seriously upon such studies as
Malcolm Hay's *The Foot of Pride*, with its apt subtitle, "The Pressure of
Christendom on the People of Israel for 1900 Years" is to see the shallowness
in assurances that such and such a procedure will not "necessarily" have evil
consequences, or that there is doubtless "hope" in this or that development.
Antisemitism lives just below the surface of our common life—in the United
States as in Germany, in France as in the Soviet Union. Dates, places, names,
groups —these are in a primary sense quite irrelevant to the menace itself.

I say all this not as a counsel of despair but in admission of the truth that
theology has no privileged place at all in the struggle, and no magic solutions.
I say it too in preface to some observations on the logical strategy of the
Christian community—the phrase "in preface to" to point to a lack of illusions
respecting what the church can or will do; the phrase "logical strategy" to
indicate that there is, nevertheless, a logic for action prescribed by the earlier
diagnosis. The ideal is that when Christians stop hating Jesus, they will stop
hating the Jews. In the measure that Christians are brought to apprehend the
divine forgiveness that overcomes hostility and guilt, the nerve of antisemitism
is cut. It requires no surrender of his faith for the Jew to agree that to the extent
Christians take to heart the gospel that Jesus reconciles them to God and man,

they must also heed the counsel, "fold to thy heart thy brother." "Is Jesus *really* your Savior? Tell me, what does he save you *from?*"—this is the Jew speaking to the Christian.

There remains a significant paradox in the relation of Christian teaching and behavior to antisemitism. If it is within the hearts of men that the primordial guilt lies, Christian dogma must carry only ancillary blame. The hope of many liberals has been that the waning of Christian orthodoxy would markedly allay defamation of Jews. Few moral men can review the centuries-old tale of Christian atrocities without at some moment wondering whether the world would not be better off if Christianity had never come into human history. Yet here as elsewhere in the affairs of men consequent evil may come to exceed calculable good. What is to be the disposition of those facets of traditional Christianity, centering in the transcendent mercy and judgment of God, that have served as powerful deterrents to antisemitism? Are we to cancel out the love that some Christians implement through their persuasion that Christ has loved them? Is it actually possible to retain a theological ethic that has been severed from its theological foundation? Is it not conceivable that traditional forms of faith may possess greater insight into the perversity of men, into the bond between inhuman behavior and human idolatry, and into the mysteries of God's work than do less traditional and more rationalistic views? Is it really the case that religious liberals necessarily know more or do more about such social maladies as discrimination against Jews than traditionalists know or do? Must we not beware of the false practicality which so subordinates truth to goodness that the quest for wisdom is compromised, the wholeness of the human spirit is fractured and goodness is ultimately profaned? I can provide no final resolution of such puzzling questions here (or anywhere)—although from the way I have phrased them it is evident where my sympathies lie. They are, at the very least, genuine and sobering questions. Further, we may be assured that if the Jewishness of Jesus is in truth a foundation of Christian antisemitism, it is also the only foundation of an answer to antisemitism. For once it is surrendered, the door is opened to the "aryanizing" of Christianity, to the diabolism of a "German Christian Movement," which dreamed that Christian faith could be accommodated to the pagan gods of space. The only means by which Gentiles are brought into the Covenant with the Lord of time is through the Jew, Jesus of Nazareth.

IV

I return to the mystery of Israel as the people of God. Any insistence upon this doctrine exemplifies a most poignant problem in ethics: Can human suffering be vindicated for the sake of a noble end? I do not see that it can—unless the yoke of election is borne as a free act of the human spirit. It is in this sense that divine election and antisemitism become, morally speaking, two sides of the one coin. Although any historic end of the chosen people does not, lamentably enough, mean the end of antisemitism, the end of antisemitism will mean the end of the chosen people. This latter is as it should be. For the mystery of Israel is that it is called to bring the world to the living God and God to the world. When this will have been done, the justice and mercy of God will be everywhere, and the oppression of his people will cease. Meanwhile, it is in order that we remember the words of the small boy in André Schwarz-Bart's *The Last of the Just*: "Oh, my God, if you do not exist, what becomes of all the suffering? It is just lost, just lost."

4

Return to the Covenant, 1963-1967

On 8 August 1963 my wife, our two children, and I sailed for England on the Queen Mary. We were to reside in Cambridge for a year. This proved to be the first of many journeys to and stays in the United Kingdom, Europe, and the Middle East. During this second leave of absence, underwritten by a fellowship from the Lilly Endowment, I was attached to Peterhouse, oldest college in the University of Cambridge, with the latter's splendid library. I also had the opportunity to work with James Parkes and his singular private library at Barley,[1] some twelve miles from Cambridge. And I made several research visits to the Continent. The European and Middle Eastern contacts and experience that began in 1963—and continued through the rest of my career—helped to broaden and deepen my understanding, with special reference to the perplexities and insolubilities of the Christian-Jewish relationship. I was enabled to utilize a number of new and recent German sources together with some French ones.[2]

---

[1] Eventually the Parkes Library was bequeathed by James and Dorothy Parkes to the University of Southampton.

[2] This wider and continuing experience is reflected in such essays as "The Protestant Christian and the Jews" (1963); "The Jewish-Christian Dialogue: Recent Christian Efforts in Europe" (1965); "The Jewish-Christian *Gegenüber*: Some Recent Christian Efforts in Europe" (1965); "End to the Christian-Jewish Dialogue" (1966); and the later book,

The weight of my publications over this short time involved one or more aspects of the Jewish-Christian relation. Significantly, the period embraced the Vatican "Declaration on the Relationship of the Church to Non-Christian Religions" (1965)[3] and the Six Day War (1967).

I

The work in Cambridge and at Barley, together with a subsequent initial research visit to Israel,[4] was to issue in *Elder and Younger Brothers: The Encounter of Jews and Christians* (1967), my second treatise in this general area. (The sexism in the title will be duly noted.)

Some review of the argument in *Elder and Younger Brothers* is prerequisite to the critique that will follow the summary. Throughout I covered four things: the decisiveness of antisemitism within the Christian-Jewish relation; the developing, reformist ferment in Christian attitudes and thinking, a movement that was now beginning to cross national, denominational, and confessional boundaries; the exigent need to grapple with the theological dimensions of the subject (the book's predominant emphasis); and a categorical rejection of the traditionalist Christian missionary position toward Jews, although in a way that testified, so I held, "to the uniqueness and integrity of Christian faith."[5] I was arguing that any calculated, concerted, or organized Christian conversionist stance toward the Jewish people comprised as such—all unwittingly, sometimes even forgivably—a desertion of the Christian faith itself.[6]

Encounter with Israel (composed with Alice L. Eckardt; 1970). Conferences I took part in included the Lutheran Consultation on the Church and the Jewish People, Løgumkloster, Denmark (1964), where I represented the Committee on the Church and the Jewish People, World Council of Churches; and the Second International Conference on Jewish-Christian Co-operation, Cambridge, U.K. (1966).

[3]   Consult Roger Brooks, ed., *Unanswered Questions: Theological Views of Jewish-Catholic Relations* (Notre Dame: University of Notre Dame Press, 1988), chaps. 1-3.

[4]   My article, "Christian Guilt," was identified by *Christian News From Israel*, in which it appeared, as a "meditation" upon what I saw and experienced in Israel in 1966.

[5]   *Elder and Younger Brothers*, p. xvii (hereinafter cited as EYB).

[6]   With respect to the fourth emphasis, full allowance was made for the possibility that individual Jews will decide to become Christians (cf. EYB, pp. 155-157)-just as individual Christians will opt to become Jews.

Opening chapters upon "the enigma of antisemitism" carried forward but also altered and refined considerably previous analyses of mine.[7] At marked issue was the trialectic of scientific (psychological, sociological), historical, and theological understanding. I was able to benefit from my previous research in the psychological and social sciences, attending for example to the question of nomothetic versus historical-idiographic apprehensions of antisemitism. A potential pitfall within nomothesis is the misleading reduction of antisemitism to one more species of "prejudice." I concentrated upon ways in which the Nazis, in effect, preached and practiced a final fulfillment of Christendom's oppression and persecution of Jews—for all the wide differences between Nazi and Christian moral presuppositions and praxis.

Christendom's traditional antipathy to "the Jews"—an organized "system of degradation" (Jules Isaac), and all in the name of God's truth—remains, I adjudged, "the major historical root of antisemitism in the Western world."[8] But in the article "Christian Guilt" (1966) I had spoken of a kind of Christian mutuality of moral apathy and failure: "Those of us who, like the present writer, stood outside the German situation retain our own private 'they' whom we like to hold up as major culprits, namely, the people who did not refuse to obey the commands of the Nazis. Yet it is entirely possible that we would have shown no greater courage, if as much, had we stood in the same place, and that we too would have been taken prisoner by the collective pathology."

Elder and Younger Brothers' following chapter, "The Mystery of the People of God," continued the dubious practice, referred to superficially in chapter three of this retrospective, of visiting the category of "mystery" upon Jewishness— granted the ostensibly reputable intention of recognizing and even celebrating the special historical relation between God and the people of God (Israel). Of course, Jewish representatives and thinkers may wish to continue to utilize the term "mystery" in conjunction with Jews and Judaism[9]—or, for that matter, actively to repudiate it (as is the case amongst secular-Jewish

---

[7] These latter included CCI (1948); "The Theology of Antisemitism" (1962); and "Anti-Semitism," in George A. F. Knight, ed., *Jews and Christians* (1965). Concrete Christian and moral resources for fighting antisemitism were enumerated in the last-listed piece.

[8] EYB, pp. 15, 8.

[9] It was a favored concept of my old friend Will Herberg.

spokespersons). All this is wholly the business of Jews and wholly their right. To refuse to admit that right (or any other kind of Jewish self-definition) is to do service to antisemitism. Further, both sides may agree that the theological story of Israel is distinctive or uniquely unique—even though "the persuasion of the mystery of the chosen people" remains "finally meaningful only to those who have faith that God has elected Israel." I was evidently aware of the danger here; the chapter in question did insist that "few undertakings are more presumptuous morally than that of an outsider seeking to counsel a whole community on what is wise or proper for it to believe." And the Christian analyst cannot totally silence "the dread thought that his...assertion of the mystery of Israel may in fact bolster the antisemitic impulse. Are not people *afraid* of mysteries? Will they not act, therefore, to bring any mystery under control, perhaps by hemming in and even destroying the representatives of mystery? This is a major reason why any interpreter who speaks in behalf of the mystery of Israel must do so with very great hesitancy." Nevertheless, "the Christian has an obligation to attest that the election of Israel...lies deep in the bedrock of Christian faith. Once the chosen mission of Israel is denied, the entire foundation of Christianity is taken away. In some way, the church is called to carry forward that mission."[10]

If the consideration of antisemitism was not the major thrust of *Elder and Younger Brothers*, but rather its point of departure, neither was it my intention to concentrate upon the "mystery" of Israel as such. Instead, in the constructive chapters[11] I undertook the task of rendering, from the perspective of Christian self-understanding, a positive theology of the ongoing Jewish-Christian encounter and *thereby* a Christian theology-as-such. The italicized adverb accords with an important critical point: Protests against "single issue" Christian theologies do not apply convincingly to a singling out of the Christian-Jewish relation. For that relation is central to the foundation and meaning of Christianity as such.

---

[10]   EYB, pp. 43, 45, 44, 46.

[11]   The five chapters involved greatly expanded a single essay, "Toward a Theology for the Christian-Jewish Encounter" in the Gerald H. Anderson edited volume, *Christian Mission in Theological Perspective* (1967). Chaps. 6-8 of EYB included adaptations of some passages from "Can There Be a Jewish-Christian Relationship?" (1965). Curiously, at least two reviewers incorrectly reported that EYB consisted of previously published essays.

The methodology I introduced in *Elder and Younger Brothers* was, first, to present reasoning and evidence for an essential discontinuity between the original people of God and the Christian church; then to offer reasoning and evidence for an essential continuity between the two parties; and finally to supply my own orientation in behalf of a dialectical point of view that mediated between, and then went beyond, unalloyed discontinuity and unalloyed continuity.

The advocate of discontinuity concentrates upon elements that separate Christians and Jews, while the claimant of continuity represents the many things that unite the two communities. Christian spokespersons for the former view emphasize the "uniqueness" and often the "finality" of Christianity, many times contending for the brokenness or even the bankruptcy of Israel's election. Christian faith is held to be the "fulfillment" or even the "successor" of Jewish faith. Judaism and the Jewish people come out as losers. Contrariwise, amongst advocates of continuity emphases may range from a concentration upon identities of faith and practice as between Judaism and Christianity, to the winsome testimony that whatever is distinctive in Christian faith "is made possible only through that faith's peculiar participation in the sacred history of the original people of God." Christian teaching and confession must never do violence to "the abiding Covenant with Israel."[12]

The apostle Paul and Paul's modern-day surrogate Karl Barth were placed under the heading of discontinuity, although attention was drawn to facets of continuity in both figures. For Paul, Israel had betrayed its calling and the church had inherited that calling. The apostle contended, as I summarized his view, that "original Israel gives birth to the Messiah, rejects him, and [thereby] enters a period of spiritual occultation from which it will reappear only at an end time."[13] In chapter two above I allude to my erstwhile interpretation of Paul as pleading that for the present, all-crucial time original Israel had not lost its elect status; in 1967 I corrected this error. The subsequent work of E. P. Sanders, among others, helped corroborate the reinterpretation. As Sanders puts it, for Paul the one thing wrong with Judaism is that it is not Christianity;

---

[12] EYB, p. 51; see also p. 143.

[13] Ibid., p. 58.

necessary to membership in the *present* people of God is faith in Jesus Christ.[14] (In academic gamesmanship it is strategically wise from time to time to find someone, preferably a scholar much more the expert than you upon the subject in question, who will put forward the identical position you argue, but if at all possible a position that you had come to hold *before* the expert got around to declaring it. It may also be well to bury the point in a footnote, thereby implying that the achievement does not really matter all that much to you; I have not quite had the character to do this in the present instance.)

In *Elder and Younger Brothers* I illustrated and evaluated the rhetoric of continuity through study of the Dutch Church document *Israël en de kerk*, certain Roman Catholic writings, and the works of James Parkes and Reinhold Niebuhr. At the end I complained that Niebuhr, like Parkes, "skirts the edge of the fallacious assumption that because particular Christian teachings have not succeeded in preventing certain evil historical-moral results, the fault is traceable to the teachings more than to their misapprehension and distortion by Christians."[15] Today I should question any such split. Where does dogma live without the application of dogma? At this one point I have moved somewhat closer to Niebuhr's and Parkes's pragmatism.

My attempt in *Elder and Younger Brothers* to further a Christian dialectical apprehension of discontinuity/continuity with respect to the Jewish people and Judaism involved a central assumption: The abiding faithfulness of God to original Israel and of Israel to God essentially qualifies the category of Christian discontinuity, but yet discontinuity asserts itself in and through the *modus operandi* that was professedly utilized in the opening of the Covenant to the gentile world: the life, death, and resurrection of Jesus Christ. I deplored the temptation that has sometimes beset the church "to surrender the unique necessity of Jesus Christ." True, for the Jew of then and now, Jesus did not transform anything and does not now transform anything: the world remains unredeemed. Jesus does not appertain in any theologically decisive or normative sense to the history of Israel (*Heilsgeschichte*). But for the Christian, Jesus Christ is integral to and indeed crucial for Israel's history. For "the acceptance,

---

14   E. P. Sanders, *Paul and Palestinian Judaism* (Philadelphia: Fortress Press, 1977), p. 552; *Paul, the Law, and the Jewish People* (Philadelphia: Fortress Press, 1983), pp. 207-208. See also on this matter A. Roy Eckardt, For *Righteousness' Sake*, pp. 42-49.

15   EYB, p. 94.

through the Holy Spirit, of Jesus as Messiah means beholding him as the one who transforms and will transform the world."[16]

More than one reviewer of *Elder and Younger Brothers* maintained that I spoke more for Christian continuity with Judaism than for discontinuity. Such reportage underestimated my emphasis throughout upon the uniqueness of the Christian faith, particularly the cardinal prescription that only in Jesus Christ is the Covenant with original Israel definitively and soteriologically opened to the world. However, perhaps these reviewers were detecting or at least intuiting something (about my future) that I, the writer, could not as yet see.

I called the culminating chapter of *Elder and Younger Brothers* "The Unfolding Covenant." I shan't weary the reader with all its ins and outs; I only reproduce parts of three summary paragraphs that pretty well convey the argument:

Only a Jew could accomplish the miracle of opening the Covenant to the pagan world. The Jew from Nazareth is also—some will insist upon adding "and therefore"—the only-begotten of the Father. Jesus Christ is known as the Second Adam. May not the Christian world think of him too as the Second Abraham, the one who is uniquely its Patriarch? For it is the man Jesus who has made universally historical the theological testimony, "It is from the Jews that salvation comes" (John 4:22)...

The medieval figure of the synagogue standing with broken staff and eyes covered has to be redeemed from its demonic original intention of teaching the blindness of "the Jews" before Christ. Franz Rosenzweig completely reinterprets this symbol to testify to Israel's use of all possible means to maintain its inner vitality, in contrast to the church, which, with unbroken staff and eyes open to the world, goes forth in behalf of the mission of universal divine election. Christians may accept this reinterpretation unreservedly...To any who protest that men cannot worship God save through the worship of Jesus Christ, the

---

[16]   Ibid., pp. 142, 107.

response is: Unless the worship of Christ means the worship of God, it is a terrible form of idolatry.[17]

A Christian theology of the Jewish-Christian relationship is called to proclaim from the Christian side what [Franz] Rosenzweig has expressed from the Jewish side: Judaism is the "star of redemption," Christianity the rays of that star. The church is "successor" of Israel *in only one respect and no other*: By virtue of the Christian gospel the dividing wall between Jew and Gentile is destroyed once and for all. The abiding Covenant with Israel is decisively and definitively opened to the world in a way that Jewish faith does not provide.[18]

The affirmation of a single, unfolding Covenant "categorically denies any subordination of Israel to the church"[19]—as it also denies any subordination of the church to Israel. Here in a word was my dialectic of continuity/discontinuity.

II

There follows a systematic critique of *Elder and Younger Brothers*. The several points are not entirely disjunctive.

1. *Rosenzweig disconnected*. To lead into the critique and to tie it to the previous section of this chapter: For some time now I have come to look upon Franz Rosenzweig as having got himself into trouble respecting both counts of his dialectic. I had been afflicted, correspondingly, with that same condition: (a) Where is the legitimacy in, *au fond*, closing off the Jewish people from world events and world responsibility? Rosenzweig's campaign to remand his people to an ahistorical, wholly "spiritual" collectivity has been rejected by many representatives of the Jewish community, attesting as they must that Jews are a *historic* people. (b) Before the facts of the church's idolatrous Christologies

---

17   It hardly seems that I understood what I was saying here. I should today label the second part of the quoted sentence an instance of theological incoherence. I was subsequently driven to deny a distinction between "the worship of Christ" and the plague of idolatry.

18   Ibid., pp. 159-160, with minor emendations.

19   Ibid., p. 151.

and its long record of antisemitism, where is the warrant for celebrating some (reputed) Christian embodiment of universal redemption? *What is all that business about the Christian church's unbroken staff and clear eyes?* Rosenzweig's notion that the gentile world can come to God only through Jesus Christ is not only repugnant to most Jews; it has to be faulted from moral, world-historical, and objective points of view. Addressing the resort to Jesus' crucifixion-resurrection as a supposed means of coping spiritually with the Holocaust, Robert E. Willis rightly objects that the passion of Christ has become part and parcel "of the very evil it seeks to illuminate."[20] His point applies far beyond the Holocaust, for it serves to indict the Christological claim *in toto*.

My embrace of Franz Rosenzweig was a sorry one. Yet he does not carry the inceptive responsibility; my own dialectical ruminations were independently to blame.

2. *Sexism with no clothes.* Jesus Christ as Second Adam, Second Abraham, the one who is uniquely the church's Patriarch, "the man" who has "made universally historical" a crucially theological testimony—all these things may simply appear as an affront to the dignity of women as human beings, as the words must also have been an affront to the movement for women's rights that was already beginning at the time. I shall return to this matter later in the retrospective.

3. *Coherence revisited.* In the initial chapter of this work, I praise coherence as an existentially valid and even indispensable intellectual and moral standard. In *Elder and Younger Brothers* I became involved in a serious menace to that norm. I was operating in the name of two (for me) inseparable theological issues, biblical authority and Christology.

The threat to coherence is intimated by David Noel Freedman, who speaks of the anomaly that while the later church was to maintain that the New Testament is the norm by which the "Old Testament" is to be judged, the viewpoint of the early church was sternly opposite: The Tanak (Hebrew Bible) was "the canonical Scripture, the unquestioned authority by which New

---

[20] Robert E. Willis, "Christian Theology After Auschwitz," *Journal of Ecumenical Studies* 12 (1975): 506.

Testament persons and events were to be assessed."[21] But did not this anomaly also mean a contradiction?—a question I did not consider in *Elder and Younger Brothers*. Stupidly, I did not even think of it. The problem is this: On the one hand, the Christian church has always honored the Tanak, in the sense that the Hebrew Bible is regarded as constituent to faith-authority. On the other hand, there is the fact that Jesus of Nazareth, while of course received by some as the Christ, had disappointed, or had been prevented in one or another way from fulfilling, the prevailing Messianic expectations within the Word of God (the Hebrew Bible)—the canonical promises—or at least (and perhaps a more apt way to put it) he failed to give reality to certain poignant expectations within the first-century community of the people of God.[22] What I wholly missed was that the foregoing instance of incoherence or self-contradiction raises inexorably the question of the objective tenability of the church's entire Christological claim (once dedication is assumed, as expressed above, to a certain mode of theological-biblical authority). As Paul M. van Buren declares, Jesus could not have been the Messiah of Israel. Israel's Messiah was to be marked and identified "as the inaugurator of the Messianic age. The Messianic age, in turn, is marked by radical historical transformation." (In a word for today, van Buren goes farther: In the face of the destroyed Jewish children of the *Shoah*, "dare any Christian say that Jesus was or is the Messiah of Israel?")[23]

However, I also utilized the foregoing Scripture/Christology dilemma more constructively—and not unsoundly, I continue to hope—in order to bear witness to the faithfulness of majority Israel to God's word and God's promise, precisely in and through a prevailing nonacceptance of Jesus as the Christ. The issue was much more than that of human probity: it was one of objective

---

[21]   David Noel Freedman, as cited in EYB, p. 133n.

[22]   However, Christians have always exaggerated the extent of Jewish concern for and interest in the Messiah. At most, Jesus came to satisfy the Messianic expectations in minority respects-one of these perhaps being the "suffering servant" of the Lord. Yet there remains overwhelming doubt that the "servant" of Isaiah 53 can be construed as an individual rather than as Israel as such or at least as a "remnant" of Israel.

[23]   Paul M. van Buren, "Affirmation of the Jewish People: a condition of theological coherence," Supplement to *Journal of the American Academy of Religion* 45 (1977): 1090. Cf. Paul Tillich: "How can someone be the Christ when he has not fulfilled the function of the Christ?" ("The Jewish Question: Christian and German Problem," *Jewish Social Studies* 33 [1971]: 270).

theological truth. For how could we ever believe that the Lord of integrity and justice would nurture the Messianic conscience of his people in a certain well-defined direction (fully allowing for their own misunderstandings and sin) only to deem his people blameworthy for persistently following in just that direction? Thus is God's probity equally at stake—unless we are to shrink divine revelation down to purely human untruth or imagination. Of course, we always have the option of denying the veracity "of the reputedly divine elements of the biblical witness that...taught Israel to hope for a Messianic consummation so different from the church's testimony." But alternatively, "we may plead—and it is a bold saying—that it was not God's revealed will or purpose that the great majority of original Israel should come to acclaim Jesus as the Christ." For any who cannot endure that God would mislead his human creatures and who yet seek after "the essential authenticity of the Hebrew Bible for faith," this plea stays compelling.[24] So we are met with both the faithfulness of God and the corresponding faithfulness of Israel. Throughout, I was endeavoring to vindicate at one and the same time the freedom/responsibility/integrity of human beings and the freedom/responsibility/integrity of God. In Professor van Buren's epitomization, Israel's No to the event of Jesus was "an act of fidelity to the one God and his Covenant with Israel."[25] For Christians to refuse to celebrate that Jewish fidelity is an act of spiritual blindness.

Our discussion to this point raises the momentous, almost unbearable question of the theological-ethical legitimacy/illegitimacy of the acceptance of Jesus as the Christ by the early Jewish-Christian community. The question is dealt with in *Elder and Younger Brothers*—e.g., these people "ranged themselves against the very tradition of faith in which they had been reared." "Are we to say, in consequence, that they betrayed their ancestral faith? There is no purely human defense against an affirmative answer. But there is a divine defense for a negative answer. It is found in the simple testimony of Paul, 'no

---

[24] EYB, p. 136.

[25] Paul M. van Buren, *A Christian Theology of the People Israel*, Part II - *A Theology of the Jewish-Christian Reality* (New York: Seabury Press, 1983), p. 33. See also A. Roy Eckardt, "Can There Be a Jewish-Christian Relationship?," p. 129.

one can say "Jesus is Lord!" except under the influence of the Holy Spirit' (I Cor. 12:3)."[26]

4. *Ought versus is.* Collaterally with the earlier points, an underlying confusion may have been nurtured in and through *Elder and Younger Brothers,* a confusion between what has been and is the case (the alleged "facts," including what is claimed to be the facts) and what is or can be normatively the case. To wit: The historical and phenomenological data[27] we have been concentrating upon concerning the dialectical relation between Judaism and Christianity do not perforce offer moral guidance respecting what that relation ought to be today or at any future time, or for that matter whether there ought to be any such relation. It is true that at present I should incline to assign precedence, from the Christian side, to continuity over discontinuity vis-à-vis Judaism and the Jewish community. But there is a dual motivation for this that is only obliquely related to "isness" or first-century and ancient "facts": (a) the conviction that Christian claims of discontinuity have long since and decisively been penetrated by immorality; (b) the consideration that the Christological claim can scarcely be received as a given (in any extra-historical or extra-phenomenological sense). As already noted, that claim is centrally problematic at the normative level. I mentioned van Buren's insistence that Jesus could not be the Messiah of Israel. However, van Buren attests notwithstanding that Jesus was and is the Christ of the Gentiles. Is not his "notwithstanding" open to exactly the same problematic negativity as his point about the Messiah of Israel? Where is the sense or the defense in declaring that the one who cannot be the Messiah is after all (normatively) the "Messiah" (if indeed only for a different

---

26   EYB, p. 139.

27   John P. Boyle explains the "phenomenology of religion" as an approach that emphasizes "a careful description of religious manifestations of all sorts with the aim of allowing the nature or essence of religion to appear" ("Paradigms for Public Education Religion Studies Curricula: Some Suggestions and Critique," *The Council on the Study of Religion Bulletin* 12 [1981]: 41). At abiding issue, of course, is whether and how such a procedure can nurture *understanding*; also whether phenomena can ever convey something about noumena. The second of these issues is the more heartrending.

collectivity or community)?[28] And even if a case could somehow be made for the latter avowal, we have hardly healed the breach between "is" and "ought."

5. *A visit to the orphanage.* In *Elder and Younger Brothers* I cited Manfred Vogel's critical response: Concern for humankind "is already cared for in the covenant of Judaism." I failed to give Vogel's judgment due weight, even going so far as to state that the Christian has no choice but "to testify that for him the preeminent fulfillment of Israel's universalism takes place" through Jesus of Nazareth.[29] Then recently I dug out two commentaries upon my book, the one by a rabbi in Boston, the other by a pediatrician in Johannesburg, each of whom independently supported the thinking behind Vogel's response.

The one reviewer adduced that I missed the mark in not recognizing that continuity may be of two kinds rather than one: Continuity may obtain via the church as well as the synagogue. Or continuity is to be found only via Judaism (the reviewer's persuasion). The first alternative is barred: "Christianity has rejected and controverted the most essential principles of Judaism...When one tradition insists that God's initial covenant with man was amplified and extended through Christ as the Messiah, while another categorically rejects this view, how is it possible to hold that both are right, or that there is essential continuity between them?"[30] (I find this last question to be out of order. For my judgment upon the side of continuity was not meant as a universal or objective statement; the asseveration that "both are right" was strictly a Christian confession.)

The other commentator adjudged that in contrast to my "tortuous conclusion" (that the Gentile can enter the Covenant by becoming a Christian), the "perfectly simple" solution is: "let him become a Jew and he, and most certainly his offspring, will be part of the Covenant." Conversion to Judaism "is the obvious means of entering the covenantal family." For Christianity "is not part of the family of Israel and its Christ is not the Jewish Jesus, but the Pagan Christ, who is none other than the mausoleum of the gods of the Middle

---

[28]   There is the further difficulty that any restricting of Christ to deliverer or Lord of the Gentiles does not come to terms with the reality of Jewish Christians (Messianic Jews) of past and present.

[29]   EYB, p.146.

[30]   Roland B Gittelsohn, "Dogmas and Dialogue" (review-article on EYB), *Midstream* 14 (1968): 72. Paradoxically enough, Rabbi Gittelsohn mostly praised EYB.

East...Christians, then, are orphans, though they do not see themselves as such." They must remain orphans, and antisemitism must continue, until they find their father.[31]

An important implication can be drawn from all three criticisms together (Vogel's and the other two), an implication that takes us back to one or more of the items already enumerated: Even were the two sides somehow to agree that "discontinuous" divine action was necessary or was at least engaged in to the end of a historical (first-century) opening of the Covenant to the non-Jewish world, where is the theological-moral necessity or rationale for persisting in that affirmation in the present? The twentieth or twenty-first century is not the first century. It is not primitive Christianity as such but rather today's Christianity that is brought before the bar of judgment.

6. *Resurrection as rupture.* The realized resurrection of Jesus Christ was assumed and avowed in *Elder and Younger Brothers.* Was not belief in Jesus' resurrection the entire religious-moral-existential raison d'être and motivation of the first Christian community? However, in 1967 I was evidently as yet incapable of discerning the other side of this historical-theological state of affairs: the possible wrongheadedness of those early Christians amidst their very fealty to the resurrection, a potentially catastrophic conclusion that would act to expunge the whole Christian claim to realized discontinuity (as well as an at least partially realized eschatology), thereby throwing into question traditionalist Christianity as such. That is to say, in the volume here under assessment I simply failed to recognize the resurrection of Jesus for its determinedly problematic quality. The most I saw was that that event meant "a fundamental transformation" of original Israel's Messianic expectations. Much more fatefully, I had not as yet comprehended the grave power of the resurrection as fuel for the reality of Christian triumphalism in the latter's linkage to antisemitism. However, as a kind of portent of a future position, I did discern that the resurrection of Jesus Christ stands at the center of the Jewish-Christian *Auseinandersetzung.*[32]

---

[31] S. Levin, "The Orphan Syndrome," *Judaism* 22 (1973): 33, 36, 37. Levin's essay does much more than review EYB.

[32] EYB, pp. 140, 88.

If there is an all-decisive discontinuity between the reputedly resurrected Jesus and the Messianic promises, we are left with one of two choices (to return to point three of the present listing): Accept the implicit witness of the Tanak that the Messiah has not come. Or deny the authority of the Tanak at this one determining place, and testify that the Messiah has come. And since the latter testimony is seen to be licit only upon the ground of the actual resurrection of Jesus Christ (so the New Testament declares), it follows that any denial that the resurrection has (as yet) taken place will negate, among other things, the entire discontinuity between the event of Jesus the Jew and Judaism. But all this I simply had not grasped in 1967.

Excursus. Please consult below "If a Man Die, Is This a Death of God?," a sermon affirming the resurrection that I delivered at the Pennsylvania State University on Easter Day in 1966.[33] If I know what I am doing at the moment, I seem to be reproducing that piece in the present volume as a kind of self-criticism *à rebours* (ass-backwards), and therefore not without some mischievousness, since I tend today to subsume the resurrection of Jesus within a Jewish province. If an individual is entitled to call upon his later convictions in order to criticize earlier ones, must he be forbidden to turn to an earlier affirmation of his in order to assess a later one? If he is not allowed to do the latter, has not "truth" been taken captive by *chronos*, viz., by the notion that "later must be better"? But all this leads into a highly telling philosophic question: What is or ought to be the relation among several competing causal variables: self-criticism, mischievousness, *chronos*, and our (or my) old friend coherence? I think it may be too easy a way out to take coherence and simply add it to self-criticism as being more or less subject to *chronos* (with mischievousness left to fend for itself). In a word: Ought not the norm of coherence sometimes be enabled to elude subordination to before-and-after processes?

7. *Portents of the trial of God.* My repeated assertion of God's faithfulness to Israel remains problematic, within two related frames of reference: the historical fortunes of Israel, and the historical deportment of Christians. As suggested in chapter three above, historical data do not have independent power to establish theological claims. Yet may not history sometimes act to bring faith

---

33 "If a Man Die, Is This a Death of God?," *The Pulpit* 38 (1967): 4-6. Interestingly (for me anyway), this was the final sermon I published.

into a state of despair? At the least, theology is not permitted to turn its back upon history (any more than it may subject itself to bad history). True, to deny the historical faithfulness of God to his/her people will bring aid and comfort to those who maintain that God has rejected Israel. Nevertheless, the question stands, and it is unrelenting: Is there empirical (historical-moral) justification for professing that God has been and remains faithful to his/her people, or do the empirical data point, horribly, to God's unfaithfulness? In subsequent years I was to be much exercised by this question.

8. *Chutzpah*? The question of the propriety/impropriety of Christians attempting to identify intellectually and behaviorally the nature and meaning of Jewish identity has dogged me from the beginning through much of the rest of my work. I have never quite forgot a query put to me approximately a quarter-century ago by a small group of rabbinical students in Jerusalem: "What do you Christians want from us anyway?" Yet for Christians to keep wholly silent upon the matter of Jewish identity may implicitly sustain the vices of abstraction and even dehumanization, and withal antisemitism.

The role or roles that Jewish faith and the Jewish people may have for the life and faith of the Christian church is another matter. Christians have both the right and the obligation to respect and proclaim that Jewish place.

So much for *Elder and Younger Brothers*—fruit of much toil and child of some folly. My wife reports to me that, according to some students and others, this was one of my better books. Perhaps a factor here was its relative conciseness. With all the books that are published these days, succinctness is often a major literary desideratum. But this is a small consolation in the presence of error.

III

A few occasional essays appearing in this period struck polemic notes.

Among other purposes, the article "Can There Be a Jewish-Christian Relationship?" sought to impugn as ideological[34] and even socially pathological the unremitting Christian charge of the responsibility of "the Jews"

---

[34] By "ideological" I have in mind the captivity of ideas at the hands of self-interest, most often collective self-interest.

for the death of Jesus.[35] And it expatiated upon antisemitic elements within the New Testament, repudiating in the process various apologetic and pedagogical attempts to exculpate those documents.[36] Many Christian efforts to exonerate the New Testament take the pertinent passages and treat them as if they were *discriminate* in character, and hence historically and morally explainable and therefore not ultimately unacceptable. What is obscured here is that the passages in question contain *indiscriminate* judgments (against *"the* Jews"). This is what makes the procedure of exoneration at once morally indefensible and intellectually insupportable. To revert one more time to *Elder and Younger Brothers*: "The Christian church remains caught in a fateful conflict between Christian morality and Christian dogma respecting [New Testament] Scripture."[37] However, this aspect of the critique is a world away from any allegation that "the New Testament is permeated *(durchdrungen)* by antisemitism."[38] That allegation is false.

Both the above kinds of rectification—upon "responsibility" for Jesus' death and upon New Testament antisemitism—have exerted some influence within recent Christian thinking, as has the rejection of church supersessionism.

"End to the Christian-Jewish Dialogue," a two-part piece in *The Christian Century*, attacked the Second Vatican Council's schema *De Judaeis*, chronicling that effort's deterioration from its hopeful beginning, under Pope John XXIII, as a brief, forthright text repudiating the ancient calumny of "deicide," to its final politicized fate as (in the words of the Roman Catholic writer John Cogley) a source of "shame and anguish" for Catholics and of "suspicion and rancor"

---

[35] See also "Toward a Theology for the Christian-Jewish Encounter," pp. 128-130.

[36] On the general subject of antisemitism and the New Testament, see EYB, pp. 121-129. The analysis in EYB ends with a celebration of the overall New Testament witness. See also "Toward a Theology for the Christian-Jewish Encounter," pp. 127-128.

[37] EYB, pp. 125-126.

[38] This allegation against the New Testament was incorrectly attributed to me by a German Catholic theologian-I here quote the exact wording of his "report" upon me-in conjunction with the Second International Conference on Jewish-Christian Cooperation in Cambridge, U.K., August 1966 (see EYB, p. 126n for specific information).

amongst Jews.[39] My article stressed that the Catholic affliction is shared within all the churches. Sandwiched between the above two polemical pieces, "Christian Guilt" spoke confessionally and hopefully of Christian repentance and reconciliation, referring to practical-existential ways by which the power of guilt may be broken.

Lastly, "Again, Silence in the Churches," another two-part article in *The Christian Century*, this one composed jointly with Alice Eckardt, assailed the churches and the Christian community for recapitulating at the time of the Six Day War (1967) the inaction and silence that they had for the most part practiced during the Nazi *Endlösung* (Final Solution). Once again Jewish annihilation was an imminent threat, and once again the Christian world (with some few exceptions) turned its back.[40] There was, as a matter of fact, much Christian support for the Arab side. In marked contrast to expressions of sympathy for Israel's plight within secular quarters, not a single church body spoke out against the publicly promised destruction of Israel or in behalf of that nation's right to defend itself. Further, as against the almost universal castigation of the Nazis a quarter century before, there now came Christian charges of Israeli "aggression." Wherever Jews are involved, self-defense is quickly identified by detractors as hidden self-aggrandizement.[41] In part two of the essay "Again, Silence" possible explanations were suggested to account for Christian anti-Israelism and antisemitism: "Whenever original Israel is

---

[39]   To exemplify a widespread Jewish response, David Polish pointed out that the final Vatican Declaration, devoid as it was of any vestige of Christian contrition or reconciliation, failed to surmount in any tangible way the dreary old charge of Jewish rejection by God until Jews see the Christian light. Not unexpectedly, the Catholic decree culminated in an evangelistic thrust ("The Statement on the Jews: An Inadequate Document," *The Christian Century* [1 Dec. 1965]: 1475-1477). See also EYB, pp. 114-115, and the verse "On the Reported Death of Deicide (c. 100-1964)."

[40]   One critic charged that my wife and I demanded blind or unequivocal support for Israel. In point of fact, we had concerned ourselves only with the question of a moral duty to oppose the effort to destroy Israel.

[41]   Henry P. van Dusen, a world Christian leader, declaimed to the immense readership of *The New York Times* (letter of 7 July 1967) that the Israeli defense forces of 1967 were not really that but were, in effect, reincarnations of the Nazis in their "assault" upon Israel's Arab neighbors. In the *Times* of 13 July 1967 I responded to van Dusen with a letter of my own (and received more than two hundred personal letters in reply, most of them sympathetic, including a considerable number from non-Jews).

assailed, certain suppressed, macabre elements in the Christian soul are stirred to sympathy with the assailants."

My current self-critical reaction to the above polemical efforts tends to be less strong than my foregoing critique of *Elder and Younger Brothers*. The reason is that I continue to believe in the substantial historical accuracy and moral validity of this polemic work. However, when the question shifts to one of psychology and practical effectiveness, that is another matter. How responsible a procedure is polemics and what does it achieve? Will it simply compound self-defensiveness in others? Does it do more harm than good? No blanket or categorical answer is available. Perhaps Christian anthropology is of some pertinence here. As Reinhold Niebuhr used to reiterate, the essence of the human being is will rather than mind (the "Hebraic" viewpoint versus the "Greek" viewpoint). This means that "education" in the "facts" or in some alleged "truth" is a highly limited instrument for good. Human self-interest and prejudice and pride are powerful forces. One comfort is that social and political action may sometimes redirect individual and collective wills. Strategies that attack at the level of volition are not always fruitless. People can and do change. Nevertheless, as I today reread such polemical essays as these I keep wondering whether they may have been, on balance, counterproductive.[42]

To end this chapter upon a rather more peaceable note, over the period 1963-1967 I continued my editorial work and my endeavors within the areas of religion and higher education, including the philosophy of scholarship in religion. "Only in recent decades has higher education in our country been granted the task of nurturing an independent intellectual tradition in religion."[43]

Such editorials as "'Theology' versus 'Religion,'" "An Identity Explored," and "Is the Study of Religion Peculiar?" carried forward and applied the general dialectical advocacy of the address "The Strangeness of Religion in the University Curriculum" (reproduced above): "Apart from objective

---

[42] Germane to the period's work in the Jewish-Christian relation were my reviews of Arthur A. Cohen, *The Natural and the Supernatural Jew*; John M. Oesterreicher, ed., *The Bridge*, Vol IV; Edward H. Flannery, *The Anguish of the Jews*; Jakob Jocz, *Christians and Jews*; Augustin Cardinal Bea, *The Church and the Jewish People*; and Heinz David Leuner, *When Compassion Was a Crime*.

[43] Editorial, "On Independence in Undergraduate Study."

intellectuality, religion is not probed resolutely; it is remanded to individual or social piety. Yet unless sacredness is truly present, essential religion is lost, and the study of religion is robbed of integrity."[44] "The tension abides, and it must abide, between academic religion and the faith of human beings."[45]

In editorials and elsewhere I argued for forms of professional identification that would reflect and foster with greater and needed effectiveness the breadth and depth of today's scholarship in religion. It was imperative that organizational structure and a publications program be strengthened in order to represent authoritatively the entire spectrum of the discipline. The American Academy of Religion had been founded in 1909 but under the rather pedantic and exclusivist name National Association of Biblical Instructors. I was the party primarily responsible for the adoption of the new name in 1964.[46] The change in name and structure was commensurate with the contemporary broadening and deepening of religion studies, together with its rapidly enhancing academic stature, in and beyond North America. Then I further contended for a correspondingly fitting change in name for the AAR's official quarterly. That campaign was also finally successful. Beginning in 1967 *The Journal of Bible and Religion* was shorn of its partially redundant label and was retitled—were we descending into the ways of the Gentiles?—*The Journal of the American Academy of Religion*.[47]

Finally, a brief analysis, presented at a Cambridge conference and published in London, pursued further the theme of sacredness/ profaneness, with stress upon the peculiar tension between these two religio-social dimensions within the pluralism and voluntaryism of American culture, and with emphasis upon the

---

[44]   Editorial, "Is the Study of Religion Peculiar?" This dialectical theme was also utilized as a point of departure for my essay "Pre-Seminary Education and the Undergraduate Department of Religion," a critique of Keith R. Bridston and Dwight W. Culver, *Pre-Seminary Education*, a study sponsored by the Lilly Endowment, the American Academy of Religion, and the American Association of Theological Schools in the United States and Canada. See also my editorial, "The Lilly Study," and a brief bibliography, "Pre-Seminary Education and the Study of Religion."

[45]   Editorial, "Is there Anything Religious in Religion?"

[46]   See editorials, "Our Public Image" and "In Defense of Religion-in-General."

[47]   Consult editorial, "The Irony of 'JBR.'" Thirty volumes had appeared under the traditional name. See the commentary by Claude Welch in JAAR 37 (1969): 319-320.

contemporary desacralization of the world. Yet does not that desacralization create a foundational crisis for the entire dialectic of the sacred and the profane? At the end I urged serious reflection upon a finding of Hans Joachim Schoeps of Erlangen, offered back in 1957: "The prevailing attitude toward the events of salvation attested to for centuries is no longer one of doubtful unbelief, but simply that of uninterested disbelief...Both Israel and Christendom today dwell on islands and must carry on their concourse from island to island, while beneath and around them there flows the stream of world history, which tends to submerge even these islands."[48]

---

[48]   "Aspects of Contemporary American Religious Life."

4A

Selected Writings

(1963-1967)

On the Reported Death of Deicide, c. 100-1964

(The Christian Century 82 [1965]: 199)

Arranged in close and splendid state,

Ecclesiastic brains have set

The errors of the record straight

For skeletons in Auschwitz met.

If a Man Die, Is This a Death of God?

(The Pulpit 38 [March 1967]: 4-6, slightly emended)

I

If Easter Day is a celebration, its context is nevertheless an event of death, the particular death of a particular human being. The expression "Good Friday" is unfortunate and misleading: Since when is an execution or a funeral a good thing? That the words are probably a corruption of "God's Friday" is of little practical help; the term "Black Friday" remains the accurate and necessary one. Some Christians testify that upon the Cross the Lord "triumphed over the powers that opposed him." But this man Jesus really died. He did not triumph over the forces that fought him; he was their victim. He was conquered by death. The context of Easter is death.

Here lies the strange appropriateness for this day of Job 14: It binds into the one company that man from Nazareth and everybody else.

> Man that is born of a woman is
> of few days, and full of trouble.
> He comes forth like a flower, and
> withers;
> he flees like a shadow, and con-
> tinues not.   (Job 14:1-2)

There's more hope for a tree:

> Though its root grow old in the earth,
> and its stump die in the ground,
> yet at the scent of water it will bud
> and put forth branches like a young plant.
> But a man dies, and is laid low;
> man breathes his last, and where is he? (Job 14:8-10)

No immortality for his soul, as the Greeks vainly imagined. No rebirth in springtime with the crocus or the daffodil. He "lies down and rises not." He lives once and is gone. His is not a make-believe "passing away"; it's a genuine, total death—the kind that produces a terrible stench, the kind that guarantees despair, the kind that shrieks to the heavens, "My God, why?" The setting for Easter is death, the past death of that one young man, the coming death of us all. The only way the Christian church can combat the sentimentalization that has corrupted the Easter season is to remind its constituency and the world that, as Lord Keynes put it, "In the long run, we shall all be dead." Our Easter finery has about as much power to save us as the Easter Bunny.

II

If the context of Easter is death, could death be its *fabric* as well?

Between Black Friday and Easter Sunday lies Holy Saturday. Why "Holy Saturday"? Not because the day is particularly sacred or set apart. But there's another meaning to "holy": the uncertain, the unpredictable. This man was put to death on the day before. That much is certain. It happened. And next week or a year from now, or a hundred years, we shall all die—this much is certain as well. But does anything else happen in between to make things different? *Will* anything happen? That's the question of Holy Saturday, the strange in-between day, the day of wondering, of brooding, of uncertainty—the day for Job's other question:

> If a man die, shall he live again?
> All the days of my service I would wait,
> till my release should come.
> Thou wouldest call, and I would
> answer thee...(Job 14:14-15)

Job's voice soon trails off into a wistful stillness. He never lived beyond Holy Saturday. He agonized, he hoped, and in the end fell silent—immured by the mystery of life and death, a holy wonderment.

And you and I? Are we to fall silent before that question, "If a man die, shall he live again?" Humanly speaking, no question could surpass this one in priority. Depending upon the answer, we shall be cast into ultimate anxiety or be armed to stand anything.

Here enters the question of God. *Not* the question of humankind. Between death and humanity there's no doubt of the sequel: Death always wins in the end. "Man lies down and rises not..." But if a man die, is God dead as well?

I can never identify the human motivations behind the editors of TIME magazine—maybe they can't either—but I don't think I shall soon forget the concurrence of their 1966 cover essay entitled "Is God Dead?" with the calendar of Holy Week last year. The account made no reference to Easter at all, but it did not have to do so. Here confronting us, and being asked by us, is the question of Holy Saturday: "If a man die, is God dead?" Perhaps the real fabric of Easter today, the only Easter we can know directly, *is* death—not alone humankind's death but God's. If God could not raise his reputed Son from the dead, and therefore failed to raise him, then death, the enemy of enemies of God and humanity alike, has the final say, and to all intents and purposes God *is* dead. A God without power over death might just as well be a corpse himself. The age of Christendom, for all its glory—its master works of art, its paeans of praise, its creedal constructions, its theological triumphs, the discreteness of its morality—is revealed as an age of delusion. How much better off we should in fact be if all knowledge of the crucifixion of this woodworker from Nazareth could have been buried amongst the myriad other crucifixions for which the Roman overlords were responsible! For even though the event did take place, it is not a saving event for us. It is only another reminder, and a most poignant one at that, of a grisly fate that stands in store for every human being.

Yet it is too late to blot out that evil Friday from our memory. So, many may react, let us make a virtue of this grim necessity. Let us not do away with the Easter time. Let us keep the memorial. On Black Friday was the death of Jesus; on Holy Saturday we agonized over what to make of it all; on Easter Day each year, death willing, we will acknowledge that God is dead. We will resolve to live out as tolerably as we can the days left to us. We will promise to fight off death as long as humanly possible. And when we finally go down to defeat, no one and nothing, not death itself, can take away our defiance. Amidst a bleak, impossible universe there will once have lived a tiny yet noble creature, a living soul wearing the very image of God. This achievement will once have been, even if in the end it was met by death, as God was once met by death.

III

Some theologians these days are insisting, or at least gambling, upon the death of God. Would it not be divinely mischievous if the language human beings are permitted to employ could somehow have taken these thinkers captive? Gerhard Eberling—not in their camp—reminds us that language possesses a power that eludes our mastery of it. Our words have a way of running beyond our control. When these theologians speak of the death of God, they can be asserting, or hoping for, God's actual demise. But the "death of God" remains deliciously ambiguous. Do we not attest in the church to the *judgment of* God—the judgment wrought by God? Do we not proclaim the *forgiveness of* God—the forgiveness bestowed by God? And when we speak of the *death of* God—are we not confessing to a death made possible by God, by his judgment and by his forgiveness?

Yet facing us here is an issue far too serious for final resolution by semantic maneuvering. Do you recall the scene in the Hochhuth play, *Der Stellvertreter* —poorly rendered *The Deputy* in the American version, correctly rendered *The Representative* in the English version—the scene where the Doctor endeavors to humiliate Father Riccardo for his faith? It's part of the Act that bears the unqualifiedly fitting title, "Auschwitz or The Question Asked of God"—the ultimate point of the drama, really. For days on end the Doctor, by simple waves of the hand, has been dispatching whomever he wishes to the crematoria, while sparing others. In a reversal of the Prologue to Job, where the Lord permits Satan to test the chief character, the Doctor has been testing God. He says:

> Because I wanted an answer—an answer!
> ...I risked what no man had
> yet risked since the world began to turn ...
> I took an oath that I would provoke
> that Old Man so measurelessly,

so totally beyond measure, that he would have to give
  an answer.
Even if it was only the negative answer, which
as Stendahl says, is all that *can* excuse Him:
that He does not exist.

Yet God has done absolutely nothing to respond or intervene. And so the Doctor
continues:

Do you find it more comforting that God in person
turns Mankind on the spit of history?...
History: dust, altars, suffering, rape,
where every reputation mocks its victims.
Creator, creation, creature, all these three
Auschwitz negates.

But which one is really dead, dead inside, God or the Doctor? Each of us
has to decide: Is God unable to answer? *Is* he dead? Or is the Doctor's
diabolism the thing that happens to human beings when they try to test
God—when they seek, in effect, to kill him? Strangely enough, the Doctor
seems himself to agree with the second option, for he has already confessed that
he is the Devil. Riccardo cries out:

If there is a devil then there is a God:
Or *you* would long ago have won.

The Doctor grips the other's arm and "bubbles with laughter":

That's how I like to see you.
The St. Vitus dance of the fanatic.

But which one is the fanatic?
  Here, then, is the other path: What if during the end-time—that is to say,
on the first Holy Saturday, that uncanny in-between time—death and the God
of life and death were locked in mortal battle—and God won?

Now it was Mary Magdalene and Joanna and Mary the mother of James and the other women with them who told this to the apostles: but these words seemed to them an idle tale, and they did not believe them.

...Then one of them, named Cleopas, answered him, "Are you the only visitor to Jerusalem who does not know the things that have happened there in these days?" And he said to them, "What things?" And they said to him, "Concerning Jesus of Nazareth, who was a prophet mighty in deed and word before God and all the people, and how our chief priests and rulers delivered him up to be condemned to death, and crucified him. But we had hoped that he was the one to redeem Israel. Yes, and besides all this, it is now the third day since this happened. Moreover, some women of our company amazed us. They were at the tomb early in the morning and did not find his body; and they came back saying that they had even seen a vision of angels, who said that he was alive. Some of those who were with us went to the tomb, and found it just as the women had said; but him they did not see." And he said to them, "O foolish men, and slow of heart to believe all that the prophets have spoken! Was it not necessary that the Christ should suffer these things and enter into his glory?" (Luke 24:10-11, 18-26)

The question for Black Friday is, "My God, why?" The question for Holy Saturday is, "If a man die, shall he live again?" And the question for Easter Day? "If a man die, is this a death of God?" If the event of Calvary *is* such a death, the way to the Empty Tomb is already marked out. The *way* to the Tomb, not the Empty Tomb itself. For, unlike the Cross, the Resurrection is the one unforced recognition of history. No one is compelled to look inside, to add this truth to the register of other historical facts. Yet the Easter question still meets each one of us: "Why do you seek the living among the dead?"

"And as for the resurrection of the dead, have you not read what was said to you by God, 'I am the God of Abraham, and the God of Isaac, and the God of Jacob'? He is not the God of the dead, but of the living" (Matt. 22:31-32). What is there to daunt us? Death, the last enemy, is put to death. The gift of eternal life is held forth to us. Hallelujah! Christ is risen!

5

Ventures Theological-Political-Ethical, 1968-1974

This span of seven years was a busy time for me, involving more than a half-hundred articles and reviews and three books.[1]

I

I edited a medium-sized sourcebook, *The Theologian at Work*, in the Harper Forum Series under the general editorship of Martin E. Marty.[2] In its

---

[1] *Christianity in Israel* (1971), a fourth item, was not really a book but an edited booklet prepared at the request of the American Academic Association for Peace in the Middle East. Included were historical and expository articles by Saul Colbi, James Parkes, Peter Schneider, and others. Special attention was directed to the problem of Christian conversionism vis-à-vis Jews and Israel. The analysis extended to Christian reactions within Israel to the war crisis of 1967.

[2] I dedicated *The Theologian at Work* to "two possible theologians: Paula and Steve," our children. I was to learn several things from this project: (a) Don't even *think* of playing God to history, especially when it comes to your own children. My daughter was to become a family therapist and my son a craftsman. (Yet are such vocations wholly separate from the theological enterprise?) (b) Don't assume that editing a book will be a less severe or less time-consuming task than writing one strictly upon your own. (c) Don't suppose that book reviewers will necessarily read what they are duty-bound to read. A review of *The Theologian at Work* in the *Journal of the American Academy of Religion* reported that I provided a "one-article sop to non-Christianity." In point of truth, I allotted considerable space to five (out of twenty-five) contributions by non-Christians. (d) Don't presume that a publisher's right

introduction I recast some of my earlier ideas upon the nomothetic/idiographic dialectic and upon the relations among theology, science, and history.[3] The book contained selections from a number of leading and representative twentieth-century theologians, primarily for utilization by students. It ranged across the theological landscape: how theologians operate; God and the knowledge of God; the problem of authority; the human place; and relations amongst the religious, antireligious, and secular domains.

During this time I wrote three major articles outside the contemporary Christian-Jewish encounter or dialogue as such. Upon the death in 1971 of my great teacher and friend Reinhold Niebuhr, I composed a tribute to him (reproduced below). In that same year I contributed an essay (also reprinted below), "The Crisis in Punishment," to a book on punitive action[4] edited by Harold H. Hart. Ever since college days and an unforgettable course with an extraordinary teacher, Louis A. Warsoff (his initials were the identifying letters of the license plate on his red convertible), I had been much interested in "the law." But I had not before been granted the opportunity to investigate and write upon a particular jurisprudential problem. My essay rambled some but it managed, I think, to grapple meaningfully, from the standpoint of philosophic and theological ethics, with the necessities and limitations of punitive restraint at the social level.

In 1972 I wrote a quite different kind of essay, "Death in the Judaic and Christian Traditions," for a special number on death put out by *Social Research*.[5]

---

hand is always in sync with their left hand. In the present case the subtitle on the book's cover read "A Common Search for Religious understanding," while the title page read "A Common Search for Understanding" (the correct wording). The discrepancy was not exactly the end of the world, yet the point is not unserious. Many theologians will insist that they seek understanding as such, not just religious understanding.

[3]   Cf. "The Contribution of *Nomothesis* in the Science of Man" (1961), and "A Note on Theological Procedure" (1961).

[4]   "Punitive action" may be defined as adverse treatment (adverse to the offending party) by civilly authorized persons in response to one or another socially offending act.

[5]   The special number was subsequently published as a book: *Death in American Experience*, ed. Arien Mack.

II

The polemic against Christian silence and inaction in and around the Six Day War, as embodied in "Again, Silence in the Churches," was re-expressed by me in an essay "Christians and Jews: Disrupted Dialogue," but with many different emphases and fresh materials.[6] In some contrast to the latter piece, "Eretz Israel: A Christian Affirmation" comprised certain personal reflections upon the Land and Jewish peopleness, during the trying months after June 1967. I put the question of whether the Christian may belong in some odd way to the family of Jews (other than in just a religious sense). If the Christian does not so belong, then Israel will have no existential place within his or her life. But if the Christian does so belong, then Israel is already alive in that person's heart and merely waits to be enfleshed through his or her words and deeds. Yet today I find myself asking: What authentication can there be for so audacious a prerogative as this (short of the individual opting to become a Jew)? One traditional response here has been that the Christian's ticket of admission, so to speak, is issued by, or at least through, Jesus the Jew. And yet, has not that ticket been voided by the Christian transmogrification of Jesus?

In "Eretz Israel" I attested to the peoplehood of Jews as an irrefrangible axiom of Jewish existence. Along the same line I suggested that philosemitism is merely the other side of the coin of *Judenfeindschaft*; it is antisemitism temporarily detoured by the power of remorse (or perhaps by expediency).[7] In philosemitism as in antisemitism Jews are treated other than as human beings.

In an additional piece, "The Jewish-Christian Encounter: Six Guidelines for a New Relationship," I criticized double-standard morality, introducing a Bill Mauldin cartoon portraying an Israeli soldier standing before the bar of the United Nations and being sentenced, "You must give up this vicious habit of committing self-defense." The truth/norm of peoplehood is subverted whenever a particular people is judged according to one given set of moral standards and

---

6   "Die gegenwärtige Situation der christlich-jüdischen Begegnung in Nord Amerika" (1968; trans. Heinz David Leuner) provided for a German audience a largely descriptive overview of hopeful and unhopeful elements in the recent and current state of affairs in Christian-Jewish relations in the United States and Canada.

7   A review by Charles Landstone of my book, *Your People, My People* in the *Jewish Chronicle* (London; 16 Aug. 1974) accused me of "excessive philosemitism," a most inaccurate charge.

another people is judged according to a quite discrepant set. Peoplehood is neither divinity nor depravity; it is instead ordinary, shared humanness. For all the renewed threats to the Jewish-Christian dialogue occasioned by Christian immorality, the dialogue following upon the crisis of 1967 was actually strengthened at one place: It was forced to acknowledge itself as much more than an "interfaith" affair. It is, at base, an encounter between representatives of a certain faith (Christianity) and spokespersons of a certain people (Jewry), the latter of whom, as individuals or in groups, may or may not be committed to the faith of Judaism. (The majority of Israeli Jews manifest little if any interest in "religion.")

The above essay stated: "Jesus of Nazareth lived and died faithful to his people and devoted to the faith in which he was reared...Were he living today we would identify him as an Israeli." Here was an instance of a detheologizing and deideologizing of Jesus that was to deepen for me as time passed. To respond here and now to this beginning development, perhaps two parallel lines are discernible. One line is the "journey toward humanization" that encapsulates this particular book, as reflective of the story of one writer. The other line is a gradual but persistent redeeming of Jesus himself via the surgery of historicization. The latter process recognizes and accepts *this man* for the one he in fact was and is, as against infecting him with (crucifying him with?) the germs of theological subreption. Is there some way for the Savior to be saved? Could the historicization of Jesus become one viable means to rescue, to reinstate, and thence to celebrate the "Incarnation"?

"The Tragic Unity of Enemies: A Report from the Middle East" (1969) was a second joint contribution by my wife and me in *The Christian Century*. Its original draft was prepared in the course of visits to Amman, to two Arab refugee camps in Jordan, and to Lebanon. The piece was at once pro-Arab and pro-Israeli. Yes, we believed it possible to think, to write, and to act in that dual and difficult way, and we still try to believe this (yet cf. below, the first and second critical comments upon the book *Encounter With Israel*). There is an "evenhandedness" that is covertly biased on the one side, but there is as well an evenhandedness that seeks to respond equally and fairly to the fears, hatreds, and longings of two parties who themselves remain foes. To the end of this second kind of evenhandedness, we strove for equality of documentation and equality of expression, against a backdrop of solidarity in misery.[8]

III

In late 1967 or early 1968 Alice Eckardt and I embarked upon a major collaborative effort, issuing in our initial book together, *Encounter With Israel: A Challenge to Conscience* (1970). For this purpose, I obtained a third leave from my university. The volume was composed at the invitation of Association Press (in those years the publishing house of the National YMCA), with Carl Hermann Voss as a helpful intermediary.[9] The aim of the book was to foster understanding of Israel and her people, as well as to contribute to responsible moral/political decision-making respecting that country and her place in the Middle East.

In our work of preparation (beyond a carload of books and articles), we visited and consulted with people from all stations of life, including not alone Israeli Jews but Israeli Arabs and Arabs within and beyond the Israeli-administered West Bank, in Jordan, and in Lebanon[10]—and involving many people who were convinced that the very existence of today's Israel is at best an egregious error and at worst a crime. We talked to diplomats, government employees, educators, religious leaders, Arab refugees and administrators of refugee camps, officials, military personnel, *kibbutz* members, political and labor leaders, social workers, housewives, students, journalists, lawyers, and others—many who were occupying high places and many who were not.

---

[8]   I presented a paper at the 1969 conference of the American Academic Association for Peace in the Middle East meeting at M.I.T. Entitled "The Reaction of the Churches," the exposition documented and appraised responses within American Christianity to the Middle East conflict. There was much description of opposing points of view, in ways reflective of academic convention.

[9]   We agreed with Association Press to furnish a manuscript of no more than 85,000 words. I have found a press cutting that quotes me as saying that since the final product contained 170,000 words, I must have neglected to advise the publisher that we meant "each." (Writers congenitally lie to publishers, as publishers congenitally lie to writers.) Now, in counting the words again-as an ex-editor and author I am naturally obsessed with word-counts-I come out with 185,000.

[10]   We visited the Gaza Strip but had no personal contact with Gazans.

The project was thus much more than a culmination or outcome of previous work. We became consumed by an intensive and lengthy scholarly and practical endeavor, directed to the laic quality and political aspects of Jewry in all their breadth, depth, and complexity. On the other hand, we gave great weight to the rights of the Arabs of Palestine: "Arab continuity of residence goes back many centuries...Many Arabs look to no homeland but Palestine...They have a strong attachment to the land." Few of these people have ever looked upon themselves as Jordanians; numbers of them feel themselves strangers in different Arab countries. Many of the very same arguments "advanced for Jewish rights to the land can be presented in behalf of the Palestinians." We must do our best to understand their anger, frustration, and longings.[11]

At one place in *Encounter With Israel*, we linked the double-standard syndrome to a hypothesis often remarked upon by James Parkes, that antisemitism has little if anything to do with Jews. As we expressed the matter:

> The drive in much of the world to demand the very most of Israel and the Jewish people, and to expect the very least of them—to require that they be saints and to insinuate that they will be devils—points to an aberration that is at once a collective psychopathological problem and a moral problem. When Jews are weak, they are condemned [and relished?] for that; when they are strong, they are condemned for that. These facts remind us that we are dealing with a moral disease that, ultimately speaking, has nothing to do with the way Jews behave or do not behave. The disease is within the minds and hearts of antisemites. To the extent that the disease is controlled, Jews begin to be treated as human beings, from whom other people normally expect neither too much nor too little. When this changed attitude is extended to the state, Israel will be at last accepted as a nation among other nations.[12]

Behind the above reasoning is the persuasion that, as Martin Luther King, Jr. had been among the first to observe, anti-Zionism and anti-Israelism cannot be separated from antisemitism. Yet, if antisemitism ultimately has nothing to

---

[11]   *Encounter with Israel*, p. 238 (hereinafter identified as EWI).

[12]   Ibid., p. 224 (slightly edited).

do with the Jewish people but instead has its abode within the gentile psyche, how may we relate this state of affairs coherently with the fact that it is Jews who are the objective victim of anti-Zionism and anti-Israelism? Help may perhaps be found in an observation of Paul Tillich. Antisemitism "creates that against which it fights. And it must create it, since it cannot find it in reality."[13] Jews are at most the *occasion* for the creation of antisemitism. They are not its cause.

Among critical difficulties with *Encounter With Israel*, or problems raised by that volume, the following five factors may be singled out. These points can be applied as well to other writings upon Israel and the Israeli-Arab conflict either by me or by my wife and me together.

(1) As I reread *Encounter With Israel* I think I glimpse therein a certain element of futility. When Alice Eckardt and I started the book, it was with some hope that our study would perhaps be received as fairminded, even by opponents of Israel. To our knowledge, that expectation was not realized. The hope was naïve. The fact is that numbers of people (many of them Christians) are simply convinced that the reality and cause of Israel are unjust—not merely particular acts of Israel, but *Israel* as such. Israel is prejudged. Accordingly, we as writers who accept the legitimacy of Israel are held to participate in the injustice. Although we tried to be fair, we soon learned that the opponents were looking upon our effort as inherently unfair. Historical work and ethical analysis appear to be highly limited in meliorating human conflicts or fostering human reconciliation.

(2) The relative and limited quality of human rights (and wrongs) is not perforce capable of overcoming all recourse to categorical, non-limited moral judgments.

In the Arab-Israeli conflict, the moral issue...is not primarily one of choosing the lesser of two evils. Nor is it a question of absolute right versus absolute wrong. Instead, the poignancy of the moral problem for any third party arises from the fact that one of the two main antagonists denies that the cause of the other antagonist can make any essential or even partial claim to justice. This state of affairs confronts us with a

---

13   Paul Tillich, "The Jewish Question: Christian and German Problem," *Jewish Social Studies* 33 (1971): 267.

peculiar moral dilemma: We are forced into making categorical moral judgments amidst a situation where there are, objectively speaking, only relative rights and wrongs. That is to say, we are compelled to choose between the parties *as if* one were entirely in the right and the other were entirely in the wrong, even though this is not in fact the case. In other words, we are at once prevented from being neutral and from offering any sort of compromise. A nation either has a right to sovereign existence or it does not. There is no such thing as a partial right to exist.

Accordingly, we who believe that Israel does possess the right to exist are compelled *at this one crucial point* to oppose any Arab [or other] denial of that right, even though we find much that is of validity in the Arab cause. Here we are in exactly the same predicament as those who deny the right of Israel to exist as a sovereign nation, including those who may even concede some slight merit in the Israeli cause. Together with our opponents, we are confronted by either/or decisions.[14]

(3) Judgments by Christians and others respecting Jewish identity, Jewish interests, Jewish faith, Jewish morality, etc. continue to be suspect. *Encounter With Israel* did not escape this difficulty; it may even have compounded it. True, my wife and I tried to keep away from the fault in question, at least at the point of praxis: "The Christian community has no right to tell Jews to do anything —whether it be to survive as Jews, or to assimilate, or do something else. We do not even have the right to tell Jews that they ought to reproach us."[15] Yet as writers we were not unentangled in internal Jewish and Israeli controversies. One major irony in the Christian acceptance and vindication of political Israel as the possession of the Jewish people is that those who retain such a stance cannot wholly avoid taking sides as between Jewish parties themselves. A foremost example of this is our rejection in *Encounter With Israel* of something we dubbed "territorial fundamentalism," the conviction among some Jews that the Land constitutes an absolute or unconditional possession of

---

14 EWI, p. 194 (slightly edited).

15 Ibid., p. 256.

the Jewish people, bestowed upon them once and for all by divine fiat.[16] The fact that most Israelis have no use for territorial fundamentalism may ease the problem somewhat but it does not dispose of it.[17]

I here suggest four considerations that may help in grappling with this third issue: (a) The criticism of Jewish territorial fundamentalism need not derive from parochial or extraneous Christian dogma. Instead, it can rest upon a universal human norm: No people has an absolute right to anything. This norm is itself consonant with the Jewish spiritual conscience, with the latter's prohibitions of idolatry and absolutization. God is not the servant of geopolitics. (b) Any danger that a given (Israeli) geopolitical claim will be absolutized may be (providentially?) offset by the presence of foes who are endeavoring to absolutize the very same territory for their own possession. A kind of uneasy but continuing balance tends to obtain here, not of political power as such, but of warring theologies that may sometimes act willy nilly to keep each others' absolutist political ambitions and claims from being implemented—in a way not wholly unlike the mutual possession of nuclear weapons by two opposing countries. (c) The equitable alternative to territorial fundamentalism is historical and moral right. That no people has an absolute right to territory does not warrant the conclusion that nations are without relative rights. Any such conclusion would be at once frivolous and irresponsible.[18] d) The critique of territorial fundamentalism—or, for that matter, of any underwriting of purely secular Zionism—cannot be permitted to obscure the many vital connections that obtain among Jewishness, Judaism, and Eretz Israel, the unities of people-faith-land.[19]

---

[16] Ibid., pp. 15, 241-243. Some Christian Zionists agree with Jewish territorial fundamentalism -not necessarily for their own sakes but in behalf of Jewry. However, within the ranks of Christian Zionists some qualify the presumed divine allocation by making it strictly provisional upon an ultimate Jewish "recognition" of Jesus as the Christ. For my wife and me, a praiseworthy or accurate meaning of "Christian Zionist" is a person who affirms the Zionism *of the Jewish people in and for themselves* or again, a person who supports the political freedom of Jews.

[17] Another case that could be used as an example here is our expression of opposition to "nonreligious Zionism."

[18] EWI, p.243.

[19] This fourth consideration is discussed in ibid., pp. 243-249.

(4) Another limitation in *Encounter with Israel* is that my wife and I did not furnish substantive analysis of the historical relations (continuities and discontinuities) between Christian antisemitism and Muslim antisemitism. Such analysis would seem to be fundamental and essential to an understanding of world antisemitism today, particularly in the context of the Middle East and with special reference to the historical-moral ease with which the Arab world was able to put to advantage many traditional Christian antisemitic policies and functions. (*Encounter With Israel* does state that Muslim Arabs have appropriated for their own purposes Christian, Nazi, and Soviet sources defamatory of Jews. "The mantle of executioner of Jews, worn for so many years by Christendom, has been taken up by the Arabs."[20])

An important and usable scholarly procedure would be to trace out the strong historical-ideological affinities, extending back over many centuries, between the antisemitism present in Islam from its beginnings and traditionalist Christian antisemitism with its own ancient and abiding hostilities to Jews. As Ronald L. Nettler has recently pointed out, the various Qur'anic attitudes toward the Jews and their religion share a singular theme: the Jews are "arrogant renouncers and falsifiers of God's Truth"—an assertion that is readily matched within unnumbered Christian sources. "Islam today, especially in its fundamentalist form, sees the struggle with the Jews as a cosmic and fateful war."[21] Here, Islam goes much farther than the Christianity of today. Muslim and Christian ideological persuasions respecting "the Jews" would appear to serve as the ultimate, shared origin and motivation of specific, contemporary forms of political and social hostility to Jews. This common persuasion makes yokefellows of Christian antisemites and Muslim antisemites.[22]

---

[20]   Ibid., pp. 219-221, 224.

[21]   Ronald L. Nettler, *Past Trials and Present Tribulations: A Muslim Fundamentalist's View of the Jews* (Oxford: Pergamon Press, 1987), pp. 7, vi, and in general chap. 1. Nettler's work is part of a new historiography that refutes the legend of Jewish life in Islamdom as relatively easy and comfortable. Consult also Norman A. Stillman, *The Jews in Arab Lands* (Philadelphia: Jewish Publication Society of America, 1979); Bernard Lewis, *The Jews of Islam* (Princeton: Princeton University Press, 1984); *Semites and Anti-Semites: An Inquiry Into Conflict and Prejudice* (New York: W. W. Norton, 1986).

[22]   We may not ignore the complication that Islam retains its own special antipathies to Christianity and Christians. But at today's all-decisive geopolitical level no comparison is possible between Muslim-Jewish hostility and Muslim-Christian hostility. It is true that over

(5) Historical study enmeshes itself in the encounter between documentation and past-present-future, thereby forever risking refutation. An example will explain the point. We included in our book the following information: "On 5 June 1967 Radio Cairo besought the Arab armies: 'Destroy, ruin, liberate. Woe to Israel, your hour has arrived...this is your end...We shall drive out of existence the shame of Zionism...There is no room for Israel in Palestine. This is your responsibility, Arab soldiers! Israel, taste death!'"[23] But what happened? Twelve years later Egypt and Israel signed a treaty of peace. To have omitted the above summons of Radio Cairo would have been irresponsible in the context of dealing accurately with the Six Day War. And yet, subsequent history did not realize the Egyptian threat; it contradicted it.[24]

The fact that significant historical change can manifest itself over, say, a two-decade period is not in itself a legitimate cause for scholarly self-reproach. (In truth, at least as I now write in early 1993, the overall Arab-Israeli conflict has not substantively altered over that time.) The best I think I can offer here is a double truism: The human being as historian has no way to establish relations with present and future history of the sort that only God can forge and master; the human being as historian is not thereby excused from chronicling data that may (or may not) prove to influence the present and condition the future.

IV

In the time following the publication of *Encounter With Israel* I continued—as did Alice Eckardt—to deal with the question of Israel in its political, theological, and moral dimensions. For example, the *Journal of Church and State* published two essays of mine, "The Nemesis of Christian

---

the centuries the Jewish people encountered less antagonism under Islam than under the church, which is a major reason why Jews, where free to do so, chose to live under Muslim rulers rather than Christian ones.

23   EWI, p. 200.

24   This hopeful observation has to be counterbalanced by the truth of a continuing antisemitic trend and campaign in the Egyptian press (see, e.g., *Egypt: Israel's Peace Partner. A Survey of Antisemitism in the Egyptian Press, 1986-1987* [Los Angeles: Simon Wiesenthal Center, 1988]).

Antisemitism" and "Toward an Authentic Jewish-Christian Relationship," both based on lectures at Baylor University.[25] The first of these pieces reviewed historiographically the place of the New Testament and of subsequent Christian history in antisemitic thought and behavior;[26] introduced the category of "the Devil" for possible aid in accounting for hatred of the Jewish people;[27] and grappled with the question of what it means to hope that Christian antisemitism can be overcome. Involved here was a nagging fear that the more such antisemitism gets exposed, the more it will prosper: "The affirmation that Christianity ought to be Jewish at its very roots may only make for a metastasizing of antisemitism—although I have often made that affirmation myself (sometimes out of desperation)."

"Toward an Authentic Jewish-Christian Relationship" sought to honor a basic dialogic norm: Without surrendering our own self-understanding or self-identity, we are to meet the other in the other's self-understanding and self-identity. More precisely—to carry forward a point made in section II above—it is as a person of a particular *faith* that the Christian meets Jews; it is as a person belonging to a certain *people* (and often, though not always, subscribing to a particular faith) that the Jew meets the Christian. A Jew may even be an atheist without ceasing to be a Jew, whereas the idea of a Christian atheist is, in principle, a contradiction in terms.

In addition, I entertained in the above essay the concept of "the trial of God" as found in some circles of Jewish thought, and here understood within

---

[25] These essays became part of the book *Jewish-Christian Relations in Today's World*, ed. James E. Wood, Jr.

[26] See also "Notes on the Protestant Bible." I allude in chap. 4 above to the indiscriminateness of New Testament judgments upon "the Jews." In "The Nemesis of Christian Antisemitism" this reasoning was carried forward against those who protest that the historical and religious context of seemingly hostile New Testament passages forbids applying the word "antisemitic" to them: "While the context of any proposition is relevant when discriminate or qualified judgments are tendered, context becomes irrelevant when indiscriminate or unqualified judgments are being made." The declaration, "Some Americans are killers," can hardly be dubbed an instance of anti-Americanism. But the avowal, *"The* Americans are killers," is vintage anti-Americanism. The latter judgment can never be redeemed by resource to a context. "The article 'the' is as decisive as the word 'Jews'—or more so."

[27] I hypothesized that a major field of "the Devil's" operations is the Christian collective unconscious.

the frame of reference of the *Shoah*. This was a step I had not taken before. At one place I even ventured to say that there is a sense in which Christians are forbidden to speak of Jewish election: "There is no way to immunize the traditional, historic testimony to that election against satanic culpability for the incredible suffering of Jews." I added: If the tenet of Jewish election is to be retained by Christians in some form, this can only be done through that teaching's detheologization, "its total moralization and total secularization, that is to say, through the avowal of election-beyond-suffering, of election-to-live, of Jewish normality. We are left with [Emil L. Fackenheim's] 614th commandment, the command to survive"—and to survive as Jews. Here again there arose the existential problem of Christian interference in things Jewish. However, at this stage I did not undertake any intensive exposition of the related issue of "the trial of God"; that was to await later writing.

In the same essay I returned to the claim of Christian participation in the Covenant with Israel, as previously suggested in *Elder and Younger Brothers*.[28] The essay read:

> Christians believe, or they hope (faith and hope are very close) —Christians *trust* that through the grace of God in Jesus the Jew, they are made fellow members with Israel in the Covenant. The Covenant is, so to say, opened upon the world. The writer of Ephesians reminds his readers that before Christ came, they were, as Gentiles, strangers to "the commonwealth of Israel," outside the "covenants of promise, having no hope and without God in the world." Yet through the grace that burst forth in Jesus they "are no longer strangers and sojourners, but...fellow citizens with the saints and members of the household of God, built upon the foundation of the apostles and prophets, Christ Jesus himself being the chief cornerstone..." (Eph. 2:11-20).[29]

In accordance with the foregoing confessional/apologetic stance, I was still maintaining that the uniqueness of Christianity is "its faith in the resurrection of Jesus."

---

28   EYB, pp. 158-159.

29   "Toward an Authentic Jewish-Christian Relationship."

"The Fantasy of Reconciliation in the Middle East" (1971) returned to the theme of tragedy and fatefulness as marking the relation of Jews and Arabs: "The only reconciliation we may firmly expect is the one bulldozed out of shared suffering, desolation, and death." By way of documenting this conviction, I cited a speech of the Egyptian president Anwar Sadat calling upon his people to continue their war to the death with Israel. Yet this same leader was later to journey to Jerusalem to carry forward a process of peace between Egypt and Israel.[30] How is that for historical prognosis! Sometimes hope is more realistic than hopelessness. I further referred to the Arab-Israeli conflict as embodying a "zero-sum" condition, according to which any gain for the one side is perforce a loss for the other side. But sixteen years later I was to argue that the erstwhile impasse may have begun to move beyond a zero-sum state of affairs.[31] At the present writing, it is an open question whether major parts of the Arab world will go the way of Egypt or the way of continued warfare with Israel.[32]

---

[30] I say "carry forward" rather than "begin" because the Egyptian-Israeli rapprochement was actually initiated through the prior advice from Israel to Egypt that Libya was plotting to unseat Sadat. The latter's personal experience that the Israelis could be trusted was what opened the way to Camp David.

[31] "Beyond Zero-Sum Thinking in the Arab-Israeli Struggle" (1987).

[32] In September 1971 there appeared in *Christianity and Crisis* under my name an article bearing the title "Anti-Israelism, Antisemitism and Quakers." This led to quite a commotion. The essay attributed to me was largely an exposé of the American Friends Service Committee's 35,000 word, anti-Israeli publication *Search for Peace in the Middle East*. In point of fact, I had insisted to C&C (fruitlessly, as matters were to turn out) that a second, thoroughly revised version of my piece comprise the one to be published—a piece that had, among other fundamental changes, removed an original allegation of antisemitism and/or anti-Zionism against the Quakers and altered the title to read "A Friendly Response to the Friends." The editor of C&C refused to honor my request and, without my consent, published the version I was now repudiating. Significantly, the journal subjected "my" contribution to rebuttal in the very same issue in which the article appeared—thus blowing its own cover. For C&C was here pointing, if unthinkingly, to its operative, anti-Israeli ideology and policy: Any contribution favorable to Israel must be subjected to immediate attack, whereas contributions favorable to the other side are to be allowed to stand without rebuttal. In short, I was the victim of a set-up (as the suspense writers would say).

Provision was made for A. Denis Baly to denounce "my" piece, and in the very number containing that article. His denunciation was bathed in a sweet-sounding title, "Search for Peace: A Modest Defense" (20 Sept. 1971). Baly's critique was marked by many inaccuracies and distortions, as enumerated in my answering piece, "More on the Middle East" (4 Oct. 1971). Yet here too C&C was not beyond resources. Appended in the same number to the above answer from me was another rebuttal by—you guessed it— A. Denis Baly. Baly's

V

Additional writings at this time carried ahead my interests in political theology, the intellectual linkage of commitments of faith to national and international life. Political theology asks: How may a given faith reckon with the phenomenon of power?

For instance, in "Politics, Morals, and the Question of Israel," I sought to apply the political realism advocated by Reinhold Niebuhr, in contrast to both political idealism and political cynicism. Niebuhr taught the fateful relationship between idealists and cynics. For the essay I created the aphorism, "An idealist is a future cynic; a cynic is an idealist who has learned something." I developed the theme that the historical-juridical-moral rationale of the State of Israel serves to avoid at once the cynicism of naked power assertion and the sentimentalities and apolitical fancies of moralistic idealism. (An instance of moralistic idealism is political pacifism.) The threefold rationale of Israel here expressed in hyphenated form is of course rejected by her enemies. Yet that foundation continues to offer moral sustenance to those who struggle against politicidal attacks upon Israel. This alternative to cynicism may also serve to buttress the political claims of the Palestinian Arabs. For once the objective justification of

---

polemic was cloaked in a stated wish "to avoid polemics." Nor was this to be the end of the matter. C&C went far beyond the stratagem of simultaneity of rejoinder. In a subsequent number the journal amassed a series of articles evaluating me and my efforts, and doing so in *ad hominem* fashion—including a self-defense and castigation of me by Landrum Bolling, architect of the Quaker Report, and, even more cleverly, contributions from several Jewish writers and one Christian missionary (29 Nov. 1971). Entirely out of the question was any *simultaneous* rejoinder by me. True, the disputation came to a close via a response of mine, but only *in a separate number* and at a considerably later date—a piece that was mutilated down to 1200 words (in the presence of the editor's threat of nonpublication). The set-up was, in a word, quite ingenious—perhaps even more ingenious than Wayne H. Cowan, editor of C&C, himself consciously knew.

The state of affairs at C&C was later made clear publicly in a demand from the surviving Niebuhr family that Reinhold's name be removed from the masthead as founding editor, in view of the journal's intensifying anti-Jewish policy ("Journal Drops Niebuhr's Name," *The New York Times*, 8 May 1972).

Chap. 11 of my book *Your People, My People* adapts, updates, and expands my analysis of the Quaker book *Search for Peace in the Middle East*.

the laic rights of Jews is allowed to dissolve, the indigenous rights of the (other) Palestinians must, paradoxically enough, dissolve as well.[33]

Collateral to the above analysis was a review-article upon Haim Cohen's work, *The Trial and Death of Jesus*[34]. Historiographically and ideologically speaking, the subject of Jesus' fate has evolved over several phases: the church's promulgation of the New Testament claim that "the Jews" had spurned and "killed their Christ" (a point of view by no means overcome in many contemporary Christian circles); the historico-critical finding of allegedly joint Jewish-Roman responsibility for Jesus' death;[35] and the more recent scholarly repudiation of any and all Jewish culpability for the trial and death of Jesus (the viewpoint of Haim Cohen, as of some Christian scholars). At this stage in my writing (1972), I had not as yet come to the view, consanguine with the third interpretation but going beyond it, that the entire issue today can be and ought to be treated as a nonquestion and thereby abandoned. In my case, this last development was to wait until the mid-1980s.[36]

VI

The period under scrutiny culminated in several publications of 1974: one book, *Your People, My People: The Meeting of Jews and Christians*; and three essays, "Theological Implications of the State of Israel: The Protestant View,"[37] "The Devil and Yom Kippur," and "Is the Holocaust Unique?"[38]

---

[33]   See also "A Political Approach to the Middle East Conflict." A rather lengthy and detailed essay, "Christendom as a Source of European Nihilism," was an expanded version of an address at a colloquium on the Holocaust at Dropsie University. Much of the material in the latter essay was adapted for *Your People, My People*, chap. 2 (hereinafter identified as YPMP).

[34]   The title of my review-article upon Cohn's book is "On History's Greatest Perversion of Justice." It was adapted to YPMP, chap. 3.

[35]   The notion of partial Jewish responsibility for the death of Jesus was given voice, lamentably, in CCI (p. 157).

[36]   On the Roman trial and death of Jesus, see my brief piece in a symposium on "Who Killed Jesus and Why?" in *Manna* (London) 12 (1986): 5.

[37]   This analysis was composed for the 1974 *Yearbook of the Encyclopedia Judaica*, which appeared in 1975.

Because the question of the singularity or incomparability of the *Shoah* (i.e., what I came later to call its "transcending uniqueness") was to receive major attention from my wife and me during the time after the period covered by the present chapter, I am postponing attention to that question until we are further along. "Theological Implications of the State of Israel" is commented upon in this chapter.

Your People, My People reflected considerable concentration upon the *Shoah* and its aftermath, and upon Christendom's contribution to that event. Among other subjects, I endeavored to provide a more intensive exposition and assessment of the Vatican Council II pronouncement on the Jews than I had earlier attempted. I further offered a highly critical analysis of a statement adopted by the General Synod of the Nederlandse Hervormde Kerk (Reformed Church of Holland) entitled *Israel: People, Land and State*;[39] also a full critique of Jean Daniélou and André Chouraqui, *The Jews: Views and Counterviews*;[40] and exposition in behalf of Palestinian Arab rights.[41]

I here examine major sections of *Your People, My People* with two purposes in mind: the relevance of that volume to the theological question of the Covenant (as opened up in chapters two and four of the present retrospective),

---

[38] Exposition of relevant parts of the essay, "Is the Holocaust Unique?," is worked into the ongoing analysis here along with other sources. There is some duplication of material as between "The Devil and Yom Kippur" and "Is the Holocaust Unique?" The latter piece raised the question, not of whether the Holocaust as such is unique (as conveyed by *Worldview*'s incipient application of that notion to my article, through the device of altering its title from "In What Sense is the Holocaust Unique?"), but of whether the Holocaust is *uniquely* unique. Is it not the case that all events are unique? History does not repeat itself.

[39] Chap. 5 of YPMP is a considerably revised version of my critique of *Israel: People, Land, and State*. This critique by me of that document was translated into Dutch by J. Schoneveld, under the title "Commentaar op de Handreiking voor een Theologische Bezinnung," and published in *In de Waagschaal* (Utrect) 7 (1973): 17-21.

[40] Additional subjects in YPMP included "Christian Perspectives on Israel" (chap. 9; based on an essay of that name) and "Christian Silence and Christian 'Neutralism': A Predictable Response" (chap. 10; based upon revisions and updating of "Again, Silence in the Churches," also upon "The Reaction of the Churches," and upon "Die gegenwärtige Situation der christlich-jüdischen Begegnung"). YPMP, pp. 178ff. is adapted from "Eretz Israel." Chap 14 of the volume concerns itself with Kurt Gerstein, Reinhold Niebuhr, Franz Rosenzweig, and Eugen Rosenstock-Huessy.

[41] On the rights of the Palestinian Arabs, see YPMP, pp. 64, 136, 170, 173, 176-178, 202.

and the volume's bearing upon the province of political and moral theology. In the retrospective before the reader a number of references have already been made to Christian antisemitism; accordingly, I will not repeat what *Your People, My People* has to say on that subject, even though some of its exposition of antisemitism is unique to that volume.[42]

The claim in *Elder and Younger Brothers* that the Covenant with original Israel is not superseded by the Christian movement is more radically maintained in *Your People, My People*.[43] In the latter volume I object to an earlier propensity of mine (in *Christianity and the Children of Israel* and even in *Elder and Younger Brothers*, though to a much more limited extent) to treat Jews "as a means to a particular Christian theological scheme (and even to a particular Jewish theological scheme), rather than approaching them as ends in themselves, as human beings whose dignity must remain wholly uncompromised." The integrity of the Jew does not rest upon any "function," divine or other. *Elder and Younger Brothers* was not wholly free of Christian triumphalism. For in that study I had singled out as a necessary function of Jewry and the Jewish faith certain elements of judgmental action against Christianity. Thus was there a failure on my part "to receive Jewish existence as an unqualifiedly normal, human reality."[44] Under the seemingly praiseworthy rubric of esteeming Jews for their place in God's economy of salvation, I was perpetuating, in effect, the Christian ideology/praxis of making demands upon them. Such a *theology of implicit demands* is inseparable, so it now seems to me, from what has been called "a theology of Jewish victimization." Where is grace in all this? Where is the humaneness of God? On today's Christian side, "the question of whether

---

42   Cf. YPMP, Part I -"The Christian Predicament."

43   Levi A. Olan incorrectly charged that I make Christianity a "better salesman" to the Gentiles than Judaism. As pointed out in the essay "A Response to Rabbi Olan," I have maintained for many years that the Jewish people and Judaism are possessed of a theological and moral integrity that is entirely independent of Christianity and the church. The Jewish nonacceptance of the Christian gospel constitutes faithfulness to God. On the other hand, Olan was quite correct in noting certain lamentably triumphalist elements in EYB, together with a tendency to read Jewish reality through the eyes of Christian utilitarianism and functionalism ("A Response to Rabbi Olan").

44   YPMP, pp. 236, 241-242. Chap. 16 of YPMP (pp. 234-249), from which the citation is here taken, reproduces, with some changes, my essay "A Response to Rabbi Olan".

Christianity can bear humanization is...assailing and indeed shattering the Christian world."[45]

I have more than once declared that if the State of Israel represents a Jewish declaration of independence from the ongoing Christian imperium, the Christian cannot consent to the break. But in *Your People, My People* I came to the conviction that for the Christian to insist upon retaining the tie to Jews, is to preserve the vices of antihumanization. A "coming of age" for the Christian community requires an unqualified readiness to enable the Jewish people to be whatever they wish to be. (The "dialogue" is, in this sense, finished, i.e., consummated.) "I think that my erstwhile insistence upon Christian membership in the Jewish family was determined in considerable measure by the necessary warfare against Christian supersessionism...Hence, that insistence was provisionally justified. But suppose that the [supersessionist] fantasy is overcome! I am not certain how to answer. Loved ones do part from one another and go their separate ways—though they need not thereby cease their loving or their caring. Indeed it may be that the parting must take place by the very decree of love and for the very sake of love."[46]

In accord with the foregoing persuasion, I once again opposed a missionary stance vis-à-vis the Jewish community, expressing the view that the conversionist effort constitutes "an attack, however unwitting, upon the Covenant of God and his people. It is the height of presumptuousness for the Christian to imply that Jews are not already members of the household of salvation." Yet how is my point of view here to be made coherent with the traditionalist affirmation in *Your People, My People* that "the uniqueness of Christianity is its faith in the resurrection of Jesus as the Christ"?[47] We shall return to that all-decisive question.

A final consideration in this commentary upon *Your People, My People* has to do with twin dangers: the theologizing of politics, and the politicizing of theology. We are brought back to the threat of Christian contumely in the understanding of Jewishness. In the 1970s I was maintaining that the sovereignty of the State of Israel cannot be arbitrated by reference to transcendent

---

45   YPMP, p. 243 (slightly edited).

46   Ibid., p. 245 (slightly edited).

47   Ibid., pp. 237, 225 (slightly edited).

"spiritual" claims or demands, nor can it be dealt with through reference to a failure to realize such demands. These two outlooks are cut from the one cloth. To politicize theology is to subject Israel to superhuman requirements—the double standard again—within the one socio-political arena that is shared with other nations. The Christian church ought to stop lecturing Israel as though the church's representatives possessed the mantle of biblical prophets. Through such lecturing, Christian preaching and teaching become instruments of human oppression. Until the church extricates itself from this arrogance, Christian moral outrages against Jews will persist.[48]

To theologize politics is to subject the secular-political sphere to the hegemony of faith; to politicize theology is to subject faith to the hegemony of politics. The first of these praxes has its source in peculiarly theological exploitation, the second in peculiarly political exploitation. In both cases the necessary dialectical tension between theology and politics is destroyed.[49] Yet we do have a way to bring extra-religious support for Israel into harmony with the religious affirmation of Israel without either falling into the idolatries of territorial fundamentalism or foisting upon Jews illicit demands of special religious and moral achievement and obedience. The authenticating of Israeli independence and sovereignty remains strictly secular. But the Christian proponent of Israeli rights may, together with the Jewish proponent, adhere to and declare the kind of faith that transcends the strictly political dimension yet does nothing to annul that domain and its values.

I went on to argue that the State of Israel is potentially possessed of both a judging role and a redeeming role in the lives of Christians. On the one hand, Israeli reality "changes the whole character of the Jewish-Christian relationship." Jews are no longer the powerless minority. They are set free. "We Christians are finally defeated, and this is very good for us. The Jewish-Christian confrontation of almost two millennia is totally transformed."[50] On the other hand, there is a sense—but not a political one—in which Israel is the

---

[48] Ibid., p. 67.

[49] Ibid., p. 62n.

[50] Ibid., p. 233.

Christians' own homeland,[51] even if, with Moses, they are only permitted to glimpse it from afar. The basis of the Christian's attestation to Jewish peoplehood (as expressed in section IV of this chapter) is the daring confession—for many Jews, a flagrantly unwarranted one—that Christians have been engrafted onto the Covenant through that Israeli of yesteryear, Jesus of Nazareth. (Only secondarily is the Christian an American, a German, a Jamaican, a Canadian, a Brazilian, a Chinese.) The spiritual affirmation of Israel means thanksgiving for divinely-given gifts and the celebrating of divinely-wrought responsibilities.

In sum, whenever we refer to the rights that Israel shares with other sovereignties, we are obliged to talk politics and morality; whenever we refer to the meaning that Israel has for us apart from other political sovereignties, we are obliged to talk theology—not apologetic theology (we are not seeking to prove something) but existential-confessional theology.[52]

VII

In the essay "Theological Implications of the State of Israel: The Protestant View," which appeared in the *Yearbook of the Encyclopaedia Judaica* (1974), I delineated five alternative choices found among Christians.[53] This typology reflected, in part, the pluralistic state of Protestantism, as also certain points at which Protestantism may dissipate itself into extra-Christian and even non-Christian outlooks: (1) The reestablishment of political Israel flouts the will of God. (2) Contrariwise: The re-creation of Israel implements the special will of God. (3) The reestablishing of Israel comprises a morally indefensible human

---

[51] EWI, p. 244. Exceptions to the denial that Israel is the Christian's political homeland include, of course, Israeli Christians. Their spiritual status is thus wholly unique. Most of these people are Arabs.

[52] In a review of YPMP, Mordecai Podet concluded that my "concentration on Christian indoctrination as a determinant of intergroup relations and of economic, political, and social movements seems narrow in an age accustomed to look elsewhere for significant social forces and to expect theology, doctrine, and religious institutions to reflect rather than originate cultural norms." Podet is incorrect in having me assign determinative power to Christian teaching. Nevertheless, Christian theologians do tend, at least implicitly, to assign greater social power to Christian teaching and the church than can be objectively warranted.

[53] See also YPMP, chap. 9 - "Christian Perspectives on Israel."

fabrication. (4) Contrariwise: The re-creating of Israel constitutes a justified human act. (5) I suggested that there may be a position supportive of Israel that in some respects links itself to types two and four, but that also goes beyond them.

The fifth position, which I was trying to work toward in the 1970s, can perhaps be identified as the eschatological-supportive type. This viewpoint is prepared to criticize the religious argument that posits unconditional Jewish possession of the Land. Yet in sustaining the fourth interpretation, the fifth view does not of necessity exclude or contradict testimonies of faith. As a matter of fact, it looks forward to, and it even covets, a reuniting of the religious dimension with the extra-religious dimension. In the essay here reported on, I spoke in behalf of the "orders of preservation," those "physical spheres of existence" that help to protect human beings in an unredeemed world (Helmut Thielicke) and may thereby be construed as indicative of the divine providence. To reintroduce *Your People, My People*: "In our less-than-perfect world, individual peoples—and small peoples especially—require political sovereignty against those who would harass, oppress, or destroy them."[54]

All Christian points of view upon the subject of Israel are open to the danger of imperialization. I should today ask, as suggested in earlier pages of this retrospective, Where do Christians get any right to pass judgment upon Jewish life and Jewish norms? However, it appears to me that a negativist response to this question need not conflict with love for Israel; paradoxically, it may help to reinstate and preserve the support of Israel. For in accepting Jews in the Jewish people's own self-understanding, Christian supporters of Israel may simply be recognizing and underwriting contemporary Jewish loyalty to Israel.

The Christian acceptance of Jewish self-understanding acknowledges the overall unity of Jewish people-Jewish faith-Land of Israel. If this triadic unity prevents the restricting of Jewishness to a form of religiousness, the presence of the second element ("Jewish faith") opposes the reduction of Jewishness to pure nationality. But the honoring of Jewish self-understanding does not in and of itself supply Christians (or Jews, for that matter) with any legitimation of Israeli sovereignty. That right is established in the same manner as the

---

[54]   Ibid., p. 201.

sovereignty of all states. We have already noted the historical-juridical-moral foundation of Israel's legitimacy. (For further elaboration of my viewpoint here, see in chapter 6A below the republished essay, "Toward a Secular Theology of Israel," 1979.) The question of political Israel remains at the forefront of the contemporary Jewish-Christian dialogue.

VIII

Reference to the article "The Devil and Yom Kippur" is somewhat unsettling for me, as was the writing of it. In chapter one above, I allude to my personal problem with self-assurance. That limitation sometimes asserts itself when, as a writer, I find myself positing realities or making claims that are either opposed or ignored by the *consensus gentium.* On both these latter counts, the Devil of today would seem to qualify for dismissal or for an uninteresting demise (except, of course, among certain more or less conservative religionists).[55] However, from this point on I shall omit quotation marks around the word Devil. This perhaps reflects self-assertiveness or orneriness on my part. My ruminations upon the Devil were, in any case, inspired primarily by the Yom Kippur War of 1973, a conflict that prompted much of the specific content and exemplification within "The Devil and Yom Kippur."[56]

I may add three other clarifying points. First, a postulate of the reputed power of the Devil is not meant to annul free will and responsibility (the Christian *silence* my wife and I lamented in 1967 was compounded by the *culpable* Christian animosity of 1973). Second, I have no particular brief for the *word* Devil. Live alternatives include "the Adversary" and "the demonic," the

---

[55] Surveys taken in several European countries in recent years have shown that most Roman Catholics do not take very seriously their Church's teaching on the Devil (*The Globe-Times* [Bethlehem, PA.], 28 Aug. 1986). However, the Devil continues to maintain a formidable place within Protestant Fundamentalism and evangelicalism. And, according to a Gallup poll of August 1991, half of the American people believe in a personal Devil (*Christian Information* of Vancouver Island, Aug. 1991).

[56] See YPMP, chap. 7, "Enter the Devil," which is based upon "The Devil and Yom Kippur." Chap. 7 of YPMP also contains assessments of Friedrich Heer's study, *God's First Love,* as does chap. 8. Harvey Cox and Paul Lehmann alike see the divine as a "politician God" whose business in the world is politics, thereby making and keeping life human (as cited in YPMP, p. 246). In fighting God and humanity, the Devil seeks to make life inhuman, i.e., anti-political.

latter term as popularized in recent theology by Paul Tillich.[57] Third, I may insert a reminder that assurances that no Devil is in fact present used to be explained in Christian quarters by reference to the Devil's cleverness. It was the Devil himself who went around convincing people that there was no such thing as the Devil. Nevertheless, if I have already lost readers in previous pages, I imagine that my introduction of the Devil here will turn off others. My friend James Parkes remained notably unconvinced by my obloquies upon the Devil; Parkes contended that the New Testament and Christian teachings as a whole are quite sufficient to account for Christian antisemitism.

As I reread "The Devil and Yom Kippur" I found myself becoming somewhat unsure of my exposition upon the Devil. At the moment, the "argument" does not appear as convincing to me, or even as heuristic, as when I first propounded it. The fact that its base is experiential does honor one criterion that is at the forefront of today's philosophy or theology of liberation. But that is hardly sufficient to supply the argument with a sound scientific (sociological, psychological) foundation.

However, not long ago I received a letter from a colleague in Michigan reporting that he had just recently read "The Devil and Yom Kippur" in an old journal. He found my analysis to be "the most sensitive, perceptive, and imaginative writing" on the subject that he had read. Whose coincidence was this, the Devil's, somebody else's, or nobody's? Earlier I referred to the Devil's special stratagem of seeing to it that certain people deny his existence. On the one hand, I can from now on appeal to my colleague's letter as a useful (and self-ingratiating) count on the side of the Devil's presence. (Are not pride and self-satisfaction themselves numbered among the Devil's tools?) Yet, on the other hand, I am still left with my current doubts respecting the presence of the Devil. For the time being, I am tempted to resort to a form of mischievousness not unlike the kind that took hold of me at one place in chapter four, and to leave the entire matter up to the reader.

For discussion purposes if nothing else, I think the puzzle has at least four sides to it: (a) To affirm the Devil may seem to convey the impression of

---

[57] Tillich's apprehension of "the demonic" is as follows: "that form of contradiction" of essential being that identifies "a particular bearer of holiness with the holy itself" (*The Interpretation of History* [New York: Scribner, 1936], pp. 84, 94; *Systematic Theology*, Vol. III [Chicago: University of Chicago Press, 1963], p. 102).

opposing the Devil, since ostensibly the Devil could have operated more effectively were the Devil's reality denied. (b) To deny the Devil may seem to have the effect of aiding the Devil, since it gives him a free hand. (c) To affirm the Devil may seem pro-Devil, since the Devil may be able to thrive on the publicity. (d) To deny the Devil may seem to oppose the Devil, on the (hopeful) ground that, by and large, people of today are too sophisticated to "believe in" the Devil, which belief is dubbed superstitious. Taken together the four variables marshall a rather formidable combination. (For worse or better, I venture to return to the subject of the Devil in my book, *How to Tell God From the Devil: On the Way to Comedy* [forthcoming].[58])

---

[58] Reviews and review-articles bearing upon the Jewish-Christian relation that I composed during the period surveyed in this chapter dealt with these books: Ben Zion Bokser, *Judaism and the Christian Predicament*; Jean Daniélou and André Chouraqui, *The Jews*; James Daane, *The Anatomy of Anti-Semitism*; Hannah Vogt, *The Jews*; Abraham Joshua Heschel, *Israel*; E. Rosenstock-Huessy, ed., *Judaism Despite Christianity*; Michael Selzer, *Zionism Reconsidered*; Johan M. Snoek, *The Grey Book*; Alan T. Davies, *Anti-Semitism and the Christian Mind*; Friedrich Heer, *God's First Love*; John M. Oesterreicher, ed., *Brothers in Hope*; Carlo Falconi, *The Silence of Pius XII*; Saul Friedländer, *Kurt Gerstein*; Haim Cohn, *The Crime of Christendom*; Hertzel Fishman, *American Protestantism and a Jewish State* (co-reviewer Alice L. Eckardt); and Saul S. Friedman, *No Haven For the Oppressed* (co-reviewer Alice L. Eckardt).

5A

Selected Essays

(1968-1974)

A Tribute to Reinhold Niebuhr, 1892-1971

(Midstream 17 [June/July 1971]: 11-18)

That a largely Jewish readership was involved here accounts for many of this memorial's emphases. I have let the materials stand (with a few minor emendations) as originally composed more than twenty years ago. Some emphases will appear dated, e.g., my comments upon the Middle East conflict and upon the state of Protestant theological and political ethics. Today, less dogmatic certainty is forthcoming within Christian theological circles than was the case in 1971. Were I writing the memorial today I would proceed rather differently, retract a number of things, and expunge the sexist language. But I would not withdraw anything of what I say concerning Reinhold Niebuhr.

I

Reinhold Niebuhr's childlike inability to realize his own greatness always brought delight to those of us who knew him well. A saint, he had no comprehension of himself as saintly. In the preservation of this ignorance, his anger proved to be of very great aid. Niebuhr was not a Messiah, yet there was something of a Messiah about him. I speak not alone of the deliverance he brought us, through his moral, spiritual, and intellectual achievements, but also, paradoxically, of his unexceptional insistence that no human being (or cause) can ever merit veneration as Messianic. Niebuhr's lifelong and valiant struggle against men's idolatries made him brother to all Jews.

Reinhold Niebuhr not only helped save me from the vices of perfectionist-pacifist Christianity but ultimately determined more than anyone else my whole outlook and professional career. I shall not forget the day in 1945 when, bathed in fright and beset by incoherence, I first appeared at his office at the Union Theological Seminary, New York. I managed to blurt out that a friend of mine, Harold A. Durfee, had suggested to me a possible topic for my doctoral dissertation, Christianity's relation to Judaism and the Jewish people, and that I wanted to have Dr. Niebuhr's reaction to this. Niebuhr received the whole idea with immediate interest and enthusiasm. After a very few moments, he rose from his chair and began pulling books from his shelves to share with me. Later he was to accept with grace a bold proposal by me that he serve as chairman of the Columbia University-Union Seminary committee for the overseeing of my project, which meant that he became director of the research. With incredible patience and overgenerous allotments of time, he guided me for two solid years through a complex field of study that was already close to his heart.

I very soon learned that my teacher's celebratedly bluff and reputedly derisive manner was utterly misleading with respect to the identity of the man within. Of course, it is essential that prophets of the Lord act and speak as though they incarnate the very wrath of God. Probably no preacher will ever excel Reinhold Niebuhr as wearer of the mantle of divine judgment. However, one test of true prophecy is the balancing of judgment by mercy. I found that behind Niebuhr's rough and forbidding exterior was a man wonderfully kind. Contrary to those who have reported that Niebuhr did not so much look at you as measure you, I have to insist that once I managed to muster confidence to meet my teacher's gaze, I found only gentleness in his eyes. He was a humble and loving person.

For any small place I may have been given, on the Christian side, within the fragile but fascinating world of relations between Christians and Jews, and between Christianity and Judaism, Reinhold Niebuhr must receive the primary gratitude, though none of the blame. He was himself always grateful that someone was carrying forward intensive work upon a subject that not only meant much to him personally but was crying out for fresh and rigorous theological-ethical study. Despite his illness he wrote to my wife and me as recently as 10 September 1970 expressing again his thankfulness that a student of his had come to share his own deep concern for Christian-Jewish understanding.

II

I have alluded to Reinhold Niebuhr's spiritual kinship with Jews. His great stress upon the human and social obligations of religion made the Jewish people natural friends of his, just as it made Niebuhr the natural friend of Jews. The aphorism he used to cite from a friend, "There are just two Christians in the entire City of Detroit, and they are both Jews," had as its background and inspiration the intimate, dreadful alliance between the churches and the forces of exploitive capitalism in the 1920s and 1930s, while the maxim testified as well to Niebuhr's developing awareness of a quite different phenomenon: the ongoing commitment of the Jewish people to social justice. Reinhold Niebuhr was the Amos of American Christianity. Instinctively, Jews were drawn to him and his message.

Their intellectual/spiritual tradition gave Jews further incentive for taking Niebuhr with great seriousness. Here was an American Christian leader whose intellect was staggering and whose scholarship and learning were prodigious, but who insisted that reason be utilized as the instrument of creative spirituality, in ways that avoid both dogmatic humanism and oppressive Christianity, while providing a firm foundation for practical social action.

Professor Niebuhr's unyielding enmity, as a Christian, to the churches' historic denigration of Judaism and to the perennial effort to convert Jews to Christianity was also widely celebrated. He fought the missionary stance on grounds of principle (theological and moral), but it was the unqualified respect for Jews and the Jewish faith within his position that earned the gratitude of the Jewish community. How can there be respect for Jews as human beings without respect for Jewish convictions, particularly religious convictions?

Among Jews, Reinhold Niebuhr will always be remembered for his courageous struggle against Nazism and for his untiring endeavors in behalf of Jews under persecution. Indeed, much of the incentive behind his opposition to Nazism and his efforts to bring about American intervention in the war with Germany was his concern for the plight of the Jews of Europe. If, as I have long held, Niebuhr underestimated the unique force of Christianity in making possible the cancer of antisemitism in the Western world (and thence in the Middle East), nevertheless he remained from start to finish a stalwart foe of antisemitism, as of other forms of human prejudice and exploitation.

Niebuhr's sympathy for the collective integrity and wellbeing of the Jewish people was bolstered by a general principle within his overall theological-moral position: In our less-than-perfect world individual peoples, and small peoples especially, require political sovereignty if they are to be protected against those who would harass, oppress, or destroy them, as they also need freedom if they are to attain fullness of life. Of equal relevance here was Niebuhr's unrelenting opposition to the kind of Christian pacifism that leaves Jews, among others, to be the victims of tyrants and other oppressors.

It was entirely logical that, early in his career, Reinhold Niebuhr became a Christian Zionist—defined strictly as a Christian who supports the Zionism of Jews. Niebuhr was an ardent champion of a Jewish state in Palestine, and later of the State of Israel. Zionism constitutes one responsible and viable answer to injustices against Jews within Christendom and secular society; a concrete implementation of the survival rights of any people (for all its temptations, the collective will-to-survive is an authentic value within the divine "orders of creation"); and a belated but compelling recognition of the historic and moral claims of Jews to their homeland. (Niebuhr contended that bi-nationalism for Palestine was impractical. It must be emphasized, however, that his insistence upon the collective integrity of peoples extended fully to the rights of the Palestinian Arabs.)

III

In one decisive way Reinhold Niebuhr towered above the other theological giants of the twentieth century: through the unique and compelling unity he forged between theology and the politico-moral domain. He was the greatest political theologian of modern times.

Niebuhr's overall point of view bears the name "Christian realism." The thrust of his abiding ethical position is disclosed in two passages: "I have spent a good part of my life validating the love ethic as final on the one hand, and trying to prove on the other hand that it must and can include all the discriminate judgments and commitments which we may broadly define as commitments in the cause of justice...I am certain that an ethic of love which dispenses with the structures and commitments of justice is ultimately irrelevant to the collective life of man" (1961). "The moral crisis is ever changing, but all changes reveal one constant factor. The moral life of man is continually in the embarrassment of realizing that the absolutes of biblical and rational norms—which enjoin responsibility for the neighbor's welfare—can never be perfectly fulfilled, either by the use of or abstention from any of the instruments of community or conflict. Therefore, religious and moral guides must teach the necessity of discriminate judgment" (1966).

Niebuhr disdained with equal force the practical cynicism of otherworldly spirituality and the utopianism and sentimentality that ever tempt the religious—and especially the American Christian—understanding of the human condition. Cynicism and utopianism are, indeed, blood brothers. This world will never be the Kingdom of God. However, the dark that ever assails us is very considerably linked to the willful corruption of our freedom. We remain responsible men, who can indeterminately transcend, though never totally vanquish, our sins. By fashioning small kingdoms of proximate justice, we enable ourselves to bear and to counteract in some measure our own pride and idolatry. One such kingdom is political democracy, grounded as it is upon Judaic-Christian anthropology: "Man's capacity for justice makes democracy possible; but man's inclination to injustice makes democracy necessary."

Niebuhr directed much of his wrath against the moralism and pietism of the churches, with their witting or unwitting tendency to nurture complacent social conformity and serve the status quo. All too readily, the churches become special centers of self-righteousness and self-deception. Worse, the churches have all-too-little comprehension of the vast and inevitable gulf between personal morality and collective morality, between individual "moral man" and "immoral society." At the social level resort must be made to essentially political decisions and action, to the end of approximating a balance of power among conflicting centers of self-interest. Order and justice are never attained by "pure love or pure reason but by an equilibrium of various forms of economic and political power." Only in this way can human social life be made tolerable, and the weak be protected from the powerful. But the equilibrium is never stable; it must be continually reacted to in order to forestall a weighting of power on one side of an alliance of forces against powerless or relatively powerless parties.

Niebuhr's dialectic moved resolutely and unceasingly from the horizontal dimension of human experience to the vertical dimension of faith, and then back again. Deprived of the motivations and power of faith, the human tale may fill itself with sound and fury, yet in the end it must signify nothing. However, any religious gospel that defaults in its worldly obligations and fails to honor righteousness and serve justice is mere sounding brass and a tinkling cymbal—once again, a signifying of nothing.

In the following passage written in 1957, in criticism of Paul Tillich, we find Niebuhr grappling simultaneously with three fundamental problems: idolatry, obligation, and meaning:

> ...The Christian faith is ultimately concerned...[with] the mystery of the reconciliation between the divine purpose and the fragmentary and idolatrous human purposes. In other words, it is concerned, not in evading idolatry, but in accepting historic responsibilities with an easy and yet uneasy conscience, since every form of human striving is bound to be idolatrous in the ultimate court. One might say that ideally the Christian faith enables men, not to escape idolatry absolutely, but to accept responsibilities, knowing that those responsibilities will involve us in idolatries from which no form of human perfection will redeem us...The insistence on divine mercy as the final answer to the human predicament does not absolve us of responsibility but frees us for performing tasks in a world which never confronts us with clear choices of good and evil.

Niebuhr was here seeking to resolve, or at least to live with, the agonizing dilemma of idolatry versus moral responsibility. There are evils worse than idolatry. Yet men still require deliverance from the evils that idolatry itself compounds. This can occur as they become beneficiaries of a peace that passes all human understanding, a peace through which the unrighteous are forgiven. Indeed, the essential power behind sustained political action is the divine forgiveness.

I see Niebuhr's position as comprising a theology of hope, not one of despair, but hope of a kind that transcends "hopes" that deceive and are ephemeral. Niebuhr exposed false hopes for what they are: temptations wanting in saving power. We may, by contrast, be set free; we may be granted a hope that endures. We will remain fallible and sinful men. But we need not deliver ourselves over to fate. We need not be defeated men.

IV

If Reinhold Niebuhr and his family were blessed by his relatively long life, the unfortunate truth remains that he was taken prematurely from us. His effectiveness was sharply reduced during the almost two decades of serious illness that preceded his death on 1 June 1971. It was back in 1952 that he suffered a serious stroke that left him considerably incapacitated.

Had Niebuhr been permitted to sustain his earlier, powerful leadership, the fortunes of American and world Christianity, as well perhaps as those of the Jewish people, would doubtless have been much happier. The contemporary period is in some ways just as threatening as the terrible epoch that saw Niebuhr at the height of his powers. Lamentably, Christian realism is now very largely in a state of disarray and of eclipse. A younger generation of Protestant liberals has drifted away from the Niebuhrian "concept of constantly contending self-interest to revolutionary, third-world romanticism" (TIME, 14 June 1971). Our origins, history, and traditions as a nation are such as forever to tempt us into the sins of self-righteousness, isolationism, and neutralism. The specter of a resurgent Christian pacifism once again moves across the world, even within the very circles that were once saved from that disease by Niebuhr's virtually singlehanded crusade. Once again, on more than one front, Christian idealism is showing its sweet and ugly face, with all the irresponsibility and naïveté of old, including the notion that the alleged powers of darkness are really not all that bad. The perennial temptation of the churches to become irrelevant to national and international problems afflicts us with renewed force. The churches are markedly paralyzed by a failure to reach and to live by those relative moral choices that are among the few sure evidences of moral integrity and health. Instead, sentimental idealization goes blissfully forward. Once again we are being assured that if we will just be nice enough, and understanding enough, the aggressors of this world will either go away or will themselves prove to be nice gentlemen, shepherding their nice, friendly peoples into international conciliation. Yet at the very same moment, cynicism, the companion of idealism, trumpets its absolutist, irrational conclusions. We are repeatedly asked, for instance, where there could ever be found a nation as pervasively rotten as the United States.

V

Nowhere are the resources and lessons of Christian realism more grievously lost than in policies toward the conflict in the Middle East.

An illustration is the recent fate of *Christianity and Crisis*. Reinhold Niebuhr helped to found that journal in 1941 and served as editor until 1966. The publication became an influential stronghold of Christian realism, especially during the war years and on into the post-war period.

In *Midstream* Eugene Rothman has documented "The Evolution of a Christian Perspective" in successive numbers of *Christianity and Crisis*. He shows the changes that have taken place in the editorial policies of that journal since the Six-Day War. Niebuhr's words in a commentary entitled "David and Goliath" (26 June 1967), "a nation that knows that it is in danger of strangulation will use its fists," were as approving as they were descriptive. The all-decisive consideration remains, Niebuhr pointed out, that the Arab Goliath has "never accepted Israel's existence as a nation or granted it the right of survival."

Already in the very same number of *Christianity and Crisis* John C. Bennett reflected the insufferable demands the Christian community has always enjoyed making of Israel (as it has of Jews for centuries): "Now that Israel has the power and the initiative in the Middle East we hope that she will put her great gifts into creating something new in her relation with the Arabs." How quickly some have turned and helped betray David to his enemies! When are we going to have the integrity to make even minimal demands of the Goliath who is obsessed with the wish to annihilate David?

The about-face of *Christianity and Crisis* became total in the policy of "evenhandedness" demanded by the [now previous] editor Wayne H. Cowan, in an editorial "The Palestinian Time Bomb" (5 October 1970). Rothman indicates how Cowan strove to substitute an ideal condition of balancing between the antagonists for the real condition of preponderance of right and wrong, with, as the inevitable outcome, total acceptance of the Arab case. As Rothman epitomizes the evolution of *Christianity and Crisis,* the final stage was "the inversion of previous priorities...[The] justice of Israel's nationhood became merely one element in the confused picture, and not a cornerstone from which other aspects of a solution might flow."

Reinhold Niebuhr would have no part in this betrayal. Until the end, he remained true to his Christian realism. For his wife Ursula and himself, he wrote in his letter to us on 10 September 1970: "We share your concern about the present state of 'cease-fire' negotiations and are astounded that our government could expect Israel to persuade Egypt to rescind its 'cease-fire' infringements involving the Russian missiles." Wherever, in our world, there is no anxiety for the welfare and fate of the Jewish people, and no intervention in behalf of Jews, there is no Christian realism. For Israel ever to rely upon the "pledged word" of others or upon vaunted "guarantees" from one or another party, rather than upon security measures and military power, would be for her to confuse earth with heaven. Here is manifest a common front between present Israeli policy and the Niebuhrian application of the theological doctrine of sin to the political domain.

Niebuhr would never tolerate the nonsense that uses Israel's success in defending herself to date as justification for preaching equal right on both sides of the conflict. It was *after* the Six-Day War that Niebuhr stressed the centrality of the Arab non-acceptance of Israel. The threat of Israel's obliteration remains the all-determining moral-political issue in the Middle East, aggravated as that conflict is by continuing Arab intransigence and most recently (as I write) by the Soviet-Egyptian defense and friendship treaty. From a Niebuhrian perspective, it follows that requisite moral decisions in the Middle Eastern conflict remain the same in principle as those required in the confrontation with the peril of Nazism. Niebuhr emphasized "the complacency and irresponsibility of American neutralism in the face of the Nazi threat," a state of affairs intimately linked to our historic self-righteousness and idealism as a nation, with our perennial and powerful impulse to try to withdraw from the world. Like conditions are becoming more and more apparent in the 1970s.

The irony of the Middle East today is that all the preachments stressing the rights of Arabs—and who would deny these rights, especially those of the Palestinians?—only strengthen those forces and interests that are bent upon the destruction of the Jews of Israel. After all, the Germans, even under the Nazis, had a relative right to endure as an independent nation. Yet the truth that there were many good men in Germany (as today there are many good Arabs and Russians) had to become irrelevant to a discriminating Christian moralist such as Niebuhr, who was himself of German background. In a sinful, fragmentary world we are left with no option but "to teach the necessity of discriminate judgment." Where party A is dedicated to the demise of party B, evenhandedness from the side of party C becomes the work of evil. This latter eventuality is embodied in the Quaker report, *Search for Peace in the Middle East.* In that document we see realized as well the ultimate alliance of idealism with cynicism and falsehood. Judge Justine Wise Polier has emphasized (*Congress bi-Weekly*, 2 April 1971) how the Friends deliberately withhold from the public information regarding the diametrically opposite positions of Israel and the Arab governments with respect to the right of the other side to life. A definition of Christianity from the Jewish philosopher Emil L. Fackenheim would have found favor with Reinhold Niebuhr: "Christianity is the religion that teaches that Jews are to turn the other cheek."

VI

There is, of course, no way of knowing when, if ever, the Christian realism of Reinhold Niebuhr will undergo the rebirth our world sorely needs. I have ventured to call his position a theology of hope. Much of the basis of this judgment is Niebuhr's summons to men to honor their indeterminate and God-given obligations as free, moral beings. The question, Is there hope?, is, in the present context, identical with the question, To what degree are we courageous enough to live as responsible men? Furthermore, I find some comfort in the small band of disciples who remain faithful to Christian realism. I find something of hope in the new and burgeoning group, Christians Concerned For Israel, of which Reinhold Niebuhr became a sponsor as one of his final public acts. And, lastly, we must never underestimate the dimensions of hope within Reinhold Niebuhr's own politico-moral insights. Thus, for example, if it is the case that vital interests of nations remain "the hidden, but always potent, motivation of national policy," it follows that self-interest may become an instrument of justice, as justice in turn can be an instrument of love. At least there is always a chance that genuine self-interest and the will-to-life may gain a tolerable victory within a nation over the impulse to self-destruction and self-punishment (as this infects, for example, the Arab world of today). There is the selfishness that does not in fact serve the self, and there is the selfishness that drives men and nations into regard for others. We may hope that the United

States will not destroy itself through the fantasy that it can betray Israel and yet emerge unscathed.

My wife and I are thankful that Dr. Niebuhr lived to receive the dedication of our book on Israel. With that unbelievable self-effacement to which I have referred, he expressed this perfect irrelevancy: "I am embarrassed by your dedication, because the book contains so much historical information of which I had hitherto been ignorant." In this same final letter (13 November 1970), Reinhold Niebuhr ended with these words: "I express my gratitude that Ursula is my wife. With affectionate regards to you and Alice, Yours ever."

The company of departed giants within twentieth-century Christian theology is completed now: Reinhold Niebuhr has gone off to join the others. We mourn for him, especially for his having been taken too soon. Yet our mourning is made bearable by our thankfulness for his life. Besides, it is unbecoming to weep in the presence of this courage, this brilliance. And besides that, Professor Niebuhr taught us to laugh. With Kierkegaard, he insisted that humor was second only to faith as a way of living with life's ironies and contingencies. However, laughter itself cries for redemption. Faith has to intercede for it. And then love must come to redeem faith along with hope. There remains, in the end, love's strange way with men: the symbiosis of righteousness and forgiveness.

The Crisis in Punishment

(In Harold H. Hart, ed., *Punishment* [New York: Hart Publishing Co., 1971], pp. 164-189)

The moral issue of punitive action is as baffling as it is fateful. The primary, overall reason for this state of affairs is that our century is witnessing two opposite, and in many respects, contradictory trends:

On the one hand, there is a widespread questioning of the efficacy of various instrumentalities of punishment; thence of the practical legitimacy of punishment; and therefore inevitably of the very ethics of punishment. Today, men raise the question, "Is not punishment per se morally wrong?" The sincerity and the force of that query must be fully respected.

At the same time, we have to remember that the very question itself is reflective of our times. Historical conditioning is involved. No pre-modern man could ever have taken this question seriously. Yet there remains little possibility of turning back the calendar. We must recognize that the older, often supernatural and next-worldly authorizations of punishment are almost completely lost in our secularizing and revolutionary culture.

On the other hand, there is a vastly increased and vital need for the prevention and restraint of socially destructive acts. We are becoming a global neighborhood. Terror is already global. We possess—or are possessed by—technical instruments that can destroy entire communities, peoples, and races. No destructive acts against humanity can surpass those committed within civil and international warfare. The rapid growth in the world's population is making more and more essential the reduction and control of intergroup strife.

These two simultaneous developments confront us with a fundamental crisis within the social domain of punishment. It is a formidable paradox that in a period of human history when universal social restraints are needed as never before, the very idea of punitive action should come under widespread and serious attack. The traditionalist tends to find only misfortune and evil in the attack upon punishment. But the liberal responds that outmoded notions and practices of punishment have themselves contributed to our social plight.

How, if at all, can the crisis be met? Any simple or final solution would be visionary. Nevertheless, a hope remains that we can overcome the dehumanizing and destructive effects on the individual and on society of unreformed methods of punishment without undermining the social functions that are necessarily, if joylessly, performed by punitive institutional structures.

Perhaps some of the difficulty is related to a lack of a sufficiently broad concept of punishment. Punishment or punitive action may be said to refer to behavior of an adverse sort (adverse to the offending party) by socially authorized persons in response to the originally offending acts. Any restraining action is punitive as long as culpability is deemed present.[1] The message is conveyed: "You may not do this." A restriction upon freedom is present. The restrained person is the recipient of a penalty.

If such words as punishment and punitiveness have become unsavory to contemporary social tastes, then let us by all means consider the use of alternative terms—so long as we do not play the trick on ourselves of disposing, unwittingly, of the reality behind the concepts.

We may distinguish three historical stages in the evolution of punishment.

1. Among some ancient peoples, the punishment for a destructive act exceeded the crime itself. Thus, if a man mutilated a bodily member (arm, leg, etc.) belonging to his neighbor, he could be put to death.

2. In biblical times, a humanizing trend appeared among the Jewish people. The punishment must fit, not exceed, the crime. In the Torah, we read of the *jus talionis*, the law of recompense: "eye for eye, tooth for tooth, hand for hand, foot for foot, burn for burn, bruise for bruise, wound for wound...the injury and disfigurement that (a man) has inflicted upon another shall in turn be inflicted upon him."[2] We have no evidence of any literal application of this kind of enjoinder; in fact, the humanization process was further enhanced, via rabbinic law,

---

[1]   Societal restraints may be imposed even when they are not punishment for destructive, culpable acts. An obvious instance is the institutional confinement of persons whose behavior has been adjudged psychopathological. Regrettably, there is often involved here a distinction without a difference. Life in a mental institution is not exactly roses.

[2]   Exod. 21:24-25; Lev. 24:20, cf. Deut 19:21.

through the substituting of appropriate monetary recompense for personal injury. The one exception was murder, where the life of the murderer was forfeit; and even here, there was humanization in that any exacting of vengeance from the children of the criminal was expressly forbidden.[3]

3. In recent times, a tendency has become manifest to permit the crime to exceed the punishment. Familiar cases in point include the effort to abrogate capital punishment completely, even in instances of first-degree capital offenses;[4] the encouragement, through parole, of the reduction of prison sentences; and the increased identification of crimes as the consequence of psychological aberrations and socioeconomic victimization —factors that are held to raise questions respecting the blameworthiness of allegedly guilty parties.

All will agree that the humanizing of the administration of justice is a good thing from the standpoint of the dignity of persons and the quality of human relationships. However, it is not impossible that this process can prove self-defeating—if no boundaries are set upon it. Death by murder is, after all, a rather "cruel and unusual punishment" from the point of view of the victim. The complaint is often heard that the rights of wrongdoers are being allowed to take precedence over the rights of victims. Ought not the targets of criminality, it is asked, be entitled to humane and civilized treatment as much as, if not more than, their assailants? However we feel about this, we may agree that the humanization of punishment, for all its virtue and continuing urgency, can hardly be permitted to erode all punishment away.

The demand for the maintenance of structures of punishment cannot be dismissed as wholly corrupt.

---

[3]   Deut 24:16; *The Encyclopedia of the Jewish Religion*, ed. R. J. Z. Werblowsky and G. Wigoder (New York: Holt, Rinehart and Winston, 1965), p. 219.

[4]   It would probably astonish the framers of the Constitution to know that the U.S. Supreme Court agreed in July 1971 to hear arguments during its subsequent term on whether the death penalty is to be construed as "cruel and unusual punishment" and accordingly as a violation of the Eighth Amendment.

True, the charge that the Establishment utilizes punitive devices for the sake of essentially immoral ends—that is, for the conservation and expansion of the exploitive power of haves over have-nots—has been substantiated many times in human affairs (for example: pre-revolutionary France or Russia). Nevertheless, all human groupings develop instruments for punishing in some way their recalcitrant or destructive members—including the very revolutionary groups that overturned their oppressive societies. The total absence of a punishing factor in human society is unthinkable because of the elementary need to protect members from destructive behavior on the part of other members. No society succeeds in removing the converse of punishment—approbation and reward—as incentives.

The objection is sometimes raised that any attempt to define as normative behavior what may only be typical behavior—to reduce what people ought to do to what they happen to be doing—is morally untenable. Just because all human groupings engage in punitive activity of one sort or another, the argument goes, it does not follow that such action is right. However, the universality of punishment is not arbitrary, but is necessitated by the nature of man. To explore the nature of man, we would have to consider such philosophical concepts as freedom of will, moral responsibility, culpability, and the need for punitive restraint.

Were men angels instead of conflicting and competing centers of self-interest, punitive structures could perhaps be annulled—on the assumption that angels are not given, mischievously, to combat. Even in a religious community where, as with Christianity, love and forgiveness constitute the basic norms and ideals, punitive action is not totally transcended or ruled out. The theologian Reinhold Niebuhr emphasizes that love cannot be fostered or fulfilled without the aid of lesser instrumentalities, the primary one being justice, understood in Aristotelian terms as rendering to every man his due. Justice, in turn, requires systems of law which entail restraint and punishment.

If all human societies must make a place for punitive action, the primary question becomes one of the moral efficacy of discrete forms of societal punishment and restraint.

Punitive action is tied to the law. The justice-injustice of punishment is bound to the justice-injustice of law.

Without law, societal punishment is irrational and indefensible; without provision for punitive action, the law is a farce. Nietzsche wrote that we have to "distrust all those in whom the impulse to punish is powerful."[5] The law, if it is just, rescues punitive action from arbitrariness, vindictiveness, and naked terror. The law, so to speak, punishes punishment—that is, the law exerts a restraining influence upon punitive behavior, restricting punishment to its service to the social order. Ideally, the law is non-discriminatory (hence the traditional figure of Justice wearing a blindfold); therefore, punishment, provided by law, must also be non-discriminatory.

Were the law to be deprived of the instruments of punishment, it would become the essence of futility, and the social order would collapse. Punishment makes possible the dignity and the integrity of law. To imagine that we could ever abolish punishment would be to entertain the fantasy that we could endure without law. The issue of punishment is, in a word, the issue of law.

The law is ever-changing—or dynamic, to use a more laudatory term; punishments change, too. An interesting example is the law of libel. In traditional British law, the principle appears: the greater the truth, the greater the libel. In U. S. law, truth is the cardinal defense against libel, a change of 180 degrees.

A fundamental means of adjudging the moral validity of specific punishments is through consideration of the justice of the laws that fathered the punishments. That there can be unjust punishment is as obvious as that there can be unjust laws. Good things are always subject to corruption. While the law as such comprises a social good, specific laws may constitute social evils.

The same holds for punitive measures. Punishment as such is good, but punishments in the specific sense are not virtuous in and of themselves. The justice of a particular punishment can be ascertained only in relation to the specific social context, and by examining its consonance or dissonance with the prevailing moral and legal standards.

Martin Luther King replied as follows to an attack upon his methods by a group of churchmen:[6]

---

5   F. Nietzsche, *Thus Spake Zarathustra*, Part II, chap. 29.

6   Martin Luther King, Jr., *Why We Can't Wait* (New York: Signet Books), p. 82.

You express a great deal of anxiety over our willingness to break laws. This is certainly a legitimate concern. Since we so diligently urge people to obey the Supreme Court's decision of 1954 outlawing segregation of the public schools, at first glance it may seem rather paradoxical for us consciously to break laws. One may well ask: "How can you advocate breaking some laws and obeying others?" The answer lies in the fact that there are two types of laws: just and unjust. I would be the first to advocate obeying just laws. One has not only a legal but a moral responsibility to obey just laws. Conversely, one has a moral responsibility to disobey unjust laws. I would agree with Saint Augustine that "an unjust law is no law at all."

King, writing from prison, then explained that a just law "squares with the moral law or the law of God," while an unjust law violates these norms. There is, of course, much controversy concerning the content of "the moral law," to say nothing of "the law of God." King's final word is relevant to this debate: "Any law that uplifts human personality is just. Any law that degrades human personality is unjust."[7] Some social reformers acknowledge publicly that they are prepared to accept the penalties of disobeying laws, even though they regard the laws as unjust. Of course, any violator's conception of what "uplifts human personality" can conceivably be a cloak for his personal self-interest. Furthermore, since we in the United States maintain a polity "of law and not of men," the burden of demonstrating the injustice of a law falls upon the disobeyer and his counselors. In discussing the case of Daniel Ellsberg and the Pentagon Papers, Anthony Lewis maintains that we ought to "obey the rules even when they seem unjust—or be willing to suffer the consequences of disobedience."[8]

Lewis's proviso that if the consequences are unfair, various legal and moral paths are open for rectifying the situation, does not meet the real issue. Everything turns on what is meant by "willing." Martin Luther King was in prison not because it was even partly right for him to be there; he was there *unwillingly* and only because the authorities held the whip hand. For if Augustine is correct that "an unjust law is no law at all," the indissoluble link

---

[7] Ibid.

[8] Anthony Lewis, "Crime and Punishment," *The New York Times* (28 June 1971).

between law and punishment means that unjust punishment is no punishment at all. It is a betrayal of punishment and it cannot be honored. A readiness to suffer for one's acts is morally tenable only when the punitive suffering is bound to laws that are in some sense just. Otherwise, the wrong party is being required to suffer. Who *really* deserves punishment—those who in conscience disobey unjust laws, or the perpetrators of the laws? Although the authorities are obliged to enforce the law through punitive action against the violation, there is no such thing as just punishment for disobedience of an unjust law.

The psychological needs of man confer a certain benediction on the socio-moral function of punishment for violations of the law. However, the psychological needs of man carry, simultaneously, a demand for the humanization of punishment.

In his little classic, *The Art of Loving*, Erich Fromm distinguishes the two types of parental love and their correspondence with human needs:

> *Motherly love by its very nature is unconditional. Mother loves the newborn infant because it is her child, not because the child has fulfilled any specific condition, or lived up to any specific expectation... Unconditional love corresponds to one of the deepest longings, not only of the child, but of every human being.*

The relationship to father is different. Father stands for law and order, discipline, and authority. Father shows the way into the world. Fatherly love is conditional love. It has to be deserved, and therefore it can be lost. Yet precisely because it is conditioned, one can do something to acquire it; one can work for it.[9]

The eventuality of punishment has its psychological foundation in conditional love, which is as essential to the human psyche as is the need for unconditional love. To be a man is to lead a double life: to yearn for acceptance despite one's shortcomings, and to give honor to justice. Without forgiveness, our dignity as pitiable creatures is impugned; without punishment, our dignity as responsible beings is betrayed.

---

[9]   Erich Fromm, *The Art of Loving* (New York: Harper & Bros., 1956), p. 41.

Man lives somewhere in between the primitive innocence of nature and the transcendent innocence of God. The human master warns the family pet that he will punish him if he is not a good dog; but were such phraseology to be construed literally, it would be a monstrous transgression against the entire dumb creation. At the other extreme, man is not divine. Among free beings, presumably only God, in whom essence and existence are reputedly one, is absolved from punishment.[10] Punishment that never ceases, punishment that is not followed by acceptance of the offender by his community, is sacrilege against humanity. Psychological need not only authorizes punishment, but demands its humanization.

The crisis we face with regard to punishment is interrelated with the split our culture has developed between rightness and goodness.

The majesty of "the right" lies in its independence from, though never its irrelevance to, consequences. Stress falls upon duty, conscience, intuition, the integrity of personal choice. In Luther's words, "Here I stand; I cannot do otherwise."

By contrast, concentration upon "the good" sooner or later involves what is "good for" something. The social consequences of behavior move to the center. Decision-making is now, so to speak, less introverted and more extroverted.

We seem to have fallen prey to a kind of sociomoral schizophrenia, which brings us inevitably to ask: "Could a society really endure without a punitive system?" The truth is that we should never have to take the question with such continuing seriousness were it not that something is amiss. It is today increasingly hard to count upon any sureties of conscience and duty for support of societal norms. We live in the plight of wanting to retain the institution of punishment for its reputed utility; and at the very same time, we are assailed by grave doubts concerning the inherent rightness of punishment. This ironic condition derives from a pervasive historical-moral wasting away of the objectivity of "the good," and hence also of "the right." At issue is the question of man's responsibility for his own acts.

---

[10]   Yet once upon a time the Hasidim in Poland, dismayed at the suffering of Jews, brought God to trial. "They knew he was present, because he was everywhere. They even had the effrontery to convict him" (Samuel Sandmel, "The New Movement," *Common Ground* [London; Summer 1969]: 13).

There is, as well, a spreading uncertainty respecting the norms and goals of human society. We appear to be left with only fragile reminders of lost certainties: the certainty, for example, of the justness of punitive action. Today, the conscientious objector and the protagonist of counter-culture proclaim: "I shall do what I find right, and to hell with your society and its pragmatic idolatries!" Obviously, the objector's "right," far from being universal, is itself riddled with subjectivity, and may, for example, comprise "the wrong" to protagonists of "law and order".

Yet, unless some identity is conserved between the social utility of the law and individual dictates of conscience, any structure of justice can hardly last. Is there a way to heal the schism between the right and the good? Is there a way to retrieve the persuasion that certain acts can be right or wrong—objectively and independently of good or bad consequences? Must decisions concerning what is right rest solely upon what it may be good for—that is, upon identifiable consequences? In this age of pragmatism, one risks the wrath of many for even daring to pose these fateful questions. It may be too late to do so. Yet, fateful moral issues do not go away just because we ignore them. Nevertheless, I am prompted to cite some witnesses who do not hesitate to make unequivocal judgments about justice and morality. The poet Chaim Nachman Bialik, recoiling from the pogroms at Kishinev in 1903, avowed that, as yet, the devil himself had not invented a fitting revenge for the blood of a little child.

To Carlo Falconi: "No one can doubt that charity [*caritas*] for innocent and unprotected victims should prevail over charity for their butcher."[11]

For John A. T. Robinson: "There are some things of which one may say that it is so inconceivable that they could ever be an expression of love—like cruelty to children or rape—that one might say without much fear of contradiction that they are for Christians always wrong."[12] These testimonies share a persuasion on behalf of "the right" which denounces the utter diabolism of crimes against helpless or suffering human beings.

To Arthur A. Cohen, there is "savor in the Psalmist's plea for revenge—a savor which, though I do not wish to enjoy it, results nevertheless from such

---

[11] Carlo Falconi, *The Silence of Pius XII* (Boston: Little, Brown, 1970), p. 24.

[12] John A. T. Robinson, *Christian Morals Today* (Philadelphia: Westminster Press, 1964), p. 16.

vital passion, such uncompromising delight in justice that it impels us to seek judgment; on occasion, to force it from heaven."[13]

Suppose that retributive justice had miraculously triumphed and Adolf Hitler and a band of cohorts had suddenly found themselves looking out of, rather than into, a crematorium. Would it have been possible for us to refrain from laughter, that laughter of derision which is also the laughter of righteousness?

If unconditioned vengeance is wrong, the moral appeal of vengeance is not wrong. I refer to the purity of rectification.

In the Talmud (*Yoma* 23a) vengeance is identified this way: A man asks his neighbor for the loan of an article and is refused. The next day the neighbor asks for something, and the offended party responds, "As you refused me yesterday so I refuse you today." But if the offended man replies, "Though you refuse me a favor, I shall not do likewise," this is anything but revenge.

One way to escape vengeance without approving evil is through a repairing of the balances of justice. The compassion that excludes an overt denunciation of evil is sentimentality, and, indeed, evil's helpmate.

The appeal of vengeance (which is not to be confused with vengeance itself) cries out for chastening, lest that appeal consume its own rightness.

When the Holy One, blessed be He, decided to drown the Egyptians at the Red Sea, Uza, the guardian Angel of Egypt stood before the Lord and pleaded: "Lord of the universe, Thou hast created the world with mercy as its measure." The guardian Angels of all the other nations sought mercy for the Egyptians. Whereupon the Angel Michael signaled to Gabriel, who flew to Egypt and removed a brick from the wall of a building. Within the brick was the immured body of a Jewish child. And the Angel Gabriel went and stood before the Lord and held the brick forward and said: "Behold: this is what the Egyptians would do to Your children." Whereupon the Holy One, blessed be He, dealt with the Egyptians in strict justice and determined that they deserved their fate. But when the Egyptians were drowning in the Red Sea, the ministering Angels began to sing songs of joy. Whereupon the Lord God rebuked

---

[13]   Arthur A. Cohen, *The Myth of the Judeo-Christian Tradition* (New York: Schocken Books, 1971), p. 118.

them, saying: "My creatures are drowning in the Sea; how dare you sing before Me?"[14]

Perhaps there is some force in the consideration that society's need for punitive action is buttressed rationally, not only by psychological need but by fragments, at least, of a childlike, intuitive vision of the right. Though we must freely grant that the content of the right varies infinitely from place to place and from people to people, the sense of right is another matter. It may be obscured and even be buried. Can it be destroyed?

No punitive measure is sadder or more debilitating than incarceration. Imprisonment is supposed to perform several functions: the protection of society against wrongdoers; the payment of one's debt to society (carryover of a traditional idea that justice is, in effect, measurable); and provision for discipline as an educative constructive value, in the sense that discipulus means pupil. But how effectively are these functions fulfilled?

The prison system has become, in effect, as much of a problem as is the crime it purports to meliorate. The brutalization that results from life in jail hardly needs lengthy documentation here, any more than does the need to be realistic in the handling of crime. The self-defeating nature of many traditional practices of incarceration is widely recognized. For often, prisons only exacerbate the very evils they are designed to reduce, and are, in effect, training schools for continued and expanded crime.

The prison receives a man...who has already demonstrated that he is handicapped in the social coping department, holds him for an interval of time, during which his handicap is encouraged to increase, and then releases him to a world that has grown harder to cope with while he was away.[15]

On the other hand, the quest for a workable alternative to the prison system has confounded reformers in every civilized land. The small consolation remains

---

[14]   Talmud Sanhedrin 39. This tale is reproduced in all Israeli army manuals.

[15]   Joseph Whitehill, "Aphorism About Prisons and the People in Them," *Friends Journal* (1-15 July 1971): 361.

that we should doubtless find ourselves in a worse plight were we to throw open all the prison gates. The evil consequences of prison life as such seem to fall among the inherently tragic prices we pay for human solidarity.

I do believe that incarceration for life, without any eventuality of release, is more cruel than capital punishment.[16] A life sentence robs the prisoner of any and every vestige of hope for the one life he will ever have. This is more than a human being ought to be made to bear.

The best remedy for evils of imprisonment is the deterrence of crime; everyone knows that an ounce of prevention is worth a thousand tons of punishment after the fact. Yet crime prevention is itself a baffling and controversial area. Despite the striking advances that have been made in this realm, as in methods of crime detection, the rate of crime continues to soar.

Human actions are, generally speaking, the outcome of a whole congeries of influences, and not merely of such single factors as the fear of travail. Psychologically speaking, while one man may stay clear of willfully destructive acts because of a wish to avoid suffering or personal inconvenience, another man (or the same man under altered circumstances) may be impelled to commit acts of malfeasance. The need for punishment can become something other than a manifestation of conditional love which permits us to work out systems for coping with our transgressions and arranging for their pardon. The need for punishment can turn morbid.

Some sociologists have naively and illogically concluded that punishment is a failure as a deterrent to crime.

In general, our massive methodological and substantive problems on the subject of deterrence are associated with two stubborn metaphysical truths: one, the simple consideration that the future must forever, and maddeningly, elude us; and two, the ancient, and in essence irresoluble, enigma of "the one and the many."

As matters stand, the proposition "punishment is no deterrent to crime" makes as little sense as the proposition "punishment is an effective deterrent to crime." Although the prevalence of destructive behavior seems to deny the

---

[16]   A later note: When I raised the question of capital punishment, I was unaware that the stratagem of murdering someone in order to get caught and put to death is sometimes practiced today (Watt Espy, "A Murderous Incentive," *The Globe-Times* [Bethlehem, Pa.], 11 Dec. 1985), but this knowledge has not changed my support of capital punishment, under some circumstances.

effectiveness of preventive measures, the fact that infinite numbers of people do not commit crimes can hardly be dismissed or ignored. The sociologists who deny the deterrent effect of punishment focus on law-breaking behavior and close their eyes to law-abiding behavior.

Were we to eliminate all punishment as ineffective in deterring crime, we might ironically find ourselves encouraging specific and even widespread outbreaks of malfeasance. This is where the unprovable claim that punishment does not deter crime is more than a harmless oversimplification of the data; it may also comprise a positive menace to the life and welfare of the body politic. The law may or may not forestall a given crime; yet the persistent nonperformance of crime on the part of most of the population may very well be occasioned by conscious or unconscious awareness of the law and its weaponry.

The power and effectiveness of punishment lie as much in the imminency of punitive action as in its actualization. And it is entirely conceivable that if punishment were to be eliminated, those who have already committed crimes for which they have been punished would commit even more and greater crimes.

These considerations are liberating as they are chastening. We are set free to struggle for the deterrence of crime through instruments of punishment, yet without any illusions that we must succeed. We simply have to do the best we can. From this sober but challenging perspective, a few examples may be given, in conclusion, of various contemporary methods of meeting responsibly the many and vexing problems of punishment and crime.

1. The American Friends Service Committee in Washington, D.C., has established a pre-trial justice program. The purpose is to aid accused parties who, even after long periods, have not been brought to trial and have suffered considerably. Up to April 24, 1971, forty-three persons, most of them ordinary felons, had been granted pre-trial release in the custody of the program's director; and certain inequities of pre-trial practices have been rectified.[17]

2. The nation's prisons are finding that severe, physically punishing methods of disciplining inmates guilty of prison infraction are, at once,

---

[17] Sam Legg, "The Quaker Way of Being Arrested," *Friends Journal* (1-15 July 1971): 362-363.

unnecessary and counter-productive. More sophisticated controls are being utilized, such as the temporary removal of personal privileges, discharges from preferred jobs, and forfeitures of earned "good behavior" times. These controls are proving much more effective than the more brutal traditional ones, in reducing both the rate of infractions and prisoner dissatisfaction.[18]

3. Whenever possible, punitive measures at the hands of one's peers are substantially more humane and meaningful than punishment through impersonal authority or by "the enemy." Does punishment in the schools contribute to better discipline? Very seldom anymore—but when it does, it is usually student-administered.

4. Efforts are being made to combat non-terminating penalties, such as are involved in "civil death." For example, a New York State law, passed in 1799, decrees that anyone sentenced to life imprisonment, even though he is paroled, continues to be deprived of his civil rights (such as freedom of movement, of employment, and of marriage). This law has been identified by one legislator as "feudal and barbaric," and attempts are under way to repeal it.[19]

I am concerned about indeterminate sentencing—a system that does not remand a prisoner for a specific period but holds him in custody indefinitely, until such time as a board of psychiatrists, sociologists, and penologists considers him fit for release. The advantages of this device are evident, yet there are difficulties. Indefiniteness is a historic weapon of penal oppression. The law is open to the least abuse when it stays with concrete, temporal penalties, which can always be decreased for good cause. Provision for maximal, specific termination points for the application of punishment is an essential of justice. If under our system of jurisprudence a man is presumed innocent until proven guilty, so too, he must be presumed innocent once he has

---

[18] *The New York Times* (15 May 1971).

[19] *The New York Times* (16 May 1971).

paid his debt. The ancient idea of the measurability of justice has its shortcomings, but it also carries protection for the malefactor.

Some communities have compensation laws that provide that victims of crimes, or their families, receive reparations through the government, either in addition to or in lieu of damages exacted from the guilty party. This arrangement constitutes a moral recognition that along with the personal responsibility of the criminal, there is also social and communal responsibility for crime. While such legislation obviously requires careful safeguards, it serves by its very nature to counteract the ever-present danger of the compounding of injustice by the very social order that is charged with the responsibility to see that justice is done. Community compensation laws preserve and apply, in a broader and deeper way, the essential truth behind the *jus talionis*: the indispensable principle of redress.

The art of rectification is the soul of law and the body of punishment. Soul and body together constitute the personality of justice.

6

Shoah (1933-1945), 1975-1982

My essay "Is the Holocaust Unique?" together with salient parts of *Your People, My People*[1] foreshadowed an intense and intensive personal and scholarly concern with the *Shoah* (Holocaust) over and beyond the eight-year period I shall next review.

I

On 28 May 1975 my wife and I flew to Europe to begin a thirteen-month stay there and in Israel. I was very fortunate. I had received a grant to become a Rockefeller Foundation humanities fellow, half the time at the University of Tübingen in West Germany, and the other half at The Hebrew University in Jerusalem, the latter involving the Centre of Holocaust Research at Yad Vashem. The Rockefeller program was designed to illuminate and assess the values, perplexities, and long-range human concerns of our contemporary world. Specifically, with Alice Eckardt as research associate we were to examine the impact of the Holocaust upon Christian and Jewish thought and life.

We studied a great amount of current literature. In the oral history aspect of the project, we held a large number of consultations with individuals and

---

[1] E.g., *Your People, My People*, pp. 219-221, 228-231, 247-249.

groups and at centers in West Germany, East Germany, Israel, France, The Netherlands, the United Kingdom, Denmark, and Norway. We carried out in-depth interviews with 143 persons (religious leaders, Holocaust survivors, scholars, officials, students) in the eight countries. A number of the interviews extended to two or more meetings. In addition, with the cooperation of the *Seminar für Zeitgeschichte* at the University of Tübingen we sent an inquiry (in German, French, or English) to 175 additional individuals and groups, for which the rate of return proved to be a high and atypical 36 percent.[2] We visited the death camp of Treblinka and the concentration camps of Bergen-Belsen and Neuengamme. We also attended a number of conferences and meetings on our subject,[3] and we presented joint lectures at the University of Tübingen (Graduate Colloquium of the *Institutum Judaicum)* and at The Hebrew University.

We did our best to stay with the specific theme of the project, although there were strong temptations within our developing researches and experiences to move beyond a strict rendering of that theme. For instance, we met with, and studied the work of, Jan Bastiaans of the University of Leiden, a psychiatrist who was conducting research upon the "post-concentration camp syndrome" among the Dutch population. Again, in Israel we were enabled to meet, and to study the researches of, Hilel Klein, a psychiatrist specializing in the effects of the Holocaust experience upon the lives of survivors and their children then living in that country.[4]

---

[2]   On the methodology utilized in our study, together with the limitations involved, consult "Christentum und Judentum: Die theologische und moralische Problematik der Vernichtung des europäischen Judentums," especially pp. 406-410; also, "Studying the Holocaust's Impact Today: Some Dilemmas of Language and Method."

[3]   An international conference on the Holocaust in June 1975 in Hamburg was the first of its kind to be held on German soil. Perhaps equally significant is the fact that none of the media attended the conference, despite a number of invitations to them. I think that were another such conference to be held today, the media would respond differently.

[4]   One of Hilel Klein's general findings was that when parents have not discussed, or have been unable to discuss, their Holocaust experiences with their children, the offspring have tended to develop psychiatric problems. Very often the children conclude that something shameful must be present in their family history.

Overall, we sought to work out an approach that was scholarly but did not sacrifice *Existenz,* and existential but did not sacrifice scholarship.[5]

Our daily experiences became a major part of the raw material out of which we were to offer, on the one hand, reports upon post-Holocaust Jewish and Christian thinking and, on the other hand, something of our own responses, if tentative and exploratory, respecting the nature and meaning of the *Shoah.* The overall endeavor was to issue in a number of interpretive and evaluative essays, and it culminated in the volume *Long Night's Journey Into Day.*

II

A number of the things I wrote during these years, on my own or in collaboration with Alice Eckardt, involved one or more aspects of Holocaust study and reflection. Several Jewish thinkers influenced me, including Eliezer Berkovits, Arthur A. Cohen, Emil L. Fackenheim, Irving Greenberg, Abraham J. Heschel, Richard L. Rubenstein, Uriel Tal, and Elie Wiesel. Most of these people had become or were to become good friends. Until today the *Shoah* has been constituent to my thinking and my writing.[6]

John T. Pawlikowski, a Servite priest and scholar of the Holocaust, has argued for the massively rational nature of the Nazi movement: "The real issue we must confront in the Holocaust is its rationality. It was a planned event whose origins lie in philosophies developed by thinkers some consider to be giants of liberal Western thought, and in theological attitudes central to

---

[5]   Cf. our jointly-written piece, "Studying the Holocaust's Impact Today," pp. 226ff.

[6]   The question is often raised of why the *Shoah* did not gain a substantial place in the scholarly and religious world until many years after the event. Recent Christian concern with the Holocaust has been largely brought about through the influence of Jewish experience and through such Jewish leadership as that of Elie Wiesel and Irving Greenberg. Reeve Robert Brenner contends that the *Shoah* did not come explicitly to the fore within the Jewish community and Jewish thinking until the late 1960s. With respect to the sudden readiness of countless survivors to speak of the Holocaust, Brenner accounts for this psychologically through reference to the events of the Six Day War (1967) and the Yom Kippur War (1973). He maintains that these events taught Jews "the significance of that new era in which so many have begun to realize and assimilate the message that each one is a fellow survivor" (*The Faith and Doubt of Holocaust Survivors* [New York: Free Press, 1980], pp. 4ff.). The *Shoah* actually received considerable attention before 1967.

Christianity almost since its inception. Its parents are in the mainstream of Western man's consciousness, not on its lunatic fringes."[7]

How and why is it that the *Shoah* may act to *possess* the lives of Christians today? One Christian analyst speaks of the Holocaust as one of two "alpine events" in and for the life of the twentieth-century church, the other being the reestablishing of the State of Israel as the Third Jewish Commonwealth.[8] The Christian world is unseverably linked to the *Shoah* because Christians and their churches were among the victimizers and Jews were their victims.

We could debate from here to eternity whether the Christians of Nazi Germany and Christian fellow-travelers of Nazism outside Germany behaved as they did *because* they were Christians or *despite* being Christians. The testimony of a contemporary German scholar is apropos: With respect to the argument that those who took part in the Holocaust were no longer Christians, this is no more than a wrongful effort to release oneself "from the responsibility for a tradition of despising human beings."[9]

The *Endlösung* was received and practiced by its faithful devotees as a tacitly soteriological event: the Final Solution was to bring redemption by ridding the world of the evil, life-destroying Jew—the only fully life-destroying reality. To employ such language when speaking of other "enemies" of the Third Reich makes little sense. As for these other "enemies"—the Gypsies, for example[10]—everything turns upon who it is that wishes to introduce such a very different subject. It is quite in order for honest humanitarians or Gypsies themselves to do so. But when the antisemites do so (and they are forever doing this) they are simply trying their best to change the subject—away from Jewish victimization. There is nothing within Christian dogma that disparages or destroys such collectivities as Gypsies and Slavs. Christian antipathy, in the sense of group antipathy originating in and through the New Testament, is

---

[7]   John T. Pawlikowski, "The Holocaust as Rational Event," *The Reconstructionist* (April 1974): 8.

[8]   Franklin H. Littell, *The Crucifixion of the Jews* (New York: Harper & Row, 1975), p. 2.

[9]   Ruth Kastning-Olmesdahl, "Theological and Psychological Barriers to Changing the Image of Jews and Judaism in Education," *Journal of Ecumenical Studies* 21 (1984): 468.

[10]   Cf. Donald Kenrick and Grattan Puxon, *The Destiny of Europe's Gypsies* (London: Chatto Heinemann, 1972), Part II - The Nazi Period 1933-1945.

restricted to Jews. Clearly, there are moral grounds for condemning the slaughters of non-Jews at the time of the Holocaust. But these grounds are part of a general human and religious condemnation of injustice and hatred. They have nothing to do with destructive Christian teachings as such.

For all the multiplicity of causes that produced the Holocaust, the Christian influence stands with the major ones. To move a little ahead to two other essays (1980, 1982), "In the *Shoah*, the consequences of the traditional Christological witness of the church are disclosed in their final horror, as those who had been baptized in Jesus' name acted to torture and put to death the non-baptized. The victimizers were either themselves Christians or agents of the antisemitic cause that had come to reign within Christendom... *The singularity of the Holocaust is measured by the specific identity of its victims.*" That singularity centers in the intention of the *Shoah:* "to annihilate every last Jew."[11]

Byron L. Sherwin helpfully distinguishes three positions within post-Holocaust Christian theology respecting the Jewish people and Judaism. In the first of these views, both theological antisemitism and its corollary, social or secular antisemitism, are seen to be endemic to Christianity. Accordingly, the Holocaust is not viewed as a challenge to Christian belief but instead represents "an affirmation of classical Christian attitudes toward Jews and Judaism." The fate of the Jews in the *Shoah* only shows that "they are the rejected people of God, doomed to degradation and death for having rejected and murdered Jesus Christ." In a second view, it is also granted that theological anti-Judaism is indigenous to the structure of Christian belief, and hence that any substantive change would imply the self-dismantling of Christian theology. However, social antisemitism must be repudiated as "behavior unbefitting civilized humanity, much less a professing Christian." Yet this position is beset by the moral difficulty that "to deplore the effect while refusing to deal with the cause" is hardly to assuage Christian antisemitism. In a third view, since "social antisemitism is the praxis of which theological antisemitism is the theory," the

---

[11] "Contemporary Christian Theology and a Protestant Witness for the *Shoah*" (slightly emended and italics added); *"Ha'Shoah* as Christian Revolution: Toward the Liberation of the Divine Righteousness." The point about the intention of the *Shoah* "helps to explain how just before his suicide Adolf Hitler had to write a remorseful letter apologizing for having failed to exterminate the Jews. Six million Jews were dead, yet Hitler realized that he was a total failure. Sufficient numbers of Jews were left to ensure a fresh metastasizing of the cancer of Jewishness. In principle, a single remaining Jew would suffice for this" (ibid., slightly emended).

only moral course is "to eliminate or radically modify the premises from which theological antisemitism flows." However, this third view is confronted by the difficulty that in all probability any such radical reformulation of basic Christian doctrines will be rejected within Christian self-understanding and by the Christian world.[12]

I think that one material reason why most of the Christian world has failed to face the questions that the *Shoah* addresses to it is the threat this would bring to its own rationale and existence. Human collectivities, religious and nonreligious, are very seldom open to committing suicide. In any case, my wife and I adhere to the third view delineated by Professor Sherwin. A possible response to the difficulty within that view as discerned by Sherwin is that in a post-*Shoah* world, pragmatic and utilitarian criteria are hardly entitled to stand in judgment upon moral truth. To be sure, the majority Christian imperium may very well refuse to alter its teachings in any radical way. But then a faithful remnant of Christians may reply to these opponents: You are hardly taking seriously the ongoing events of history. You are only opening yourselves to the judgment of the God of history.

The ultimate polemic against Christianity and the Christian world is not some sort of intellectualist argument over this or that teaching or practice. It has to do with burning children, gassed women and men, destroyed homes and towns. This suggests that it is forbidden to the church to respond to the polemic through theological or historical argument. The only legitimate Christian response is to change Christian teaching and practice, in the name of humanity and justice and in the very face of majority Christian opinion or disinterest.

Johann-Baptist Metz of the University of Münster declares: "What Christian theologians can *do* for the murdered of Auschwitz...is, in every case, this: Never again to do theology in such a way that its construction remains unaffected, or could remain unaffected, by Auschwitz. In this sense I make available to my students an apparently very simple but, in fact, extremely demanding criterion for evaluating the theological scene: Ask yourselves if the

---

[12]   Byron L. Sherwin, "Jewish and Christian Theology Encounters the Holocaust," in Byron L. Sherwin and Susan G. Ament, eds., *Encountering the Holocaust: An Interdisciplinary Survey* (Chicago: Impact Press, 1979), pp. 424-425.

theology you are learning is such that it could remain unchanged before and after Auschwitz. If this is the case, be on your guard!"[13]

The counsel Professor Metz offers his students may be applied to the thinking and praxis of all Christians. For example, to take what Metz says and direct it against me: There is a serious problem with my claim, alluded to in chapter five above, that non-Jews are brought into the Covenant with Israel through the event of Jesus. The fault lies in my tacit confusion of the past with the present, in my perhaps implying an identity between the pre-*Shoah* era and the *Shoah* and post-*Shoah* time. And it will become apparent in chapter seven that I have not completely overcome this fault. Of course, we may still indicate that the Jesus-event was what served to open the Covenant to non-Jews. But to say this is to present or re-present a historical truth of the past. We do not live in that past. We live in the age of the Kingdom of Night. Accordingly, we may put the matter this way: *Once upon a time*, the Jesus-event opened the Covenant to non-Jews; today we Christians are confronted by other decisive events: the *Shoah* and a reborn State of Israel.

(There was a Catholic chapel at Auschwitz for the "convenience" of members of the SS.) Why do I put this datum in parenthesis? May not a reversal of things be in order?—to set out that fifteen-word parenthesis or observation in the form of the entire, non-parenthetic text of this book, and to put *everything else* in parenthesis—though not such a sentence as the following: When the Devil appears, he characteristically comes in the name of God.

III

"How German Thinkers View the Holocaust," an article in *The Christian Century* by Alice Eckardt and me, served as a preliminary account of our impressions and findings in 1975-1976.[14] The Holocaust is, of course, "ancient history" for many younger Germans—as it is for many older ones, ideologically and psychologically speaking. Only some 30,000 Jews are left in the Germany of the 1990s. In the essay we ventured the oversimplifying

---

[13]   Johann Baptist Metz, *The Emergent Church: The Future of Christianity in a Postbourgeois World*, trans. Peter Mann (New York: Crossroad, 1981), p. 28.

[14]   For additional analysis of the German and European situation in the 1970s, see "Christentum und Judentum."

paradox (of some validity at the time) that in East Germany people were encouraged to be anti-Zionist but discouraged from expressing antisemitism, whereas in West Germany there remained noticeable antisemitism along with considerable sympathy for Israel. Jürgen Moltmann of Tübingen University conveyed to us the opinion that the German people had for the most part repressed and suppressed their dark history: "The guilt was never given expression, and so it could not be forgiven." Psychologically and morally speaking, the Holocaust was occupying a generally minor place in the consciousness and conscience of people in the countries we visited (except, of course, in Israel). However, as exemplified in *Christen und Juden* (1975), a pronouncement of the Evangelical Church of Germany, some movement was to be found toward repentance before the fact of the Christian community's culpability for, and role in, the German Nazi "program." The pronouncement speaks of the deep trauma that the Holocaust created for Christians, of the destructive power of Christian antisemitism, of the church's recent rediscovery of its Jewish roots, of the abiding integrity of Judaism, and of the special duty of Christians to support the independence and security of the State of Israel. Yet there was present within public opinion, though not in *Christen und Juden*, a tendency to universalize the Holocaust (= to subject it to abstractness) by trying to subsume Jewish suffering under the general human suffering of 1939-1945. This unrightful trend was apparent to us as well in such countries as France and Poland. Emil L. Fackenheim makes a telling observation: "Rather than face Auschwitz, men everywhere seek refuge in generalities."[15]

An additional document reflective of hope for the church in Germany and for Germany itself was the later pronouncement of the Synod of the Protestant Church of the Rheinland, "Toward Renovation of the Relationship of Christians and Jews" (1980). The synod confessed the co-responsibility and guilt of German Christendom for the Holocaust, defined as "the defamation, persecution, and murder of Jews in the Third Reich." The synod was the first Christian body to do this. Its very precise and delimited rendering of "Holocaust" stands in refreshing contrast to the waffling of that reality at the hands of the universalizers, who are often antisemitic. Furthermore, against detractors of Israel, the synod went on to maintain that "the continuing existence

---

[15] Emil L. Fackenheim, as quoted in Franklin H. Littell, "A Milestone in Post-Holocaust Church Teaching," *Christian News from Israel* (Jerusalem) 27 (1980): 116.

of the Jewish people, its return to the Land of Promise, and also the creation of the State of Israel are signs of the faithfulness of God toward his people."[16]

During the period 1975-1982, I was arguing that a moral crisis had everywhere come to beset Christian symbolism and redemptivist claims, a crisis that manifested itself, and continues to manifest itself, in and through the dreadful fact of the *Shoah* and its aftermath. For example, in "Jürgen Moltmann, the Jewish People, and the Holocaust," I commented upon that German theologian's attempt to trinitarianize and Christianize Auschwitz.[17] Moltmann wrote that "even Auschwitz is taken up into the grief of the Father, the surrender of the Son, and the power of the Spirit." He contended that Jesus' abandonment and deliverance up to death meant *absolute* Godforsakenness, the very torment of hell. And he attested that the resurrection of Jesus embodies liberation for all humankind, a "new element of life and salvation." Indeed, according to Moltmann, only from and through the crucified and resurrected Jesus does the resurrection hope extend to all the living and all the dead.[18]

As I understood the issue here, it involved the promulgating of Christian triumphalism under a cloak of opposition to triumphalism. Here are two passages from the article "Jürgen Moltmann":

The Christian faith, which is supposed to bring human freedom, is [in Moltmann] transmuted into an apologetic weapon, all the while identifying itself as transapologetic. Christians are reputedly enabled, with the aid of the gospel, to expose the falsehoods, evils, and wiles of

---

[16] The Synod continued: "We believe in the permanent election of the Jewish people as the people of God and realize that through Jesus Christ the church is taken into the covenant of God with His people" ("Toward Renovation of the Relationship of Christians and Jews: The Synod of the Protestant Church of the Rheinland, 1980," in Helga Croner, ed. and comp., *More Stepping Stones to Jewish-Christian Relations: An Unabridged Collection of Christian Documents 1975-1983* [New York: Paulist Press, 1985], pp. 207-209).

[17] In that article I distinguished between Moltmann's heavily triumphalist and supersessionist work *The Crucified God* and his subsequent study *Kirche in der Kraft des Geistes*, which somewhat qualifies his Christian imperialism. In *The Crucified God* Moltmann levels the traditionalist, if specious, charge of Jewish "responsibility" for Jesus' death. The article "Jürgen Moltmann, the Jewish People, and the Holocaust" was adapted for use in *Long Night's Journey Into Day*.

[18] Jürgen Moltmann, *The Crucified God*, trans. R. A. Wilson and John Bowden (New York: Harper & Row, 1974), pp. 278, 148-151, 186, 163.

those who do not assent to the gospel of "liberation." But a grim specter stands over the world Christian community: What of the terrible eventuality that many of those whom Christians seek to identify as unfree may in truth be completely free people, while those they seek to portray as free people (namely, themselves) are in truth slaves—for example, slaves to a pre-Holocaust (and Holocaust-preparing) past that extends all the way back through Martin Luther to the apostle Paul and the fateful dichotomization of "gospel" and "law".

There may be, however, an exit from this moral plight, a means whereby the *Endlösung* is itself transfigured. It is possible for Christians to be born again:

There is *metanoia*, total revolution: Christians may come under the power of genuine liberation, or, in Moltmann's Pauline terminology, under "the power of the Spirit." Emil L. Fackenheim raises the question of whether the link between Christian affirmation and Christian antisemitism has become, after Auschwitz, *the* central question for Christianity.[19] The Catholic theologian Rosemary Ruether finds the resolution of the moral-theological problem only in the church's unqualified repudiation of its original sin, that is, its antithetical theology (*gegensätzliche Theologie*) and its "realized eschatology." Ruether asks, "Is it possible to say 'Jesus is Messiah' without, implicitly or explicitly, saying at the same time 'and the Jews be damned'?" She answers: only if the Christian affirmation is relativized into a "theology of hope," which will free it of anti-Jewish imperialism, and indeed of all religious imperialism.[20]

The elements of hopelessness that suffuse and thereby corrupt Jürgen Moltmann's theology begin to be counteracted and cleansed by an authentic theology of hope.

---

[19]   Emil L. Fackenheim, "The Nazi Holocaust as a Persisting Trauma for the Non-Jewish Mind," *Journal of the History of Ideas* 36 (1975): 375.

[20]   "Jürgen Moltmann" (somewhat emended and condensed).

IV

The liberation of Christians from anti-Jewishness, in and through their liberation from a triumphalist anti-Judaism, brings us hard against the issue of Jesus' resurrection. In "Jürgen Moltmann" I offer a short critique of the advocacy of a consummated resurrection of Jesus, or more positively an affirmation of an eschatological or futurist rendering of that event. But I did not begin to concentrate upon this critique and affirmation until the essay "Covenant-Resurrection-Holocaust" (1977), based upon a paper read to the Second Philadelphia Conference on the Holocaust. This piece carried forward and developed, though briefly, the intimation in "Jürgen Moltmann" that if we are ever to be enabled to live with ourselves, with God, and with Jewish sisters and brothers, we shall have to subject the (proclaimed) resurrection of Jesus to a radical prolepticism. For it is very difficult to separate the avowal of a consummated resurrection of Jesus from other Christian views that undergird the "teaching of contempt" for Jews. The dogma of the resurrection "is the relentless doctrinal force behind every other derogation of Jewry. It is the ideological menace that helped, in the end, to create one Holocaust and could perhaps help to create new ones." With the Holocaust, the triumphalist aspects of the dogma of the resurrection of Jesus are revealed "as a seal of hostility and guarantor of the destruction of Jews."[21] By contrast, to identify Jesus' resurrection in proleptic (anticipatory) terms may help to counteract the Christian triumphalism that has perpetuated anti-Judaism and theological antisemitism.

The most obvious and serious response to my critique of a traditionalist resurrection of Jesus is that to engage in such an act is to repudiate or at least to abandon the Christian gospel at its very center.[22] At this juncture I should

---

[21] The passage quoted last here is from a different essay, "The Holocaust and the Enigma of Uniqueness: A Philosophic Effort at Practical Clarification" (1980), slightly emended.

[22] The Christian church remains in a special plight vis-à-vis the "religions of the world" and the question of religion. For the claim the church makes is not a "religious" one that can be readily relativized and assimilated to the "family of religions." The church's claim is factual and allegedly definitive, a claim of the same order as the claims of history and science—even though the facts by which the church identifies itself as a witness are subject to differing interpretations. (Historical and scientific approaches are not free of human interpretation either.) The church's claim to ultimate objectivity is not easy to reconcile with

simply say that human ideas, not excluding those that claim to be vehicles or counterparts of divine revelation, are not spared judgment at the hands of their human consequences. But once the resurrection of Jesus is subjected to the criterion of truthfulness, the implications for morality come immediately to the fore. The abolition of a triumphalist resurrection has decisive consequences for the moral problem. For once the resurrection of Jesus is understood proleptically, it is possible that the poison of anti-Judaism and antisemitism may be drawn out of the Christian enterprise. Another eventuality is to apprehend the resurrection in discretely Jewish terms, an alternative to be considered later in this book.

The issue before us comprises a special and fateful case of the capture of a particular human cause by *ideology*, the afflicting of human ideas by a given collectivity's self-interest. The phenomenon of ideology is closely linked to what Gregory Baum and others have identified as *false consciousness*, the arrogant but ultimately fruitless denial that human thinking and praxis are conditioned by certain established and inherited ideological influences.[23]

The treatment of the resurrection as an ongoing and contemporary crisis for the Christian church was to be continued in subsequent publications of mine. For the present, I leave the matter with a question: If it is so that God uses the wrath and evil of human beings to praise her (Ps. 76:10), may she not also use the errors of humankind to the same end, not excluding such obliquities of Christian doctrine as a triumphalist resurrection of Jesus?

V

"The Shadow of the Death Camps" consisted of personal reflections growing out of my Holocaust research abroad and at home up to that point

---

the "personal" and admittedly relativist affirmations with which some religions (particularly those originating in India) remain more or less content.

23   In response to my paper "Covenant-Resurrection-Holocaust," John Carroll White identified "the experience of a resurrection event" as "not nearly the obstacle to the reconstruction of theology that Eckardt makes it out to be." White confuses the entire issue, which is solely one of the reality or nonreality of the resurrection event itself, and not an issue that can be reduced to "experience" ("Resurrection, Pluralism, and Dialogue: A Response to A. Roy Eckardt," in Josephine Knopp, ed., *Proceedings of the Second Philadelphia Conference on the Holocaust*, pp. 140-148).

(1977). Over the months, my objective knowledge of Christian culpability for the Holocaust was more and more penetrated by an existential outlook that allied itself with current Jewish and Israeli experience. For example, I reported with approval David Wolf Silverman's interpretation that Israel's decision to rescue its hostages in Uganda (4 July 1976) was firmed up through the separating of Jews from non-Jews by their terrorist captors. Here, in Silverman's words, was "a direct consequence of the lived presence of the Holocaust. The three decades that separated the Auschwitz platform (where Dr. Mengele, the Angel of Death, selected Jews for the gas chambers) from the Entebbe Air Terminal were spanned in an instant." Again, as a response to the question of Christian moral credibility, I cited Gregory Baum on the Christian side: "What Auschwitz has revealed to the Christian community is the deadly power of its own symbolism." The "anti-Jewish thrust of the church's preaching" is not a historical, psychological, or sociological matter; "it touches the very formulation of the Christian gospel."[24]

According to one of my old notions (inspired by Reinhold Niebuhr), the teaching that Jesus Christ reconciles human beings and God is authenticated in Christ's power to overcome human idolatry. I finally came to see the moral and theological contradiction therein. The teaching that Jesus Christ—the individual, finite person as such—overcomes human idolatry is *itself* idolatrous, and hence indefensible. Only the power of God can overcome human idolatry.

The summons to remember the Holocaust is eminently necessary and pervasively moral, an obligation that is laid upon Christians as well as upon Jews. Yet we can never overcome the fear that such remembrance may rekindle or keep alive human resentment and even hatred. Caesar C. Aronsfeld points out that when people are compelled to prostrate themselves or humble themselves, they may eventually turn upon the party they think of as making this demand.[25]

"Christians and Jews: Along a Theological Frontier" was originally presented as the 1978 Hugh Th. Miller Lectures at the Christian Theological Seminary, Indianapolis. It sought to develop a twofold theme: "faith under the

---

24 "The Shadow of the Death Camps."

25 Caesar C. Aronsfeld, as cited in "Remembering the Holocaust: A Psycho-Moral Question."

judgment of history" and "history under the judgment of faith." I pointed to the tension that is present in the human situation between worldly humaneness and spiritual affirmation. Today I should plead for the greater priority of worldly humaneness. The dialectic of history and faith was to be foundational to my study *For Righteousness' Sake* (1987).

A serious fault in the lectures "Christians and Jews" is their Christological effrontery: "Jesus of Nazareth is the Savior of the world (John 4:42). The apostle Paul testifies in II Cor. 5:19, 'In Christ God was reconciling the world [*kosmos*] to himself'—but note, *the world*, in contradistinction to Israel, which is not part of the world, but part of the promise, indeed the first-born of God. Israel already lives with God and serves him." The implication here is that while a missionary stance toward Jews is denied, such a stance is sustained vis-à-vis other non-Christians. I can no longer speak this way. My earlier distinction between the illegitimacy of the Christian mission to Jews and the legitimacy of the Christian mission to non-Jews has proved insupportable. Christian absolutism with respect to the peoples of the world is just as imperialist as the church's traditionalist stance toward Jews (though of course it is not supersessionist in the way that it has been toward Judaism and the Jewish people). Because of its idolatry, the Christian teaching of the once-and-for-all "divinity" of Jesus Christ must be fought by more faithful Christians.[26] The moral and theological destructiveness of that teaching is present as well in relations between Christians and non-Jewish non-Christians. The most that can be said in support of the Christian missionary enterprise is its ongoing and potential dissemination of the message of the one judging and loving God, Yahweh, and of the centrality of neighbor love. The validity of the Christian mission is thus grounded upon or subject to the validity of the Jewish mission to humankind, to the end of cleansing the world of its paganisms and idolatries, and elevating to a deciding place the norm of human justice.

The Miller Lectures also entered upon the question of "the Covenant and the trial of God."[27] The *Shoah*-event puts certain shattering questions to us:

---

26   Two important studies here are John Hick, ed., *The Myth of God Incarnate* (Philadelphia: Westminster Press, 1977); and John Hick and Paul F. Knitter, eds., *The Myth of Christian Uniqueness: Toward a Pluralistic Theology of Religions* (Maryknoll: Orbis Books, 1987).

27   This issue is alluded to briefly in chap. 5 above.

What does it mean to affirm the abiding faithfulness of God to original Israel? Does not the character of the event make any such affirmation obscene? At the heart of the issue of the Holocaust is the question of whether God afflicts comfortless Jews, and therefore whether he (*sic*) represents the Devil. In the Kingdom of Night (as at other times) Jews have asked themselves whether God has taken upon himself the role of the Evil One.[28]

At this specific place in "Christians and Jews" I think I may have been on somewhat firmer ground than in what I had to say respecting the Christian mission. I noted how in Elie Wiesel's *Souls on Fire* Rabbi Levi-Yitzhak demands that God ask forgiveness for the hardships he has visited upon his children. "This is why the phrase Yom Kippur also appears in the plural, Yom Kippurim; 'the request for pardon is reciprocal.'" However, Eliezer Berkovits insists that nothing can exonerate God for the suffering of innocent human beings.

When I was young, to challenge or criticize God was unthinkable. It was not that I looked upon such a thing as wrong: rather the very possibility never occurred to me or my friends. It was not until "Toward an Authentic Jewish-Christian Relationship" (1971) that I raised the question in my writings of "the trial of God," the culpability of God. Nothing in my Christian upbringing acted to raise that question—not even the terrible death of my brother at the age of twenty five. Instead, it was my encounter with Jewish thinkers and sources, particularly those who were carrying forward the Hasidic tradition, that helped make the question a life-and-death one for me. I was to learn from my Jewish colleagues that to challenge God is a constituent element within authentic and responsible faith.

But how is it possible to forgive an unforgivable God? We shall return to this all-determining question.

VI

"Contemporary Christian Theology and a Protestant Witness for the *Shoah*" (1980) deplored the fact that while a number of post-Holocaust thinkers within Christian circles are calling for the reform of Christian teachings, many of these

---

28   "The Devil and Yom Kippur."

people yet appear unprepared to attack and renounce those specific church doctrines that by perpetuating anti-Jewishness, continue to cause all the trouble. I once mentioned to Robert A. Everett this problem of Christians who come out at the very same place they were before. Everett's comment was: "They rethink but they do not decide."[29]

As already stated, I have come to believe that traditionalist, triumphalist renderings of the resurrection of Jesus from the dead stands at the center of this unhappy and destructive state of affairs. However, I am hardly one to talk. It took me more than thirty years to reach the ineluctable though depressing conclusion that here indeed is to be found the root of Christian supersessionist imperialism vis-à-vis the Jews and Judaism (as well as imperialist arrogance with respect to other non-Christians).

To cite the article here under review: The apostle of a triumphalist resurrection "announces [to the Jews], in effect, 'It is not the Christian theologian to whom you Jews are to listen. The theologian is, after all, a fallible, sinful human being. You are better advised to pay attention to *God* and to what he does. Let God decide the matter. But God's decision proves to be on the Christian's side, not yours. It was God who raised Jesus from the dead. So the Christian is proved right and you are proved wrong. In the resurrection God *confirms* the Christian gospel, the Christian cause.'"

The ideology that suffuses the religion of Christianity has here arrived at a final destination: the Christian claim gets underwritten "by God himself." That claim works unceasingly to convince itself of its own absoluteness. Hence, there appears no way within its own resources for it to reverse itself. Yet a stern possibility remains: What if God has other ideas upon this entire subject? With this question, a glimmer of human hope returns.

Nevertheless, there is no point in any attempt by me or someone else to make a judgment of Jesus' non-resurrection (until now) compatible with the New Testament. Although at various places the New Testament writers differ with one another upon the exact form of Jesus' resurrection, they are wholly at one in believing that the event took place and is absolutely central to the Christian faith. This is *the* New Testament position. As Paul writes, "If you confess with your lips that Jesus is Lord and believe in your heart that God

---

[29]   Conversation with Robert A. Everett, 20 Nov. 1978.

raised him from the dead, you will be saved" (Rom 10:9). Again: "If Christ has not been raised, then our preaching is in vain and your faith is in vain" (I Cor. 15:14).

In the essay under discussion it is argued that an authentic Christian reform will take its origin from the dialectic between the nature of the *Shoah* and the meaning of "Protestant." Uncounted words have been written upon the reality and identity of the Holocaust; nevertheless—and incredibly—the uniqueness of that series of events can be stated in just a few words, through recourse to the Holocaust's intention. I return to a point earlier made:

> The singularity of the *Shoah* is tied to the singularity of the determination that not a single Jew is to be permitted anywhere on this planet, including Jewish infants and Jewish fetuses and, therefore, Jewish corpses. Theologically expressed, with the *Shoah* there comes into being, as never before, the total effacement of the people of God... Because the *Shoah*-event bears the character of an absolute, the *Shoah* performs [an act of absolute] division. It splits humankind into two parties: those who take the *Shoah*-event with absolute seriousness or will eventually do so, and those who do not or will not.[30]

A person either assents to the presence of Jews in the world, or rejects that presence. There is no third way.[31]

We may recall a question posed by James H. Cone: "If God is good, why did God permit millions of blacks to be stolen from Africa and enslaved in a strange land?" In this question, the continuity between black suffering and Jewish suffering is evident. Yet there is also discontinuity. Blacks have not been accused of being children of the Devil, as Jews have in the Gospel of John

---

[30] "Contemporary Christian Theology and a Protestant Witness for the *Shoah*" (slightly emended).

[31] See the essay "Travail of a Presidential Commission."

(8:44) and in the Christian tradition.[32] At this point the Christian gospel and Nazi ideology instead converge.

Until our time, the concept "Protestant" has conveyed two meanings, the negative meaning of a "principle of protest" (Paul Tillich) and the positive meaning of *pro*-plus-*testari*, "to be a witness for." Upon the negative side, the Protestant reality protests against all human idolatries, all human absolutization. Upon the positive side, the Protestant reality, as traditionally identified, witnesses to the coming of Jesus as the Christ, and to his crucifixion and resurrection.

But then there was to come to pass *die Endlösung der Judenfrage*, the ultimate answer to the question of the Jewish people, i.e., *we shall not allow any more Jews to live*. This historic decision and this historic event force a question upon every Christian: Which of the two sides are you on, the side of Jews or the side of "no Jews allowed"? It is clear that the "principle of protest" has enabled many Christians to battle against anti-Jewish evils within Christianity. But it is equally clear that the inability of even some reforming Christians finally to overcome anti-Jewishness and anti-Judaism is grounded in their *pro*-plus-*testari*, their witness to the resurrected Jesus.

A word upon the fate of Paul Tillich may perhaps be helpful. In *The Protestant Era* Tillich posed the shattering question, "Will the Protestant era come to an end?" He did not give an answer, although he set the answer, as all Protestants are obliged to do, within "the interpretation of Protestantism" itself, "its promises, its failures, and its creative possibilities."[33] It is most ironic that the late 1940s should be the time in which Tillich posed his question. For even though, chronologically speaking, Tillich was then living after the *Shoah*, from theological, moral, and psychological perspectives he was speaking as though the *Shoah* had not taken place. He failed to recognize, as most other Christians do not yet recognize, that in the time of the *Shoah*

---

[32] Consult, e.g., Joshua Trachtenberg, *The Devil and the Jews: The Medieval Conception of the Jew and its Relation to Modern Antisemitism* (Cleveland-New York: World Pub. Co. [Meridian Books], 1943; Philadelphia: Jewish Publication Society of America, 1961).

[33] Paul Tillich, *The Protestant Era*, trans. James Luther Adams (Chicago: University of Chicago Press, 1948), p. xii.

the Protestant era does reach its end, as also the Catholic era and the Christian era as a whole. That is to say, with the coming of the *Shoah* the positive or celebrative aspect of the Protestant and Christian witness is made finally and totally answerable to the prophetic-critical dimension of Protestantism. This, Paul Tillich was never able to grasp, because he did not, in subsequent years, take the singular significance of the *Shoah*-event into his life and thence into his theology. He could not follow the judgmental power of the Protestant principle into its final and necessarily radical extremity. For it is in the name of the Protestant ethic itself that Protestantism is judged and found wanting, which means in the name of justice and love, and in behalf of the final coming of the kingdom of God. In the *Shoah* the messiahship of Jesus is transmuted through the total obliteration of the messianic people of Jesus; the crucifixion of Jesus is transformed through the crucifixions of the children of God; and the resurrection is transubstantiated into the anti-triumphalist, coming resurrection of Jesus and all the people of God...

A teacher of Elie Wiesel once said to him, "Only the Jew knows that he may oppose God, as long as he does so in defense of His creation." A parallel suggests itself. On the day of the *Shoah* and its aftermath, only the Protestant knows that he may oppose Jesus as the Christ, as long as he does so in defense of history and truth, in defense of the people of God and thereby of Jesus himself.[34]

Thus may we hold to the anguish-filled paradox that a meaningful and licit contemporary Protestant and Christian theology of the *Shoah* is distinguished by its post-Protestant and post-Christian character. However, I am not by any means assured that the essay just discussed meets adequately the following two

---

[34]   "Contemporary Christian Theology and a Protestant Witness for the *Shoah*" (slightly emended). It is the case, as Paul Tillich insisted, that the "principle of protest" is deprived of its truth and power once its own standing-ground is removed. Tillich avoided this outcome by declaring that Protestantism in its protesting dimension is supported by the bedrock of "the New Being that is manifest in Jesus as the Christ." But what if this latter *pro testari* is no longer to be permitted? We may respond: The requirement of moral witness is "cared for within the truthful and transcendent economy of Judaism. Judaism is herself the mother of the 'principle of protest,' through the prophets Moses, Amos, Hosea, Isaiah, Jeremiah, Jesus, and the rest. And the bedrock, the truth that makes the Protestant principle possible and precludes its self-annihilation, is the judging love of God, enemy of all idolatry and friend of all creation" (ibid.).

questions: What discrete, objective grounds or principles are there for affirming that a particular event (yes, let us say: the *Shoah*) is able or has the right or power to speak in judgment upon a previous event (yes, let us say: the resurrection of Jesus)? And what is the methodology or what are the methodologies to be employed in dealing with the first question? Psychological? Philosophic? Moral? Sociological? Theological? A combination of two or more of these?

A final note: As we shall see, I was at last to come to a view of Jesus' resurrection that was more than prolepticist.

VII

In 1980 *The Annals of the American Academy of Political and Social Science* put out a special number called "Reflections on the Holocaust." A contribution by my wife and me was titled "The Holocaust and the Enigma of Uniqueness: A Philosophic Effort at Practical Clarification." There was included, among that essay's other emphases, much additional attention to the question we have been exploring in this chapter: the Holocaust's singularity.

The article was rather heavy upon metaphysical reflection, although it gradually built up to a moral-existential stress.[35] Its point of departure was Yehuda Bauer's concern that a responsible encounter with the Holocaust must not give way to mystification, to some form of transnatural fuzziness. Yet we may agree as well that such an encounter must not lose or obscure the essential peculiarities of the *Shoah*-event.[36] To face up to this problem, Alice Eckardt and I called upon the dialectical relation between nomothesis and idiography (introduced into this retrospective in chapter three above)—meaning, on the one hand, a generalizing response to events/phenomena and, on the other hand, a response to the historical distinctiveness of individual happenings.

---

[35] Not discussed here is an eight-sided attempt within the essay to support and work out its theoretical structure, with special reference to our claim that the analysis as a whole can be identified as scientific.

[36] Of relevancy here are Yehuda Bauer and Nathan Rotenstreich, eds., *The Holocaust as Historical Experience* (New York-London: Holmes & Meier, 1981); and Richard L. Rubenstein and John K. Roth, *Approaches to Auschwitz: The Holocaust and its Legacy* (Atlanta: John Knox, 1987). The latter study has much to say upon Christianity and the Holocaust, but is unaccountably silent upon most contemporary Christian work in this area.

Three meanings of uniqueness were then suggested, making up a kind of continuum. The sequence of these meanings drives us into greater and greater particularity and incomparability:

(a) *Ordinary uniqueness*. All historical events are unique, emerging as they do within the shifting conditions of an overall spatio/temporal flux. To point out that the *Shoah* is unique in this sense is to utter a truism as elementary as it is unnecessary.

(b) *Unique uniqueness*. "As the mind reviews the dramas of human history and seeks after the meaning of that history, it resorts to the category of insignificance/significance. The mind freely concludes that while many happenings appear to be more or less trivial, other happenings possess singular importance and may, indeed, be characterized as 'epoch-making': they make the epoch in which they transpire." That the *Shoah* of the Jewish people is in this sense a uniquely unique event hardly requires argument. As Professor Bauer himself writes, for "the first time in human history a sentence of death had been pronounced on anyone guilty of having been born, and born of certain parents." Bauer emphasizes that a failure to recognize that the Jewish situation was unique is itself an instance of the mystifying of history.

(c) *Transcending uniqueness*. One way to situate a qualitative shift to a third form of uniqueness

is to speak of a radical leap from objectness to subjectness,[37] a total existential crisis and involvement for the party who engages in one or another affirmation of transcending uniqueness. This extraordinary about-face is accompanied by a marked transformation in modes of language.

Now, in place of relatively calm, descriptive references to the merely unprecedented character of the Holocaust or to its singularly catastrophic nature, the witness...is heard to testify that such an event is simply unbelievable [i.e., it has to be believed within and through its

---

[37] The terms "objectness" and "subjectness" were proposed by us, in contrast to the more customary "objectivity" and "subjectivity" as a means of offsetting somewhat any connotations of "arbitrariness" or "taste" within the popular usage of "subjectivity." Representatives of transcending uniqueness will simply deny that they have "sold objective (real) truth for the pottage of mere whim or personal preference" ("The Holocaust and the Enigma of Uniqueness").

very unbelievability]. The witness asks, How could there ever be such an event as this one? Often the witness will plead that the only really sensible response to the Holocaust is a kind of holy, or unholy, awe and even a consuming silence...

The response that finds in the Holocaust a transcending, crushing uniqueness is representing the dimension of the *numinous*, as described by Rudolf Otto in *Das Heilige*. This psychospiritual state, called the numinous by Otto, presents itself as *ganz andere*, wholly other, a condition absolutely   *sui generis* and incomparable, whereby human beings find themselves utterly abashed. There is a feeling of terror before such an awe-inspiring mystery, but a mystery that also fascinates infinitely.[38]

A revolutionary change here comes to fruition. The role of ordinary observer is transformed into the anguish of life-and-death witness. Our essay concluded: "Improper mystification is indeed a pitfall whenever we seek to characterize the Holocaust as transcendingly unique in any objective, impersonal sense. But the transcending uniqueness of the Holocaust is made manifest in an existential way by virtue of the special relation that many human beings have to that event. It is at this juncture that a *social ethic* for the post-Holocaust era comes together with a *sociology of knowledge* applied to the Holocaust. Herein lies the Holocaust's uniqueness, in an absolute sense—a binding sense—for our time."[39] In a word, the overall *Shoah*-event may be conceptualized under the heading of *the existential radicalization of uniqueness*—the very opposite of mystification, and hence a constructive, assenting response to Yehuda Bauer's concern.[40]

---

[38]   "The Holocaust and the Enigma of Uniqueness" (slightly emended). The English version of Otto's *Das Heilige* carries the misleadingly intellectualistic title *The Idea of the Holy*, trans. John W. Harvey (New York: Oxford University Press, 1958). See also Mircea Eliade, *The Sacred and the Profane* (New York: Harper & Row, 1961), pp. 8-10.

[39]   "The Holocaust and the Enigma of Uniqueness" (slightly emended).

[40]   Further to the issue of the Holocaust's uniqueness is "Was the Holocaust Unique?," although that brief article (1984) falls in the province of chap. 7 of this retrospective. The piece is mentioned at this juncture since it is primarily a rebuttal of Pierre Papazian's treatment of *Long Night's Journey Into Day*—for example, his preposterous claim that the Eckardts find the Holocaust "beyond human understanding" and unique as genocide. The

VIII

As consultants to President Carter's Commission on the Holocaust, Alice Eckardt and I participated in that body's factfinding and study mission in the Summer of 1979 to Poland, the Soviet Union, Denmark, and Israel. Our article, "Travail of a Presidential Commission: Confronting the Enigma of the Holocaust" (1981) constitutes a report and commentary upon that journey.

To move on to another item: In her response to my article, "*HaShoah* as Christian Revolution: Toward the Liberation of the Divine Righteousness," Sarah S. Miller sought to subsume the Holocaust-event under the rubric of other terrifying events.[41] In so doing, Miller fell prey to a numbers game. She failed to comprehend the reality of the *Shoah* as the numbers-game-to-end-all-numbers-games, through its decree that for all time to come the number "Jew" must equal absolute zero. Again, Miller's viewpoint makes about as much sense as the charge that a grave marker dedicated to one's parents thereby insults all other deceased parents. To deny the singularity of the Holocaust is, in effect, to deny the integrity of the Jewish community and Jewish life. It cannot be repeated too many times that the singularity of the *Shoah* lies in the *identity* of the victims, not in their numbers.

"After the Holocaust: Some Christian Considerations" dealt further with the singularity of the Holocaust and the Christian contribution to that event. A purely extra-Christian, sociological-historical accounting of the Holocaust does little if anything to explain to us "why in the heart of' Christendom the very people from whom originated the holy scriptures, the apostles, and the confessed Lord of the church were not only singled out for annihilation but were, with rare exceptions, abandoned by the churches and Christian

---

plain truth is that on our view, the transcending uniqueness of the Holocaust is tied to the horrible fact that this series of events is very much *within* human understanding. In his work *The Tremendum* the late Arthur A. Cohen witnesses that the *immensity* of the Holocaust is what is mysterious, is what fabricates the ultimateness of its horror—in contrast to the *nature* of the Holocaust, which is not mysterious. The *tremendum* is ultimate but not final, not absolute (*The Tremendum: A Theological Interpretation of the Holocaust* [New York: Crossroad, 1981], pp. 29, 49).

[41] Sarah S. Miller's response appeared in the same number of *Quarterly Review* as my original article: 2 (1982): 67-69.

people."[42] This essay included several specific proposals for altering traditionalist Christian teachings.[43]

I have identified *Long Night's Journey Into Day: Life and Faith After the Holocaust* as a culminating study for the years 1975-1982. A word of explanation is in order. Begun in 1975, this was the second book that Alice Eckardt and I did together. The first edition was published in 1982. Over the period 1985-1988 my wife prepared a revised and expanded edition. In accord with the history of the book, it is probably wise to postpone added reference to it until chapter eight of this review, since the study is best judged as embodying a position that Alice Eckardt and I were still taking in 1988. However, in keeping with the date of publication of the first edition (1982), and as a way of linking *Long Night's Journey Into Day* to a dominant thrust of the present chapter, I include one salient and controversial passage from the original version:

> Wherein lies the singularity of the Holocaust? Our answer is a simple one. (What are we saying? There could be no paradox more reason-defying than this: to propose a simple interpretation of the modern world's most impossible event...Yet we contend that the truth is a simple one.) The Holocaust is the final act of a transcendingly unique[44] drama. It is the hour that follows logically, inexorably, and faithfully upon a particular history of conviction and behavior. It is a climax that succeeds the drawing up, over many centuries, of the requisite doctrinal formulations. It is the arrival of the "right time" (*kairos*) following upon all those dress rehearsals, those practice

---

[42] "After the Holocaust: Some Christian Considerations" (slightly emended).

[43] Additional occasional articles during this period that bear upon the subject of the *Shoah* are the following: "Christian Responses to the *Endlösung* (1978); "Can Christians Confront the Holocaust?" (1978); and a contribution to the "Symposium: Germans and Jews Today" (1981).

[44] I have ventured to change "uniquely unique" as used in the original edition to read "transcendingly unique." This accords with earlier analysis in the present chapter. However, the change somewhat oversimplifies the actual state of affairs; aspects of "unique uniqueness" as I above describe that possibility remain with respect to the viewpoint of the passage here reproduced. ("Uniquely unique" was retained— unfortunately—in the 1988 revised edition of *Long Night's Journey Into Day*.)

sessions of the Crusades, the Inquisition, and the like. The Holocaust is the consummation of all of them. Yet within this very simplicity...there implodes all the demonic complexity. Only in our latter years could we [who are Christians] finally ready ourselves for the eschatological deed, the *Endlösung*. Only the final destruction remained to be carried out...All that remained to be done was to "manage" and to follow out the correct technical procedures. Antisemitism "became professionalized and mass murder became an administrative process."[45] The German Nazis...lived out and applied a deep historical inevitability. Here was the implementation of the dominant theological and moral conclusions of the Christian church, as also of the philosophical ideas of certain so-called great men of Western culture (Voltaire, Nietzsche, Fichte, and others), now aided by technological instrumentalities not previously marshalled or available. All in all, *we were only following orders—the remorseless commands of nineteen centuries.*[46]

This passage may make the reader wonder a little about possible influences upon me of such a determinist as Spinoza, mentioned in chapter one. The last thing we meant to imply in the passage is that the Nazis were not to be held accountable for their deeds. Philosophic and social determinism must never be permitted to foreclose human responsibility (or divine responsibility). The same may be said for any philosophy or theology of the Devil.

IX

During this block of time I wrote several pieces upon subjects other than the Holocaust as such. "Consider the Animals" (1976) dealt with the different, though not wholly discrepant, subject of humankind's relation and obligations to the so-called higher animals. That essay was to be adapted as an epilogue to

---

[45] Nora Levin, *The Holocaust: The Destruction of European Jewry 1933-1945* (New York: Schocken Books, 1973), p. 91.

[46] *Long Night's Journey Into Day*, 1st ed., pp. 56-57 (slightly emended). This passage is retained in the revised edition (pp. 66-67). *Long Night's Journey* builds in part upon previously published essays.

the volume *For Righteousness' Sake.* "The Achievements and Trials of Interfaith" (1978; reprinted below) was part of a symposium in the journal *Judaism* upon the subject of Christian-Jewish relations in the United States over a fifty-year period. Alice Eckardt and I offered therein a critique of threats to interfaith amity from the theological right and the theological left. We maintained that genuine interfaith amity is possible only within a context of non-absolutist faith-claims. My short piece "Panel Response," on the role of religion in (allegedly) promoting peace in the Middle East (1979), is somewhat reminiscent of "Attack Upon Religion." For the contention overall was that "religion usually fosters sympathy for other people within personal, non-threatening situations; but religion generates hostility toward other people within collective, group-threatening situations... All in all, whether we concentrate upon Judaism, upon Islam, or upon Christianity, *when we remain on the political level* there appears a fundamental contribution by religion to conflict and war rather than to peace. This is one of the major reasons why politics is often more moral than religion."[47]

The title of my essay, "Toward a Secular Theology of Israel" (reprinted below), could just as well have read, or perhaps would have better read, "Toward a Theology of Israel as a Secular Reality." A colleague who read that essay responded that the relation between historical events and faith needs much more attention than I here gave it. He was quite right, I think. As earlier noted, the history-faith relationship was to receive major attention in my systematic study of that problem, *For Righteousness' Sake* (1987).[48]

A final piece during this period was my eulogy "In Memoriam James Parkes" (reproduced below). I have read somewhere that my point of view on the Christian-Jewish relation reflects that of Parkes, and that I am among those who are continuing Parkes's work. That finding is incorrect. To be sure, at many points Parkes and I have been in agreement—with special reference to the moral demands of Christian praxis. Yet while I always admired Parkes, for his

---

[47]   "Panel Response" (slightly emended).

[48]   Such contemporary Jewish thinkers as Eliezer Berkovits, Irving Greenberg, and Pesach Schindler hold that in the age after the *Shoah*, divine commands involving special moral or spiritual responsibilities for the Jewish people are licit only insofar as they presuppose and honor the politically sovereign integrity of Israel. However, many Jewish figures (including those here listed) express fear of and opposition to idolatries associated with the land. Cf. Lev. 25:23: "Mine is the land."

wisdom as well as his courage, he did not influence me substantively in my overall philosophic and theological position. I have much honored him as a historian—what philosopher or theologian is not secretly envious of great historians?—and I have benefited from and often cited important elements of his work (particularly upon the history of Christianity and its place in the crime of antisemitism). Yet I suppose that had Parkes not been on the scene, I would have relied upon other historians of these matters. And I would have gone my own philosophic and theological way. James Parkes was a modernist-educationist-progressivist who taught the "equality" of Christianity, Judaism, and Humanism. I have always felt that his rendering of the Trinity (the very center of and key to his theology) is to be questioned, together with (I have more lately come to believe) his position on the Incarnation. However, my final word upon Parkes remains one of great esteem. It is fitting that this chapter upon the *Shoah* and its lessons should end with a reference to him. For James Parkes fought literally to his death anything and everything anti-Jewish.[49]

---

[49] In 1981 I composed a rather lengthy historiographical and bibliographical analysis, "Recent Literature on Christian-Jewish Relations," covering the previous decade. It appeared in the *Journal of the American Academy of Religion* and in the *Jewish Book Annual*. Reviews of books over the period covered in this chapter included Arnold Forster and Benjamin R. Epstein, *The New Anti-Semitism*; Irving Howe, *World of Our Fathers*; Charlotte Klein, *Anti-Judaism in Christian Theology*; Roland B. Gittlesohn, *The Modern Meaning of Judaism*; Paul M. van Buren, *Discerning the Way*; Clemens Thoma, *A Christian Theology of Judaism*; Arthur A. Cohen, *The Tremendum*; and Eugene B. Borowitz, *Contemporary Christologies*.

6A

Selected Essays

(1975-1982)

The Recantation of the Covenant?

(In Confronting the Holocaust: The Impact of Elie Wiesel, eds. Alvin H. Rosenfeld and Irving Greenberg [Bloomington-London: Indiana University Press, 1978], pp. 159-168)

I offer a few comments upon just one phrase within a tale from Elie Wiesel. The words read: "in the kingdom of night, when it [the Torah] was taken back."[1]

I am unsure who utters these words. Is it the beggar of Jerusalem, in whose tale they appear? Is it Katriel? Is it the personage called "I" in the novel? Perhaps we are not to know for certain. It is painful and it is hard to comprehend the beggar. Yet he has put forth his hand, and we are obligated to reckon with him.

More than once I have made reference to the above phrase, for it has pursued me over the nine years since it was first expressed.[2] I find that I have even overstated the wording. I have written that, according to the beggar's testimony, "at Sinai God gave Israel the Torah, and then in 'the kingdom of night,' the Holocaust, he took it back again."[3] But the phrasing of our text is more circumspect than this. Thus the passive voice is utilized: "they were given the Torah," and then "it was taken back."

The present opportunity for constructive searching ought not be dissipated in semantic maneuvers. Therefore, I shall be categorical. In the precise context

---

[1]   Elie Wiesel, *A Beggar in Jerusalem*, translated from the French by Lily Edelman and the author (New York: Random House, 1970), p. 200.

[2]   At the end of the novel Wiesel dates the work "Jerusalem 1967-Christiansted 1968."

[3]   A. Roy Eckardt, *Your People, My People: The Meeting of Jews and Christians* (New York: Quadrangle/The New York Times Book Company, 1974), p. 228. This wording is closer to Jacob Glatstein's affirmation in a poem "The Dead Do Not Praise God," but Wiesel's phrasing appears to echo Glatstein.

of our phrase, there was a kind of *kairos*, a kind of appointed time-space, if a dread one, when a recantation of the Covenant ostensibly occurred. That time-space was "the kingdom of night," the *Endlösung* ("Final Solution"). According to our theologieal tradition, God responds to human events with total seriousness. He is, indeed, deeply involved in such events. This means that if the Torah was "taken back," certain human beings must have had a part in that event. Of course, insofar as the power to recant depends alone upon the power to bestow, any final recantation could only come from God himself. But *has* God recanted? Or did he receive back the Covenant only to offer it once more, to incarnate it in some fresh or strange form? These questions try our souls.

I

An initial interpretation is that of simple negation. The bond with Israel is severed. For that matter, there never was any bond. He who bears witness to this interpretation will insist, nonetheless, that all we have is one legend being called forth by a previous one. Our context reads: "Just like long ago, at Sinai, when they were given the Torah. Just like a generation ago, in the kingdom of night, when it was taken back." But in truth, so attests the proponent of this first view, no Torah was ever given. How ludicrous, then, to declare that it could be returned. No owner is to be found to receive it. In the end as in the beginning, the great world, out there, remains a dark and empty thing.

How can we, contemporary people *par excellence*, arbitrarily strike out this first possibility? The logic may be marked by wistfulness, yet, hauntingly, it stands its ground: There was in fact no singular kingdom of night, for there never was a singular kingdom of day. (Perhaps there might arise little kingdoms of night, relative kingdoms of night, but there is none possessed of *Einzigartigkeit*, of absolute and transcendent uniqueness.)

II

A second possibility is that God (who is here, here in all his hiddenness) recanted because of the acts of his people. Israel betrayed the divine statutes and had to be judged.

In *A Beggar in Jerusalem* there is much laughter. For the most part it is terrible, maniacal laughter. According to Rabbi Nachman of Bratzlav, somewhere in the world there is a certain city that encompasses all other cities. In the city is a street that contains all the other streets of the city; on that street is a house dominating all the other houses; it contains a room that comprises all the other rooms of the house. "And in that room there lives a man in whom all other men recognize themselves. And that man is laughing. That's all he ever does, ever did. He roars with laughter when seen by others, but also when alone."[4] Is there something special for him to laugh about now? (By now I mean, of course, 1933 to 1945.) Yes. The man is especially laughing at this moment because of the very context of the phrase that occupies us: It was *in the kingdom of night* that the Torah was taken back. I think—and hope I am not unkind—that someone who identifies the *Endlösung* as an act of judgment by God upon his people is subject to confinement in that room, where he will have to listen, without surcease, to the laughter of that man.

III

There is a third alternative, the inclusion of which is prompted in part by recent residence in Germany. This alternative clearly transcends any intention either of the beggar or of his creator. Yet the alternative does muster a certain theological relevance by virtue of the reputed historical opening of the Covenant to the non-Jewish world. I shan't examine here the shattering possibility that the Torah was finally taken back because of the eternal assaults of Israel's enemies upon her, although some later remarks will bear upon that evenuality.[5] What

---

[4] *A Beggar in Jerusalem*, p.30.

[5] In attendance at our conference was a good friend who is a Christian. After hearing my paper, she observed to me that the absence in it of any real reference to the terrible Christian treatment of Jews as a possible basis for the recantation of the covenant of demand could be received by Jewish hearers in the following way: We are confronted here by one more typical Christian case of a readiness to find evil everywhere but within the Christian community. My friend's comment points up a substantial moral fault in my presentation. But had I acted to remedy this fault in revising the paper for publication, I would have hidden, culpably, the unfortunate truth about the original presentation. I can only point now to the element of irony in the situation. Having assailed Christian responsibility for antisemitism and the Holocaust over a period of years, I had early decided to omit this element from my paper. My intent was—doubtless with gratuitous pridefulness—to forestall the reaction, "Here is that

I will allude to is a possibility that takes into some account the Christian viewpoint. Yet I do not intend to violate the Jewish presuppositions of *A Beggar in Jerusalem*.

My allusion is to the possible taking back, or replacement, of the Torah in association with the event of the cross of Jesus of Nazareth. The interjection of Pauline theology is evident. This theological complication could be elucidated in any number of ways. There is, for example, the Christian theological truism that long before the kingdom of night, the Covenant with original Israel had already been taken back. That is to say, the Torah was soteriologically fulfilled or even abrogated on the basis of faith in Jesus as the Christ. Reputedly, Jesus is the divine Word, or the Torah—as the prologue to John's Gospel has it.

I shall only mention some recent argumentation from Jürgen Moltmann of the University of Tübingen. In a work entitled *The Crucified God*, Professor Moltmann—a dominating figure among contemporary Christian theologians—puts the cross of Golgotha in unique association with Jesus' (allegedly) total Godforsakenness. Jesus' abandonment and deliverance up to death are held to constitute the very torment of hell.[6] This is a way of declaring, in effect, that the twentieth-century kingdom of night marshals no crucial theological significance, but possesses at most only ancillary significance, simply because the very hell of Godforsakenness long preceded it and, indeed, furnishes prototypical substance for the Holocaust itself. The *Endlösung* is viewed under the aspect of Golgotha, rather than the possible other way around. In consequence God need not have any special concerns with the reputed kingdom of night. Any relating of that kingdom to the taking back of the Torah becomes meaningless, or at least gratuitous, from this Christian perspective.

I shall never forget the account that follows, as it was read in a memorable paper of Irving Greenberg's at the Conference on the Church Struggle and the Holocaust, held in Hamburg in 1975. The scene is Auschwitz in the late

---

Eckardt playing his same old tune once again." Perhaps the lesson here is that an ostensibly ingenuous resistance to repetitiveness and boredom can contain evil seeds within itself.

[6]   Jürgen Moltmann, *The Crucified God* (New York: Harper & Row, 1974), pp. 148, 151.

summer of 1944. The gas chamber near the crematorium was out of order; it had been wrecked in a Jewish commando operation in August. "The other gas chambers were full of the adults and therefore the children were not gassed, but just burned alive. There were several thousand of them. When one of the SS sort of had pity upon the children, he would take a child and beat the head against a stone before putting it on the pile of fire and wood, so that the child lost consciousness. However, the regular way they did it was by just throwing the children onto the pile. They would put a sheet of wood there, then sprinkle the whole thing with petrol, then wood again, and petrol and wood, and petrol—and then they placed the children there. Then the whole thing was lighted."[7]

Jürgen Moltmann, though he writes today, lives virtually in the time before the kingdom of night. His is pre-Holocaust theology—understandably so, within its own frame of reference. For him the event of Golgotha remains the solely decisive event of salvation-history. Yet how is it possible for us to remain bound by that single event? How can we stop at that place? Are we not called to find in the subsequent unfolding of events an acting out of the divine-human encounter, and hence of the human understanding of God?

Even though my own rejection of the Christian supersessionist view of the Jewish Torah preceded my involvement with the Holocaust, that involvement has effected a crisis in my thinking on the Covenant (as it has for some others). It is just not so that the event of the cross of Golgotha remains an absolute horror upon which the Christian faith will and should build, dialectically, its faith. It is no longer possible, if it ever was possible, to make the passion of Jesus of Nazareth the *locus classicus* of Christian faith. Jesus was a man with a mission, a courageous man who set his face to go up to Jerusalem. Professor Moltmann is a theologian of Germany. But he does not comprehend that there is in this world an evil that is more horrible than every other evil. This is the evil of children witnessing the murders of other children, while knowing that they also are to be murdered in the same way, being absolutely aware that they face the identical fate. The Godforsakenness of Jesus has become non-absolute,

---

7   This account is adapted, with some changes, from a representation in an unpublished paper by Irving Greenberg at the International Conference on the Church Struggle and the Holocaust, Haus Rissen, Hamburg, BRD, 8-11 June 1975.

if it ever was absolute, for there is now a Godforsakenness of Jewish children that is the final horror. It was *in the kingdom of night* that the Torah was taken back: this fact determines eschatologically all other presumed transformations of the Covenant.

IV

A fourth eventuality is that God recanted because he found that he could no longer live with himself. The kingdom of night proved too much, even for him. In *A Beggar in Jerusalem* a young madman, one of only three survivors who had escaped the deportation, asks: "How does God justify himself in his own eyes, let alone in ours? If the real and the imaginary both culminate in the same scream, in the same laugh, what is creation's purpose, what is its stake?"[8]

In recent thinking, Jewish and Christian, no one has put these kinds of questions more relentlessly or persuasively than Richard L. Rubenstein. I now raise the question, not of the impossibility or objective negation of all divine-human covenants, but instead of the obliteration of Israel's Covenant of demand (this in contradistinction to a Covenant of promise, of assurance).

From the standing ground of our fourth alternative, a moral indictment is entered against the very King of the universe. For once upon a time God mandated that his elect be "a kingdom of priests and a holy nation" (Exod. 19:6). Yet at the last, in the kingdom of night, his chosen ones were transubstantiated into vermin, and to less than vermin—and by his permission.

The end of the Covenant of demand is the consequence of the juridical-moral trial of God. The charge entered against him is no less than implicit Satanism. No plea of innocence is open to him. No appeal is available to him. All that is possibly left for him is an act of penitence.

This penitential act is suggested in Elie Wiesel's *Ani Maamin: A Song Lost and Found Again*. God stays silent there, it is true, before the remorseless pleadings and terrible denunciations of him by Abraham, Isaac, and Jacob. Yet when Abraham snatches a little girl from before the machine guns and runs like the wind to save her, and she tells him weakly, that she *believes* in him, in Abraham, then at last a tear clouds the eyes of God (though Abraham cannot see

---

[8]   *A Beggar in Jerusalem*, p.28.

that). When Isaac beholds the mad Dayan singing "of his ancient and lost faith," of belief in God and in the coming of the Messiah, yet a second time God weeps (though Isaac cannot see that). And when Jacob finds a death camp inmate declaiming that the Haggadah lies, that God will not come, that the wish to be in Jerusalem will never be granted, but that he will continue to recite the Haggadah as though he believes in it, and still await the prophet Elijah as he did long ago, even though Elijah disappoint him, then yet a third time (though Jacob cannot see it) God weeps. "This time (he weeps) without restraint, and with—yes—love. He weeps over his creation—and perhaps over more than his creation."[9]

According to this fourth viewpoint, the original sin of God—a sin in which Christians, Muslims, and others were to become most ready and available accomplices—was the sin of applying absolute divine perfection to the lives of ordinary human creatures. But it may be that the penitence of God has come. Is he, perhaps, promising now to do his best not to sin again, not to have anything to do with allowing such torment? For the loathsome myth of the Jew as "suffering servant" will surrender its horror only as the erstwhile Covenant of demand is given a fitting burial.[10] Was the Torah of demand in fact taken back in the kingdom of night? If so, release came with it.

V

A fifth possibility is the reincarnating of a Covenant of promise through a new, or a renewed, political-secular bond. In the kingdom of night, there is the recantation of the Torah; after the kingdom of night, a transformation, a *metanoia*, is needed if the Torah is to be reconstituted, if it is to be vindicated.

Our final theme may be identified as the christology of the resisters. "Christology" stands here only for messianic thinking as such; no invidious comparisons are entailed. And the "resisters" are simply those Jews who fought back. The general christological/messianic significance of the Holocaust has

---

9   Elie Wiesel, *Ani Maamim: A Song Lost and Found Again*, translated by Marion Wiesel (New York: Random House, 1973), pp. 89-103.

10   A. Roy Eckardt, "Is the Holocaust Unique?" *Worldview*, XVII, 9 (September 1974), 34-35.

been obscured in a certain measure by a fixation upon death and suffering. Thus it was possible for a typological link to be more or less assumed between the Jew of Nazareth, who reputedly went as a lamb to the cross, and the Jews of the *Endlösung*, who allegedly went as lambs to the slaughter. Most Jews, obviously, had no choice but this. They were trapped. In their very death agonies the Torah was obliterated. However, the recent historiography of Yehuda Bauer, Yuri Suhl, and others has made us forcibly aware of the Jews who responded to their would-be annihilators through combat.[11] This historiography is of some aid in the formulating of a fresh christology.

We have remembered the burning of the Hungarian Jewish children at Auschwitz. Now let us recall a different kind of burning, but one that is just as constituent to the Holocaust. I refer to an event inspired by the revolt of the Warsaw Ghetto. On the second of August 1943, at the annihilation center of Treblinka, a sprinkler normally used for disinfectant had been filled with petrol. The contents were sprayed about the grounds of the camp. At a signal, hand-grenades were thrown and a great fire was soon raging. The arsenal exploded. Two hundred or more Jews managed to escape. Most of them were later captured and killed. A major objective of the revolt was to destroy the murder center. At least obliquely this aim was achieved. In October of 1943 the Germans razed the remaining parts of the camp.

I speak here only of the men who actively fought the German Nazi antichrist— not of the children and the rest who went to their doom. Who are these other Jews? Many of them are two persons in one. Here is a man who, by betraying his brothers, had lived. For he had been one of the "winners" in the competitive "race of the dead," physical endurance contests held at Treblinka and elsewhere that made his survival literally realizable through his brother's extinction. But now, through his sacrifice, others would live, would escape, would know. Only in rising against the enemy could he emerge from the absolute despair that was his for having bought his life with the lives of

---

[11] Yehuda Bauer. *They Chose Life: Jewish Resistance in the Holocaust* (New York: Institute of Human Relations, American Jewish Committee; Jerusalem: Institute of Contemporary Jewry, The Hebrew University, 1973); Yuri Suhl, editor and translator, *They Fought Back: The Story of the Jewish Resistance in Nazi Europe* (London: MacGibbon & Kee, 1968); Reuben Ainsztein, *Jewish Resistance in Nazi-Occupied Eastern Europe* (London: F. Elek, 1974).

others. (Neither of these things is to be said of Jesus of Nazareth. He did not live by having to destroy his brothers. And he did not engage, subsequently, in that act of resistance which enabled others to live.)

Messiahs retain special followers, a special apostolate. Who, in the present context, are these apostles? In the Christian tradition, the works and person of the disciple do not exactly replicate the saving function of the Christ. The disciple's cross is not the savior's cross. Yet there is always a link, an act of witnessing. Today the heirs of the Holocaust saviors are the members of the Israel Defense Forces. These men and women are not Holocaust messiahs, for they have not committed the requisite and qualifying sin of betraying their fellow Jews. Yet they remain special messianic heirs. For they carry forward the other aspect of the messianic office. They enable Israel to live.

Among its many other roles, the sovereign State of Israel remains the assenting voice, the perpetuation of the *Widerstand*, the *Résistance*. It comprises, so to say, the dowry brought to the new marriage, to the new Covenant of promise. It is the rainbow set again in the clouds. Yet the rainbow that was seen after the recession of the flood waters meant the divine remembrance of the covenant with all living creatures (Gen. 9:16). One messianic query reads: "Are you he who is to come, or are we to look for another?" (Matt. 11:3). Has a messiah come? Traditionally, the Christian answers "yes," the Jew answers "no." But the German Nazi *Endlösung* brings a partial reversal: the Jew may answer "yes "—though not, of course, a "yes" to the one from Nazareth, lest he fall prey to the cynic's definition of Christianity: that religion which teaches that the Jewish people are to turn the other cheek. And the Christian? As the poor pagan redeemed—hopefully—into the Covenant of promise (cf. Ephes. 2:12-13), the Christian has answered "yes" to the messianic query. But what is this to mean in the frame of reference of the kingdom of night? Is he or is he not a child of Israel? Is he among the company of those who act to return the Torah? Or is he a resister against that? Is his history restricted to only a part of the history of Israel, or does the Christian's history enshrine Israel's total history which is pierced by, but then prevails over, the German Nazi *Endlösung*?[12]

---

[12]   Following upon the conference at which this paper was read, the Jewish Telegraphic Agency and Herbert J. Farber Associates alleged in a news release that in my paper I personally opposed the teaching of Jewish election as a dangerous one that has led to attacks

VI

All that has been sought here is to single out the "taking back" of the Covenant, its possible recantation, and then to ask: Where? Where was it taken? To oblivion? If not to oblivion, then to what place?

There is a passage from Reinhold Niebuhr, written twenty-five years ago, that, I think, conjoins him and Elie Wiesel. It brings as well a little focus to these poor midrashim upon the phrase of that strange beggar who reaches out to us from the deep shadows of Jerusalem. "Nothing that is worth doing can be achieved in a lifetime; therefore we must be saved by hope. Nothing which is true or beautiful or good makes complete sense in any immediate context of history; therefore we must be saved by faith. Nothing we do, however virtuous, can be accomplished alone. Therefore we are saved by love."[13]

---

upon Jews. This was the only point they reported on my presentation. Anyone reading the foregoing phenomenological and pluralistic discussion will note the false and misrepresentative character of this published report.

[13] Reinhold Niebuhr, frontispiece to *Justice and Mercy*, edited by Ursula M. Niebuhr (New York: Harper & Row, 1974).

The Achievements and Trials of Interfaith

(Co-author Alice L. Eckardt; *Judaism* 27 [1978]: 318-323)

Interfaith has worked quite influentially in the United States. The Christian contribution to it has been made possible by a creative avoidance of theological absolutism on the one side, and of "liberal" universalism on the other side. Within right-wing absolutism, which presumes to possess final truth, and left-wing universalism, which negates the particularities of human life, there reside twin threats to interfaith amity. We shall elaborate upon this state of affairs.

The role of the Christian church in the interfaith movement could come about only through a transcending of certain teachings that traditionally ensured anti-Judaism and even antisemitism. Only in the measure that historic allegations of Jewish perfidy and ignorance were displaced in the church by the norms of love of neighbor and social justice, could Christians enter into interfaith relations as true partners of non-Christians. Significantly, this could occur in the measure that the high moral demands of prophetic Judaism overtook the Christian conscience. Those of us Christians who, as young people, were destined to pledge ourselves to interfaith amity now look back with grateful hearts to pastors who initiated us into the marvelous company of Amos of Tekoa, Isaiah of Jerusalem, and Jesus of Nazareth. Furthermore, the American churches—Protestant and Catholic—were markedly influenced by ideals of religious pluralism and liberal relativism, forces that counteracted Christian absolutism and triumphalism. A most effective antidote to the intolerance that has dogged historic Christianity is a democratic social order that contravenes religio-political tyranny over human beings. Fortunately, our land, despite its Christian majority, is not a Christian country in any theocratic or political sense. It is a secular-pluralist country, carrying in its Constitution and its ethos built-in protections against Christian and other forms of religious tyranny.

Theologically expressed, the above historical-moral achievements may be identified as the judgment of God upon the idolatries and sin of the very people who claim to be special representatives of his truth.

II

The attainments of interfaith contain vital lessons for today and for the future. It is no accident that right-wing Christians have played a very minor role, and often, instead, an obstructionist one, in interfaith understanding and friendship. Thus, Christian Fundamentalism comprises a major and continuing means for perpetuating anti-Jewish influences. This is not due to any calculated design; these people are as decent as anybody else. The cause of their affliction is a tenacious refusal to abandon a non-critical, literalist rendering of the New Testament. In 1936, the Nazis circulated a children's picture book featuring the watchword *"Der Vater der Juden ist der Teufel,"* the direct source of which is John 8:44. Christian Fundamentalism remains a naive but dangerous companion of Nazi ideology. Any assertion of "the divine inspiration of all Scripture," a pillar of Fundamentalism, cannot escape a proclivity to antisemitism.

Christians and Jews dedicated to intergroup amity and human justice will lament the contemporary, massive growth of "evangelical" and "born again" Christianity. This development comprises a return to the very absolutisms that the Christian interfaith movement had managed to surmount. The new "evangelicalism" is spiritual retrogression, a weighty blow to the moral advance of American religion. "Christian Yellow Pages" bigotry is the natural consequence of the exclusivist we-they mentality of "born again" religion.

In addition to its insufferably individualistic piety and its consequent failure to work out a responsible social ethic, "born again" Christianity is a relapse into fateful forms of unreason. The current turn to "evangelicalism " is part and parcel of a social irrationalism that is regnant as well in astrology, attestations of the paranormal, and the rise of neo-Nazism. Flights into unreason furnish an atmosphere out of which destructive social and political movements come. Words of Paul Kurtz, originally directed against "the new nonsense" of paranormal claims (Uri Geller *et al*) are applicable to the new Christian "evangelicalism":

There is always the danger that once irrationality grows, it will spill over into other areas. There is no guarantee that a society so infected by unreason will be resistant to...the most virulent programs of dangerous ideological sects (TIME, 12 Dec. 1977).

The spectacle, today, of thousands of Americans gathered at religious "revivals" ("Christ circuses," one dissident calls them) bears an unhappy kinship to the mass hysteria of the Nazi meetings that ended with the slaughter of Jews. Whenever religious absolutism joins forces with human unreason, the corpus of human justice is menaced.

The most we can do here is to see to it that Christian "evangelicalism"—freedom for which is, of course, warranted by the Constitution—is kept from achieving forms of political power and influence that are disastrous for freedom.

III

It is instructive to apply the moral principles of interfaith to questions of human dignity and human right.

Sometimes it is countered that "evangelical" Christianity has learned its lesson and is now rediscovering the social dimensions of faith. This asseveration is being made by "born again" apologists themselves.

The fatal difficulty is that the mating of social responsibility with religious absolutism engenders a flawed political theology. A perfect illustration is the new "Christian Zionism." True, current "evangelical" support for Israel constitutes a vital judgment against indifference among Christian "liberals" to the fate and well-being of Jewry. But the fact stands that the ideology of "Christian Zionism" is an imperialistic one (not unlike the concept behind such impossibly juxtaposed words as "Jewish Christology"). "Christian Zionism" embodies the theologizing of politics. The State of Israel is theologized into a preparation for such a religious eventuality as the "Second Coming." "Christian Zionism" is not genuinely political; that is to say, it does not, and cannot, acknowledge Jewishness on the latter's own terms. An earlier Christianity claimed that the dispersion of Jewry from its land was divine punishment. The "Christian Zionists" teach the obverse of the identical notion. To assert that the restoring of Jewish-Israeli sovereignty comprises a special act of divine grace is acceptable, to be sure, as an instance of religious-confessional celebration. But we can never permit such testimony to slide over into the political domain. The stumbling block is the necessary and just intrusion of the category of the future. For, if a political interpretation of the reconstituting of the Jewish commonwealth must be that God has moved to restore Israel today, thus revealing His mercy, it follows that the destruction of Israel tomorrow would have to be comprehended as an act of divine disfavor, one that manifests God's judgment.

The only licit non-Jewish authentication of Jewish sovereignty (or, for that matter, Jewish authentication) is an insistence upon the historical, juridical, and moral validity of Israel. Any attributing of special right, divine or other, to the State of Israel, constitutes a most fateful menace to the future of the Jewish body politic. Ironically, the theologizing of politics, whose advocates may fancy that they are fostering human dignity, constitutes, in truth, a formidable assault upon that dignity. For, in the sphere of international affairs, the natural reaction to any protagonist's claim of *divine* right, and a wholly legitimate reaction, is recourse to political sanctions and power, not excluding the waging of war, in the name of human right. In alternate terminology, the creating of the Third Jewish Commonwealth has to be demythologized of any idea of the beginnings of, or the coming of, ultimate redemption.

The foregoing argument comprises one application to the socio-political domain of the identical norms that have traditionally guided the American interfaith movement and dialogue. Each partner is possessed of equal dignity; neither is possessed of special right.

IV

Threats to interfaith amity today are hardly the monopoly of "evangelical" triumphalists. An equal threat comes from the Christian theological left—a more subtle threat, because the left so often masquerades in the name of shared social values and human cooperation (whereas many Christian rightists are at least honest enough to make plain that, since they "possess" the truth, they are under no obligation to have concourse with the unwashed and the unfaithful).

The liberal relativism that has contributed so praiseworthily to intergroup harmony is, unfortunately, counteracted by forms of "liberal" universalism, particularly within the Protestant corpus. This viewpoint is typified today by radical anti-Israeli and even antisemitic trends within the Quaker movement. Fortunately, the "Friends" do not marshall decisive political influence. The hypocrisy of some of these people is illustrated in their concern over Jewish "nationalism," but not over other relevant nationalisms. Thus, one Quaker professor asserts that Israel is to be "evaluated" and her future "determined" by her "practice or lack of practice of justice, mercy, and righteousness."[1] The revealing element in this preachment is not what is being demanded of Israel, but what is not being demanded of her foes. Evidently, policies of hostility among the Arab states toward Israel as well as toward various minorities within Arab countries, are not unjust, unmerciful, or unrighteous, and, hence, remain perfectly acceptable. That this professor should refuse to apply his Quaker-pacifist demands to the Arabs suggests that his hidden purposes are not, in fact, the fostering of peace, but, instead, the dissolution of an Israel turned into defenselessness through the implementing of his brand of "Christian" perfectionism. Significantly, his apologetic, originally appearing in a Quaker journal, has been republished by an Arab-front group, "Americans for Middle East Understanding."

The great disillusionment of Jews with the Christian community in 1967 and subsequent years has been eased somewhat by recent evidences of support and sympathy, e.g., by "Christians Concerned For Israel" and by numbers of Christian "evangelicals." These examples represent implicit and explicit opposition to Christian "liberal" universalism.

A further illustration of Christian menaces to interfaith amity, and, in light of its source, a weighty one, is a recent pronouncement by William P. Thompson, President of the National Council of Churches, who expresses total agreement with the view that the crux of the Middle East problem is the cause of the Palestinians (*The New York Times*, 4 Dec. 1977). Thompson's prejudices are made clear by his failure to include a second all-decisive issue in the Middle East: the security of the State of Israel. This latest judgment from an NCCC official is simply one more in a long series from that ecumenical agency, expressed positions that have done a great deal to jeopardize Christian-Jewish friendship.

---

[1]   Calvin Keene, "Prophecy and Modern Israel," *The Link* 10 (Summer 1977): 1-3.

V

A special lesson of the Nazi Holocaust, particularly for Jews, just as, one would hope, for perfectionist Christians, is that without group security and political power, a people will sooner or later be dead. This realization has itself helped Jews get over a certain minority outlook of "by-your-leave." Bernice S. Tannenbaum, President of Hadassah, recently spoke for all Jews (and all Americans) when she wrote:

> As free people living in a free country, we take directives from no one. When we react, we do so out of shared priorities and common destiny, not at the   behest of any government, including that of Israel. Independence also   means independence from rote subservience to whichever administration happens to occupy the White House at a given time (*The New York Times*, 13 Nov. 1977).

The Jewish community in our land is learning that, if competing and conflicting self-interest is integral to the American ethos itself, there is no moral justification whatsoever for forbidding Jewish forms of self-interest while condoning other forms. This principle applies as much within interfaith encounters as anywhere else.

Some Jewish leaders may have been troubled by the lack of interest of many Jews in interfaith. They reason that this condition reflects a withdrawal, an inward-looking trend that is not good for the future of Diaspora Jewry. To the extent that the new independence of Jewry reflects a collective "coming of age," this subjectivist development is not to be lamented. However, in the Holocaust it became evident that intimate relationships between Jews and Gentiles (Christian or non-believing) were a precondition of protests on behalf of Jews and of self-sacrificing endeavors to save them. Separation and non-communication of Jews and non-Jews do nothing to challenge attitudes among the latter. Today, contacts with the non-Jewish community may often be painful for Jews, and one can understand and sympathize with decisions to draw back. But is it in the ultimate welfare of Jews to do so? To whom does one turn in the event of trouble and possible persecution?

The Holocaust, originally an unspeakable trauma for Jews vis-à-vis the Christian world, is today a subject of shared concern, interest, and study within interfaith circles. In June of 1976, the Board of Homeland Ministries of the American Baptist Churches agreed that its congregations ought to observe the Day of Remembrance of the Holocaust (*Yom ha-Shoah*); it now appears on all American Baptist church calendars.

Conferences on the Holocaust and university courses on that subject can have a powerful impact upon human attitudes and motivations. It is essential that these efforts not ignore the Christian contribution to, and complicity in, the "Final Solution." It is equally essential that they not overlook Christian efforts to make amends, including revolutionary trends within contemporary Christian thinking.

Out of a penitent recognition of the destructive power of the church's "teaching of contempt" (Jules Isaac), numbers of thinkers are giving themselves to a radical reform of Christian doctrine. A major thrust of the new thinking is the identifying of the Christian community as adopted brothers and sisters within the Jewish-Israel family, the total opposite of traditional Christian supersessionism and triumphalism.

VI

We cannot overestimate the spiritual and moral benefits that Christians receive from ties to Jewry. Of infinite value for Christians is the weaving together of life and faith on the part of the Jewish community, an achievement that many Christians are found to welcome with a kind of unbelieving joy. It is most essential for Christians to be reminded that human ideas concerning God need not be an obstacle to moral obligations. This they are often enabled to see through their association with Jews. The sense of community, so fundamental to Jewishness, involves an especially valuable lesson, both in its own right and as a means of counteracting Christian individualistic piety.

All in all, the American interfaith movement of late years has gained a maturity that carries it far beyond the platitude and the pious gesture; today we have become much more ready to come to terms, candidly and reflectively, with the forces and pressures that divide us, but, also, with those that unite us.

An insistence upon the divine judgment on all human claims to truth, and a declaration of the legitimacy of discrete collective entities as elements in the good creation of God, comprise the very soul of interfaith endeavor. Here we discern part of the greatness of the American "experiment" and, indeed, something of the peculiar contribution of this country to human solidarity. This way of believing and behaving rests, in turn, upon certain religious foundations, including, especially, prophetic Judaism and a Christianity that, against its own idolatrous absolutisms, has somehow succeeded in carrying forward that prophetism.

The achievements and the trials of interfaith are beautifully summed up in an injunction of the Kotzker Rov: "Worry about your own soul and the next person's body, and not the reverse."

Toward a Secular Theology of Israel

(In *Religion in Life*, XLVIII, 4 [1979]: 462-473)

Where, if anywhere, is to be found the authentication of the State of Israel? Much of the long and intense debate over Zionism within Christian and Jewish circles has focused upon this issue. From a rational or morally even-handed point of view, the question today is ludicrous. No such query is posed concerning the sovereignty of Iran or Egypt, Nigeria or Uruguay, Jordan or Lebanon, India or the United States—or even concerning the legitimacy of the regimes in these countries. This fact does not, regrettably, quash the ongoing conflict over Israeli legitimation. The intrusion of a double standard between Israel and other national sovereignties[1] suggests that any discussion of the foundations of Israeli autonomy is a peculiarly negative concession to human intransigence rather than a positive celebration of human attainment. But this state of affairs makes all the more obligatory careful assessments of the debate and a decision on one side or the other.

The question of the Zionist claim may be approached by considering various denials of the integrity of Israel as a political reality, denials that either question Israel's existence in principle or support her on grounds that prove indefensible. For present purposes, two such negations are given attention. It is from opposite directions that these views converge upon our subject. They are alike formidable, for each sustains a certain plausibility and appeal.

I

One position is associated with the Christian theological left. There is the phenomenon called "liberal"-universalism. Quotation marks are used in order to avoid confusion with genuine forms of liberalism. Within authentic liberalism the demands of a "liberal"-universalism are not visited upon Jews, since Jewry

---

1   Within Christian circles this double standard appears as a psycho-theological carryover of the persuasion that the Jews, having been rejected by God for their unfaith, are condemned to endless wandering without a country of their own.

is there fully enabled to make its own decisions respecting the meaning of Jewishness. But Christian representatives of a "liberal"-universalist viewpoint set the universalist possibilities of faith in severe judgment upon the reputed temptations and evils of Jewish particularity. The modern roots of this outlook lie in the Enlightenment, in that opposition to nationalism which denominates "humanity" as its center of value. Nationalism is regarded as the single, most powerful foe of universal, "spiritual" norms. National identity is regarded as a barrier to ideal human relationships, a barrier that a truly enlightened people of God will transcend.[2]

The attraction of this position lies in the honor it gives to the anti-parochial reaches of human moral achievement. As a matter of fact, the modern history of Judaism itself has not been entirely free of the "liberal"-universalist gospel. Thus, in one period the Reform movement was forcibly anti-Zionist, precisely on the ground that the Jewish people are emancipated, or ought to be, from all nationalist enticements. Jewish laic[3] and historic particularity was annulled in principle. Jewishness was assimilated to a form of religiousness: Jewish identity was reduced to adherence to the religion called Judaism. It was only through bitter practical experience at the hands of antisemites and non-Jewish anti-Zionists that Reform leadership was driven to recognize that there is much more to Jewishness than religiousness, and that universalistic moral and spiritual norms, when not fleshed out in the particularities of existence, comprise a menace to human life itself. "Citizens of the world" are inevitably subversive of legitimate human-collective needs and values. Particularity is the *sine qua non* of universality. The alternative is fascist and totalitarian homogeneity, where the "parts" of a human collectivity are subjugated and even destroyed for the sake of the "whole." The very survival of the religion of Judaism, a faith that boasts many universalist aspects, is threatened whenever provision is

---

[2]   A. Roy Eckardt, "Theological Implications of the State of Israel: The Protestant View, "*1974 Yearbook of the Encyclopaedia Judaica* (Jerusalem), pp. 161-62.

[3]   The concept "laic" is a proposed replacement for "ethnic" in characterizing the overall reality of the Jewish people. "Ethnic" is rather too narrow. "Laic" is the adjectival form of *laos* (peopleness). Strictly, "laic" means "lay" or "secular." But this very usage is applicable to Judaism as a whole, which is a lay religion, without priests or clergy. Even more significantly, the Jewish *laos* is totally secular in an all-decisive respect: a people wholly of this world (*saeculum*) is involved. Cf. James Parkes's conceptualization of the Jewish people as a "natural community," in, among many references, *Prelude to Dialogue* (London: Vallentine, Mitchell, 1969), p. 193.

lacking for the secular-laic identity of Jews. Fittingly, the Jewish community in its entirety has long since repudiated false universalism. (It is a delightful irony that today every candidate for the American Reform rabbinate is asked to spend a year of her or his studies in Jerusalem.)

In the Christian camp the form of anti-Zionism and anti-Israelism that stems from leftist or "liberal" sources has behind it an influential tradition.[4] According to that tradition, the great moral heritage of the "Old Testament" prophets is held to be violated whenever and wherever "nationalism" becomes regnant. No form of idolatry is more serious or more destructive than that deriving from nationalistic pretensions. However, it is essential to keep before us that while Christian "liberal"-universalism views itself as emancipated from narrow interests, in truth it bears within itself the antithesis of its own moral norm. For when we turn to the real conflicts of human life, the universalist norm is very often revealed as "mere ideology" (in the Marxist sense): moral ideas and ideals are captured by collective self-interest. In a great many cases it is the custodians of preponderant power who have been preaching to the powerless the evils of nationalism. Such counsel becomes, in effect, an instrumentality for depriving the afflicted and the weak of equality and justice.

The ideology of "liberal"-universalism remains as a foremost contemporary influence within left-of-center Protestantism (in some contrast to Roman Catholicism) in perpetuating negativistic thought and behavior toward Jewry as a fully laic reality. One Quaker teacher recently wrote that the State of Israel is to be "evaluated" and her future "determined" by her "practice or lack of practice of justice, mercy, and righteousness."[5] The telling fact in the professor's preachment was not what he sought to demand of Israel but rather what he failed to demand of her foes. The truth that so often only Jewish "nationalism" is singled out for reproof, but not the national interests and politicidal designs of Israel's enemies, indicates that the real motivation cannot be a pure moral judgment against nationalism as such, but rather the taking of an adversary stance vis-à-vis the Jewish people. Thus, the nationalist claims of

---

4   There are full documented reminders of this judgement in Hertzel Fishman's *American Protestantism and a Jewish State* (Detroit: Wayne State University Press, 1973).

5   Calvin Keene, "Prophecy and Modern Israel," *The Link*, x, 3 (1977), 1-3.

the Palestinian Arabs are celebrated, or at least readily conceded, rather than being called to reckoning by universalist standards.

If "liberal"-universalism is easily assimilated to the service of less-than-universal causes, its primary import, in the context of this analysis, is its betrayal of the Jews as a historic particular people. Yet we cannot evade the truth within its warning against nationalist idolatries. In consideration of the challenge of "liberal"-universalism, the question with which we began is changed to read, Is there an authentication of the State of Israel that does not threaten the rights of non-Jews?

II

From within the Christian right we are met by a point of view that appears, at first blush, to have consequences quite different from those of "liberal"-universalism. For now, in place of criticism or even outright rejection of the Jewish national cause, we hear expressions of great sympathy for and solidarity with Israel.

Reference is made to Christian Zionism, a position variously found among conservative Christians, including especially those of an "evangelical"[6] and fundamentalist bent. Christian Zionists as a group are distinguished by an insistence that the return of the Jewish People to Zion is to be comprehended in positive theological terms. The establishing of the Third Jewish Commonwealth is a special work of God, a sublime act constitutive to the very process of divine salvation (*Heilsgeschichte*).

Christian Zionist ideology takes two alternate forms: a surrogate religious apologetic for Israel and an assimilating of Jewish historical fortunes to the Christian imperium.

In the one version the will of God is insinuated unqualifiedly into the political process, although without any necessary insistence upon Christological sanctions. An example is Evangelicals United for Zion, which through its organ *Perception* and other means seeks "to stimulate real interrelation between the Evangelical Christian and Jewish communities based upon a biblical bond of

---

[6]　The quote marks reflect a double consideration: it is the group under discussion that calls itself "evangelical"; yet many Christians oppose this group's version of the gospel (evangel) and hence its preempting of the term "evangelical."

love for God's land and His people, Israel."[7] Insofar as "evangelicals" perpetuate the reputed promise of God that Abraham and his children's children are to inherit *Eretz Yisrael*, they naturally incline to sustain the socio-political cause of Israel. (This point of view parallels in some degree right-wing religious Zionism among Jews, as typified in the intractable *Gush Emunim* for a greater Israel.[8])

The other form of Christian Zionism focuses upon Christology. The return of the Jews to their land is construed instrumentally, in accordance with certain alleged timetables of heaven. The renewal of Israel becomes part of a divinely scheduled preparation for the Parousia, the return of Christ in glory. Carl F. H. Henry told a recent Conference on Biblical Prophecy meeting in Jerusalem: "We live already in the last days because of the Resurrection of the Crucified One. The dramatic and unmistakable message of the New Testament is that the very last of those days is soon to break upon us."[9] The reestablishment of Israel in 1948 is often treated as proof that the Parousia is imminent. Sometimes the transpiring of the latter event is held to make possible the Jewish acceptance of Christ. An article in the "evangelical" monthly *Eternity* contends that if God has indeed acted to resettle the sons of Isaac in *Eretz Yisrael*, the sons of Ishmael (the Muslims) can scarcely be expected to dislodge them. The writer goes on to attest that although the Jews have not returned to the Land "in faith," tomorrow they will "look upon Him whom they pierced," and the entire nation of Israel "will be converted in a day."[10]

The appeal of Christian Zionism derives from its refusal to exclude God's active will from the common life. Here is embodied a vital judgment against those Christians who either remain indifferent to the collective fate of Jews or are positively hostile to Zionism and the State of Israel. Christian Zionism's support of Israel constitutes a practical denial of the error of "liberal"-

---

[7]   *Perception*, October 1978, p. 4.

[8]   Right-wing Jewish Orthodoxy is not necessarily Zionist. The *Neturei Karta* are an ultrareligious yet militantly anti-Zionist sect—and they live, strikingly enough, within the State of Israel (the Mea Shearim section of Jerusalem).

[9]   As quoted in *Newsweek*, June 28, 1971, p. 62.

[10]   *Eternity*, July, 1967, as cited in Solomon S. Bernards, "The Arab-Israel Crisis and the American Christian Response," *The Lutheran Quarterly*, August, 1968, p. 272.

universalism with its inordinate "spiritual" demands. But the "liberal"-universalist concentration upon the moral perils in nationalist dedication points, functionally speaking, to an equally serious fault within Christian Zionism.

The overall trespass of Christian Zionism in either of its forms is its theologizing of the political order.[11] This has several paradoxical effects, all of which are baneful. The foremost of these is an unintended eroding of Israel's collective integrity. Scattered all through the Christian tradition is the claim that the fall of Jerusalem and the "dispersion" of the Jewish people comprise a judgment of God upon an unbelieving Israel. Now along come the Christian Zionists to hold for the opposite side of the identical coin. They proclaim that the contemporary return of the Jews to their land is a special sign of God's mercy and even a disclosure of his own intimate and singular plans. But these fabricators of God's mercy have entangled themselves in the same game played by the historicizers of God's judgment. Both parties misappropriate the events of history. The implication is as ominous as it is obvious: Israel's physical destruction tomorrow would have to be treated as a sign of God's returning wrath. This is the kind of predicament we arrange for ourselves whenever we practice the heresy of fancying that the events of history can contribute to or exemplify the truths of faith—the very opposite of the biblical teaching that it is the Lord of history who assigns his own final meanings to the exigencies of time and place.

Another consequence of Christian Zionism is its exacerbating of human strife. As James M. Wall writes, "The use of religious validation to settle secular conflicts is a misuse of religion and a disservice to politics."[12] One quite logical counter to the claim that Yahweh once gave Palestine to the Jews in perpetuity is the protestation that Allah has since awarded the land to his true people the Muslims, as embodied today through the great majority within the Arab nation. The Muslim rejoinder is not unlike the traditional anti-Jewish

---

[11]   Not all Christian Zionists do this. Thus, Dr. G. Douglas Young, director of Bridges for Peace and former president of the American Institute of Holy Land Studies in Jerusalem, is an exceptional evangelical Christian whose dedication to Israel is through-and-through political. Young has grasped the meaning of a Christian secular theology of Israel. This is made clear in his serial *Dispatch from Jerusalem.*

[12]James M.Wall, "Israel and the Evangelicals" (Editorial Comment), *The Christian Century*, November 23, 1977, p. 1083. This editorial marshalls devastating criticisms of the Christian Zionist handling of the Middle East conflict.

affirmation within the Christian church that the "new covenant" fulfills and replaces the "old covenant." A chronologized theology has little choice but to award the medal of victory to the Muslims (over Christians as well as Jews) for having come in last. Last is best. Such theologizing constitutes, of course, a political *reductio ad absurdum*. The expectable reaction to its Muslim version on the part of the Israelis has naturally been to fight. However, the pragmatic-theological and psycho-theological advantage must fall to the Muslims, because the Jews do not possess a counterpart to the *jihad* (religious war) of the *Qur'an*. As for the Christians of the Near Orient, the future of their communities amongst 150 million Muslims is, like the future of the Jews, most problematic.

An equally serious consequence of Christian Zionism's assimilating of the political world to the assertions of faith is its paradoxical undermining of the integrity and credibility of the religious order. True religion functions as a pointer to the transcendent and mysterious ways of God. "For my thoughts are not your thoughts, neither are your ways my ways, says the Lord" (Isa. 55:8). In Christian Zionism the thoughts and ways of God are massively domesticated—a procedure that is properly reserved for human life with cats and cows. Various parties, Jewish or Christian, may continue to believe that the establishing of the Third Jewish Commonwealth brings special evidence of God's grace and indeed contains the seeds of ultimate redemption. Such testimony may be listened to as an instance of strictly confessional celebration. I do not question the insistence upon God's presence within the common life. But it is one thing to glimpse, in a wholly existential way and as through a glass darkly, the hand of God within the happenings of history, and quite something else to mobilize that witness of faith (hope?) for apologetic or polemic purposes, to the ultimate end of theocratizing a political structure. The *Deutsche Christen* of the Nazi era politicized their theology; the Christian Zionists of today theologize their politics. The result is the same: the integrity of the religious order is undercut.

The identical effect occurs through the very insistence upon a religiously absolutist rendering of Israel's right-to-be. Once God is made into a weapon of geopolitical claims, the opposition is furnished with an excuse to cry "Idolatry!"—and this reaction is not unjustified.

We are advised that right-wing Protestantism is at last coming to honor the moral obligations first made vital to some of us by the Christian "social gospel."

If the "evangelical" position on the politics of the Middle East is any harbinger, "evangelicalism" would be better advised to go home to its "pure gospel." Christian Zionism is a perfect case of the way in which the combining of social action with the dictates of religious absolutism engenders a flawed political theology.

Despite all their seeming disparity "liberal"-universalism and Christian Zionism are conjoined by a failure to provide responsible political counsel. For significantly, it is not only the Christian right but also the "liberal" left that theologizes the political order—the one by imperializing the particularities of human affairs, the other by nullifying them. The "evangelicals" coerce Israel into becoming *a political church*, a theocratic tool. The "liberals" force Jewish integrity onto the Procrustean bed of *an apolitical church*, a strictly "spiritual" entity. In both instances the Jews are forbidden to be what they are, a laic reality with all the limited rights of any collectivity of this world. Thus is the authentication of Israel menaced from two different directions.

III

Our question now becomes: How are the elements of truth in the "liberal"-universalist and Christian Zionist positions to be honored as at the same time we avoid their temptations? The answer to this question is grounded, generically speaking, within a secular form of theology, i.e., a theology oriented to this world, the human order. To force convictions of faith upon the political domain is only to cut the ground from under Israel's real legitimation and to assault, unwittingly, Jewish collective life.

Several points are offered, as a means of bringing out the position behind the foregoing critiques.

1. The particularity of Israel is to be comprehended within the "orders of creation" (*Schöpfungsordnungen*), or at the least as "emergency orders" (*Notordnungen*). Emil Brunner identifies the orders as ways in which the will of God meets us, even if only in fragmentary and indirect fashion.[13] These orders extend to the family, economic life and labor, the community of culture, the law, and the nation-state. Helmut Thielicke utilizes the phrase "emergency

---

[13]Emil Brunner, *The Divine Imperative* (New York: Macmillan, 1942), p. 291.

orders," and thus speaks more cautiously than Brunner. The orders provide "physical spheres of existence" that help protect men in a fallen world. They are orders of "preservation."[14]

An application of Brunner's reasoning is that "liberal"-universalism has ranged itself against the very nature of the divine creation. In ruling out Jewish sovereignty, the "liberals" reject one incarnation of the ways of God with men. An application of Thielicke's reasoning is that discrete peoples must have political sovereignty if they are to have needed protection against the will-to-power of others. This need applies especially to small peoples. "Liberal"-universalism thus represents a threat to human beings within our far-from-perfect world. But Christian Zionism incorrectly concentrates upon Israel, to the tacit exclusion of a concerned policy respecting other peoples and nations. The linking of the nation-state to the protective authorization of God is not an argument for Israel *qua* Israel; yet, unless we fall into a double standard, the right of Jewish sovereignty is seen as one instance of a universal right.

2. Within the real world, i. e., the world of political relations, the legitimation of the State of Israel is a matter of the historic rights of the Jewish people within the larger area known as Palestine. (The original British Mandate of Palestine extended through present-day Jordan; Israel today possesses only 25 percent of that area. Of equal significance, the majority of the population of Jordan today are Palestinians.) Objectively speaking, the historic rights of Jews match, and in many comparisons surpass, the claims of any sovereignty in the world. Emphasis here falls upon the unbroken residency of the Jews in the land for more than three thousand years, a residency that was finally acknowledged, in a power-political sense, by the international community of nations in 1947.

The historical and moral attainments of men are not contradictory of attestations to the will of God—provided that God is understood in humanizing, creative, and providential terms. This principle applies everywhere. Thus, one tenable rejoinder to a possible allegation that "our" country really belongs to the Indians and ought to be "given back" to them is that such a demand does not take into account the "white man's" stewardship of the land over a considerable period of time. This is not in any way to ignore our terrible treatment of the Native Americans or the need for continuing acts of justice in behalf of these

---

[14]Helmut Thielicke, *Theological Ethics*, I (Philadelphia: Fortress Press, 1966), pp. 276, 439-40.

people. The state of affairs within Palestine is a comparable one. Israel's stewardship of the land easily meets that of the United States. This stewardship extends to the developing of a democratic social order that contravenes various forms of tyranny, including religio-political forms.

3. Every argument for Israel's historic and moral rights is an argument for the independence of the Palestinian Arabs. The United Nations' acknowledgment in 1947 of the Jewish claim was restricted, of course, to part of a division of that section of Palestine lying west of the Jordan River, with a Palestinian Arab polity being equally recognized. Significantly, the admission of Israel to the United Nations in 1949 was consummated quite independently of the Arabs' reaction to the UN decision. Israeli sovereignty was acknowledged in a way not at all conditional upon the Arab response to the Plan of Partition. Thus, the Jewish historical and moral claim was capped by a fresh juridical factor at the international level.

The lingering tragedy of the Middle East is that the Arab side refused the United Nations' partition. For as the Peel Commission of a decade earlier had reported, here was a clear case of "a conflict of right with right." It is sometimes contended that by their rejection of the 1947 partition, the Palestinian Arabs forfeited their claim to the land. Since the refusal was not grounded in a democratic plebiscite, this argument is not easy to sustain. However, the moral validity and practical workability of a given act of geographical partition depends wholly upon the readiness of each primary party to acknowledge the other's legitimacy. The question of such mutuality continues as the single foundational issue in the Middle East conflict.

4. The desacralizing of political claims is an essential of peace among nations, because this helps to temper the imperious pretensions and uncompromising character of theological asseveration. This is especially a problem in the Middle East where religion remains a massive, ever-increasing obstacle to a final settlement. The line goes: We are simply obeying the divine will and decree. How dare you charge us with selfish interests! In contrast to this unyielding posture, the essence of politico-secular procedures is the art of compromise.

5. The character of the Christian-Jewish relationship, normatively considered, is such that the Christian position on Zionism and the State of Israel is enabled to pattern itself upon the prevailing Jewish position. Support for a

Jewish state would hardly be distinctively Christian were it limited to humanitarian grounds or purely politico-moral justifications.

Were it so that the Christian church has now supplanted the Jewish nation as the elect people of God, the concept "Israel" would thereby refer to a "spiritual community" rather than a laic reality. The very idea of political sovereignty for God's people would be not only proscribed but emptied of all meaning. But a wholly different persuasion is open to us: The Covenant of God with the Jewish people, original Israel, is not broken, and cannot be broken because God does not renege on his promises (Gen. 17:13, 19; Lev. 24:8; II Sam. 23:5; I Chron. 16:17; Ezek. 37:26; etc.). Indeed, Christians, those erstwhile pagans, have been made "fellow-citizens" with God's people (Eph. 2:19). The Christian church consists of those who have been "grafted in" to the tree of salvation which is Israel (Rom. 11:17). The Christian community is composed of those human beings who have been permitted to become, in Krister Stendahl's phrase, a "peculiar kind of Jew."[15] We have been joined to that Israel which is the potential humanizer of all her children. Accordingly, any attempt within the church to cancel out the special divine relation with Israel may be seen as "theologically self-annihilative for the Christian community itself."[16] (Part of the contribution of Christian Zionism is its insistence upon the peculiar and ineluctable relationship that Christians have with Jews.)

It follows from the above that the question of Zionism and Israel ought to be raised and answered by Christians as younger brothers and sisters in the same manner as it is raised and answered by Jews as elder brothers and sisters. And it is exactly here that we encounter a remarkable thing, of supreme moment for the entire challenge of a secular theology. When Christians turn for guidance to their elders in the faith, they quickly learn that the dominant Jewish persuasion is such that it avoids the very kinds of theologizing we have ourselves criticized. For the great majority of Jews do not take refuge in "religious arguments" for the Third Jewish Commonwealth but instead seek to

---

[15]Krister Stendahl, "Judaism and Christianity II—After a Colloquium and a War," *Harvard Divinity Bulletin* (New Series), I (1967), 5.

[16]A. Roy Eckardt, "Theological Implications," p. 160. The interpretation of the Christian-Jewish relationship here sketched is treated intensively in two volumes by the present author: *Elder and Younger Brothers* (New York: Schocken, 1973) and *Your People, My People* (New York: Quadrangle/New York Times, 1974).

live out their lives for the sake of the responsibilities of this world. And an even more remarkable thing is that most Israelis seek neither solace nor direction in theologization—they who are passing their days within the gates of Zion itself! It is a wondrous paradox that the new Israel of the Middle East should itself be an increasingly secular reality. How infelicitous it is then—no, how wrongheaded—when Christian spokesmen keep on trying to religionize Israel. It is most noteworthy that the main trunk of the tree of Israel, as it lives and grows today, bends neither to the theological left nor to the theological right.

The most remarkable element of all is the Jewish and Israeli transcendence of the theological absolutism that divides human beings from one another. The dominating Israeli-Jewish rationale for the existence of Israel is a secular-political one. This becomes quite evident to any who have resided, as I have, in Israel. Fortunately for the Israelis, as for the well-being of their Arab neighbors, the theologization of Israel from within the country itself remains a minority exercise, and it is effectively kept under public control. The last thing most Israelis would tolerate is a theocracy. Out of much bitter history these people know that the nation-state is anything but a law unto itself. Political sovereignties are subject to the universal norms of justice. Were this not insisted upon, we should find ourselves subject to the error of the Christian Zionists. A genuinely secular theology will never sanction more than relative and partial claims to political autonomy.

To express the matter in categories of theological challenge, How could we ever sanction a split between the being of God and the creation of God? The most perennial and influential of all Christian temptations is to return to the old paganism, that fateful polytheism which keeps company with the Marcionites. What is the political meaning of the *shema*? Herein lies the ultimate question of Zionism. The remedy to all dichotomous theologies is found in that majestic confession of Judaism: "Hear, O Israel, the Lord our God, the Lord is One." The only true universalism is one that moves dialectically between the unity of the one God and the integral particularities of his creation. Because God is one, the concept of secular theology is not only meaningful but obligatory, a requirement laid upon us all. In Zionism and the State of Israel the world of God and the world of human politics are endeavoring to converge—a paradigm for humanity as a family.

6. Having suggested several pathways toward a secular theology of Israel, I have to offer a qualifying point, lest the above proposals assume the countenance of perfectionism.

The relation of the religious and political orders will continue to manifest varying degrees of tension. This fact may be viewed both positively and negatively —positively in that each of the sides is possessed of integrity; negatively in that each side is conditioned by the demands of the other. From a theological viewpoint, judgment must be rendered against any political order that absolutizes itself or its claims, idolatrously equating itself with God. From a political standpoint, judgment must be levied against the spiritualizing of the people of God, whereby the wardrobe of their "whole armor" is limited to truth, righteousness, and faith (Eph. 6:11-17) and does not include tanks, guns, and bombs. Eugene B. Borowitz counteracts all such spiritualization: The equating of justice and love, particularly *agape* (as in the thinking of Joseph Fletcher), means that the laying down of my life permits you to "continue in your sinfulness. The appeal of such a doctrine of love to all exploiters and oppressors of the weak is a commonplace of social and historical analysis." This is why "justice looms so large" in the biblical prophets[17]—justice as the *weapon* of love, never to be confused with love itself.

There is within this world no ultimate peace, no final resolution of human conflict, no end to the struggle between moral claims and human will-to-power, and hence no wholly consummated marriage (*basar*, one flesh) of the sacred and the profane. The persistence of the duality of religion and politics is itself a reminder of this. The very fact that the reestablished Jewish Commonwealth of today has not dispelled an untidy dualism of religiousness and the state helps to underscore the point. This dualism is found in every human collectivity—Christian, Muslim, *et al.*

The seer John finds no Temple in the heavenly Jerusalem because there and then God will be all-in-all (Rev. 21:22). Only in that transcendent time and place will the separating categories of life be obliterated, for that is the Day of the Messiah. A secularizing theology is a needed corrective to such enticements as we have here reviewed and criticized. But it does not put an end to enticement as such, for to hope in that fashion would itself be to ignore the

---

[17]Eugene B. Borowitz, "On the New Morality," *Judaism* XV (1966), 333.

tension of the two orders. The men of Caesar and the King of the universe do not march to the one drummer.

In sum, while the movement toward a secular theology of Israel may manage to become an obligation within our human journey, pointing to the ultimate norms and hopes of faith, a fully realized secular theology of Israel is not possible. Abraham and his children's children must abide in their search for the secular city "whose builder and maker is God" (cf. Heb. 11:10).

In Memoriam James Parkes, 1896-1981

(*Journal of Ecumenical Studies* 19 [Winter 1982]: 97-104)

Two prevailing memories I have of James Parkes involve spirits, though in rather different forms. I still see him, as of the third weekend in August 1963, captivating our children Paula and Steve with tales of a mischievous "impersonating Elemental" that dwelt in his boyhood homestead on Guernsey, still among the more Norman of the Channel Islands. (Read for yourself Parkes's account of "The Bungalow Ghost" in his autobiography, *Voyage of Discoveries.*) Heir to a venerable if whimsical line of persuasion, Parkes adhered to strictly empirical data—compounded, one is tempted to interject, by the marvelous fogs of Britain— to become an *orateur,* though always a chary one, for that elusive *coterie* known as ghosts. My other memory is of the expression that would light up James's handsome face when he poured the wine at dinner. His beaming in so artless a way was made possible by a standing order he had worked out with a London merchant, who agreed to keep his *clientèle* supplied with very good French wines at no higher than "seven and six" per bottle. (In those years that cost was anything but the *boutade* it would be today.)

Parkes's mother died while he was still a boy, following a long illness that left his father very poor. His brother and sister were both killed in the First Great War. He was himself gassed severely while serving as an infantry officer on the Ypres Salient. Physicians who afterwards attended him doubted that he would live out his twenties. He was eventually to be reduced, due to a "Depuytren's Contracture," to typing entire manuscripts with a pencil end held in a hand he could not unclench. Yet Parkes was well on his way to eighty-five when he died at Bournemouth on 6 August 1981. I once dared remark to him that I had recently been laid low by a coronary. He sniffed, and responded, "Oh I've had several of *those!*"

An individual of genius and of far-ranging interests, Parkes painted with marked creativity, and he knew the history of architecture and how to fabricate tapestries as well as he knew religious history and theology. It was as a boy of twelve or thirteen that he began to develop a marked interest in theology, politics, and history, all in their interrelatedness. His sense of humor was "something else." Back in 1933 he produced a handbook titled *International Conferences*, which contained the decree, "For the purposes of a conference, all museums are the same museum, all Gothic churches are the same Gothic church, all castles are the same castle, all palaces are the same palace."

For his Columbia University-Union Theological Seminary doctorate Robert A. Everett prepared a dissertation on Parkes's life and thought. When the student's mentors-to-be wondered aloud whether Parkes had actually "written enough" to qualify as a thesis subject, Everett could call attention, with more than a little scorn, to the master's list of publications totaling 329 entries by the year 1977.

II

A great man has left us. Contra the chronic ignorance, near and far, of his legacy, James Parkes remains the preeminent historian-prophet of the Christian-and-Jewish worlds. (The hyphens are of the essence here.) Beginning in the year 1925, through his professional work in several student organizations, Parkes was appalled by the regnant antisemitism of Christians and others throughout Europe. The consequence was his determination to give himself to study and resolution of what was then known (with built-in shamefulness) as the Jewish problem. His first book, *The Jew and His Neighbour*, appeared in 1930. Lest his developing and controversial reputation within that area needlessly compromise his endeavors beyond it, he fashioned the *nom de plume* John Hadham, under whose identity he wrote many volumes of a different genre, popular works in Christianity. (The surname was inspired by love for the Hadham villages of Hertfordshire. Even had the villages been ugly, who would not be beguiled by such an appellation as Much Hadham?) The first of the Hadham books was *Good God* (1940), the universalist and perfectionist soteriology of which so antagonized the Student Christian Movement Press that they rejected the manuscript, but the work went on to sell over 100,000 copies under the Penguin imprint. The one man was to become two best-selling authors. (His fiancée demanded, and received, two engagement rings, one from James, the other from John.)

Parkes read in five languages; his books have been translated into seven. The other major works in his primary subject include *The Conflict of the Church and the Synagogue: A Study in the Origins of Antisemitism*, 1961 [1934]; *End of An Exile: Israel, the Jews and the Gentile World*, 1954; *The Foundations of Judaism and Christianity*, 1960; *A History of the Jewish People*, 1963; *Antisemitism*, 1964; and *Whose Land: A History of the Peoples of Palestine*, 1971. Much of his writing involved him in the case for, and the meaning of, a Jewish state. He became deeply involved in the question of Zionism and the Zionist cause.

The contribution of James Parkes to your life and mine has come out of his pioneering, singular, and unrelenting warfare against the antisemitisms of the Christian (and, subsequently, non-Christian) world and in behalf of the God-given, abiding integrity of Judaism and the Jewish people. Parkes saw well that antisemitism has little, if anything, to do with Jews; it is a Gentile problem from beginning to end. (Appropriately, he was honored with an assassination attempt by the official Nazi *Antisemitische Weltdienst* when he resided in Geneva.) A whole generation ahead of almost everybody else on these vital issues, Parkes was no reductionist or cushy latitudinarian when it came to church doctrine. An Anglican priest (as well as an Oxford Ph.D.), he always thought of himself as an orthodox Christian, but he kept nourishing and redeeming his orthodoxy through the resources of biblical-prophetic judgment and praxis. (Here is one explanation among several of why he always found Karl Barth's views so perverse and "abominably heretical.") During the Nazi horror, Parkes, at his rambling home/library in Barley, Royston, Herts., gave shelter to so many Jewish and other refugees, including numbers of children, that at one point there was scarcely room for him to sleep. In later years he was to resolve that a right Christian witness dictated his absence from church during Holy Week upon the eminently moral/ logical ground that that is the time when, *à outrance,* unholy things (viz., untruths) are uttered and acted out respecting the Jewish people and Judaism.

Parkes's watchword from the start to the finish of his career was: You cannot build good theology upon bad (i.e., false) history. For centuries Christian scholarship and church teaching had been disseminating a massively false but world-determining "history," born from the twin allegations that "the Jews" were guilty of deicide and that the Judaism of Jesus' time was already *spät Judentum,* a dying, even malignant thing, corrupted by inhuman legalism and rife with hopelessness. James Parkes stood in the vanguard of those who identified this entire ideology for the terrible calumny it was—and is.

On Parkes's selfsame watchword, good Christian teaching has to be relentlessly truthful concerning the actual history/life of the churches. In an address to the London Society of Jews and Christians, Parkes observed that the hatred and denigration of Jews and Judaism

> have a quite clear and precise historical origin. They arise from Christian   preaching and teaching from the time of the bitter controversies of the first century in which the two religions separated from each other. From that time up to today there has been an unbroken line which culminates in the massacre...of six million Jews. The fact that the action of Hitler and his henchmen was not really motivated by Christian sentiments, the fact that mingled with the ashes of murdered Jews are the ashes of German soldiers who refused to obey orders when they found what those orders were, the fact that churches protested and that Christians risked their lives to save Jews—all these facts come into the picture, but unhappily they do not invalidate the basic statement that antisemitism from the first century to the twentieth is a Christian creation and a Christian responsibility, whatever secondary causes may come into the picture.

How many future Christian clergy and teachers of my generation ever heard a word about any of this from their own ministers and teachers? I never did, through all the years of "liberal" divinity school and "liberal" graduate school courses—until at last Reinhold Niebuhr rescued me and enabled me to uncover the facts for myself. Of course, Parkes has not been the only scholar (Christian or Jewish) or decent/devout church leader to point to the sin-ridden realities of church history. But the historic and all-decisive truth remains that he was among the very first to do so and, uniquely, upon the sure foundation of his own original, all-revealing researches into the ancient-to-recent Christian past. Indeed, well before the Nazis gained power in Germany he was already exposing the dread tale of Christian denigration and persecution of Jews and Judaism. Parkes acted to create a whole new anti-ideological historiography, subsequently to be elaborated and applied by such Christian scholars as Margaret Brearley, Alice L. Eckardt, Edward H. Flannery, Eva Fleischner, John Pawlikowski, Peter Schneider, Paul M. van Buren, and Clark W. Williamson.

III

Parkes's views of Judaism and Christianity were distinctive and, perforce, disputatious. In total opposition to preachments declaring that the Christian church has superseded Israel in the divine economy, he bore scholarly and personal testimony to the living, dynamic, and incomparable quality of Judaism. He was especially struck by the great creativity and joy that suffused the period from Ezra to the completion of the Talmud—a period extending to a time much after "the new Israel" initiated the pretense that it had replaced "the old Israel." For Parkes, in Judaism and Christianity we are met with two quite different kinds of religion. He emphasized that at the center of Judaism is the "natural community." Although it would be absurd to assert that Judaism has no concern for the individual person, that faith's concerted stress falls upon humankind as social being, related to other human beings "through righteousness and justice." And while Christianity is not unaware of the social aspect of humanity, it has consistently subordinated that dimension "to the personal aspect of life." Thus it may be adjudged that Judaism concentrates upon "the elect nation" while Christianity directs itself to "the elect from every nation." The reasoning here points as well to the legitimacy of a Jewish state. Such a state finds its religious and thence political basis within the natural community. (In the specific instance of the State of Israel, the justifications of historical continuity, legality, and moral necessity are to be added to the above foundation.)

Judaism is a way of life, the religion of the attainable. Its task and contribution focus upon the norms and patterns of daily living. Christianity is a way to personal salvation and is in a certain sense, therefore, the religion of the unattainable. In an early article, Parkes wrote:

God speaking to men in community through Sinai speaks with a different voice from God speaking to the hearts of men as separate persons from Calvary; and just as the church found a satisfactory doctrine of God only in the frank acceptance of the paradox of the Trinity in Unity, so we shall only find a satisfactory doctrine of man when we found it squarely on the paradox of man's dual existence as person in himself, and as member of the community in which alone his personality can exist.

This one of four essays appeared under the significant general title, "The Permanence of Sinai as God's Revelation of Man in Society." The point is that Parkes was proposing an anthropological rationale and formulation for the shared legitimacy of Judaism and Christianity. In completion of the picture, humankind is in addition "a seeker called to explore and use all the riches this world provides."

Correspondingly, to the understanding of God as the source and sustainer of societal Israel, and as personal redeemer, must be added a third channel (*not* persona): the action of the spirit of God in political, secular, and scientific life, or, put differently, humankind's calling and power to understand and have responsible dominion over the world. In sum, Judaism, Christianity, and scientific Humanism are to be co-related with the threefold action of God and the threefold understanding of humanity.

It should be apparent that in Parkes's trinitarian authentication of Judaism, Christianity, and Humanism he did not abandon a Christian frame of reference. Since, as he himself taught, the two faiths of Judaism and Christianity differ essentially, it follows that the Jew will speak in a quite alternative way. I am not Jewish and I cannot represent Judaism, but I believe that I am correct that the spokesperson for Judaism will testify that all three of the roles or channels Parkes depicts are underwritten within Judaism proper, without any need to introduce or call upon Christianity or Humanism. Jews will agree that, yes, their faith is fundamentally communal. But that faith also provides a fully personal dimension (cf., for example, the sublime Psalms of David). And, thirdly, Judaism has itself opened the way for humanity as seeker and ruler of the world, through its original teaching that God grants humankind dominion over the creation.

It is not at all to the end of faulting Parkes's advocacy that I have alluded to a possible Jewish rejoinder to his position. That would be inappropriate in a tribute to him, but it is, in any case, not the point. I make the reference as a means, first, of underscoring Parkes's own insistence that the Jewish and the Christian outlooks are fundamentally different; and, second, of illustrating the kind of dialogue between Jews and Christians that meant so much to him and to which he devoted a large part of his life.

It remains evident, I trust, why Parkes was utterly repelled by any attempt to "convert" Jews to Christianity. The Jewish and Christian faiths are not only profoundly different; they are also of permanently equal validity.

IV

James was distressed when I saw fit to introduce "the Devil" into the question of antisemitism and the struggle against it (ghosts, *sí*; the Devil, *no*). As I was more and more going the route of realpolitik vis-à-vis an antisemitism metastasized far beyond the churches and religion, Parkes remained the Christian educationist, the rectifier of churchly sin. Contending as late as 1979 (and correctly so, as far as it goes) that "the basic root of modern antisemitism lies squarely in the Gospels and the rest of the New Testament," he drew from this the restricted and sanguine conclusion that with the aid of a radical reform of the church's liturgy and its biblical hermeneutic, Jews can be shown as "a normal, contemporary people with a normal, contemporary religion." A few years earlier James had written to me that, "if for two thousand years you read the New Testament in church as the 'Word of God,' I think this is enough explanation of that subconscious and instinctive hostility which is the 'abnormal' part of antisemitism." On the other hand, Parkes did not seem to object to my usage of the concept "demonic." However we may feel on the wisdom of directing energies to the reform of Christian liturgy, Parkes was surely right that the life of local Christian congregations can be a powerful force for either evil or good.

We have to keep in mind that Parkes was a wondrously reasonable man, and it was thus natural for him to expect everyone to be reasonable. He looked to the rationality of theological endeavor as judge of and guide to practical decision-making. Yet he forever insisted that religious understanding and claims must be assessed and chastened, not only by historical truth, but also by moral demands and ethical criteria. His threefold, dialectical devotion to reason, faith, and ethics prompted me once to denominate him an Anglican of the Anglicans. He rather enjoyed the characterization.

Parkes would often protest that while Christians have comprehended the *person* of Jesus, they have grievously denied the significance of the *religion* of Jesus, the religion of Judaism. Here erupts, in fact, the nightmarish, betraying irony of the whole history of Christianity. (One may venture to wonder, in the name of the very truthfulness that Parkes pursued so unflinchingly and at such great personal hardship, what the "person" of Jesus can ever mean in abstraction from the religious faith that possessed him and for which he gave his life.)

V

I have told of a few incidents in the life of James Parkes. I must make place for some lines from his autobiography, which may better than anything else take the full measure of the man (also perhaps of the woman he married):

> Among our post-war visitors was one unusual guest, known to us as The Old Man of the Road. Some tragedy early in life had turned him into a "tramp," and he had been on the road ever since the First Great War. He took much pride in keeping himself clean; he knew that he could have a bed in our garden house when he wanted, that he could come to us when he felt ill, and that there would always be a meal for him. Once or twice we sent him to hospital, where he never stayed long. He loved the country, would tell us of its beauty and bring Dorothy some offering of flowers or fruit culled on his way. His visits continued till we knew he was too old for the road, and we then found a place for him where he died peacefully and well loved in an old people's home.

In 1949 Parkes was elected president of the Jewish Historical Society of England, only the second Gentile to be so chosen by that date. He received fitting academic honors from, among other institutions, the Hebrew Union College-Jewish Institute of Religion, The Hebrew University of Jerusalem, and University College, London. In the mid-1960s he bequeathed his unique library of some 10,000 books, periodicals, pamphlets, and papers to the University of Southampton. He was survived by Dorothy, a redoubtable colleague in her own right. James has gone off now, *kiveyakhol*, to look up good Pope John XXIII, Reinhold Niebuhr, Cornelius Rijk, Kurt Gerstein, Heinz David Leuner, Peter Schneider, and the other departed saints of Christian redress and Christian-Jewish reconciliation. Parkes contended that either no human being survives physical death or everyone does. If all do, "then it is into a world of growth and further understanding, not into a static world of heaven or hell."

James Parkes had few peers within the category of historian-cum-theologian. Nor do I know a more superb teller of tales. It may not be all that long until, over a good transfigured sherry, Parkes will be regaling the others with his stories—perhaps pausing to find Barth and remind him (but only the one quick time, I think) of his opinion of him. From Parkes's early years to his death (and beyond?), he has been living out the motto of his family crest, *Vous pouvez me rompre mais je ne plie pas* ("You may break me, but I do not bend"). His prodigious intellect was matched by his valor, his prophetic indignation, his steadfastness, his hopefulness. But greatest of all was his empathy. He was not a Jew, yet he was a Jew.

7

A Continuing Encounter, 1983-1986

The Jewish-Christian meeting continued to occupy much of my thinking, research, and literary effort in the early and middle 1980s.

I

The distinctiveness that was apparent within my point of view respecting the Christian-Jewish encounter applies much less today. It would be wrong for me to presume that the changes noticeably in process on the Christian side are somehow related to my efforts. Through the years I have been relatively more aware of adverse criticisms of my work than of sympathetic ones. Sometimes, though, an individual's contribution gets staked out dialectically in or through opposition to it.

A small but persisting company of today's theologians, historians, and church leaders—most of them blessedly younger than I—have come to speak and write of the destructive, even genocidal, implications in traditional Christian teachings and attitudes toward the Jewish people. Differences of conviction remain respecting what individual Christians and the Christian community ought to do and what changes ought to be made in Christian teaching and praxis. I take it that most Christian thinkers and representatives of the church would not agree with me that the antisemitic or at least anti-Judaic aspect of Christianity is endemic to that faith[1] (along with, of course, Christianity's pro-Judaic aspects). And not too many Christians would be happy with my proposals for Christian change. However, the ranks of Christian reformers and revolutionaries appear to be growing. In the meantime, I continue to believe that the final, decisive judgment against the Christian tradition is its immoral elements, as proved or at least exemplified in its historic hostilities to the Jewish people and Judaism.

As we have noted, through the centuries church representatives have done all they could—aided and abetted by elements constitutive to the New Testament—to hold "the Jews" blameworthy for Jesus' death. However, within recent years, a denial of the legitimacy of this accusation has become part of an agenda shared by increasing numbers of Christian scholars. Over a considerable part of my writing career, I joined various theologians and historians in refuting this specific charge against the Jewish people, with aid from documented historical research and findings.

Of late I have come to the view that this approach is wrongheaded and that a quite different procedure is demanded: an insistence that the issue of responsibility for Jesus' death is a nonquestion.[2]

This persuasion is illustrated in a response by me to an effort by Harvey Cox that keeps alive the old canard of implicating the Jewish community in the death of Jesus.[3] Cox fails to realize or to grant the New Testament's tendentiousness and hence the need for alternative, critical scholarly procedures. The following paragraphs sum up my current position:

> Jesus was a messianic revolutionary, who was executed with unnumbered other Jews by the Romans under Pontius Pilate (anything but the flunky of alleged Jewish conspirators that Mr. Cox tries to make him). Jesus the Jew died as the beloved, though failed, deliverer of his people from the hated Roman oppressor. The New Testament

---

[1]   "Behind all the cooperativeness and good feeling that seek to penetrate planned meetings, the many conferences, and even casual associations between Christians and Jews, there lurks the specter of antisemitism. It is the hidden agenda of all such encounters" ("Post-Holocaust Theology and the Christian-Jewish Dialogue [1987]).

[2]   My newer emphasis is, however, foreshadowed in EYB, pp. 116-119.

[3]   Harvey Cox, "The Trial of Jesus," *The New York Times*, Op-ed page, 5 April 1985.

documents culpably shift Roman responsibility for Jesus' crucifixion onto "the Jews." That finding is an all-decisive truism of responsible historical scholarship, which Professor Cox fails to make clear.

But the infinitely more fateful question is why the Christian world must keep driving itself to raise the issue of Jewish linkage to Jesus' death. The psychological and moral problem here extends just as much to expressions of Jewish innocence as to claims of Jewish "guilt." What is there in the collective Christian psyche that demands repeated, unrelenting concentration upon the "place" of Jews in Jesus' trial and crucifixion? Where is the moral legitimacy in keeping this kind of pot boiling? It is not even a half-century [as of 1985] since the Japanese attacked the United States, yet there bygones can wholly be bygones, and Americans can enjoy every available Japanese automobile, camera, and gadget.

After 2,000 years the question of responsibility for Jesus' death is a nonquestion, or ought to be. It ought to have been buried long ago, together with all other efforts at hostility to Jews. Rather than concentrating upon reputed Jewish (and Roman) "malice" in the death of Jesus, Harvey Cox could more responsibly expend his time in fighting the Christian malice toward Jews that the churches inculcate every "Holy Week."[4]

II

In "Antisemitism is the Heart" (1984) I tried to sum up certain major lessons garnered from many years of study and writing in Christian-Jewish relations. Much has been said in previous pages upon the demonry of antisemitism. I contended in this particular essay that the Christian-Jewish dialogue of today "is a product of parthenogenesis: the single parent is Christian

---

[4]   "Responsibility for Jesus' Death is a Nonquestion," letter by A. Roy Eckardt, *The New York Times*, 16 April 1985. Cf. my brief piece, "Who Killed Jesus and Why?"; *For Righteousness' Sake*, pp. 63-73; and "Post Holocaust Theology and the Christian-Jewish Dialogue," pp. 15-16.

antisemitism."[5] Many times the various movements that seek to liberate women, the poor, black peoples, et al. also act to negate the national liberation movement of the Jewish people: Zionism and the State of Israel. Anti-Israelism appears to be the main contemporary application of Christian and other antisemitisms. But Christian hostility to Israel is not itself explainable until we seek out the theological rootage of antisemitism. Although there were promptings back in 1977, it was primarily during the four-year period under review that the conviction fastened definitely upon me that the really deciding focus of the Christian-Jewish encounter is the resurrection of Jesus. I do not mean (the obvious point) that the resurrection is the dividing line between Christians and Jews, though that is of course true. I mean rather the powerful and fateful connections among Christian resurrectionism (in its traditionalist understanding), Christian supersessionism, and Christian theological antisemitism. The theological foundation and thence the ultimate motivation of the scourge of antisemitism within the Christian world appears to be, as earlier suggested, the church's dogma of the triumphal resurrection of Jesus. The potentially chief moral anguish for the Christian community today is thus not so much Christianity's traditional "teaching of contempt" brought into reputed legitimacy by "the Jews'" (alleged) "rejection of their Lord"—although, to be sure, such teaching has by no means been vanquished. The really salient Christian burden is not the Friday before Easter, but Easter itself—a kind of proclamation that appears, on the surface, ever so innocent and ever so sublime (the latter with particular respect to the reputedly glorious triumph over the human evil of death). On the surface, there is no contempt for anybody.

The question keeps asserting itself: How can the resurrection of Jesus be proclaimed as a special saving act of God without the Christian exclusivism and imperialism that helped lay the railroad tracks to the murder centers? The way that the Christian church ultimately reckons with its supersessionist resurrectionism will determine whether its moral credibility post-*Shoah* is to be entirely lost. For in the measure that the resurrection of Jesus is proclaimed as the special and once-for-all salvational intervention of God in human history,

---

[5]   In a review of Stuart E. Rosenberg's *The Christian Problem*, John T. Pawlikowski decries the "total absence of any sense that some fundamental Jewish rethinking needs to take place" along with Christian rethinking, "if the dialogue is to advance" (*Journal of Ecumenical Studies* 24 [1987]: 676). Pawlikowski is challenged to name a single substantive area of potential Jewish "rethinking" that can be compared with the need for Christian rethinking.

there appears to be little or no way, upon Christian theological and moral grounds, to attack the evils of Christian exclusivism.

A saving mark of some Christian post-*Shoah* thinking and praxis is its moral revulsion against supersessionism vis-à-vis the Jewish people and Judaism. However, as yet few Christian theologians and spokespersons seem prepared to venture out upon the frontier of an untrammeled *theology of moral coherence and moral responsibility* that will subject all Christian dogma to judgment in and through the great events and experiences of recent and current history—or, to use religious language, in and through the grace and guidance of the Holy Spirit.

While on the subject of moral coherence, I suggest that one difficulty in my allusion to historical events as a judge of faith is how to reconcile that view with the contention in chapter three of this retrospective that "historical data cannot in themselves serve to interpret the meaning of history or to discern meaning in history." However, in my study *For Righteousness' Sake* (1987) I was fully to address the dialectic of history and faith.

On the Jewish side, an important lesson of the *Shoah*—as conveyed by such scholars as Emil L. Fackenheim, Irving Greenberg, and Richard L. Rubenstein—is the crisis that that event brought to the historic teaching of Jewish martyrdom. The newer stance within some notable Jewish thinking is that such martyrdom has come to an end. As I have sought to mediate this view, the *Shoah*-event makes morally obscene the traditional apologetic of Israel as the Lord's powerless, suffering servant. Instead, the *Shoah* is to be comprehended and treated excrementitiously, i.e., through the realization that the loathsome purpose of the entire Nazi program was to turn the holy nation of Israel into excrement.[6] "Therefore, after the *Shoah* collective Jewish martyrdom would only make feces of the Name of God...*The* enemy is human suffering." And whenever it is alleged that God insists upon human suffering, the voice is not that of God but of the Devil.[7] The frame of reference here is, of course, our particular age. Human experience of, say, the year 40,000 or 50,000 will have

---

[6]   Consult *Jews and Christians*, pp. 30-33. That volume is hereinafter referred to as JAC.

[7]   "Antisemitism is the Heart" (slightly emended).

different things to teach; Jewish martyrdom could once again become thinkable and licit.

III

The query posed by the title of my article, "Is There a Way Out of the Christian Crime? The Philosophic Question of the Holocaust," follows directly from the essay just commented upon. On the basis of my recent thinking and writing, I shall try to show how the answer to the question of this next item's title can be Yes. (The subtitle of the essay rests upon its utilization of the classical dialectic of thesis-antithesis-synthesis.)

The Christian crime of today is that of an ongoing antisemitism and anti-Judaism that refused to end when the Holocaust took place. Within the churches, Christian supersessionism remains quite alive and quite well. It is as if the *Shoah* never happened. The historical/theological legitimization of Christian triumphalism vis-à-vis Judaism and the Jewish people follows from the continuously and contemporaneously asserted claim that in Jesus Christ eschatological reality has entered human history in final, salvational form. Of ultimate significance is the dogma that the event of Jesus' resurrection "is not a mere human idea or human spiritual 'experience,' but is exclusively a deed of God."[8]

Between Christian absolutism and the everyday life of the devoted and sincere Christian, the shadow of the *Shoah* interposes itself, with shattering consequences. A poignant eventuality is suggested: the *forlornness* of today's Christian. Is that to be the necessary consensus?

The Christian of conscience would appear to be utterly ashamed, utterly bereft, utterly alone. Is not that the lesson of the *Shoah* to the Christian world? For the Christian crime has not ceased. What is to be the lot and the fate of those who do not intend to abandon, or for one or another reason do not find themselves able to abandon, a life of crime, or I should say a faith of crime? Have they not betrayed their own human dignity? Are they not destroyed, in a spiritual and moral sense, under

---

[8]   From rabbinic times, the resurrection of the dead became a fundamental Judaic doctrine ("Death in the Judaic and Christian Traditions").

the relentless blows of an unanswerable moral assault upon their faith? Is there no way out of the Christian crime?

A possible response to the foregoing questions entails the additional query of whether post-*Shoah* Christians are *only* forlorn, or whether they may be, at once, forlorn and not forlorn. In chapter five above, reference is made to the passage in the Letter to the Ephesians (2:11-20), according to which Christians are the outsider pagans who have had no hope but who are then brought by divine grace into the Covenant with the people of God, becoming members of God's household. While it is the case that Christians continue to earn condemnation for their antisemitisms, and rightly so, "they are also received by a voice that says 'I accept you.'" And yet, does not this act of acceptance force our dialectic into immorality? "On the one hand, the Christian crime lives on (thesis). On the other hand, the Christian is said to be accepted (antithesis)...Is it not morally reprehensible to assert these two things together? How can there be acceptance of those who only continue in their transgressions? Worse: Is it not wrong to be granted forgiveness while abiding in one's sins? Worse still: Is not God himself/herself a transgressor in accepting the Christian, and thereby condoning evil?...Is there no way beyond thesis and antithesis into a bearable synthesis?"

The foregoing philosophic and theological questions, together with those that follow below, have been among the central ones in my recent work. We have noted more than once the crucial place of Jesus' resurrection for the Christian-Jewish encounter.

The authentication, if authentication is needed, that the resurrection of Jesus cannot in fact embody eschatological fulfillment, even a fragmentary realization, lies in that event's indirect but powerful contribution to the deaths of millions of human beings, including great numbers of children... Is Christianity immune or is it not immune to world-historical events since Jesus? Is the Christian faith falsifiable by history? *Has* Christianity been falsified by history? These questions create a life-and-death dilemma: If the traditional Christian faith is *not* falsified by history, then how is supersessionist anti-Jewishness ever going to be vanquished? But if the Christian claim *is* falsified by history, does this not mean that the Christian assurance of God's acceptance of the unacceptable is extinguished? To express the two sides of the dilemma as a single question: How is it possible for there to be Christians who, at one and the same time, unqualifiedly accept the Jewish people and are themselves unqualifiedly accepted by God? Or is it fatefully the case that the final choice for the Gentile has to be between Christian antisemitism and pagan forlornness?

The theological/moral/historical procedure that I more recently tendered in behalf of a possible synthesis entails setting in juxtaposition the traditionalist, triumphalist resurrection of Jesus and the reestablishing of the State of Israel: "In 1948 there was constituted the Third Jewish Commonwealth. The Psalter tells us that 'he who sits in the heavens laughs; the Lord has them in derision' (Ps. 2:4). Could it be that a divine comedy is being staged for the sake of, among others, the Christian world?"

The Christian crime continues on. Of course, Christians are always free to give up the life of crime. But are they not then driven into "the most terrible eventuality of all: the aloneness of no longer being accepted"? Is it not so that the life-and-death remedy for the aloneness of those outside the original Covenant with Israel is supposed to take place in and through the saving resurrection of Jesus? "In the last resort, i.e., in the final extremity of life, the question is posed: Is this God of Israel a defeated God? Is this God of Israel himself/herself barren of resources? If so, Christian forlornness is accompanied by the forlornness of God. And the end is the end of human hope."

As the ravaging twentieth century draws near its close, the Christian community's existential challenge

is whether there is a historical word from God that saves the Christian church from forlornness and at the same time saves it from the unabated victimizing of Jews. Is there a special historical event that judges and redeems the victimizing resurrection? Is there an event of God that in the very moment that some Christians may be undergoing the dreadful trauma of necessarily rejecting the resurrection in its victimizing aspects will nevertheless bring assurance, an event through which it may be said once again, "I accept you"?

Such an event *could be* the State of Israel as a contemporaneous act of the God of Israel,...a sign and a witness that God continues to accept human beings *totally apart from* the resurrection of Jesus Christ. In this connection the Christian theologian Robert A. Everett suggests that the political Israel of today may be received as sacramental for Christians.[9] Israel may be saying to Christians that their traditionalist victimization of Jews and Judaism is not constituent to their acceptance by God and hence need not be constituent to their acceptance of themselves. They do not need any such "works-righteousness" (or "works-*un*righteousness"). They can live wholly by grace.

The possibility of propounding "a non-eschatological, nontriumphalist Christian teaching of the resurrection is here left open, and with it the possibility that the resurrection of Jesus may yet find a place in Christian teaching."

To sum up this tentative, affirmative response to the question of whether there is a way out of the Christian crime: "Two events, the resurrection of Jesus and the restoration of the State of Israel, are linked inexorably, the one in its [historical] destructiveness, the other as judge and redeemer of that destructiveness. In principle, the causal place of the [triumphalist] resurrection, and hence of Christianity, in the Holocaust of the Jewish people is put to shame. And the Christian faith...is restored to full integrity. Peace is finally brought between the thesis of criminality and the antithesis of acceptance. A strange synthesis is manifest, and it is not an idea but a deed."[10]

IV

Among possible difficulties or complications in the argumentation just sketched is that the God who forgives may also be himself/herself unforgivable. This leads me into another essay, "The Holocaust and (*Kiveyachol*) the

---

[9]   Robert A. Everett, conversations with author, 16-17 Jan. 1985. See also Philip Culbertson, "Eretz Israel: Sacred Space, Icon, Sign, or Sacrament?," *Shofar* 6, 3 (1988): 36-44.

[10]   "Is There a Way Out of the Christian Crime?: The Philosophic Question of the Holocaust" (slightly emended). For parallel exposition, consult JAC, pp. 87-91, 153-156.

Liberation of the Divine Righteousness," based upon a paper delivered at the International Conference on the Holocaust and Genocide, Tel Aviv, 1982.[11] (The Hebrew term in the title is translated "so to speak" or alternatively "as one might be allowed to say.") Here are the article's two opening paragraphs:

> According to a survivor of Auschwitz, a certain story was told in that camp of death about a Hasidic *rebbe* who argued with a disciple, "You know, it is possible that the *rebbono shel olam* [Master of the Universe] is a liar." "How can that be possible?," asked the disciple in dismay. "Because," the *rebbe* answered, "if the *rebbono shel olam* should open his window now and look down here and see Auschwitz, he would close the window again and say, 'I did not do this.' And that would be a lie."[12]
>
> But why would it be a lie? Does not the blame for Auschwitz fall upon human beings? Eliezer Berkovits of today's Jerusalem supplies a comprehensive, decisive rejoinder in but a single sentence: "God is responsible for having created a world in which man is free to make history."[13] Berkovitz's answer is unanswerable, is it not? For what human being is ever granted the power to ask or to resolve to be born?[14]

The essay as a whole comprises a kind of midrash (commentary) upon the quoted sentence of Rabbi Berkovits. The midrash assumes the standpoint of righteousness (as a norm) in the presence of, *kiveyachol*, "the divine sin." The

---

[11] That essay and "*Ha'Shoah* as Christian Revolution" are largely duplicative.

[12] Menachem Rosensaft, contribution to symposium on "Jewish Values in the Post-Holocaust Future," *Judaism* 16 (1967): 294.

[13] Eliezer Berkovits, "The Hiding God of History," in Yisrael Gutman and Livia Rothkirchen, eds., *The Catastrophe of European Jewry: Antecedents-History-Reflections* (Jerusalem: Yad Vashem, 1976), p. 704.

[14] "The Holocaust and (*Kiveyachol*) the Liberation of the Divine Righteousness" (slightly emended). I see that it was actually back in 1972 that I raised the question of final responsibility for the human presence in this world: "Within the Judaic-Christian domain the raising of the question of theodicy will never cease, for the simple reason that no human being ever asks to be born or to be subjected to the specter of death" ("Death in the Judaic and Christian Traditions").

historical intentionality of the *Shoah* cannot be dissociated "from what it was that made the event fatefully possible in the first place, namely, the Covenant, the setting apart of Jews as 'a kingdom of priests and a holy nation' (Exod. 19:6). Presumably, God is anything but uncaring of the future, and ought to be able to foresee the consequences of his [*sic*] own methods and decisions. God is of course identifiable as the culprit behind all Jewish suffering, but the *Shoah* remains uniquely unique[15] as a most monstrous, eschatological incarnation of that suffering." By the same reasoning, "God ought to have realized that the Incarnation-Crucifixion-Resurrection was going to be fabricated into a Christian supersessionism and triumphalism" that would have dire consequences for the Jewish people.[16]

To bring to trial "the hiding God of history" (Berkovits) may be "the one hope left, in the shadow of the Kingdom of Night, for an honest and authentic witness to God, for rescuing and sanctifying the Name of God—at least once it is agreed that the way 'God proves himself holy' is 'by righteousness' (Isa. 5:16)."[17] That is to say, in the courtroom the prosecution's chief witness against God is—God.

The pristine, compelling, altogether artless reason why the Jews of the concentration and murder camps had to ask: Where is God now? Why does he not liberate us? was that according to Jewish faith, God is the Lord of history, the one who penetrates and is sovereign over the events of time/place. *Therefore*—a nightmarish conclusion—God's non-deliverance of six million Jews must have meant either God's absence, or God's failure to act, or even God's inability to act. That God should accordingly be brought to trial places that decision among the most moral judgments that could ever be made—this, against the (relatively) immoral insistence that human beings are not to question God.

As noted in chapter six above, Rabbi Berkovits concludes that within the dimension of human time and human history, the ways of God are simply unforgivable. My midrash tries to reckon with this unbearable state of affairs. I here go back to "*HaShoah* as Christian Revolution: Toward the Liberation of

---

15   The term "transcendingly unique" would have been more felicitous here, on the basis of our discussion in chapter six, part VII.

16   JAC, pp. 50-51.

17   Ibid., p. 51 (slightly emended).

the Divine Righteousness," which contains, antecedently, an analysis of the problem of the unforgivableness/forgivableness of God.[18] There is no need to reproduce the entire argumentation—or, better, the entire witness. The following passages convey something of my overall outlook:

> Abraham J. Heschel has spoken of the "overwhelming sympathy with the divine pathos" that the prophet Isaiah developed...For me [Eckardt] the penultimate height of faith—not the final height, for that would be redemption—is to find oneself genuinely sorry for God. In the Woody Allen film *Love and Death* Boris Grushenko claims that the worst thing we can say theologically is that God is an underachiever. Boris failed to go far enough. The worst thing we can say, and, not alone for that very reason *but much more because of the dread realities of Auschwitz-Birkenau and Belzec and Chelmno and Maidanek and Sobibor and Treblinka*, we have to say it, is that God is a klutz—the ultimate klutz—so much so that he has got himself strung out upon a cross that is never going to be struck down. He *would* have to go and make himself a world! Now he is stuck with it, and with us, and he is left with no choice but to keep on undergoing the agony of it...If all this is not the height of klutzyness, I do not know what is. The Creator of all the universes made radically vulnerable—and under his own auspices!
>
> Is there anybody around who is willing to attend to the anguish of God, and to bring comfort to him...? We humans may not amount to very much, and we are but tiny nothings in all the galactic vastness, but can't we at least spare *a little compassion* for this purpose? *Someone* ought to go to the side of the Eternal Victim. Should no one come forward, all of existence must be riddled with madness...
>
> So God is unforgivable—and we may forgive him...[19]

---

[18] The analysis of the "trial of God," of God's unforgivableness, and of how it may be responded to, appears at greater length in *For Righteousness' Sake*, pp. 315-325. That I should repeat this kind of conceptualization at several places reflects a continuing concern, perhaps even a sort of obsession, with the question of the "trial of God."

[19] "Ha'Shoah as Christian Revolution: Toward the Liberation of the Divine Righteousness" (with some emendations and additions).

The suddenness of the jump from unforgivableness to forgiveness here may strike readers as violently arbitrary or otherwise unwarranted. Perhaps the jump may be received as a kind of tour de force—hardly in the meaning of a stroke of genius but only as a most plaintive way of trying to face responsibly a highly poignant and otherwise unresolvable state of affairs. However, the forgiveness may also be looked upon as consistent with humankind's implementation of the gift of *imago dei*, as expressed below in section VI of this chapter.

"I have heard it said that at the conclusion of one of the trials of God, after the Accused had been found guilty as charged, a certain Hasid stood before the assembly and said: 'Let us pray.' And it is told, at the close of *The Gates of the Forest*, that Gregor, whose real identity was that of Gavriel but whose faith had been carried off in the transports to the East, came to pray. He prayed for, among others, the soul of his father, and he prayed as well for the soul of God."[20]

But is there not a flaw?: Where did I ever get the right to forgive God? Is not such forgiveness the province only of the victim? Is this flaw, then, a fatal one? We come back to this question in chapter eight.

V

To return to the eventuality of losing readers, I make reference to two essays from this period, the one short and the other long. I wrote a brief piece in *The Christian Century*, identified by the journal (rather oddly) as an "editorial" and entitled "Requiem for a Dream," in mourning over the re-election of Ronald Reagan. And I contributed a chapter, "The Christian World Goes to Bitburg," to *Bitburg in Moral and Political Perspective*, edited by Geoffrey H. Hartman. The latter piece was an assessment of President Reagan's decision to honor, among others, fallen members of the Nazi SS at Bitburg, Germany on 5 May 1989.[21]

---

[20] Ibid. The reference in the citation is to Elie Wiesel, *The Gates of the Forest*, trans. Frances Frenaye (New York: Avon Books, 1966), p. 223. Consult also Wiesel, *The Trial of God*, a play in three acts, trans. Marion Wiesel (New York: Random House, 1979). For companion analyses of the "trial of God," consult JAC, pp. 49-56; *For Righteousness' Sake*, pp. 320-322.

[21] The chapter in the Hartman volume is also to be found as an appendix to the revised edition of *Long Night's Journey Into Day*.

VI

I come more discretely to the one book I did in this period, *Jews and Christians: The Contemporary Meeting.*

At the beginning of that book—a popularly written survey, with accent upon the American scene—I mention a fundamental presupposition of my work in Christian-Jewish relations through the years: It is not right to use a Christian point of view to argue to the insufficiency or invalidity of Jewish existence, and it is not right to use a Jewish point of view to argue to the insufficiency or invalidity of Christian existence.[22]

Fundamental to *Jews and Christians* is the counsel of Emil L. Fackenheim: In the aftermath of the *Shoah*, the first priority for Christians "may be theological self-understanding. For Jews, it is, and after Auschwitz must be, simple safety for their children."[23] I tried in *Jews and Christians* to reckon phenomenologically with the structure and the stuff of today's Christian-Jewish vis-à-vis, with paramount attention to our religiously and socially pluralistic situation; to set forth several practical areas of current controversy and/or collaboration (among others: authority in religion, religious liberty, religion-state relations, sex and marriage, violence and nonviolence, and women's liberation); and to offer some valuational judgments upon the dialogue from a moral-philosophic standpoint.

As a contribution to moral philosophy, the book focuses upon the moral consequences of belief systems and utilizes philosophic methodologies. "Jewishness" and "Christianness" are treated in their continuity and discontinuity— continuity, on the ground that religion is involved in both cases; discontinuity, on the ground that while Christianness falls primarily under the category of religion, Jewishness embodies a more broadly laic reality. (In a review of *Jews and Christians*, Norman Solomon of the Selly Oak Colleges took forceful exception to my distinction between Christian identity and Jewish

---

[22] JAC, p. 3.

[23] As cited on p. 34 of ibid. The citation is from Emil L. Fackenheim, *To Mend the World: Foundations of Future Jewish Thought* (New York: Schocken Books, 1982), p. 284.

identity, maintaining that like any religion, Christianity is "distorted when presented as a belief system rather than as a broad cultural matrix."[24])

I paid considerable attention to what I called "The New Jewish Stand" with its elements of group determination and group self-affirmation, as encouraged in good part by the norms and opportunities of an open, pluralist culture. The Jewish people are standing up before the non-Jewish world; Jewish thought is standing up before God and the domain of faith; and a number of Jewish thinkers are standing up in behalf of a distinctly Jewish "mission and witness."[25]

Since Judaism is not hamstrung by the absolutism and imperialism of "the only begotten Son," it is perhaps better suited than Christianity to bring to the world the message of the one living and redeeming God. It is highly doubtful that the Christian church's alleged "universalization" of Israel's witness can be received as legitimate or compelling. Such "universalization" could perhaps have begun to ring true had the church been able to surmount its absolutism and imperialism. As matters now stand, a reputed Christian universalization is compromised by the church's advocated dualism between those who are "saved" in Christ and those who are not "saved." Judaism is able to avoid this dualism by, on the one hand, its laic character and, on the other hand, its principle of a justice that is truly universal.[26] Yet the Jewish community as a whole is anything but emancipated from all provincialism.

In *Jews and Christians* I also concentrated upon today's "Commotion in the Back of the Church," referring by this to Christian voices that are being raised in behalf of urgently needed change and humanization, in opposition to Christian exclusivism and antisemitism. The evaluative emphases of the book focus upon

---

[24] Norman Solomon, review of JAC in *Jewish Christian Relations* 20 (1987): 61. Solomon evidently missed such qualifications as this: "The act of participating in Christian peopleness in a cultural sense, and sometimes a national one, has upon occasion overridden the stipulation of an active or distinctive faith" (JAC, p. 5).

[25] See JAC, pp. 56-60.

[26] The difficulty with the Protestant Reformation emphasis upon humankind's inability to "save" itself is not primarily a theological or soteriological one, nor is this emphasis in any necessary conflict with Judaism (wherein Yahweh along "saves"). Instead, the stress upon human inability creates moral dangers, a support for human irresponsibility. The entire insistence upon humankind as sinful has to be balanced by an insistence upon humankind as good (as is the case in the Christian anthropology of Reinhold Niebuhr).

Christological reform and revolution, since the heart of the Jewish-Christian conflict is Christology. It is at the point of Christology that the prodigious question of moral and religious credibility most besets the Christian community.[27] I did point out that if "it is unjust and untruthful to claim or to insinuate that Christian teaching and the church were the sole creators of the Holocaust," it yet remains essential that we identify the German Nazis as heirs of "an earlier collectivity of males": Christian writers, priests, and theologians.[28]

This brings me to interpose a reference to the essay "Christians, Jews, and the Women's Movement" (the one article from this period that is reproduced below), wherein I seek to implement a recently acquired knowledge of, and commitment on the side of, women's liberation.[29] I have come to agree with Madonna Kolbenschlag that "women's experience will be the hermeneutic of the future."

Of immediate pertinence to the self-criticism that is constituent to this retrospective is the inclusion within *Jews and Christians* of adverse judgments by me upon my own position and work, with particular reference to the destructive elements that make up the one side of the ambivalence that all Christians share:

> Will not the hidden impulses that are stirred up and the hostility induced in some Christian readers [and even in the writer?] by the morally inspired attacks contained in this volume [*Jews and Christians*] upon the sins of Christians and upon certain Christological claims outweigh any possible "good" that might be done through sanctioning the attacks? Do not such attacks comprise a life-and-death threat to the Christian psyche? ...[Were] it not for "those Jews"—so the Christian

---

[27] On the Christological issue, see JAC, pp. 82-87 and *passim*.

[28] Ibid., pp. 29, 31.

[29] *Black-Woman-Jew* (1989) reflects this commitment. In *Religious Studies Review* (18 [1992]: 318) Kathryn M. Huey misrepresents B-W-J by offering Diane Tennis's return to "the reliable Father" as though it were my view. "Christians, Jews, and the Women's Movement" was originally presented as a lecture at the Oxford Centre for Postgraduate Hebrew Studies. A fuller version appears in JAC.

unconscious may lament—the very need for Christian "revisionism" would never have come to beset us...

In a word, the protest of more than one Jew of today is unanswerable: "After 1900 years, is it not about time that you Christians just let us alone? Forget all about those vaunted 'Jewish-Christian dialogues'! Stop producing those well-intentioned books! Stop rousing the demons! Just let us alone!"[30]

But I seem to have put myself into a kind of pickle. Whimsy has intruded, or perhaps my earlier friend mischievousness is at work. For the very lines that appear as an instance of self-reproach in *Jews and Christians* may only smack of self-congratulation as I now duplicate them in *Collecting Myself*. And yet, to fail to reproduce the foregoing confession would mean unfaithfulness to the facts. In either case, Reinhold Niebuhr was right; he used to stress, in good classic Protestant fashion, that there is simply no way whereby the human self can deliver itself from itself.

Having reread all my books and articles as well as checked the present retrospective down to this point, I am not certain that I gave conclusive evidence (as of 1986) of having finally overcome the Christian habit of passing judgment on things Jewish. (If nothing else, I keep bringing up the eventuality.) Yet it has been my ambition to kick that habit entirely.

Lastly, *Jews and Christians* addresses itself to the question: What is there, if there is anything, to provide the Christian faith with distinctiveness and integrity, once that faith's Christological triumphalism and supersessionism are repudiated, once the victimizing absoluteness of the Christian tradition is surmounted?[31] A prevailing moral-theological dilemma of *Jews and Christians* reembodies the "historic dilemma of Christian existence: How are Christians ever to claim participation in an unbroken divine Covenant with Israel without

---

[30] JAC, pp. 146, 147 (slightly emended).

[31] In a review of the first edition of *Long Night's Journey Into Day*, Clark M. Williamson made the important point that some Christians who are antisemitic can very well be that way without having any decisive belief in or concern with the resurrection of Jesus. I may offer a companion point: Some Christians who are devout believers in Jesus' resurrection are anything but antisemitic.

at the same time theologizing Jews, without subjecting the Jewish people and Judaism to Christian religious imperialism?"[32]

As suggested in previous pages, I have come to reject a theology (or ideology) that teaches the peculiar or exclusivist essential of Jesus Christ. A consequence of this rejection is the religious and/or human and/or scholarly need to locate somewhere else the distinctiveness and the contribution of Christian faith.

I went on to propose in *Jews and Christians* that the answer may lie in the *image of God*. In the Talmud, Rabbi ben Azzai declares that the fundamental Jewish teaching is the human being as created in God's image.[33] I suggested that Christians can be those people who, as they live out their days upon the very threshold of Israel (Judaism and the Jewish people), are granted a chance to honor the dictum of Rabbi ben Azzai. In 1948 I wrote that to surrender the affirmation that Jesus is the Christ is to surrender the Christian faith. During the period 1983-1986 I came to declare that Christian integrity and truth ought to seek after another foundation. In the 1950s I was saying that Israel is the church just outside the church; by the late 1980s I was coming to say that Christianity is Israel just outside Israel. To honor Rabbi ben Azzai's dictum is one way to cope with the historic dilemma of the Christian life alluded to above:

> Jews and Judaism are not being theologized; at the same time, Christianity is not being reduced to Judaism; and a peculiarly covenantal task for Christians is being pointed up...[A teaching] that derives from the doctrine that humankind is made in the image of God comprises the basis for the reconstruction of a uniquely integral and distinctive Christianity, a Christianity that will have vanquished its Christological idolatries...And once the image of God is celebrated in its universal dimension, the *imitatio dei* can go freely to work...[34]

---

[32]   JAC, p. 148.

[33]   See Irving Greenberg, "Developing the Image of God or, Judaism: 24 Hours a Day, 7 Days a Week," *Perspectives* (New York: National Jewish Resource Center, Feb. 1985): 5-6.

[34]   It is not at all implied here that a human being must be either a Jew or a Christian to be freed of idolatry. All human beings are made in the image of God. The human dignity that this conveys extends to the right to stand up to God, and even to demand moral

The integrity and the irreplaceableness of Christianity center *in Christian people* and what they do rather than in an exclusivist dogma. John Hick identifies the peculiarity of Christianity as the response of discipleship to Jesus of Nazareth.[35]

In the above way, Christians may become part of the world people of God. Thus, I managed at one point to surmount my fear of the 1940s and later that to abandon "Jesus as the Christ" is to surrender the Christian faith. I thought that, on the contrary, such an abandonment can open the way to a restoration of Jesus of Nazareth as historical and historic head of the Christian church.[36] However, in *Reclaiming the Jesus of History* (1992) and other writings of the 1990s I sought to reaffirm the Christian teaching of the Incarnation and Resurrection in a new way, thereby qualifying what I am saying at the present juncture.

Jesus was a specialist in celebrating the image of God, even though his Sermon on the Mount provides (of contextual necessity?) only half the potential roster. In that sermon many sorts and conditions of people embody the image of God and are blessed: the poor in spirit, the mourners, the meek, those who covet righteousness, the merciful, the pure in heart, the peacemakers, the persecuted (Matt. 5:3-10). I proposed in *Jews and Christians* that what we are left to do is to "assemble the pitiable others: the wealthy in spirit, the merrymakers, the arrogant, those who hunger and thirst for unrighteousness, the unmerciful, the impure in heart, the warmakers, the persecutors—plus the tax collectors, the prostitutes (Matt. 21:31), and the prodigals. Now, at last, the guest list of the Kingdom of God is filled."[37]

---

accountings from her. At this point, the *imago dei* and the "trial of God" converge.

[35] JAC, pp. 152, 153 (slightly emended). The reference to John Hick is to his book *The Center of Christianity* (San Francisco: Harper & Row, 1978).

[36] The Christian movement "denied Jesus' life by deifying him" (Hyam Maccoby, *Revolution in Judaea: Jesus and the Jewish Resistance* [New York: Taplinger, 1980], p. 195).

[37] JAC, p. 153 (slightly emended).

VII

In chapter two of the present volume I allude to my "pioneering" place in the Christian-Jewish encounter. And at the start of the chapter here ending I mention that today my work and point of view in that area are not as distinctive as they used to be. Thus, my ongoing judgments against Christian absolutism and triumphalism are not the exiguous thing they once were. Harvey Cox furnishes one description of the change:

Admittedly the "supersessionist" position [Cardinal Joseph] Ratzinger takes—that the Christian church has definitely replaced Israel as the new "people of God" [a position still held by untold numbers of Christians —A.R.E.]—has been the dominant one for centuries. But starting about two decades ago,[38] spurred by the painful recognition that the "supersessionist" view may well have contributed to the antisemitism that culminated in the Holocaust, scholars began rethinking both the biblical evidence itself and this inherited theological depreciation of the Jews. The consensus of this work, including that of Catholic scholars, now tilts very heavily against the supersessionist view.[39] What has called it into question is both the accumulating

---

[38]   Harvey Cox is somewhat off the historical mark here. Three, perhaps even four decades would be more accurate.

[39]   On 30 June 1987 the United Church of Christ became the first major American denomination to renounce theological and moral supersessionism. Here is the text of its Declaration on Judaism:

We in the United Church of Christ acknowledge that the Christian Church has, throughout much of its history, denied God's continuing covenantal relationship with the Jewish people expressed in the faith of Judaism. This denial has often led to outright rejection of the Jewish people and to theologically and humanly intolerable violence.

Faced with this history from which we as Christians cannot, and must not, disassociate ourselves, we ask for God's forgiveness through our Lord Jesus Christ. We pray for divine grace that will enable us, more firmly than ever before, to turn from this path of rejection and persecution to affirm that Judaism has not been superseded by Christianity; that Christianity is not to be understood as the successor religion to Judaism; God's covenant with the Jewish people has not been abrogated. God has not rejected the Jewish people; God is faithful in keeping covenant (as published in *The New York Times*, 1 July 1987).

One year later the Episcopal General Convention meeting in Detroit followed suit and repudiated Christian supersessionism (*The New York Times*, 24 July 1988).

evidence of current biblical scholarship and the weight of Catholic and Protestant theological interpretation. The continuity between Judaism, Jesus, the Palestinian "Jesus Movement," and the first decades of the church is becoming increasingly clear with every new archeological find and each new discovery of an ancient manuscript.[40]

The Christian change respecting Judaism and the Jewish people as described by Cox is paralleled in a wider frame of reference by a comparable development respecting Christianity and the world religions. In an exposition of "The Non-Absoluteness of Christianity," John Hick traces some of the major factors in the shift from the persuasion that the Christian gospel is "absolute," "final," and "normative" for all humankind to the abandonment of absolutism by "many, perhaps most, thinking Christians during the last seventy or so years."[41] Professor Hick's finding is on the overly optimistic side. In any case, and with all due awareness of the fallacy of *post hoc, ergo propter hoc*, there is a certain comfort in being reminded that one's own viewpoint is perhaps not quite the "indefensible" or "heretical" thing that some critics have claimed.[42]

---

[40] Harvey Cox, "Liberation Theology vs. Cardinal Ratzinger," *Tikkun* 3 (May-June 1988): 105.

[41] John Hick, "The Non-Absoluteness of Christianity," in John Hick and Paul F. Knitter, eds., *The Myth of Christian Uniqueness* (Maryknoll, NY: Orbis Books, 1987), pp. 16-36. See also my *Reclaiming the Jesus of History*, chap. 10 - "Jesus Christ and the Great Ways of Humankind."

[42] During the time-segment encompassed in this chapter I reviewed Patricia Treece, *A Man for Others*; served as consulting editor for a special number of *Quarterly Review*, "Focus on Jewish-Christian Relations"; took part in a symposium in *Midstream* on the subject "Was the Holocaust Unique?"; contributed a foreword to Stuart E. Rosenberg's book *The Christian Problem*; and composed the article "An American Looks at *Kairos*," an analysis of racism in South Africa.

7A

Selected Essay

(1983-1986)

Christians, Jews, and the Women's Movement

(*Christian Jewish Relations* [London] 19 [June 1986]:13-22)

Women's experience will be the hermeneutic of
the future.
Madonna Kolbenschlag

I should like to offer the thesis that in the long run today's women's
movement may prove to have as much significance for the Christian-Jewish
relation as the Holocaust and the refounding of the State of Israel—or larger
significance.

Writing in a recent number of the *Union Seminary Quarterly Review*,[1]
Deborah McCauley, a Christian, and Annette Daum, a Jew, bring home the
truth that a most weighty handicap of the Jewish-Christian dialogue to date is
its overwhelmingly patriarchal or androcentric character and thrust. A prevailing
consequence is that dialogue's domination by problems of exclusivity over
testimonies to inclusivity.

The histories of the human world have always shared an ideology and praxis
for the special treatment of females. Such special treatment ranges from
idealization to calumniation, from virtual divinization to demonization. The
close affinity within these diametrically opposite attributions lies in the fact that
males have fabricated them, and the labels are never assigned to males as males.
Thus, there are "fallen women" but of course no fallen men. Ann Patrick Ware
of the National Coalition of American Nuns comments upon a recent seminar
called "Images of Women in Christian and Jewish Traditions": the very title
"confirms the perception that what women are and do is not normative but
derivative. Can one imagine a session entitled 'Images of Men ...'? Men are
men, but women must represent something. Women's actions, words,
appearance constitute an 'image' of women, not a reality."

---

[1]   Deborah McCauley and Annette Daum, "Jewish-Christian Feminist Dialogue: A
Wholistic Vision," *Union Seminary Review* 38 (1983): 147-190.

In a word, women are "the other": those who are "forever" on trial—rather like God herself.

Issues raised by the contemporary women's movement

The contemporary women's movement and the issues it raises impinge upon today's encounter of Christians and Jews in many decisive ways. In this article I shall limit myself to only three of them.

The Jewish tradition lives with the Christian tradition in the one prison cell of sexism.

The rampancy of sexism within the Jewish tradition and Judaism helps offset, substantively as well as psychologically, a stress upon the overall moral asymmetry of the Jewish-Christian relation, a stress ordinarily necessitated by the presence and power of Christian antisemitism and triumphalism.

Jews who are tempted into self-righteousness by Christian hostility may be reminded that all is hardly well within the Jewish scene. With the church, the synagogue retains a liturgy and imagery that, very largely, is still sexually exclusivist. A young graduate student friend from Wisconsin recently converted from Christianity to Judaism. She said to my wife and me, "At last I am part of a tradition of which I can be proud." Comparatively taken, her testimony is faithful to the historical record. An original impetus for her decision was her distress over the sin of Christian antisemitism. However, many Jewish women cannot feel as she does. Christians, out of disillusionment with their faith or through happy encounters with Jews, are sometimes tempted to idealize Judaism or the Jewish community. Soon or late they must come hard against a still-prevalent sexism there. If, as John B. Cobb Jr. declares, "the ugliest of all Christian crimes" is "our crime against the Jews," a grievous wrong within Judaism concerns the status of women. (In point of moral fact, is not sexism the *only* serious count to be entered against Judaism?)

Rachel Adler writes that the "problem" of Jewish women is their identification as peripheral Jews within Jewish law and practice:

> The category in which we are generally placed includes women, children and Canaanite slaves...[Members] of this category have been "excused" from most of the positive symbols which, for the male Jew, hallow time, hallow his physical being, and inform both his myth and

his philosophy... Children, if male, are full Jews *in potentio*. Male Canaanite slaves, if freed, become full Jews, responsible for all the *mitzvot* and able to count in a *minyan*. Even as slaves, they have the *b'rit mila*, the covenant of circumcision, that central Jewish symbol, from which women are anatomically excluded. It is true that in Jewish law women are slightly more respected than slaves, but that advantage is outweighed by the fact that only women can never grow up, or be freed or otherwise leave the category.[2]

Because the Christian church whose history is suffused with triumphalism and hostility to Jews has always been a male-dominated community, a conversion to womanism may have implications for the struggle against antisemitism.

Would Christian contempt for Jews and Judaism have become as bad as it did were the church not male sexist? Any affirmative protestation here assumes that males and females are equally adept at such a sin as antisemitism—a response that is a long, long way from being convincing. As a matter of fact, many womanists discern close links between Christian supersessionist antisemitism and characteristically male chauvinist behavior. For the entire structure of Christian imperialism was reared by males. The Holocaust, for all its unprecedented and unique reality, and for all its ensnaring of women practitioners, is at one with the common and perennial infamy of male wars and male destructiveness. As Rabbi Leonard Aaronson writes, "the human male is a killer and a rapist." In the United States today every two minutes or less a woman is raped; every eighteen seconds or less a male beats the woman he lives with; every five minutes or less a male molests a child; and every thirty minutes or less a daughter is sexually attacked by her father.

Letty Cottin Pogrebin of *Ms.* magazine reckons with the bond between antisemitism and anti-womanism: "If you are not an ally of women, you cannot be considered an ally of Jews!" Pogrebin contrasts the AQs (Ally Quotients) of two Christian clergymen, Jesse Jackson and Jerry Falwell. Jackson's anti-Israel

---

2   Rachel Adler, "The Jew Who Wasn't There," in M. M. Kellner, ed., *Contemporary Jewish Ethics* (New York: Sanhedrin, 1978), pp. 348-349. Adler's reference to slavery could seem anachronistic in light of that institution's abandonment by Jews long ago. Her response, I should imagine, would be to point out that the passage of time has not freed women. Hence, the comparative allusion to slavery remains as fitting as ever.

"evenhandedness" and antisemitic slurs appear to lower his AQ in comparison with Falwell's expressed support of Israel. However, as against Jackson,

> Falwell and his ilk have made no secret of their moral imperialism: they intend *by law*, not just public suasion, to "Christianize America," impose prayer in public schools, revitalize family patriarchy, outlaw reproductive freedom and give the fetus more rights than the woman in whose body it exists.
>
> They have proved their enmity by word and deed. In comparison, Jackson is at worst an indiscreet bigot,...and at best an unknown quantity, a man whose commitments on the Jewish question have yet to be tested. But on the woman question, Jackson has come a long way: he has moved from anti-choice to pro-choice on reproductive rights, and from the knee-jerk male supremacy of the old black power movement to a position of sensitivity on women's needs.[3]

In sum, there is hope for Jesse Jackson and little or no hope for Jerry Falwell. Attitudes to women are here established as the litmus test for actual and potential Christian attitudes to Jews. The surmounting of Christian imperialism as such means hope for both the male acceptance of women as equals and the Christian acceptance of Jews as equals.

Antisemitism is by no means absent from the women's movement.

This circumstance helps counteract, or ought to, any impetus to idealize either the feminist movement or women—or, perhaps more accurately it points up the power of patriarchal destructiveness to determine the psycho-intellectual condition and praxis of women. Historically speaking, the presence of antisemitism in the women's movement (to cite McCauley and Daum again) "is rooted in anti-Judaic male theology of the past, and was incorporated into the movement for suffrage in nineteenth century America." An example of the latter is the influential and blatantly antisemitic work of Elizabeth Cady Stanton, *The Women's Bible.* Some of today's Christian feminists "have fallen prey to the ancient masculine trap of triumphalism." Judaism and Jewry have

---

[3]   Letty Cottin Pogrebin, "Women as the Litmus Test," *Present Tense* 12 (1985): 46-47.

always been the primary "other" onto which Christianity has projected those parts of itself to which it will not lay claim. In this scenario, Judaism becomes the bad parent whom Christianity as the adult child blames and punishes for those parts of its personality it does not like and for which it refuses to accept responsibility. The phenomenon of patriarchal projection is made manifest in Christian and post-Christian feminist writings which either explicitly or implicitly blame Judaism for the initial and formative development of the misogyny and sexism we experience in both Christianity and Western civilization.[4]

This particular variation within antisemitism is exemplified in the misrepresentation found amongst some non-Jewish feminists concerning the binding of Isaac by his father Abraham, wherein the "sacrifice" of the child is transformed into a renunciation of matriarchal protection in the furtherance of a patriarchal system. The plain truth, of course, is that the story teaches the rejection of child-sacrifice. Womanist antisemitism is also brought to the surface and compounded via the claim that Jesus of Nazareth was a feminist. True, he was also a male. To date, the feminist claim for him is seldom utilized, as it could very well be, in order to show that Jesus' evident sympathy for women was typifying a moral impulse strictly within Judaism. Most often the claim concerning Jesus becomes a negativistic-ideological stress upon the faults of traditional Jewish behavior, as against the presumed virtues of the central figure in Christianity. One complicating factor, which probably does not help things, is that it is sometimes Christian males who put forward the (alleged) feminism of Jesus in (alleged) contrast to Jesus' peers. In any event, the so-called feminism of Jesus was soon to be buried by a church whose sexism exceeded, if anything, the continuing sexism of the Jewish world.

Many of the most promising revolutionary movements of our time are unable, or do not wish, to keep themselves free of antisemitism (cf. the bond between the Sandanistas and the PLO). In our present, specific context the antisemitism of the women's movement returns us to the moral asymmetry that obtains between Jewishness and Christian identity as a whole. However, in

---

4   McCauley and Daum, "Jewish-Christian Feminist Dialogue," p. 182.

fairness it has to be remembered that some of the antisemitism in the women's movement comes from people who have abandoned Christianity.

The future of Judaism and the women's movement

I shall try next to do some tying together, first through a constructive critical comment directed to the future of Judaism, and second through a word upon the contribution of the women's movement to the future of the Jewish-Christian meeting.

As Jewish feminists again and again point out, no problem is more conspicuous, stubborn, or serious than the rite of circumcision, involving as it does, traditionally and contemporaneously, *"the* physical sign of being in covenant with God."[5] If, as the Mishnah states, Abraham was not called perfect, i.e., a completed human being, until he was circumcised, it follows that women have no way to become completed human beings. (Christian baptism is free of the taint of sexism: here is a place where the moral asymmetry between Judaism and Christianity is reversed.)

However wholly unacceptable is the apostle Paul's Christian supersessionism vis-à-vis Judaism, his emphasis upon the ultimate irrelevance of circumcision may be interpreted as a strangely prevenient Christian judgment upon the Jewish tradition. This is said strictly in the context of the discrete problem of sexism and not at all with respect to Paul's woeful negativism respecting the place of Torah as a whole (cf. the work of E. P. Sanders). Paul's emphasis allies him, in an astonishing way, with womanism. I say "astonishing" because Paul was anything but a womanist. What I have in mind is the apostle's allusion to Jews and Gentiles: "Neither circumcision counts for anything nor uncircumcision, but keeping the commandments of God" (I Corinthians 7:19). This passage may be applied to our present subject.

In a biblical frame of reference, Paul is on the face of it talking nonsense, since circumcision *means* keeping God's commandments (Genesis 17:10). But in the late twentieth century the apostle's contention, applied to a Jewish feminist hermeneutic, gains contemporary power and application. In Romans 2 Paul declares:

---

5   Ibid., p. 164.

If a man who is uncircumcised keeps the precepts of the law, will not his uncircumcision be regarded as circumcision? ...For he is not a real Jew who is one outwardly, nor is true circumcision something external and physical. He is a Jew who is one inwardly, and real circumcision is a matter of the heart, spiritual and not literal. His praise is not from men but from God.

The plain implication of the previously-cited words of Rachel Adler is that the observance of Torah and the commandments is a right wholly inherent to Jewish women. Paying full heed to her lament over the marginalizing of Jewish females, we may venture to rewrite, in her behalf and theirs, the Pauline affirmation of Romans 2:

Clearly a woman of Israel remains uncircumcised. But through her honoring of the precepts of Torah, this uncircumcision is seen to have no consequence. Her uncircumcision is to be deemed the same as circumcision...For she is not a real Jew who is one outwardly, nor is true circumcision something that only males can achieve. She is a Jew who is one inwardly, and real circumcision means being treated as a human being, with full dignity and rights. Her praise is not from men but from God.

In contemporary parlance, the one way that Jewish men and Jewish women are made equal adherents of Judaism is through equally keeping the Torah. "Neither circumcision nor uncircumcision counts for anything." The answer to "uncircumcision" is found, and can only be found, in the unqualified opening of Torah-observance to women. (We are led to an incredible conclusion, to be taken not literally but with the seriousness of laughter: the apostle Paul never knew it but he was, preveniently, though only at this single place, an unwitting supporter of today's Jewish feminism.)

The women's movement in dialogue

My second series of comments relates to a possibly creative and redeeming contribution from within the women's movement to the Jewish-Christian meeting, with special emphasis upon Jewish-Christian reconciliation. Reference is needed to a number of variables: the meaning of revolution; the disparity between Jewishness and Christianness; the problem of male saviorhood; the encumbrance within Christian feminism; the consanguinity of antisemitic, Christological and sexist idolatries; and the final nemesis for antisemitism. Let us consider the way in which all these variables converge within the redeeming reality of Jewish womanism.

As summarized by George E. Rupp, three major attitudes vie for attention:

Antiwomanist ideology

On this position the androcentric or patriarchal tradition is inviolable and true. Contemporary womanist awareness and demands are no more than illicit self-exaltation.

Dialectical reform

Neither the androcentric tradition nor the new womanist awareness is to be wholly accepted or wholly rejected. Justice is to be sought between whatever is valid in the tradition and whatever is compelling in womanist awareness and demands.

Pro-womanist revolution

Now the androcentric tradition is seen to be evil and is to be totally rejected. Womanist awareness and demands have true and final authority, morally speaking.[6]

This tripartite structure may of course be utilized in the treatment of any and all sorts of social issues. In what follows, the androcentric tradition is repudiated, and the third alternative is embodied in ways that stand in adverse judgment upon the second alternative. But one complicating point requires mention first. The difference between radical womanists, who tend to have little hope for religious faith, and reforming womanists, who are more hopeful for faith, impinges upon the differences between Jewishness and Christianness: Are the people who are involved Jews or are they Christians? For as everyone knows, or ought to, the loss or absence of faith does not exclude a Jew from Jewishness whereas Christian faith is requisite to Christianness. Accordingly,

---

[6]   George E. Rupp, "Commitment to a Pluralistic World," in L. S. Rouner, ed., *Religious Pluralism* (Notre Dame: Notre Dame University Press, 1984), p. 219.

a radical Jewish womanist and a radical Christian womanist, as just characterized, are not in identical predicaments vis-à-vis their respective communities, nor do they, accordingly, have the same potential opportunities.

From the standpoint of the revolutionist Christian women's movement, Pope John Paul II's argumentation upon why only males can be priests, namely, it was in male form that God became incarnate, is turned against itself. That argument is viewed as self-refuting and self-condemning. For is not the best evidence of the untruthfulness and immorality of the traditionalist Incarnation-claim its pretension to male saviorhood? Insofar as males are radically exploitive of women, how could a male ever be their savior? A malignant disease does not cure itself. The androcentric reality of the Roman Catholic priesthood (as of the Orthodox Jewish rabbinate) is a violation of the truth, at once revealed and existential, that all human beings are made in the image of God.

There are resources within the women's movement for meliorating Christianity's intolerance of Judaism and Judaism's (much less) intolerance of Christianity. Female inclusivity is a winsome and powerful weapon against male exclusivity. Yet, as we have noted, Christian feminism is itself not free of the taint of antisemitism that afflicts Christianity as such. Accordingly, our present subject requires a much more discrete and much more profound approach.

There is the radical Christian womanism that cuts through the chains of a "Savior" who does not save, one in whom, and in whose maleness, women are in fact victimized. The avowedly Protestant Christian feminist Dorothee Sölle and the avowedly post-Christian feminist Mary Daly can embrace in their repugnance for what the latter has called "christolatry," the "idolatrous worship of a supernatural, timeless divine being who has little in common with the Jewish Jesus of Nazareth."

The point is that within and through the very struggle of Christian women *and men* against the Christological victimization of women, there is also carried forward the struggle against the victimization of Jews. The contemporary radical womanist attack upon the idolatrous deification of a male human being as reputed Savior constitutes a unique and unprecedented world-historical and potentially world-transforming event, equaling or excelling the Holocaust and a restored State of Israel. The reason for saying so is that this new event cuts not merely in one epochal moral direction but in two. On the one hand, it attacks the deification of not just any human being but the specific deification that created anti-Jewish supersessionism; and, on the other hand, it attacks the world-destroying sexism that came to penetrate Christianity (because of its male "Savior") in continuity with the sexism of Judaism. The inner bond between Christian antisemitism and Christian anti-womanism is disclosed. The single root cause of both these phenomena in the Christian world is the triumphalism of a male "Savior" aided and abetted by all his male followers through the long centuries. The whole of Christian history exhibits a single affliction, with two faces. There is the idolatrous divinizing of a human being which establishes antisemitism at the heart of Christianity, and there is the idolatrous male-izing of divinity which establishes anti-womanism as equally central.

If anti-Judaism and antisemitism are, as Rosemary Ruether has it, the left hand of Christology, androcentric sexism stands at Christology's right hand. Thus does the radical women's revolution become a resource, if an unintended one, for vanquishing the historic Christian derogation of things Jewish. This is not to imply that the women's movement is a means to an end. Were that the case, we should remain in the abyss of the exploitation of females. The contribution of the women's movement to overcoming Jewish-Christian moral asymmetry is an event of free grace, and it is to be received and celebrated as such.

Yet there remains what appears to be a fatal catch: We are still confronted by a considerably sexist Judaism. If that faith has always kept itself immune to human divinization, it has hardly escaped the sin of sexism. And the thoroughly Jewish Jesus remains, after all, a male. A final tragedy for the Christian church would be its deliverance from the Christological idolatry that ensures antisemitism only to land in the idolatries of a continuing Jewish sexism. This suggests that the real hope and the real future for Christianity is linked to the Jewish women's revolution—just as the Jewish ideal of justice and the sanctification of life is linked to the future and the prosperity of the Jewish feminist movement. For only the empowerment of Jewish womanism—which, unlike Christian womanism, is not hung up psychologically and spiritually upon the problematic of the saviorhood/non-saviorhood of a male being—can overcome, at one and the same time, all three of the evils that assail us: the mortal sin of Jewish and Christian androcentrism; Christian supersessionist and exclusivist imperialism against Jews and Judaism; and the antisemitism of the women's movement. Therefore, to the extent that Christian feminism frees itself from traditional Christian anti-Jewish, patriarchal triumphalism, it becomes the liberated emissary and partner of Jewish womanism. The prodigal daughter returns to her mother's household.

Overall, it may be suggested that the hope of today's Christian-Jewish dialogue is contingent upon its transfiguration into a Christian-Jewish-womanist trialogue. And, of infinitely greater import, the human, moral, and theological hope of the Christian church may be seen to lie in Jewish womanism.

8

Later Times, 1987ff.

With some measure of relief, I come to the final segment of this review and assessment of my literary ventures.

I

During the period beginning in 1987 I have been putting out eight books along with a number of occasional essays. In addition, I had a part in the reworking and expanding of *Long Night's Journey Into Day*. The rate of production here may seem more auspicious than is actually so. The fact is that as far back as 1980 I gave up teaching and administrative duties in order to devote all my time to writing. The job of a writer is to write. In my case, a threefold rule, seldom broken, has proved of much help: no talking on the telephone within the work day, seven days a week; no writing of letters within those same periods; no imbibing of spirits until after hours. Speaking of spirits, we who are Methodists are ofttimes dubbed legalists; I have just supplied three examples to justify attaching that label to me.

Some continuity obtains between this final segment of years and my earlier emphases. As examples, a chapter in *For Righteousness' Sake* occupies itself with one Christian's analytic and moral response to the rabbinic tradition, while a final chapter of that book has a not unfamiliar ring: "Trial of Faith, Trial of

God"; *Black-Woman-Jew* has as a major component the story and the problematic of Jewish liberation; and *Reclaiming the Jesus of History* bears directly upon the Christian-Jewish dialectic. My handling of that dialectic in later years has sought greater breadth and greater depth of context than it had managed to gain before; this is exemplified in various volumes of this final period.

Another introductory word, perhaps unnecessary since it is very much a truism: Ordinarily, the closer the date of a given piece of scholarly or creative (= idiomorphic?) writing approximates the present, the less is the party responsible able (or willing) to provide self-criticism—not perforce because the more recent creation is objectively less disputable or more convincing than earlier efforts, but simply because insufficient time has as yet elapsed for the writer to recognize or admit deficiencies or to change his mind. An all-necessary distancing from the work is not yet available. In this connection, readers will have noticed that as this book has gone forward, the element of adverse self-criticism has lessened and the element of descriptiveness and perhaps even self-apology has intensified. A further limitation or difficulty is that the writer may simply believe that what he will have contributed of late is as sound as he can make it, or that this phase of his effort may be turned to as a standard or instrument for evaluating previous endeavors. An additional complication or datum is that writers have a continuing responsibility to respond to critics when it appears that others have distorted or otherwise misrepresented their public creations.

Consonant with the foregoing paragraph, this chapter is more or less restricted to, on the one hand, commentary introductory or collateral to the writings (particularly the books) of this period and, on the other hand, remarks apropos of the essays offered below in chapter 8A.

II

To begin in a blanketing way, I have long sought to come to terms with or at least to live with the absolutist/relativist enigma within philosophic theology and the implications that this enigma has for how we know things and how we are to live responsibly.

My early polemic against "Christian relativism" in behalf of a "Christian absolutism" that would wage a truthful and effective war against antisemitism and other evils has long since turned to stone. True, the polemic was never unqualified by me, since I kept trying to control and even to obliterate the arrogance that tends to accompany absolutist theologies.

It was H. Richard Niebuhr who taught me the meaning, power, and necessity of theocentric relativism. From that standpoint, it is, in Niebuhr's words, "an aberration of faith as well as of reason to absolutize the finite." All our "relative history" of finite persons and movements proceeds "under the governance of the absolute God." To substitute some finite reality—any finite reality—for God is *idolatry*.[1]

There is, in consequence, much irony in the fact that Professor Niebuhr failed to carry to a full and coherent conclusion the dictates of his own theocentric relativism. This occurred at the all-crucial place of his Christology:

> Ernst Troeltsch came to see, not alone that we know the absolute God solely through the relativities of history, but that we know God only in a historically relative way. Niebuhr follows in this train. He finds "the great source of evil in life" to be "the absolutizing of the relative, which in Christianity takes the form of substituting religion, revelation, church or Christian morality for God"...Niebuhr works hard against the absolutizing of any embodiment or concretion of faith. But he does not reach his goal. For we note the absence of Jesus Christ from his list of unacceptable substitutions for God...[His] emphasis upon "the authority of Jesus Christ" vis-à-vis the authority of culture seriously qualifies his insistence upon the moral perils in absolutization...[Niebuhr] does not always listen to himself. For his strictures against defensiveness and self-defensiveness stop short of judgments concerning Jesus. Thus, in his affirmation that the *unity of humankind* is to be found in Jesus Christ, Niebuhr stays absolutist and supersessionist. When he bespeaks "that ultimate reality" which is "decisively revealed in Christ," the last thing he is talking about...is historical relativism—or even "historical relationism," a term he later preferred. And when he declares as a "fact that Christ is risen from the dead, and is not only the head of the church

---

1   *For Righteousness' Sake*, pp. 232, 234 (hereinafter referred to as FRS); H. Richard Niebuhr, *Christ and Culture* (New York: Harper & Row, 1951), p. x.

but the redeemer of the world," Niebuhr is both absolutist and supersessionist...

True, [he acknowledges that] a "deformation of radical monotheism
in Christianity occurs when Jesus Christ is made the absolute center of
confidence and loyalty." Yet the issue is not met by repeated insistence
that the lordship of Christ must not be substituted for the lordship of
God, since this very point is offset by Niebuhr's equal insistence upon
theological affirmations respecting Jesus (including his resurrection) that
are not to be made about anyone else. When he pens the words, "some
imagined idol called by his name takes the place of Jesus Christ the
Lord," he is ignoring *his own discernment* that there is idolatry in
ascribing lordship to any being other than the Creator of heaven and
earth.[2]

H. Richard Niebuhr's failure to be wholly true to his own witness against
absolutist idolatry may help point the way toward a contrastingly new and
affirmative Christology, in opposition to and replacement of what he himself
used to call "the unitarianism of the Second Person." A fresh Christology will
honor the theocentric relativism that Niebuhr preached but never quite
reached—to the end of an authentic Christian theocentric historicism. The
rudiments of such a Christology are offered in my study *Reclaiming the Jesus
of History*.

III

In recent years I have renewed my early and ongoing concerns with issues
other than, and in some respects wider than, the Christian-Jewish encounter. My
work of the late 1980s and early 1990s focuses upon seven broad, partially
overlapping areas:

1.   Contemporary Moral Philosophy: the history-faith relationship and the
     ethics-faith relationship as these may be perceived and treated from the
     perspective of a Christian moral philosophy (section IV of this chapter).

---

2   FRS, pp. 235-236 (slightly emended). See ibid., pp. 237-238 for a suggested
explanation of H. Richard Niebuhr's inability to carry through his historical relativism to the
fullfillment he was himself demanding.

2. Liberation Thinking: the philosophy and theology of human liberation; most particularly, female liberation (section V).

3. The *Shoah:* contemporary thinking upon the Holocaust (section VI).

4. Christology: recent and current thinking upon the Jesus of history, and the Christological import of such thinking. The attestation to God's Incarnation and God's Resurrection (section VII).

5. The Quality of Humor: the philosophy and theology of human laughter and comedy, with their implications for Christian doctrine and witness.

6. The Fundamentals of Christianity: the abiding essentials of day-to-day Christian faith and life.

7. The Threefold Relation of God-Devil-Laughter: the possible place of comedy in distinguishing "God" and "Devil." (Items 5-7 are elaborated upon briefly under section VIII of this chapter.)

IV

I seem to remember that it is a breach of literary etiquette for an author to identify a particular work as his *opus magnum.* The appellation ought to come, if it comes at all, from a party other than the writer. This leaves me with a problem: I have not succeeded in hiring anybody to carry out this task for me, and I doubt that "she who must be obeyed" will agree to do it. However, once the meaning of *opus magnum* is limited to "chief work" (contra "great work") I take it that the writer may assume the right to describe one of his books in that way. In my case, I should plead that the phrase be applied to *For Righteousness' Sake,* the most comprehensive of my books and a culmination of my life's work. (*Black-Woman-Jew* is of the nature of a sequel to that book; *Reclaiming the Jesus of History* carries ahead and develops one of that earlier volume's themes; and *Sitting in the Earth and Laughing* perpetuates and amplifies, with much mischief, the elements of humor in *For Righteousness' Sake.*)

As I have reread *For Righteousness' Sake* and compared and contrasted it with others of my books, I have felt that in this instance things fit together rather well, at least from the standpoint of the preeminent norm of literary and substantive coherence. I think that if the penny dropped anywhere, it dropped here. (Unfortunately, I have not had the benefit of many critical reviews; the book has gained little attention.[3]) Of equal or greater importance, *For Righteousness' Sake* unfolds a dialectic wherein the Christian-Jewish *Auseinandersetzung* is not the ultimate rationale or frame of reference of the endeavor as a whole but yet wherein my efforts do not leave, or do not quite seem capable of leaving, that arena.

A specific impetus behind *For Righteousness' Sake* was the conviction that the typology offered by H. Richard Niebuhr in his noted and notable work *Christ and Culture* was incomplete and could profit from greater comprehensiveness. I became convinced of the need to present a more capacious range of views than we have had in religio-moral philosophy (or in the history of religious ideas)—Christian, Jewish, Muslim—and in ways that manifest the power and the limits of these views, with respect to practical decision-making in today's world. Just as Niebuhr had supplemented and corrected the twofold schema of "church" and "sect" put forward by Ernst Troeltsch, so I took as my task to supplement and correct Niebuhr's fivefold typology by means of an eightfold typology. (To keep the pace of this particular numbers game going, any replacement of *For Righteousness' Sake* will want to supply us with eleven types: 2—>5—>8—>11.)

H. Richard Niebuhr's typology delineates major possible relationships between "Christ" and "culture": Christ against culture, the Christ of culture, Christ above culture, Christ and culture in paradox, and (Niebuhr's own position) Christ the transformer of culture. By augmenting the number of types to eight, and by reidentifying and expanding the two overall variables of "Christ" and "culture" into the more comprehensive categories of "faith" and "history," or "faith" and "the human world," I endeavored to furnish a systematic treatment of the possible relationships, this in the interests of more catholic decision-making.

My types (I also dubbed them *normative images)* were:

1. Faith against the world.
2. Jesus of Nazareth.
3. Concretions of righteousness and goodness in the rabbinic tradition.

---

[3]   In a review of FRS, Alan Davies incorrectly states that the "real topic" of the study is the Holocaust (*Journal of Ecumenical Studies*, 25 [1988]: 285-286). Again, Davies engages in such misrepresentations as: Not to agree with Eckardt "is to make God and oneself an antisemite."

4. Faith for the world.
5. Faith above history.
6. History and faith in tension.
7. Faith transforming history.
8. History transforming faith.

For Righteousness' Sake was directed to the query, "In what sense may decisions for and against various views of the faith/history relation be themselves treated as raw materials for our own moral decisions?" The concrete method of study I utilized was "the anguishing contemporary question of the relation between faith and history" along the highways and byways of human culture, and in the frame of reference of an even more anguishing question of today: the righteousness of God. The several interpretations reviewed and assessed "constitute developments from, fulfillments of, variations upon, and in some instances partial negations of, an originative persuasion that human history stands open to commands and judgments of transcendent, apodictic (absolute) quality—a persuasion we may denominate 'the message of the divine righteousness.'"[4]

The second, third, and eighth positions listed supplement and refine H. Richard Niebuhr's schema. In consonance with various opinions of mine expressed earlier in this retrospective, the eighth alternative is the one to which I feel myself drawn, at least for the present. I also refer to that position as "Christian theocentric historicism"—"historicism" not in the inglorious sense of a philosophy that seeks to exempt itself from its own demands of historical relativity, but instead a hopefully *self-critical* view judged and underwritten by its theocentrism. Will Herberg rightly apprehends historicism as a positive concept that in its depth and breadth permits it to be, in Bernhard W. Anderson's words, "the touchstone, or criterion, for determining theological authenticity."[5]

A paradoxical feature of my own intellectual/spiritual journey is that, for all the substantive aid I have received from Reinhold Niebuhr and his "history

---

[4]   FRS, pp. 3-4, 5, 13-14.

[5]   FRS, p. 247. The citation is from Bernhard W. Anderson, introductory comment to Will Herberg's essay, "Historicism as Touchstone," in Herberg, *Faith Enacted as History: Essays in Biblical Theology*, ed. Anderson (Philadelphia: Westminster Press, 1976), pp. 190-198.

and faith in tension," and from H. Richard Niebuhr and his "faith transforming history," and for all their influence upon me, I should yet locate myself within the family "history transforming faith." However, I think that this outcome is made possible because "history transforming faith" has no ultimate quarrel with either "history and faith in tension" or "faith transforming history" but instead makes peace with them through a free acknowledgement of their rightness. Here enters the grace of theological pluralism. And that pluralism need not stop with the acceptance of categories six and seven. Is it not the case that each and every one of the competing types go to add up to a history of their own that may in turn serve in the transformation of faith?

One serious problem with the closing pages of *For Righteousness' Sake* is that in the matter of the "trial of God," including God's ostensible unforgivableness, I did not go any farther than I have in chapter seven, section IV of the present retrospective. I raised the question of who, if anyone, has a right to forgive God, but I proffered no answer. However, that question is addressed constructively in "For the Sake of Rachel and For the Sake of Sarah" (1989).

Please consult the excerpt from *For Righteousness' Sake* below, "People of Eight."

V

Fairly early in my professional life I was stressing that "basic moral strategy, to be effective, must be primarily social and political rather than primarily religious. Religious faith can foster and support ethical incentive and purpose, but zeal for action remains ineffectual until it is wedded to socio-political instrumentalities."[6] From the standpoint of liberative moral philosophy and theology, these words may suggest a judgment against me, since it was only relatively late in my work that I was brought to the study and advocacy of liberation praxis as such. (Strictly speaking, in liberative understanding "praxis" is more than practice alone. It is that critical relation "between theory and

---

[6]   *The Surge of Piety in America* (1958), pp. 124-125.

practice whereby each is dialectically influenced and transformed by the other."[7])

One analytic complication here is that in *For Righteousness' Sake* I treated Christian liberation teaching and thinking under the heading of "faith transforming history," in some distinction from my own "normative image" of "history transforming faith." There is much objective justification for this. For on balance, and with particular reference to Latin American liberation theology, "faith transforming history" takes precedence over "history transforming faith."[8] Gustavo Gutiérrez expresses the point dialectically: While "Christ's liberation cannot be reduced to political liberation," that liberation is yet "present in concrete historical and political liberating events."[9] Latin American liberation is very much a church movement. On the other hand, the continuities between liberation thinking and "history transforming faith" can be readily exemplified—as in my study *Black-Woman-Jew: Three Wars for Human Liberation*. Also, the analytic complication referred to above becomes somewhat redundant in and through the efforts of individual liberation figures, many of whom are dedicated to the transformation of the secular world in behalf of faith and many others of whom are pledged to the transformation of faith in behalf of secular life. Still others could not care less about all such distinctions. Most liberationists are consumed with zeal to set free the exploited, the humiliated, from various kinds of bondage. Liberation, overall, means a transformation of and deliverance from oppressing and inhuman structures—personal, social, economic, political, religious, cultural.

Black-Woman-Jew, a study in contemporary history, represented three world-liberative causes—each for its own sake though not without critical evaluation. Emphasis fell not alone upon the numerous differences among the three but also upon the unnumbered affinities within them. In each instance the views of many representative figures were considered and assessed.

---

7   David Tracy, *Blessed Rage for Order: The New Pluralism in Theology* (New York: Seabury Press, 1978), p. 243; FRS, p. 6.

8   See FRS, pp. 200ff.

9   Gustavo Gutiérrez, *The Power of the Poor in History: Selected Writings*, trans. Robert R. Barr (Maryknoll, NY: Orbis Books, 1983), pp. 68, 63; FRS, p. 200 and cf. pp. 231-232.

The black person, the woman, the Jew ask together: How am I to respond to a world that wishes to define me as a nonperson, that regards my group as an illegitimate or less-than-good form of existence? I drew special attention to relations between black religion and black power; to the war for black liberation in South Africa[10]; to black woman's liberation from the twin scourges of racism and sexism; to Jewish woman's liberation from sexism and antisemitism; to the essential place of women's liberation as judge of and guide to any and all liberation movements; and to Jewish liberation, not alone for its own sake but as a unique resource in humankind's perennial quest for moral universality. I held that the selfsame standards of response (acceptance, interpretation, evaluation) that are utilized respecting black liberation and women's liberation are to be applied to Jewish liberation (or, for that matter, to any other form of human liberation). The essay "One *Ruse de Guerre* on the Devil" is indicative of the singleness of standard that is developed in *Black-Woman-Jew*.

The gathering revolution in Christian theology occasioned by the *Shoah*, the reemergence of the State of Israel, and the church's reappropriation of its Jewish roots may neither be separated from nor exalted above other revolutionary trends within contemporary Christianity: the development of liberation theology coupled with the struggle to end the oppression of the world's masses; the growth of the women's movement, including opposition to a male chauvinist sacerdotalism; and the struggle against a white racist church. From a general politico-moral standpoint, there is no difference in principle between the question, Is God antisemitic?, and the questions, Is God a rich capitalist? Is God a white racist?[11] Is God a male chauvinist?

Once this solidarity-for-justice is recognized and celebrated, we are nevertheless obliged to distinguish first things from second things (without in any way derogating the importance of the secondary struggles). Historically and substantively speaking, it was the separation of the church from its Jewish foundation, from Jewish prophetism, and from the Jewish struggle against idolatry, that, more than any other factor, enabled the church to fall into its

---

[10] Chap. 5 of *Black-Woman-Jew* is comprised substantially of the essay "An American Looks at *Kairos.*"

[11] Cf. William R. Jones, *Is God a White Racist? A Preamble to Black Theology* (Garden City: Anchor Press/Doubleday, 1973).

many and various sins of omission and commission that had subsequently to be fought with the weapons of liberation theology and praxis.

The essays reprinted in chapter 8A below include one item first contained in *Black-Woman-Jew:* "Double Jeopardy for Black Women: Racism and Sexism." I here and now dedicate this essay to Professor Anita Hill.

VI

As previously indicated, during the years 1985-1988 Alice Eckardt prepared a revised, updated, and expanded edition of *Long Night's Journey Into Day*, grounded in new research and new events. The work in its final form was thus some thirteen years in preparation. For the new version we changed the subtitle to the more appropriate *A Revised Retrospective on the Holocaust.* Pergamon Press (Oxford) joined Wayne State University Press in publishing this edition, in time for the July 1988 international conference on the Holocaust, "Remembering for the Future," held in Oxford and London. Having read the first edition of the book, Dr. Elisabeth Maxwell of Oxford had come to us seeking counsel respecting how the lessons of the study might be implemented, particularly in the United Kingdom. In response, Alice Eckardt proposed that an international scholars' conference be held in that land. The above-mentioned meeting was the consequence, underwritten as it was to be by Elisabeth and Robert Maxwell and worked upon tirelessly by my wife and many others over many months. The conference was to be attended by some 600 scholars from 24 countries, figures indicative of greatly expanded academic and lay interest in and concern with the Holocaust. Some 60 percent of the scholars who came were non-Jews. (A follow-up conference was planned for Berlin in March, 1994.)

Emil L. Fackenheim has described the *Shoah* as a "negative epiphany." *Long Night's Journey Into Day* is an exercise in memory, impassioned by the human search for redemption and contrasting with the failures and irresponsibilities of amnestia, intentional obliviousness. The multiple approach used is historical-moral-philosophical-theological. The book pleads for a radical reexamination and reformulation of the Christian theology and praxis that helped bring the *Shoah* to pass. We suggested that those who reject the power and constraint of the *Shoah* as a demand for the revolutionizing of faith are living and dying as though that event never happened. The study probes the moral, theological, and political issues that the Holocaust raises for Christians and Jews. Salient themes (most of which have already been given some voice in this retrospective) include the ethical and methodological dilemmas faced by Holocaust scholars;[12] the incomparability of antisemitism; the singularity of the *Shoah*;[13] the widespread Jewish resistance to the Nazi murder machine; the "necessity" of the Devil; the trial, repentance, and faithfulness of God; Christian culpability for and in the Holocaust; the self-sacrificing acts of righteous Gentiles; the linkage of *Shoah* and State of Israel; the issue of relating the *Shoah* to other acts of mass murder;[14] the dialectic of Christian teaching and the *Shoah*; and intensive study and assessment of the views of contemporary Christian and Jewish thinkers.[15] Throughout, we seek to honor Irving Greenberg's ennobling principle that no statement, theological or other, can be made "that would not be credible in the presence of the burning children."[16] "Supersessionist theology is a carrier; it carries the germs of genocide, but the genocide only of Jews." Included in our study is a polemic against the "suffering servant syndrome" when applied to Jews.[17]

---

[12]   There is reliance at this point upon the essay "Studying the Holocaust's Impact Today." Any and all writings on the *Shoah* by American Christians as perhaps also by Jews run hard against Eugene B. Borowitz's observation that for American Jews as a whole the Holocaust is very largely past history (cf. Borowitz's essay, "On the Jewish Obsession with History," in Leroy S. Rouner, ed., *Religious Pluralism* [Notre Dame: University of Notre Dame Press, 1984], p. 20).

[13]   "The decision that there were to be no more Jews on Planet Earth constituted an absolute convergence of quantitative and qualitative reality" (*Long Night's Journey Into Day*, rev. and enlarged ed., p. 56; references to that edition are hereinafter identified simply as LNJID). See in general LNJID, chap 5 - "Singularity."

[14]   Our position on this specific issue is that the remembrance of one such singular event as the *Shoah* does not block, but instead must be enabled to nurture, the remembrance of other singular events, catastrophes, and crimes.

[15]   The extensive critique in LNJID, pp. 102-123, of Jürgen Moltmann's position is largely based upon "Jürgen Moltmann, the Jewish People, and the Holocaust."

[16]   As cited in LNJID, p. 128.

[17]   LNJID, pp. 132, 144-147. In the course of an essay "Emil Fackenheim and Christianity After the Holocaust" (*American Journal of Theology & Philosophy* 9 [Jan.-May 1988]: 134-135) Michael McGarry decries certain critical Christological statements in LNJID (utilizing only the first edition). McGarry alleges that, according to the Eckardts, Christians must give up their belief in the resurrection of Christ *if they are to be true to* Jewish partners in the dialogue. In the process, he misstates our point of view, praxis, and contribution. In

VII

Returning next to issues of Christology, I think as I now write that my critique of resurrectionist Christian faith in earlier pages of this retrospective is overdrawn. In pondering further this momentous and devastating question, I have come to believe that there is a world of difference between triumphalist, victimizing resurrectionism and nontriumphalist or antitriumphalist and nonvictimizing resurrectionism. This possible reorientation accords with the hope offered in chapter seven above that it may yet be feasible for Christian theology to propound a non-supersessionist resurrection, and with this to restore Jesus' resurrection to its historic and definitive place in Christian teaching. This entire question is addressed in *Reclaiming the Jesus of History*, particularly in chapter eleven, which ventures a positive affirmation of the Christian teaching of Jesus' resurrection. (The substance of that chapter is reproduced below in the essay titled *"'Why Do You Search Among the Dead?'"* That essay repeats certain earlier materials of mine; these are retained for purposes of emphasis and reminder.)

Reclaiming the Jesus of History reviews and assesses a number of current scholars and interpreters, including Marcus J. Borg, James H. Charlesworth,

---

point of truth, the Eckardts have never written a single word to support the libel that we take the position we do to the end of fostering some kind of Jewish-Christian dialogue. Any such politicizing of Christian moral theology would indeed constitute a grave sin. We may be guilty of many sins but this is not one of them. Further to this matter, consult Alice L. and A. Roy Eckardt, "A Reply to Michael McGarry," *American Journal of Theology & Philosophy* 11 (May 1990): 1-3.

The revised edition of LNJID contains two appendixes: my essay "The Christian World Goes to Bitburg"; and Alice L. Eckardt, "We Are Called to Remember in Worship: Creating Christian Yom HaShoah Liturgies," reproduced from Marcia Sachs Littell, ed., *Liturgies on the Holocaust* (Lewiston, NY: Edwin Mellen, 1986). In connection with Ronald Reagan's visit to Bitburg and his honoring of Nazi dead, Martin Stöhr and Rolf Rendtorff, two Christian theologians of Germany, mourned the truth that, just as in the Nazi period, the German bishops and Christians of all denominations (in Stöhr's words) "did not stand by the Jews" (as cited in Ilya Levkov, ed., *Bitburg and Beyond: Encounters in American, German, and Jewish History* [New York: Shapolsky, 1987], p. 502).

Not otherwise mentioned or utilized in this chapter are "Post Holocaust Theology and the Christian-Jewish Dialogue"; "Hilberg's Silence" (with Alice L. Eckardt); and "Salient Christian-Jewish Issues of Today: A Christian Exploration." The substance of the last-mentioned essay is taken from FRS, chap. 12; JAC, chaps. 5, 7, 9; "Is There a Way out of the Christian Crime?"; and "Christians, Jews, and the Women's Movement." During this period I also reviewed Jacob Neusner, *Death and Birth of Judaism*; and Ilya Levkov, ed., *Bitburg and Beyond*.

John B. Cobb, Jr., Paula Fredriksen, Donald Goergen, John Hick, Paul F. Knitter, John Macquarrie, Sharon H. Ringe, E. P. Sanders, and Paul M. van Buren; considers such contemporary movements as Christian liberationism, Christian feminism, Christian pluralism, and Christian incarnationism in their implications for Christology; concentrates upon continuities and discontinuities between the "Jesus of history" and the "Christ of faith"; seeks to retrieve the teaching of incarnation vis-à-vis Jesus; and offers a neokenotic, theocentric Christology of its own.

I believe that the reasons we may honor Jesus—not, I trust, in an idolatrous way but in a suffusedly human and faithful way—rest upon, and ought not violate, what Jesus said, what he did, and what happened to him, yet also upon what we may attest that God did in and through him. In the last-mentioned connection, in the course of my study *No Longer Aliens, No Longer Strangers* I endeavor to rediscover and reaffirm the Christian teaching of the Incarnation of God in Jesus Christ in a nonsupersessionist, nonexclusivist way.

VIII

The final turn that my literary journey has been taking is the theme of comedy. This has not come as a total surprise to me, for I have spent a great deal of my life laughing and being ludicrous (*bouche à feu* against depression? against the epidemic dark?).

In the course of this latest period I have been exercised about the relation between the humble (great?) domain of comedy and the great (humble?) realm of philosophic theology. My study *Sitting in the Earth and Laughing: A Handbook of Humor* directs itself to the sense, nonsense, and mystery of humor in ongoing individual and social life, addressing a variety of perspectives: philosophic, psychological, social, and religious. Alternating with chapters of serious study are sections of comedy, fantasy, and nonsense from my own pen and from others. I have been learning that the world of humor/comedy is not readily controllable by a writer (or by anyone else); it has its ways of exploding into a universe of its own.

Somewhat unanswered within *Sitting in the Earth and Laughing* is the question of historical/moral/aesthetic links and disparities between Jewish humor and Christian humor. I grapple with that issue in an essay reproduced at the end of chapter 8A of the present retrospective, "Comic Visions, Comic Truths," under whose provenance Incarnation-Crucifixion-Resurrection are joyfully attested to as Three Jokes, three eschatological starts. For in and through the providence of comedy, Christian imperialism may find itself put to shame.[18] It is a dream of mine that my writing upon humor/laughter/comedy might somehow manage to make it as my one, if only, contribution to a postmodern Christian theology. In this connection the volume *How to Tell God from the Devil: On the Way to Comedy* attempts to utilize the resources of comedy for drawing needed life-and-death distinctions between things truly divine and things truly devilish. The same is the case, though with quite different emphases, in *On the Way to Death: Essays Toward a Comic Vision.*

No Longer Aliens, No Longer Strangers seeks to provide a brief enchiridion of essential elements in Christian faith and living: the Christian understanding of the human being; the church as people of God; the person and behavior (praxis) of God; the standards that govern Christian morality; a few applications of the Christian ethic to daily life; the quality of Christian humor; and reflections upon death and eternal life.

A massive problem I keep on facing is the relating of intellectuality, spirituality, and ethics. While I am not always experiencing personally a split among these three norms, I have a strong impression that my writings taken as a whole do not always elude or overcome that rift. I could take refuge in the finding that the mind/spirit/morality trichotomy is endemic to the human condition, but that would be a cop-out. It is probably better to acknowledge these nagging incoherencies in my case than to try to wriggle out of them with the weapon of words.

---

[18] Greatly expanded from a paper presented to a symposium honoring Emil L. Fackenheim in Toronto, 22-24 March 1992, "Comic Visions, Comic Truths" was read before the Christian Scholars Group on Judaism and the Jewish People, Baltimore, 17-18 April 1993. The substance of this paper appears in my forthcoming study, *How to Tell God from the Devil: On the Way to Comedy*, under the title "A Stop Along the Road to Hear Three Jokes: Comedy and the *Campesino*." See also my essays "Divine Incongruity: Comedy and Tragedy in a Post-Holocaust World" (1992) and "Is There a Christian Laughter?" (1992).

8A

Selected Essays

(1987-1993)

People of Eight

(Adapted from *For Righteousness' Sake* [1987], pp. 225-234, 239-240)

How, if at all, may we "mend the world"?[1] In principle, there are two generic choices: through the world itself, and through something "beyond the world." Everyone expects—well, almost everyone—that the proponent of faith will opt for the second choice, and, indeed, insist upon it. But what if the representative of faith says: "Through the world itself"? Is that understanding out of the question? Is it to be ruled out? Is its protagonist being "unfaithful"?

I

Thus, do we come, at the last, to "history transforming faith." or, in terminology a bit more forceful, a Christian *theocentric historicism*, as aimed especially at the life and thought of the church. We have alluded at various points to *historicalness*, the acceptance of and response to the crucialities of time and place. Historicalness is not itself just "history," although of course decision-making takes place wholly within history. When bringing together the realities of "historicalness" and "history" we may find it useful to employ the word *historicity*.

The concept "Christian" in the phrase "Christian theocentric historicism" refers simply to Christian auspices, the praxis that is available, as a gift to the Christian community, but yet is independent of Christianity as of every other religion. Christian triumphalism and supersessionism would devastate the ethic involved.

I identify representatives of this view as "eighth people" or "people of eight."

Today many concepts vie as aids in encapsulating the intent and the hope of Christian and other thinkers: e.g., "post-liberal," "post-modern," "post-Christian," "post-secularist," and "post-conciliar" (still in gladsome memory of

---

[1]   Emil L. Fackenheim, *To Mend the World: Foundations of Future Jewish Thought* (New York: Schocken Books, 1982).

good Pope John and *aggiornamento*). Common to viewpoints that appropriate
"post" as a prefix, though of course not lacking elsewhere, is a felt obligation
to begin anew, to construct a living bridge between a certain spiritual past and
the moral challenges and agonies of humankind today, to point the way responsibly to the future. So it is with the "post-liberal" position that I espouse. This
latter usage of "post-" may, with other such usages, sound presumptuous. For
the viewpoints to which "post-" wants to attach itself sometimes retain a vitality
that keeps them from being sent to oblivion via the pretensions of a four-letter
prefix. The "liberal" outlook may well be a case in point. Is Liberalism as dead
as all that? The living gift of Liberalism is its demand that religious claims be
subjected to the judgments and life of morality. To speak in behalf of a "post-
liberal" outlook does not have to mean casting Liberalism away but can instead
mean acting to redeem it by infusing it with a realism and a transcendence of
which it still stands in need. In this respect my "post-liberal" position is a
species of Christian "revisionist" moral philosophy. As David Tracy writes:

> the neo-orthodox insisted that the liberal analysis of the human situation
> was able to account at best for human finitude and possibility, but was
> utterly unable to account for those negative elements of tragedy, of
> terror, indeed, of sin in human existence...With the relative strengths
> and limitations of liberalism, orthodoxy, neo-orthodoxy, and radical
> theologies in mind, the revisionist theologian is committed to continuing
> the critical task of the classical liberals and modernists in a genuinely
> post-liberal situation...[He] is committed to what seems clearly to be the
> central task of contemporary Christian theology: the dramatic confron-
> tation, the mutual illuminations and corrections, the possible basic
> reconciliation between the principal values, cognitive claims, and
> existential faiths of both a reinterpreted post-modern consciousness and
> a reinterpreted Christianity.[2]

In the present essay I offer a prologue to our final normative image, the
third of those images not specifically delineated within H. Richard Niebuhr's
typology.

---

[2]   David Tracy, *Blessed Rage for Order: The New Pluralism in Theology* (New York:
Seabury Press, 1978), pp. 28, 32.

II

For the sake both of review and of the analysis still to come, it may be helpful to assay a few of the more prominent comparisons and contrasts between our eighth image and the images that have gone before.

Eighth people can be freely accepting of one or another aspect of all seven of the other points of view. Among the supports for this statement, four interrelated points may be singled out: (a) Every normative image is inseparable from human experience of one kind or another. Indeed, all the images have a place within historical determinations of faith. Even a denial of history's consequentialness cannot be made other than within time and place; thus does that denial paradoxically pay tribute to history's power. To paraphrase First John's comment on sin (1:8), "If we say we are not conditioned by history, we deceive ourselves, and the truth is not in us." All this has a disarming way of making us "members one of another." (Who among us does not *fear* infirmity and death?) (b) All the normative images we are studying are linked in one or another way to the responsibility of unfolding and representing the divine righteousness. (c) Because both "history" and "faith" are taken by eighth people to be, in principle, equally licit and commanding, this establishes continuity, of varying degrees, with most other images or types. (d) "The relativities of all things human and the mysteries of all things divine are too great ever to permit any one solution to become *the* Christian answer. That answer must be sought again and again in every particular context and time by finite men responding to the absolute God."[3]

These four reasons explain, at least partially, how people of eight can be fully open to philosophic and theological-ethical pluralism. Each item witnesses to the cruciality of history for faith. Yet history comprises no more than half the total dialectic of faith and history. And eighth people know well, as other protagonists ought to know, that within the bounds of history, no final resolution of the problem of faith and history is possible. (To acknowledge that a given faith evolves over the course of history is to honor the overall dialectic of faith and history. For the process of development involves [a] independent influences arising over time from *within* the faith, and [b] independent influences arising

---

[3] Lonnie Kliever, *H. Richard Niebuhr* (Waco: Word Books, 1977), pp. 58-59.

over time from *beyond* the faith, i.e., from external history. Thus are eighth people enabled to acknowledge the contribution of all normative images to a general theological ethic.)

Let us return to the individual images covered thus far.

The two non-dialectical views of "faith against the world" and "faith for the world." In their thinking/praxis eighth people do not support unqualified rejection of the secular order, however sorry that order's present and constitutive state. As H. Richard Niebuhr points out, around the edges of the radical movement of "Christ against culture" the Manichean heresy is forever developing.[4] On the other hand, people of eight do not accept a mere conciliation or accommodation of faith to the secular realm. They oppose any betrayal of transcendence. In Troeltsch's language, they are neither a "church-type" nor a "sect-type." They join other mediating views in a life that moves constantly, and with fear and trembling, between the world and their faith.

However, the possibility of confusing or identifying "history transforming faith" with another image is markedly greater in the case of "faith for the world" than of "faith against the world." A reason for this is discernible in or through the passage cited above from David Tracy. Within the post-liberal posture a certain reminiscence is found of the two interests of Friedrich Schleiermacher: to be both a Christian theologian and a modern person, "participating fully in the work of culture, in the development of science, the maintenance of the state, the cultivation of art, the ennoblement of family life, the advancement of philosophy."[5] (Just here are we not haunted, quite involuntarily, by the specter of the Faith Movement of German Christians?) This much cannot be gainsaid: Exactly because of their historicist leanings, eighth people are not exempt from a certain temptation, in singular ways, to assimilate their faith to history, under the power of false consciousness. Because their deontological ethic of response/responsibility is peculiarly vulnerable to the idolatries of the world, they must fight these idolatries with the same fervor that they battle moral irresponsibility.

Part of the life insurance available to people of eight consists in the fact that these people do not receive history as an absolute, after the fashion of its

---

4   H. Richard Niebuhr, *Christ and Culture* (New York: Harper & Bros., 1951), p. 81.

5   Ibid., p. 93.

Hegelian or extra-Hegelian disciples, but instead in all its relativity and fragmentariness. In this regard, the demands of responsible decision-making upon the stage of history are such that certain events may have to be judged and found wanting at the hands of other events. In consequence, previously authoritative happenings may be told to abdicate their authority. That this can and does occur helps to show that the process of history is being assigned, not absolute status, but instrumental and pragmatic status. The simplest refutation of any absolutizing of history lies in the truth that history not only helps answer some of our problems, it also creates greater problems, if only by compounding the insufficiency of our responses to it.

The other part of the eighth people's insurance policy is that they have no intention of abandoning their faith in the God who judges all pretension and idolatry.

In light of "faith for the world's" constituent stress upon human reason, a word on that theme is in order. It is, after all, the presence of the instrument of human reason that enables us to identify the present work as an exercise in *moral philosophy*. In the view of Lockean rationalism, Christian teaching may be according to reason and above reason but never contrary to reason. A historicist faith is accepting of this principle. However, the attestations of historicism extend broader and deeper than those of rationalist empiricism. It will be recalled that for Locke, reason entails deductions from the natural faculties of sensation and reflection. By concentrating upon events and the meanings of events, and, most particularly, extraordinary events, historicism goes beyond this form of rationalism. It speaks from the standpoint of a faith that is according to history and above history, though not contrary to history. There is, nevertheless, a final link between reason and history. I refer to the dimension of transcending reason, which not only examines reason itself but responds creatively and sometimes ecstatically to transcending events.

In seeking to develop the legitimacy of "history transforming faith," I shall resort both to argument and to testimony. The difficulty of balancing logical-rational discourse and existential avowal is a perennial one. The illegitimacy of switching from argument to unsupported asseveration (a peculiarly tempting device whenever the going gets rough) is often pointed out. I do not envision any final victory over this condition, in literature or in life, for the difficulty ultimately defies resolution through mere human thought or action. To commend reasoned analysis or reasonableness (including "common sense") as the criterion of certain kinds of knowledge and truth cannot itself be rationally vindicated. To pretend otherwise is to beg the question because we are forced to assume the integrity of reason in the very effort to "prove" (i.e., test) that integrity. As G. K. Chesterton succinctly put it, "reason is itself a matter of faith." All arguments finally rest upon, yet also lead into, some kind of "I believe." The other side of this state of affairs is that confessions of conscience lose their imperative force when they are turned into logical argumentation. And, happily, the fact that reasonableness, if it is to be honored, must itself be accepted on faith does not necessarily negate its validity or its usefulness. All in all, the most we can manage to do is to make our subjective testimonies as objectively reasonable as possible, and our objective arguments as vitally subjective as possible.

Jesus and the kingdom/righteousness of God. A preeminent paradox is that a Christian "return into history," to Jesus and the origins of Christianity, turns us completely around, directing us to the end-time, the coming of the reign of God, which Jesus himself proclaimed. But we recall as well that in Jesus this proclamation is related to, or counterbalanced by, his ethic of Torah-cum-Prophecy. In these concrete ways the Christian church is bonded historically to Jesus. He is the foundation of Christian historicism. Insofar as Jesus points beyond himself to the reality and authority of God, his historicity is the paradigm for the Christian life. Instead of recasting the figure of Jesus to satisfy a traditionalistic "authority" for him, "history transforming faith" will seek to apprehend the "authority" of Jesus in reconciliation with the historical truth about him.

The talmudic and rabbinic tradition. We have been apprised of the dialectical ways in which this vast Jewish tradition interweaves the three categories of changing historical experience, certain advocated concretions of day-to-day morality, and a transcending Torah and faith.

Faith above history. I have maintained that the overall relation between faith and history is architectonic in the sense that history is at the foundation of human life, and that faith comes along to build upon that foundation. However, in contrast to "faith above history," the historical-moral demands and opportunities of the divine righteousness apply to all members of the religious community.

History and faith in tension. Eighth people freely acknowledge the sinfulness and tragedies of the human condition whereby history and faith are placed into inevitable and abiding tension. (Practitioners of "faith against the world" are anything but strangers to the knowledge of sin; yet, as H. Richard Niebuhr points out, they are tempted to exempt their own holy commonwealth from sin's dominion.[6]) We live in an unredeemed world. It is so that people of eight support the socially and politically ameliorating emphases within Christian realism. However, Reinhold Niebuhr's Christian realism tends to take the message and life of Jesus and the event of the Cross and shift their foci "from historical fulfillment to the religious problem of ultimate reconciliation with God." At this point it would appear that Christian realism does not wholly surmount the spiritualizing proclivities of traditionalist Christianity. From the perspective of today's theology of liberation, the Exodus experience of God's historical deliverance of his people from oppression is to remain paradigmatic.[7] Herein is suggested a means of avoiding "excessive spiritualization" (Gutiérrez). In this vital respect, the theological aspects of Christian realism appear paradoxically more supersessionist respecting Judaism than does liberation theology. I say "paradoxically" because Reinhold Niebuhr is in truth much more sympathetic to Judaism and the Jewish people than are today's liberation theologians (even though Niebuhr himself did not overcome all Christian triumphalism).

Faith transforming history. Because images seven and eight share a transformationist perspective and yet in constituent ways are not the same, extra attention to that relationship is appropriate.

In the first of the two transformationist positions, faith goes to work seeking to change the historical and created order. The engine of that image is revolutionary praxis broadcast to the wide human world. In "history transforming faith" the imperatives of historical events and patterns become instruments for making religious faith more responsibly moral. The engine of this image is revolutionary praxis targeted upon the *ecclesia.* A shared commitment to the reconstruction of human life makes close allies of the two

---

6   Ibid., p. 118.

7   Dennis P. McCann, *Christian Realism and Liberation Theology: Practical Theologies in Creative Conflict* (Maryknoll, NY: Orbis Books, 1981), p. 203.

advocacies. The discrepancies between them revolve around, on the one hand, the *vantage ground* and, on the other hand, the primary *object* of the praxis. Thus do they vary in their strategies.

The Christian priest in South America who concentrates his efforts upon prayer and Bible study groups (*communidades de base*) to the end of political action, and the secular Christian who from the outset devotes herself to strictly political labor here, there, or somewhere, are doing two measurably different things, if not at all conflicting ones. In addition, eighth people are distressed when utopianism, an agathological expectation of success, comes to afflict "faith transforming history," with special reference to the grandiosity of its hopes and programs. In its tendency to lean toward a deontological ethic and an ethic of responsibility,[8] "history transforming faith" does not play up expectations of success, since "duty" and what is "right" together with what is deemed "fitting" comprise its determining moral incentives. In this regard, the very wording "history transforming faith" carries a tiny suggestion that the exigencies of time and place will ultimately have their say and their way, not simply with aid from individual human beings but at times in spite of them.

All things considered, the variations within the two tranformationist outlooks remain partial, for world and church can never be rigidly dichotomized, any more than can faith and history. As Gutiérrez states, a liberating theology concerns itself not alone with the transformation of history, but also therefore with the portion of humanity that is gathered into the ecclesia.[9] The latter concern is the special one taken on by "history transforming faith." The scope is much more delimited but the task is hardly easier.

Within contemporary liberation theology, traditional Christian supersession-ism and triumphalism are retained at the broadly political level, and this not alone through the usual influences of historic anti-Jewishness and anti-Judaism[10] but also under the power of moral-theological persuasion. For even

---

[8] Agathological ethics, deontological ethics, and an ethic of responsibility are distinguished in *For Righteousness' Sake*, chap. 1, pp. 8-9.

[9] Gustavo Gutiérrez, *Teología de la liberación*, octava edn. (Salamanca: Ediciones Sigueme, 1977), p. 40.

[10] See, e.g., Jon Sobrino, *Christology at the Crossroads: A Latin American Approach*, trans. John Drury (Maryknoll, NY: Orbis Books, 1978); cf. Clark M. Williamson, "Christ Against the Jews: A Review of Jon Sobrino's Christology," *Encounter* 40 (1979): 403-412.

though history remains a struggle, yet "the promises of the Exodus paradigm" are held to be "fulfilled ultimately through the work of Christ the Liberator," as through the process of conscientization the Christian *comunidades de base* (reputedly) align their aspirations and praxis with Christ's liberation.[11] Such religious imperialism is unacceptable to people of eight.

In certain of its aspects the movement for women's liberation further exemplifies "faith transforming history." There is the oft-used symbol of Eve and Lilith standing together ready to re-create the Garden of Eden. Such symbolism represents fittingly the sort of faith that yearns to transform history. But the figure is appropriate as well to "history transforming faith," since the rebuilding of faith is vitally constituent to the rebuilding of the Garden. But the question remains: Where are we to find the weapons for rebuilding faith?

People of eight oppose spiritualization with its implied denial of the integrity of the created, historical order, the tacit dismissal of that order's relevance and value. In this respect they are at one with today's radical feminist struggle. However, in relative contrast to the skeptical, even cynical attitude within radical feminism respecting the redeemability of Western traditions of religious faith, eighth people fight hard to keep from abandoning all hope for political-moral change within traditional-institutional structures. Many of them will continue to work, however critically and while shedding many tears, from the side of the religious community. Thus may they ally themselves with Christian and Jewish reformist feminists, in some contrast to revolutionary, anti-religious feminists.

The basic differentiation between "history transforming faith" and the feminist movement as such (though never in any sense of non-support of the womanist cause) centers in the elementary disparity between *principle* and *history.* All feminism proceeds essentially under the authority and inspiration of a principle: the principle of the goodness of woman. Of course, womanist praxis cannot be dissociated from history, a history comprising in the first instance the woeful tale of patriarchalism. But the tale ought never to have happened. The truth of female goodness has not been taught by history. It is authenticated, we must say, in and through the very goodness of creation, of Being itself. People of eight tend to operate prevailingly under the promptings and often the

---

11   McCann, *Christian Realism*, p. 204.

impulsions of historical event (though not excluding the history of nature.) I have to stress that the difference is not absolute. Thus, the historicist's answerability to events can scarcely be severed from certain prevenient convictions or principles respecting the meaning of the right and the good, not to mention the very meaning of history itself. But yet it would be wrongheaded to fail to distinguish between the determining power of transhistorical principles and the commanding voice that may be heard from within one or another happening of time and place. The fact that the quality and character of the moral conclusions and prescriptions of the two parties involved may prove to be affinal and sometimes even identical will perhaps incline us to lose the point. The point not to be missed is that the advocate of our final normative image gambles upon the determinative quality of history for her or his faith-decisions and moral decisions, however shattering the outcome. Accordingly, the anguishing practical problem for people of eight is not the seriousness of history as such but instead, *the truly fearsome challenge of which patterns and events in history may be deemed crucial for day-to-day decision-making.*

The Christian conversionist type is H. Richard Niebuhr's own option.[12] (The conversionism that H. Richard Niebuhr propounds is highly dynamic. Life, the world, the church—all manifest a state of permanent revolution. Christianity itself "is 'permanent revolution' or *metanoia* which does not come to an end in this world, this life, or this time."[13] Niebuhr it was who taught me the meaning of theocentric relativism. According to that persuasion, "it is an aberration of faith as well as of reason to absolutize the finite." But yet "all this relative history" of finite persons and movements "is under the governance of the absolute God."[14]

Must we not adjudge that the use of the term "absolute" in connection with God has today become problematic? Again, I think that H. Richard Niebuhr's individual position as an identifiably median one could be more balanced dialectically between God and world. Lonnie Kliever observes that for Niebuhr "man's relationship to God is determinative of his relationship to neighbor,"

---

[12] Kliever, *H. Richard Niebuhr*, pp. 58-59.

[13] H. Richard Niebuhr, *The Meaning of Revelation* (New York: Macmillan, 1941), p. ix.

[14] Niebuhr, *Christ and Culture*, p. x.

which means that "theological reflection has a certain priority in the work of the moral theologian."[15] Niebuhr's tendency to "favor" God over world is reflected in the fact that his polemic against a Christianity of the world is rather more forcible and consistent than are his criticisms of Christian otherworldliness.[16]

Three interrelated judgments are offered: (a) We may affirm, in equal measure, that the relationship to God is determinative of the relationship to neighbor, and that the relationship to neighbor is determinative of the relationship to God. (b) Granted that the theocentric imbalance within H. Richard Niebuhr's thinking was able to meet responsibly his own historical situation back at mid-twentieth century, we are challenged to apply the category of responsibility to the time a generation and more afterwards. (c) A possible consequence of points (a) and (b) taken together in a contemporary context—a wholly limited and relative context: let 2090 bury its own dead—is that while God and neighbor are equals when it comes to mutually determinative relations, yet, in paraphrase of George Orwell, the neighbor is for the present rather more equal. According to a talmudic witness, no less a personage than God is said to have once yearned: "Would that my children might forget me if only they remembered my commandments!" (*Chagiga* 1.7).

It is true that the mature H. Richard Niebuhr coveted a theology that combines "the radical sovereignty of God and the radical historicity of men. Only such a theology could do justice to historic Christianity and modern existence."[17] But "sovereignty" and "historicity" are not on the one level of power and priority. We have cited Niebuhr's statement that "for the conversionist, history is the story of God's mighty deeds and of man's responses to them." People of eight assent to this, but then they add two things. First, history is also the story of humankind's deeds (some mighty ones, many pitiful ones) and of God's responses to those deeds. Second, history is in addition the tale of human reaction to essentially human action and need. If the Christian conversionist

---

15   Kliever, *H. Richard Niebuhr*, p. 64.

16   Cf., e.g., H. Richard Niebuhr's essay, "Towards a New Otherworldliness," *Theology Today* 1 (1944): 78-87.

17   Kliever, *H. Richard Niebuhr*, p. 64.

looks for the transformation of culture in and to the glory of God,[18] the Christian historicist looks for the transformation of the church in and to the glory of "the least of these" our sisters and brothers (Matt. 25:40). Yet this latter witness is no mere "faith for the world," since eighth people are aware of the poverty of the world's riches and the idolatries of the world's poverty, as they are aware too that the eschatological reign of God is the only sure *finis/telos* of all human striving and all human hope.

A few remarks respecting the church are relevant. Martin Luther rejected the claim that the church was the custodian of God's will and activity upon earth.[19] True to that Reformation witness, H. Richard Niebuhr came to abandon "expectations and exhortations for some ideally pure and united church as God's instrument of renewal." Eighth people are no more idealistic than is Niebuhr respecting the church. But the fundamental concern of *For Righteousness' Sake* is with normative images. The eighth image implies regulative demands upon the church in order that the Christian movement may do a lot more to fulfill its obligations to the world. Niebuhr does believe that "the reformation of the church and the reformation of the world must proceed apace as a permanent revolution of the world of culture (man's achievement) within the world of grace (God's Kingdom)." Here continuity is once again present between "faith transforming history" and "history transforming faith," a continuity that extends as well to the moral images represented in Jesus of Nazareth and in the rabbinic tradition. Niebuhr's own emphasis upon the reformation of the church is of constitutive influence upon the viewpoint of "history transforming faith." In all four normative images just mentioned there is agreement that responsibility to God "is incompatible with a spiritualism limited to immaterial goods, with a moralism that values only the virtuous man or nation, with an individualism that disregards mankind as a whole or its societies, and with all idolatries that substitute some finite concern for God as the center and source of life's value."[20] If humankind's worst sins are in fact religious ones, we have a necessary warrant for the permanent revolution of faith. (I hope that I do not

---

[18] Niebuhr, *Christ and Culture*, p. 196.

[19] John Dillenberger and Claude Welch, *Protestant Christianity Interpreted Through Its Development* (New York: Scribner, 1954), p. 22.

[20] Kliever, *H. Richard Niebuhr*, pp. 54, 39, 55.

anywhere imply that there is no support in Niebuhr for "history transforming faith.") The continuing imperative of the Christian faith is the reformation of church as of society. This means that each new generation is called to develop new sacred and secular expressions of the reign of God. *Yet there remains a basic difference between H. Richard Niebuhr and eighth people: over whether the transformation of faith is to fall primarily under the aegis of faith itself or primarily under the aegis of secular historicalness.*

III

How, then, may we summarize the theological and moral advocacy of people of eight? "History transforming faith" is a critical response, but not a wholly rejective one, to the autonomism of humanity that is grounded in the Renaissance and the modern era. That response endeavors to serve the values of human dignity and freedom. Yet in opposition to any elevating of humankind to practical sovereignty over God, eighth people posit history as a tool of God in her abiding synergy, her righteous love affair with human beings. (See Figure 1.) It appears to be our lot to live in a time of special revelations. This means

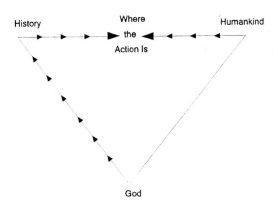

Figure 1

that the sacred keeps taking on the visage of the secular. The trick is how to discern within secular history—the experiential history of the world—some clues to the rightful conduct of human life. Accordingly, "what I say to you I say to all: Watch" (Mark 13:37). There will be uncertainties, wrong turnings, sins, unresolved anguish. Withal, the responsible maturing of faith consists in a permanently transforming political praxis with special concentration upon a transforming of the house of faith. Eighth people distinguish themselves from other representatives of dialectically median views through their testimony that *history does not abolish faith: it transforms it.* The fresh worldliness of these protagonists is not secularistic; it is secular. It may not appear to be very "religious." It lives upon secularity, at the very moment that it is casting out secularism. It suggests a radical form of incarnationism. It is, dialectically speaking, a "genuine worldliness" or even, daringly, a "Christianity without religion" (Dietrich Bonhoeffer).[21] These are its rallying cries. Thus do the people of eight stake out an autonomous claim within the unending dialectic of faith and history.

I have avoided and avoided an unavoidable question: Is our eightfold imagery really the most comprehensive one that we can have? Or are there eventualities of ninth, tenth, etc. normative images? (How about these: "The world for faith"? "History above faith"? "Faith transforming faith"?) A coherent historicism ought to allow room for progress beyond its own schemas. Were historicism to try to stop history, it would be committing suicide.

The potentiality of an additional image of "faith transforming faith" is actually hinted at in this book. I refer to the transformation of Christianity through the teachings and power of an abiding Judaism and abiding Jewishness. But there are at least two problems. First, I am unsure that this would mean an integrally alternative type, since Jewishness is already representative of a worldly historicism as much as a religious faith. Second, how could Christianity ever be reduced to Judaism?

---

21   Eberhard Bethge, *Dietrich Bonhoeffer: Man of Vision, Man of Courage* (New York: Harper & Row, 1977), pp. 614, 375, and *passim.*

Double Jeopardy for Black Women: Racism and Sexism

(Adapted from *Black-Woman-Jew*, 1989, pp. 51-59, 197-198.)

We consider the black woman: her standing and her stance in the struggle for human liberation.[1] The reader of *Black-Woman-Jew* will have noted the maleness of most representative black thinkers and leaders introduced to this point. This fact does more than describe a rampant state of affairs; it also opens the way to critical responses from black women and to their own distinctive contributions within liberative thought and praxis.

I

Paula Giddings describes the historical background:

By the eighteenth century an incredible social, legal, and racial structure was put in place. Women were firmly stratified in the roles that Plato envisioned [either whore or mistress or wife]. Blacks were chattel, White men could impregnate a Black woman with impunity, and she alone could give birth to a slave. Blacks constituted a permanent labor force and metaphor that were perpetuated through the Black woman's womb. And all of this was done within the context of the Church, the operating laws of capitalism, and the psychological needs of White males. Subsequent history would be a variation on the same theme.[2]

---

[1] On the history of black women in the United States, consult, *inter alios*, Paula Giddings, *When and Where I Enter* (New York: Morrow, 1984); Gerda Lerner, ed., *Black Women in White America* (New York: Pantheon Books, 1972); and Jeanne Noble, *Beautiful, Also, Are the Souls of My Black Sisters* (Englewood Cliffs NJ: Prentice-Hall, 1978). On the genesis of contemporary black feminism in the USA, see "A Black Feminist Statement: Combahee River Collective," in Cherríe Moraga and Gloria Anzaldúa, eds., *This Bridge Called My Back* (Watertown, MA: Persephone, 1981), pp. 210-212.

[2] Giddings, *When and Where I Enter*, p. 39.

The distinctive plight of black females today is summed up by Audre Lorde: For nonwhite women in the United States "there is an 80% fatality rate from breast cancer; three times the number of unnecessary eventuations, hysterectomies and sterilizations as for white women; three times as many chances of being raped, murdered, or assaulted as exist for white women." Giddings observes that the unemployment rate for black women is higher than for black men and white women and white men. Almost half of all American families below the poverty line are headed by women, but a much higher percentage of these are black and/or Hispanic, as against white. Michele Wallace refers to the three Americas of which some interpreters speak: white, middle-class black, poor black. What they usually fail to note is that poor black America is largely composed of black women and children. Barbara Smith points up an essential difference between white female experience and black female experience: White women may come to a realization of oppression at 25, 22, or perhaps 18; but for black women and women of color, "oppression is a lifelong thing." "A Black Feminist Statement" of the Combahee River Collective elucidates certain goals: "Our situation as Black people necessitates that we have solidarity around the fact of race, which white women of course do not need to have with white men, unless it is their negative solidarity as racial oppressors. We struggle together with Black men against racism, while we also struggle with Black men about sexism." And Eleanor Johnson enumerates fundamental questions that black feminists raise:

A basic premise in Black feminist thought is that the personal is political. Is it a coincidence that Black women on welfare learn to be ashamed, isolated, and silent? Is it an accident that Black lesbians remain hated and feared, thus maintaining invisibility? What of gay men who, in order to survive, become walking "fem" comedies for the Black community? What causes a black woman to continue to struggle with Black men for mutual love and respect, in the face of overwhelming abuse, neglect, and misunderstanding? Why is it that Black people are generally able to tolerate differences in culture and race in such a racist society? What of the Black woman who speaks of her would-be-abortion-turned-sterilization without visible outrage? What causes Black folks to hang in there to re-explain and re-educate white folks about who we are and why we are?[3]

II

The black woman is subjected to double jeopardy: racism and sexism. In her is wedded the *high visibility* of a "woman of color" and the societal invisibility of a woman.

If the black woman is a lesbian, the jeopardy is triple. There is the special, fiery sexism that empowers homophobia, the fear of and aversion to homosexuality. It is argued that homophobia compounds a fourfold evil: it divides black people who are ordinarily political allies, cuts off political growth, stifles revolution, and perpetuates patriarchal domination.[4]

Racism is an objectively structural phenomenon—not primarily a matter of prejudice, one instead of institutionalized caste privilege. It will be important to have in mind the question of whether sexism is a comparable instrument of advantage, built into the historical-empirical-ideological structures of American life. (It is odd that in *Portraits of White Racism* David Wellman makes only one or two passing references to sexism.)

Still today, to most black women black liberation connotes (if it connotes anything) power for black men. And still today, women's liberation suggests (if it suggests anything) power for women who are white. So—in a liberative frame of reference—why should black women trust black men? And why should black women trust white women? But also, why should black women trust white men? I include successively (1, 2, 3 below) these three variations within a shared

---

[3] Audre Lorde, "An Open Letter to Mary Daly," in Moraga and Anzaldúa, eds., *This Bridge*, p. 97; Giddings, *When and Where*, pp. 351, 354; Michelle Wallace, *Black Macho and the Myth of the Super-Woman* (New York: Dial, 1979), p. 177; Barbara Smith, "Across the Kitchen Table: A Sister-to-Sister Dialogue," in Moraga and Anzaldúa, eds., *This Bridge*, p. 114; "A Black Feminist Statement," in ibid., p. 213; Eleanor Johnson, "Reflections on Black Feminist Therapy," in Barbara Smith, ed., *Home Girls: A Black Feminist Anthology* (New York: Kitchen Table-Women of Color Press, 1983), pp. 223-224.

[4] Cheryl Clarke, "The Failure to Transform: Homophobia in the Black Community," in Smith, ed., *Home Girls*, p. 207. A section of Home Girls is comprised of materials (fiction and nonfiction) by black lesbians (pp. 145-213).

"hermeneutics of suspicion." For is it not the case that the sexist, the White Lady,[5] and the racist aggressor are closely allied menaces?

(1) The sexism of the black power movement is often lamented by black women. In Cheryl Clarke's words: "While the cult of Black Power spurned the assimilationist goals of the politically conservative black bourgeoisie, its devotees, nevertheless, held firmly to the value of heterosexual and male superiority...It is ironic that the Black Power movement could transform the consciousness of an entire generation of black people regarding black self-determination and, at the same time, fail so miserably in understanding the sexual politics of the movement and of black people across the board."[6] Josiah Young paraphrases the complaint of a Xhosa woman during a recent forum on black theology. "When you men are praying, I must go outside. I cannot pray with you because you do not consider me an equal before God. You talk about the white men, but it is *you black men* who oppress me. Really! What has your black theology of liberation to say about that?"[7] Black and other nonwhite American women may be heard speaking in similar terms, whether in Atlanta, Los Angeles, New York, or places in between.

A caution is in order: Whenever the white oppressor refers to the oppression of black females by black males, it may well be that white racism has moved into the neighborhood. Furthermore, no assessment of black female/black male relations can ignore the persisting powerlessness of the black male.

Let us introduce the work—highly controversial—of Michele Wallace. Wallace's argumentation has two sides, (a) black macho; and (b) the myth of the black superwoman. The materials that follow throughout point (1) are primarily an exposition of Wallace's point of view, together with some response from me.

(a) Wallace's premise—undocumented—is that over the past half century and more "a growing distrust, even hatred" has developed between black men and black women. The black woman finds herself "in the grip" of black macho, which harbors misogyny: Black men tend to view themselves as more oppressed than black women; they tend to believe that black women have contributed to

---

5   On the "White Lady," see Wallace, *Black Macho*, part II, *passim.*

6   Clarke, "The Failure to Transform," in Smith, ed., *Home Girls*, pp. 198, 199.

7   Josiah U. Young, *Black and African Theologies* (Maryknoll NY: Orbis Books, 1986), p. 80.

that oppression; and they are tempted to see themselves as "sexually and morally superior and also exempt from most of the responsibilities human beings [have] to other human beings..." It is simply a fact of today's American scene that, for whatever reasons, many black men are forsaking the roles of husband and father. (Wallace does not limit to black males her finding of nonresponsibility or irresponsibility. The "black woman thinks of her history and her condition as a wound" that exempts her "from human responsibility...[She] feels powerless to do anything about her condition or anyone else's." Wallace is endeavoring to get blacks of both sexes to honor a clear imperative: "Either we will make history or remain the victims of it.")[8]

The myth of "the joint participation of the white man and the black woman in a ruthless attempt to castrate" the black male has been nurtured for more than a century. (The relation between myth and fact is not always made clear in Wallace. However, we can agree that even when the ground or origin of a given myth is nonfactual, the myth still has the power to influence belief and behavior.) The stereotype of the black man as the brutal buck who was after the white man's woman has meant (insofar as it has been believed) an attack upon everything the white man owns and dominates. We do know that it was mostly after slavery that the myth developed of the lascivious black man as a threat to pure white womanhood. White culture and Americanization helped condition the black male to look upon himself in largely physical terms. The black man of the ghetto was forced by the white man into becoming a rebel without a cause. Wallace argues that a "profoundly deep hatred of himself and his woman" came to afflict the black male, out of "four hundred years of relentless conditioning." "The manhood America finally conceded to blacks was the manhood of a psychopath or, changing the skin color and motivation here and there, of a James Bond movie...Black men kicking white men's asses, fucking white women, and stringing black women along in a reappearance of the brutal Buck on the silver screen....A black man can walk down the street with a white woman unmolested. What a victory for the black revolution. He can marry a white woman, *if he's got the money*, and no one will try to stop him." On the other hand, "in a male chauvinist society each man is somewhat threatened by every other man's virility. Because white men were the oppressors and black

---

Wallace, *Black Macho*, pp. 13, 15, 161, 175, 177.

men were oppressed, white men had an even greater cause to fear the black man's virility." Like the white perspective, the black male perspective has "supported the notion that manhood is more valuable than anything else...The majority of blacks are left with only the booby prize of an outmoded manhood that mocks their powerlessness."[9]

For Wallace, black male sexism is symbolized and embodied in the involvement of some black men with white women.[10] Whatever its possible elements of truth within a given culture, the charge that black men are peculiarly attracted to white women is a staple of white racism. (The white male attraction to or utilization of black women is blotted out or excused via ideological manipulation.) Black women naturally reject any double standard that condones black male/white female liaisons as it yet tries to "reserve" black women for black men. (White male/black female involvements are fewer in number and notoriety. The effort to limit black women to black men is often identified as implicitly sexist, due to the imbalance in the populations of the two sexes. Some one million black women in the USA will never find husbands.) To interpret and apply Wallace here: What could be more horrible for the black woman than the fear that black men prefer white women? On his part, the black man who "lands" a white woman may be tempted to reckon that he has somehow escaped his oppression and been accepted in the white world. This psychological expectation (or fantasy) does not obtain in unions of black women with white men, not just because these are fewer but because of the stubborn and insinuative power of sexism (in its white incarnation). Yet sadly, neither type union is free of the specter or the memory of bondage to whiteness.

The ultimate question within possible black womanist judgments respecting black men is whether black women are to engage in "racist" condemnations of black men (thereby afflicting themselves as well) or whether they are to comprehend the black male as a victim, with them, of white racist structures. A complete either/or may not be achievable—because it is so hard to extricate sexist structures from racist ones or racist structures from sexist ones. However, the second orientation (the black male understood as a victim together with the

---

[9] Ibid., pp. 23, 32, 26-28, 38, 48-49, 71, 79, 80.

[10] Ibid., p. 14. For a review/assessment of theories accounting for the reputed preoccupation of black men with white women, see Noble, *Beautiful, Also*, pp. 317-325.

black woman) appears to be the more weighty and accordingly the more moral one. It may be readily granted that the destructiveness of white culture could afflict and influence the black male more than the black female, since (Wallace argues) that destructiveness goes beyond racism as such. Involved as well is the peculiar destructiveness of the male-as-male. In this respect, it is evident that American white sexist culture has greatly contributed to black male sexism. Black men have been conditioned immeasurably by the white male power structure. Wallace maintains that the black power movement had revenge as its motive, and that a kind of superiority (black manhood, black macho) rather than equality was the primary motivation.[11] However, I do not see that this annuls the morality or justice of the movement. Sometimes good consequences develop out of dubious or corrupted intentions. Further, revenge need not always be evil.[12]

I venture to interject a plea, one that arises from the fact that when white men persecute "their" women (as they so often do), they may experience blame from a white world as men and more particularly as men-with-power but never as white men. (Only those who are not white can discern the evil of whiteness.) Black men lack the luxury of the white man. When they persecute "their" women, they experience blame not as males but strictly as blacks. The blame is racist through and through. A dreadful double standard here unfurls itself. Before its presence and its power a plea is initiated in behalf of the black man and of the moral demand to meet him in nonracist ways.

(b) The fundamental mythological image that Michele Wallace finds emerging around the black woman is thus described: "Less of a woman in that she is less 'feminine' and helpless, she is really more of a woman in that she is the embodiment of Mother Earth, the quintessential mother with infinite sexual, life-giving, and nurturing reserves. In other words, she is a superwoman." It was after the American Revolution that the myth came to develop of the invulnerable black female—stronger than white women (to justify her labor); physically equal to any black man (so he would not have to feel a need to protect her); emotionally callous (avoiding any attachment to the husband who

---

[11] Wallace, *Black Macho*, pp. 34-35.

[12] Cf. Alice Walker, "Only Justice Can Stop a Curse," in Smith, ed., *Home Girls*, pp. 352-355.

might be sold away); and sexually promiscuous (to supply the labor force). The utilization of this mythology in the defamation of the black male is found by Wallace to have incalculable power. Every aspect of the myth

> was used to reinforce the notion of the spinelessness and unreliability of the black man, as well as the notion of the frivolity and vulnerability of white women. The business of sexual and racial definition, hideously intertwined, had become a matter of balancing extremes. That white was powerful meant that black had to be powerless. That white men were omnipotent meant that white women had to be impotent. But slavery produced further complications: black women had to be strong in ways that white women were not allowed to be, black men had to be weak in ways that white men were not allowed to be.[13]

May any objective validity appertain today to the myth of the black super-woman? A powerful dialectical reinforcement would appear to have eventuated itself between "black macho" and the "superwoman." But it is noteworthy that Wallace is much more prepared to apply the category of misleading myth to the latter than to the former. Both realities, together with their mutual reinforcement, are essentially products of the persecuting white world. Wallace welcomes young black women of today who know themselves as victims rather than as superwomen. Yet black women naturally "want very much to believe it [the myth]; in a way, it is all we have." And Wallace confesses that even for herself, it is hard to let the myth go.[14] I kept waiting for her to say comparable things concerning black macho, but she never does. Nevertheless, her call to blacks to take hold of history is not sexist. It applies to all.[15]

(2) How is it that black women are driven to a hermeneutics of suspicion regarding white women?

---

[13] Wallace, *Black Macho*, pp. 107, 138.

[14] Ibid., pp. 174, 107.

[15] For a sustained critique of Wallace's *Black Macho*, consult Linda C. Powell, "Black Macho and Black Feminism," in Smith, ed., *Home Girls*, pp. 283-292; see also Clarke, "The Failure to Transform," in Ibid., pp. 203-204. Both these sources fault Wallace for failing to face up to the issue of homophobia.

That the black female lives under a tyranny of whiteness is seen in the universal bias of rating the beauty and merit of black women upon their shade of skin and the straightness of their hair and features.[16] The standards for American women, physical and other, are those of white women.

Today much of the black female hermeneutics of suspicion is occasioned by, paradoxically enough, the feminist movement itself. For one thing, that movement partially "redefined womanhood for white women in a manner that allowed them to work, to be manless, but still women," whereas the black woman "was left with only one activity that was not considered suspect: motherhood." More generally, the world of the liberated white woman has by no means been bought into by black women as a whole—nor have blacks been enabled to buy into it. Problems of the white suburban housewife have been at once irrelevant and alien to most black women.[17]

Furthermore, the feminist movement has been under positive attack by black women, for reasons intrinsic to the black situation. Many black women look upon the white women's movement as a mask for white privilege and ideology. While much white feminism has been seeking alternatives to the traditional family structure, the black woman is fighting desperately to salvage that structure—as at the same time she has to struggle against its continuing domination by males and to battle the stereotype of black woman as the domineering matriarch.[18] In addition, "we don't think work liberates you. We've been doing it so damned long."[19]

Barbara Smith depicts deftly the tie that binds the feminist struggle to the war against racism: "The reason racism is a feminist issue is easily explained by the inherent definition of feminism. Feminism is the political theory and practice to free all women: women of color, working-class women, poor women, physically challenged women, lesbians, old women, as well as white economically privileged heterosexual women. Anything less than this is not

---

16 Wallace, *Black Macho*, p. 158.

17 Ibid., pp. 173, 174; Giddings, *When and Where*, p. 300.

18 Renee Ferguson, "Women's Liberation Has a Different Meaning for Blacks," in Lerner, ed., *Black Women*, pp. 587-588, 590.

19 Margaret Wright, "I Want the Right to Be Black and Me," in ibid., p. 607.

feminism, but merely female self-aggrandizement."[20] A difficulty is that so much white feminism fails to live up to Smith's specifications. (This is in addition, of course, to the "ordinary" but inveterate practice or representation of white racism on the part of white females. In this connection, there had been a great deal of prejudice against black women in the white women's suffrage movement.[21]) The ongoing situation is described by Cherríe Moraga: "Racism is societal and institutional. It implies the power to implement racist ideology. Women of color do not have such power, but white women are born with it and the greater their economic privilege, the greater their power. This is how white middle class women emerge among feminist ranks as the greatest propagators of racism in the [feminist] movement."[22]

Other contributors to *This Bridge Called My Back* repeatedly give voice to a polemic against the apologists of the women's movement and other white women:[23]

Judit Moschkovich, in re: the talk by Anglo-American women of developing a new feminist or women's culture: "This new culture would...be just as racist and ethnocentric as patriarchal American culture."[24]

Audre Lorde: "To speak to white women about racism is wasted energy, due to their destructive guilt and defensiveness."[25]

Doris Davenport: "Most feminist groups in the U.S. are elitist, crudely insensitive, and condescending...I honestly see our trying to 'break into' the white feminist movement as almost equivalent to the old, outdated philosophy of integration and assimilation." Davenport adds to her commentary several areas of aversion to white women as such: They are repulsive, aesthetically speaking, and have a strange body odor; culturally, they are limited and

---

[20] Barbara Smith, as cited by Moraga and Anzaldúa, eds., *This Bridge*, p. 61.

[21] Giddings, *When and Where*, chap. 7.

[22] Moraga, in Moraga and Anzaldúa, eds., *This Bridge*, p. 62. See also Noble, *Beautiful, Also*, pp. 300, 301.

[23] See in general Moraga and Anzaldúa, eds., *This Bridge*, pp. 61-101.

[24] Judit Moschkovich, "'—But I Know You, American Woman,'" in ibid., p. 83.

[25] Lorde, "Open Letter to Mary Daly," in ibid., p. 97.

bigoted; socially, they are juvenile and tasteless; and politically, they are naive and myopic (especially feminists).[26]

Finally, "A Black Feminist Statement": Disillusioning experience in various liberation movements (civil rights, black nationalism, the Black Panthers), as well as experience "on the periphery of the white male left," led to a need "to develop a politics that was antiracist, unlike those of white women, and antisexist, unlike those of Black and white men."[27]

The last few words here return us to (1) above and direct us to (3) below. There is a tendency sometimes for women who are not white to laugh at the white women's movement: "*You* are oppressed? You must be joking." Is there, then, no hope for some measure of black female/white female solidarity? Cherríe Moraga suggests an opening. Women from a privileged class "will dare to look at *how* it is that *they* oppress" when they have once "come to know the meaning of their own oppression."[28]

(3) A hermeneutics of suspicion toward white male reality is implied in much that has been said above concerning the black woman. The several forms of distrust are interrelated. The black woman, simply by virtue of *being* black woman, is a standing refutation of white male rule in its dual aspects of race and sex. "There is such a thing as racial-sexual oppression which is neither solely racial nor solely sexual, e.g., the history of rape of Black women by white men as a weapon of political repression."[29] In South Africa today, when a woman marries she is regarded as a minor.[30]

III

The black womanist message and movement trumpets its own integrity and creates its own positive contribution—the very opposite of the distrust we have

---

26   Doris Davenport, "The Pathology of Racism: A Conversation with Third World Wimmin," in ibid., pp. 86, 89, 87.

27   "A Black Feminist Statement," in ibid., p. 23.

28   Cherríe Moraga, "La Güera," in ibid., p. 23.

29   "A Black Feminist Statement," in ibid., p. 213.

30   Winnie Mandela, *Part of My Soul Went with Him*, ed. Anne Benjamin, adapted by Mary Benson (New York: W. W. Norton, 1985), p. 131.

just been pained yet forced to chronicle. Normatively speaking, black womanism means *black* black womanism.[31] For the *black* black woman, originating bearer of every baby, is the creational-historical criterion of all blackness. The "lightening" or "whitening" of blackness can only come from extraneous, alien sources. *Black* black Africa is a powerful judgment against the dissipating of blackness throughout non-African territory.

Barbara Smith points up the essential way in which autonomy differs from mere separatism. Autonomy arises out of a position of strength, in contrast to the separatism that comes from a position of fear. "When we're truly autonomous we can deal with all kinds of people, a multiplicity of issues, and with difference, because we have formed a solid base of strength with those with whom we share identity and/or political commitment." Black feminism is held to be "the logical political movement" for black women "to combat the manifold and simultaneous oppressions that all women of color face." There must be a multi-issued and multi-level strategy for fighting women's oppression. This suggests a political orientation conducive to coalition building.[32] Black womanism is fundamentally inclusivist. But just as black women have always been vital to the black movement as a whole, so the black movement is vital to the progress of womanism. And the black woman's role, integrally linking as it does the inner relation between race and sex, is of the utmost importance.[33]

The issues to which black womanists are dedicating themselves are legion: reproductive rights, equal access to abortion, sterilization abuse, health care, child care and rearing, children of broken families, rights of the disabled, violence against women and children, sex education, rape, battering, sexual harassment, welfare rights, lesbian and gay rights, economic exploitation, educational reform, housing, legal reform, women in prison, aging, police brutality, labor organizing, anti-racist organizing, nuclear disarmament,

---

[31] Consult Alice Walker's essay, "If the Present Looks Like the Past, What Does the Future Look Like?," in *In Search of Our Mothers' Gardens* (San Diego: Harcourt Brace Jovanovich, 1983), pp. 290-312.

[32] Barbara Smith, in Smith, ed., *Home Girls*, pp. xxxii, xxxiii, xl-xli. Part of the citation here is from the Combahee River Collective Statement (see n. 1 above).

[33] Giddings, *When and Where*, pp. 340, 348.

maintaining the environment, and black feminist cultural work (literature, music, theater, and publishing).[34]

Barbara Smith has always felt that the ability of black women "to function with dignity, independence, and imagination in the face of total adversity—that is, in the face of white America—points to an innate feminist potential. To me the phrase, 'Act like you have some sense,' probably spoken by at least one Black woman to every Black child who ever lived, is a cryptic warning that says volumes about keeping your feet on the ground and your ass covered." Smith then alludes to Alice Walker's definition of "womanist" as making "the connection between plain common sense and a readiness to fight for change."[35] Must we not adjudge that issues of human dignity eventually converge upon issues of right language?

Alice Walker says: "I just like to have words that describe things correctly. Now to me 'black feminist' does not do that. I need a word that is organic, that really comes out of the culture, that really expresses the spirit that we see in black women. And it's just...womanish. [Her voice slips into a down-home accent.] You know, the posture with the hand on the hip, 'Honey, don't you get in my way.'" In addition, Walker argues that "womanism" is not just different from "feminism"; it is better: "Part of our tradition as black women is that we are universalists. Black children, yellow children, red children, brown children, that is the black woman's normal, day-to-day relationship...When a black woman looks at the world, it is so different."[36]

Womanist 1. From *womanish*. (Opp. of "girlish," i.e., frivolous, irresponsible, not serious.) A black feminist or feminist of color. From the black folk expression of mothers to female children, "You acting womanish," i.e., like a woman. Usually referring to outrageous, audacious, courageous or *willful* behavior. Wanting to know more and in greater depth than is considered "good" for one. Interested in grown-up doings. Acting grown up. Being grown up. Interchangeable with

---

[34] This list is adapted from Smith, ed., *Home Girls*, pp. xxxv, xxxvii, xxxviii.

[35] Ibid., p. xxiv.

[36] Alice Walker, as cited in David Bradley, "Novelist Alice Walker: Telling the Black Woman's Story," *The New York Times Magazine* (8 Jan. 1984), pp. 35, 36.

another black folk expression: "You trying to be grown." Responsible. In charge. *Serious.* 2. *Also*: A woman who loves other women, sexually and/or nonsexually. Appreciates and prefers women's culture, women's emotional flexibility (values tears as natural counterbalance of laughter), and women's strength. Sometimes loves individual men, sexually and/or nonsexually. Committed to survival and wholeness of entire people, male *and* female. Not a separatist, except periodically, for health. Traditionally universalist, as in: "Mama, why are we brown, pink, and yellow, and our cousins are white, beige, and black?" Ans.: "Well, you know the colored race is just like a flower garden, with every color flower represented." Traditionally capable, as in: "Mama, I'm walking to Canada and I'm taking you and a bunch of other slaves with me." Reply: "It wouldn't be the first time."[37]

(An evaluator for a feminist journal recently expressed puzzlement over the use of "womanist" and "womanism" in a manuscript of mine. Evidently she was oblivious of the kind of perspective that Alice Walker brings. I'll wager a guinea that the critic is white. James Cone points out that many Third World women theologians disdain the word "feminist" to describe their work. They think of it as a Western term.[38] Because of the weight of usage I will continue in this book to employ the words "feminist" and "feminism," along with "womanist" and "womanism.")

Nelle Morton, a white feminist, dislikes the phrase "woman's movement" as being too organizational. By contrast, "woman movement" opens up "a whole, moving, pervasive way of perceiving—an emerging, accelerating, enlarging, powerful, growing potential that cannot be contained by the use of the possessive 'woman's.' When I say 'woman movement,' 'woman word,' 'woman space,' or 'woman sensibility,' I imply something in constant ferment."[39]

Could the black womanist critique of white feminism cut the ground from under the case for the freedom of women-as-women? No way! As Frances

---

[37]   Walker, *In Search*, p. xi.

[38]   James H. Cone, *For My People* (Maryknoll NY: Orbis Books, 1984), p. 253.

[39]   Nelle Morton, *The Journey Is Home* (Boston: Beacon Press, 1985), p. xxix.

Hooks has it, "Black women hold the key to the future of America." (Only of America?)

"Why Do You Search Among the Dead?"

(*Encounter* [Indianapolis] 51 [Winter 1990]: 1-17)

The birth, life, crucifixion, and resurrection of Jesus ordinarily furnish the determining content of Christology. However, the final item in the list distinctively perpetuates debate within Christian theological and scholarly circles at a decisive point: Ought the resurrection be treated or accepted as a historical event, or ought it be received or placed within some alternative category? Is the resurrection part of the worldly history of Jesus, or is it to be construed as metahistorical?[1]

In Christian scholarship and testimony upon the resurrection of Jesus we immediately face two extreme positions, not to mention additional viewpoints that fall between the extremes. For analytical purposes, the two extremes may be identified as indicative of subjectiveness and of objectiveness.

J. K. Elliott represents the former extreme. He concludes that "whereas we can assert with conviction that the resurrection belief founded the church, we cannot readily assert as fact the resurrection itself...[The] resurrection of Jesus was an event only in the minds and lives of Jesus' followers. It cannot be described as an historic[2] event. The Easter story is a faith legend, not an objective eye-witness report; but it is a myth that the Christian church through the centuries has found to be a continuing inspiration."[3] (Elliott's book is published by the Student Christian Movement Press.)

At the opposite extreme is the point of view of objectiveness. This position is represented in the Gospels, wherein "the Easter stories are all told as if they

---

[1]   See Paul M. van Buren, *A Theology of the Jewish-Christian Reality*, Part III - *Christ in Context* (San Francisco: Harper & Row, 1988), chap. 5.

[2]   By "historic" Elliott means "historical"; he does not deny the historic, i.e., significant, quality of the resurrection.

[3]   J. K. Elliott, *Questioning Christian Origins* (London: SCM Press, 1982), pp. 78, 92. Elliott's equation of "legend" and "myth" is somewhat careless. Legends are suffused by falsehood in a way that is not perforce the case with myths.

were historical events on the same basis as, say, the crucifixion."[4] In the Gospel of Luke the post-resurrection Jesus replicates the pre-crucifixion Jesus. For it is the risen Jesus himself who protests to the eleven disciples and to "those who were with them," "See my hands and my feet, that it is I myself; handle me, and see; for a spirit has not flesh and bones as you see that I have." Jesus then proceeds to eat "a piece of broiled fish" (Luke 24:33, 39-40, 42). However, within the Gospels as in the Apostolic Writings as a whole there are differences and conflicts respecting the form and content of the objectiveness.[5] Thus, in contrast to the Gospel of Luke the apostle Paul maintains that when the dead are raised, the body in question differs from the body that has died: "It is sown a physical body, it is raised a spiritual body" (I Cor. 15:35-50). The only way to reconcile Luke and Paul would be to treat the risen Jesus as a special and different case within the abstract or generic category of those persons who have been dead.

Why is the claimed event of the resurrection to be singled out as *the* issue within the Christian-Jewish encounter, or more precisely within the problem of Christian triumphalism and supersessionism? The reason is that in the Christian *Anschauung* the resurrection constitutes a class by itself. To turn for a moment to the general history of religions: Under the rubric of sacred or numinous events as such, we are apprised of certain events that concentrate univocally upon the action and power of the *divine*; certain others that emphasize the action and power of *humans* (the Hinayana Buddhist paradigm, for example); and finally those that exhibit synergism, a *combination* of the action and power of both kinds of agents (the human and the divine, perhaps with Moses and God at Sinai as an example *par excellence*). Objectively stated, the resurrection of Jesus boasts the first of the three eventualities: God alone is the agent—this upon a most rudimentary and (humanly) anxiety-inducing experiential foundation: human beings can do nothing whatever to extricate themselves from death. It is this that puts the resurrection of Jesus (and of course *any* alleged resurrection) in a singular class.

---

[4] Ibid., p. 77.

[5] Mark (chap. 16) and Matthew (chap. 28) are not as somaticist as Luke and John.

I am going to recount and assess the stages through which my own thinking and conviction upon Jesus' resurrection have passed. To this end, I shall apply a Hegelian form of dialectic:

Thesis: Pedestrian Acknowledgement

Antithesis: Critical Questioning upon Moral Grounds

Synthesis: Antitriumphalist Affirmation

It will be recalled that while in Hegel's theoretical schema "thesis" is reputed to reveal one aspect of things, and "antithesis" a contrasting aspect, the two are then raised (*aufgehoben*) to the higher synthesis of a third stage.[6] What I mean by this allusion when applied to my own situation—and I mean nothing else—is that I do not now wholly repudiate either the thesis of pedestrian acknowledgment or the antithesis of critical questioning upon moral grounds; each of these is—I hope—gathered up, for their partial truths, into the third stage.

I. Thesis: Pedestrian Acknowledgment

As I look through my earlier writings, I am struck by the rather casual and unthinking way in which, over a number of years, I received and handled the resurrection. I remained quite oblivious to such moral issues as the promulgation of that doctrine might raise. In my first book I ignored the subject entirely, though in an avowal of "loyalty to Christ as the transcendent Truth who stands above the relativities of history," I was obviously giving voice to a high Christology. In another book I unabashedly equated the "incarnate and resurrected Christ" with "the Word of God," though I did add that the resurrection of Jesus "stands at the apex of the Jewish-Christian *Auseinandersetzung*," and I did recognize that the resurrection entails "a fundamental transformation of Messianic expectations." In a later book I continued to agree that "the uniqueness of Christianity is its faith in the resurrection of Jesus as the Christ," although I did supplement such bald statements as this with an awareness that "from a Jewish point of view the Christ has not come and was not raised from the dead." Further along in the same study I seemed to hint at future misgivings in and through counsel to the church "to proclaim the death of the resurrected Christ, in the name of the Christ who may one day come"—

---

6   See William Kelley Wright, *A History of Modern Philosophy* (New York: Macmillan, 1941), pp. 327ff.

counsel the wording of which strikes me today as somewhat on the incoherent side.[7]

All in all, my "thesis" stage appears in retrospect to mirror a prosaic, unreflective attitude.

II. Antithesis: Critical Questioning on Moral Grounds

This second stage requires a background, autobiographical note: My personal and scholarly interest in the overall relation between Christian and Jewish thinking and life, and more especially in the human evil and destructiveness fabricated by Christian triumphalism and absolutism, did not result from a confrontation with the *Shoah* (Holocaust) as such, but preceded the latter concern, a concern that did not develop until considerably later. However, the *Shoah* was subsequently to exercise salient influence upon me—particularly through the mediation of Eli Wiesel, Irving Greenberg, Emil L. Fackenheim, and Eliezer Berkovits—and the *Shoah* has been the single most determining element in my encounter with the resurrection of Jesus. The phenomenon that originally nurtured my interest in the Christian-Jewish relation, beginning in 1944-1945, was Christian antisemitism as such. But since that phenomenon and the *Shoah* are ineluctably bound together, there is no point in disjoining the *Shoah* from my original work and its motivations. Nevertheless, it was the anti-Jewish problematic within Christianity and Christian history that finally led me, and also my wife, to the subject of the *Shoah*.[8] I speak of all this here only in order to underscore the fact that the question of Christology and its moral/immoral potentialities is much more than a modern or contemporary issue. It has ancient and abiding and tragic roots.

By way of further clarification of my antithetical stage: The nature of the confrontation (to the death?) between the *Shoah* and Christian theological doctrine is elementary and transparent: It is the issue of *transhistoricalness*. For the way to try to shelter or shield Christianity as something transhistorical is to

---

[7]   A. Roy Eckardt, *Christianity and the Children of Israel* (New York: King's Crown Press, Columbia University, 1948), p. 149; *Elder and Younger Brothers* (New York: Scribner, 1967; Schocken, 1973), pp. 127, 88, 140; but cf. pp. 139-140; *Your People, My People* (New York: Quadrangle/New York Times, 1974), pp. 225, 238, 248.

[8]   Alice u. Roy Eckardt, "Christentum und Judentum, Die theologische und moralische Problematik der Vernichtung des europäischen Judentum," *Evangelische Theologie* 36 (1976): 408.

turn it into a faith that, as Alan T. Davies has maintained, "does not see history as open to God's presence in the way Judaism does." Upon this view, such happenings as the crucifixion and the resurrection become transhistorical events that rule out "further orienting experiences..."[9] Yet to any such view the *Shoah* as a fully historical consequence of Christian praxis (and of course of other influences as well) answers: No, you cannot turn your back upon such new orienting experiences.

My antithetical stage developed at a time of shattering unrest and a searching of conscience among Christian scholars and theologians (a period that remains with us). For Jean Daniélou, among many others, had expressed the final logic of Christian anti-Jewishness: The offense of the Jews is that "they do not believe in the *risen* Christ."[10] The citations that follow may be set in polemical juxtaposition to Daniélou's claim.

The Canadian Catholic churchman and theologian Gregory G. Baum declared: "What Auschwitz has revealed to the Christian community is the deadly power of its own symbolism." The "anti-Jewish thrust of the church's preaching" is not a historical, psychological, or sociological matter; "it touches the very formulation of the Christian gospel." Baum was speaking here of Christian triumphalism and supersessionism respecting the Jews and Judaism, the sort of thing that "assigns the Jews to the darkness of history," rejected by God and all peoples, in ways that could only end in the murder camps. In the Nazi *Endlösung* "the theological negation of Judaism and the vilification of the Jewish people" within the Christian tradition were, at the last, translated into the genocide of the Jews. "The message of the Holocaust to Christian theology...is that at whatever cost to its own self-understanding, the church must be willing to confront the ideologies implicit in its doctrinal tradition."[11]

Baum's judgments were paralleled by the Episcopalian theologian, Paul M. van Buren: "The roots of Hitler's final solution are to be found in the

---

9   Such is the claim of Alan T. Davies, as reported in David Glanz, "The Holocaust as a Question," *Worldview* 17 (Sept. 1974): 37.

10   Jean Daniélou, *Dialogue With Israel* (Baltimore: Helicon, 1966), p. 99 (italics added).

11   Gregory Baum, *Christian Theology After Auschwitz* (London: Council of Christians and Jews, 1976), pp. 8, 9, 11, 12; Introduction to Rosemary Radford Ruether, *Faith and Fratricide: The Theological Roots of Anti-Semitism* (New York: Seabury Press, 1974), p. 8.

proclamation of the very *kerygma* of the early Christians...[The command out of Auschwitz] is that we accept a judgment on something false lying close to the very heart of our tradition..."[12]

And the United Methodist historian-theologian Franklin H. Littell wrote:

> The cornerstone of Christian antisemitism is the superseding or displacement myth, which already rings with the genocidal note. This is the myth that the mission of the Jewish people was finished with the coming of Jesus Christ, that "the old Israel" was written off with the appearance of "the new Israel." To teach that a people's mission in God's providence is finished, that they have been relegated to the limbo of history, has murderous implications which murderers will in time spell out. The murder of six million Jews by baptized Christians, from whom membership in good standing was not (and has not yet been) withdrawn, raises the most insistent question about the credibility of Christianity.[13]

To all these colleagues, there is a common foe: supersessionist elitism. Before the fact of the *Shoah* the question emerges: Is the Christian message morally credible? In the post-*Shoah* world many Christian spokespersons have expressed a readiness to "rethink" Christian teaching, to avoid Christian imperialism. Yet for more times than we ought to allow, such expressions of concern appear as no more than nice or pleasing sentiments lacking any concreteness. When a demand is made for specifics, the reformer may back off. And whenever a critic from within the Christian community raises the moral question concerning *specific* Christian teachings, viz., Christological teachings, he or she may be dismissed as a "radical" who is undermining the faith. It is as if the *critic* were on trial, and not the Christian message.[14] Until the self-

---

[12]   Paul M. van Buren, "The Status and Prospects for Theology," address to the Theology Section, American Academy of Religion, Chicago, 1 Nov. 1975, as cited in A. Roy Eckardt, "Christians and Jews: Along a Theological Frontier," *Encounter* 40 (1979): 93.

[13]   Franklin H. Littell, *The Crucifixion of the Jews* (New York: Harper & Row, 1975), p. 2.

[14]   An illustration of this attempt to dismiss one or more Christian post-*Shoah* theologians for "going too far" or being "too radical" is Michael B. McGarry's review of A.

identified reformer does something concrete to reconcile the resurrection of Jesus and the apodictic requirements of human morality, he or she can hardly take refuge in objections respecting what is or is not the *sine qua non* of the Christian faith. Unless and until calls for post-*Shoah* Christian reform are implemented in specific measures or specific advice, these calls remain mere words, noisy gongs and clanging cymbals.

In the frame of reference of the resurrection, the overall moral-psychoanalytic issue may be formulated as follows: On the one hand, a consummated resurrection of Jesus may be said to constitute a basic theological (Christological) threat to or indictment of Judaism and the Jewish people; on the other hand, any denial of Jesus' resurrection may be said to comprise a life-and-death threat to the Christian faith and the Christian community. On the one hand, "once the resurrection is identified as a special act of God, a divine event or divine fact, how can Christian vilification, imperialism, and supersessionism vis-à-vis Judaism and the Jewish people ever be vanquished? For the issue between the two sides is seen to be, not a relatively harmless disparity of mere human symbolism, spiritual conviction, or 'religious experience'—probably amenable to the soothings of 'relativization' or 'confessionalism'—but a matter of saying Yes or No to God himself, Sovereign of all things."[15] Yet on the other hand, are we then compelled to identify the Christian as visited by forlornness, as lost and without hope in this world? (cf. Eph.2:11-22).

In checking over my own writings I note that it was back in 1976 in a critical analysis entitled "Jürgen Moltmann, the Jewish People, and the Holocaust" that I first made more than passing reference to the problematic of the resurrection. The context of the passage that follows is Moltmann's explanation that while his book *Theology of Hope* begins with "the *resurrection of the crucified Christ*," his succeeding work *The Crucified God* turns back "to look at the *cross* of the risen Christ."[16] Here is my response:

Roy Eckardt, *Jews and Christians* in the journal *America* (23 May 1987): 428-429.

[15]   A. Roy Eckardt, *For Righteousness' Sake: Contemporary Moral Philosophies* (Bloomington: Indiana University Press, 1987), pp. 304-305.

[16]   Jürgen Moltmann, *The Crucified God*, trans. R. A. Wilson and John Bowden (New York: Harper & Row, 1974), p. 5.

We may have the temerity to envisage a next step: the non-resurrection of the crucified Jesus, and the crucifixion of the non-resurrected Christ. This potential development may be formulated in at least two alternative ways: (i) Absolute Godforsakenness (until the still-future resurrection, which means the future resurrection of Jesus, as of others). (ii) The pure faith of Christian Judaism (not to be confused with Jewish Christianity which is the faith of Jews and not of Gentiles). If we are to "turn back" with radical and total resoluteness, then we must really turn back: to the crucified Jew, and thereby to the suffering Jews (of whom Jesus remains, to be sure, in a real sense the *Stellvertreter)*.[17]

However, in the remainder of the above source I did not follow up upon the subject of the resurrection but concentrated instead upon the issue of the crucifixion and the *Shoah*[18]—although at the end I did suggest that ultimate Christian liberation from complicity in the Nazi *Endlösung der Judenfrage*, "Final Deliverance from the Jews," necessitates "the total secularization, demythologization, and humanization" of Christian theology.[19]

In 1977 I read a paper that may clarify a little—though hardly do anything to authenticate—the above-cited materials vis-à-vis Moltmann. My presentation took as its point of departure the historical-moral finding, for some time now a truism of scholarship, that Christian teachings and ideology helped prepare the way for the coming of the *Shoah*. (None of this is to forget that the Christian gospel, insofar as it incarnates the love of God and neighbor, retains an opposite consequence of fostering human solidarity and justice.) In the 1977 piece I declared that "the all-decisive avowal of Christianity is the resurrection of Jesus Christ," citing Paul's word to the church in Corinth, "If Christ has not been raised,...your faith is vain." (I Cor. 15:14), and adding that to my knowledge the possible vainness of the Christian faith has never been linked to the denial

---

[17]   A. Roy Eckardt, "Jurgen Moltmann, the Jewish People, and the Holocaust," *Journal of the American Academy of Religion* 44 (1976): 686.

[18]   Subsequent paragraphs of the appraisal of Moltmann question whether his attribution of absolute evil to the crucifixion, "the very torment of hell," can stand up in the presence of the *Shoah* (p. 687). The analysis concludes with a recognition and critique of changes in Moltmann's thinking in his subsequent volume, *Kirche in der Kraft des Geistes*.

[19]   Eckardt, "Jürgen Moltmann," p. 691.

of any other church doctrine.[20] I continued that some in the Christian community fancy that they can oppose anti-Jewishness "while holding fast to the central Christian dogma, the consummated resurrection of Jesus Christ." In a word, I was maintaining that the teaching of Jesus' resurrection cannot be separated from other Christian doctrines that Jules Isaac gathers under the rubric of the "teaching of contempt."[21] But then I concluded on a note of faith or trust or hope—falling, as I now look back upon the essay, into something of a *non sequitur* or at least a superfluity—by affirming a resurrection yet in the future:

The man from the Galilee sleeps now. [I wonder how I knew that.[22]] He sleeps with the other Jewish dead, with all the distraught and scattered dead of the murder camps, and with the infinite dead of the human and nonhuman family. But Jesus of Nazareth shall be raised. So too the young Hungarian children of Auschwitz shall be raised. Once upon a coming time, they shall again play and laugh. The little ones of Terezin shall see another butterfly.[23] "The wolf shall dwell with the lamb, and the leopard shall lie down with the kid, and the calf and the lion and the fatling together...They shall not hurt or destroy in all my mountain; for the earth shall be full of the knowledge of the Lord as the

---

[20] Some of those who are loudest in their zeal for the resurrection are sometimes prepared to pass over and tacitly to cast aside other elements that are equally indigenous to the Apostolic Writings, e.g., Satan, or Jesus' birth by parthenogenesis. In effect, most of us pick and choose between beliefs. We practice "selective Christianity." Among the most woefully discretionary, and hence anticatholic, of all Christian bodies is the Vatican, which, at the level of praxis, consistently chooses the rights of males over the rights of females—and upon what is for the Catholic hierarchy invincible grounds: Jesus Christ was a male and he chose only males for his disciples.

[21] Jules Isaac, *The Teaching of Contempt: Christian Roots of Anti-Semitism*, trans. Helen Weaver (New York: Holt, Rinehart and Winston, 1964).

[22] There is no absolute "guarantee" against a bodily resurrection of Jesus. Cf. Eckardt, *For Righteousness' Sake*: "How could we ever dub [any] supposed event 'impossible' when we remain in the vulnerable position of not being able to establish final criteria for adjudging what can and cannot occur in history as in nature? In point of truth, no human being can say absolutely what is possible and impossible in our world" (pp. 306-307).

[23] Cf. *...I never saw another butterfly...Children's Drawings and Poems from Terezin Concentration Camp 1942-1944*, ed. Hana Volavková, trans Jeanne Newcová (New York: McGraw-Hill, 1971).

waters cover the sea" (Isa. 11:6, 9). The last enemy, death, shall be sentenced to death (I Cor. 15:26; Rev.21:3, 4). One day we shall be together in the regnancy of God, so hope tells us, the hope that lives upon faith and love. We shall sing and we shall dance. And we shall love one another. Accordingly, it is not assured that we shall read and write theological papers to each other.[24]

I have not completely given up the above stress upon the future. Here is a comment of mine upon Ulrich E. Simon's declaration that without the resurrection, the *Shoah* is pure hell:[25] "He is right—in principle. But for the sufferers, as for the survivors and descendants, the only way that hell can be defeated is through a future resurrection, when God will be victorious over every satanic and evil power, including death itself. *For no past event, however holy or divine could ever redeem the terror of the present: only a future happening can do this.*"[26]

Shattering questions remain: How can the resurrection of Jesus be proclaimed as a special act of God without the Christian triumphalism that paved the way to Belzec and Sobibor? Is not the resurrection in and of itself a form of Christian supersessionism? How can the Christian church escape supersessionism and triumphalism while continuing to proclaim as a realized fact the resurrection of Jesus Christ? In its claim that the resurrection of Jesus concretely means God's triumph over death, is not the church inevitably implying its own triumph over non-Christian faith? In the resurrection does not God (reputedly) *confirm* the Christian gospel in the sense of a definitive embodiment of objective truth? Does not the resurrection appear as a divinely-wrought displacement event? Is it possible, or how is it possible, to proclaim Jesus' resurrection in a nontriumphalist way?

The above questions come forcibly to mind as one consults many Christian advocacies of the resurrection. One example is a study of John Frederick

---

[24]   A. Roy Eckardt, *Proceedings of the 2nd Philadelphia Conference on the Holocaust, 16-18 Feb. 1977*, ed. Josephine Knopp (Philadelphia: National Institute on the Holocaust, 1977), pp. 39-45 (slightly emended).

[25]   Conversation with Ulrich E. Simon, London, 20 Feb. 1976.

[26]   Eckardt, "Christians and Jews," p. 125.

Jansen: "In the resurrection and vindication of Jesus the earliest church saw the completion and goal of Israel's faith in God." That faith "finds its ultimate expression" in the Easter faith of Christianity. "The whole of God's story with his people" is "fulfilled in the resurrection of Jesus...All people do not yet accept Easter's pledge, but one day 'every eye will see him, every one who pierced him' (Rev.1:7)...Ultimate vindication includes ultimate judgment. The risen Jesus 'is the one ordained of God to be judge of the living and the dead' (Acts 10:42)." The New Testament message "sees in Easter the surety of the future of Jesus Christ as Lord of all and Lord forever." The Easter faith reminds us that "the future of Jesus includes the future of Israel...Israel's future is bound up with the future of Christ."[27]

Subsequent writings by me carry forward the moral critique of the proclamation of a consummated or triumphalist resurrection of Jesus. For example, in 1978 I developed that critique in and through an assessment of Wolfhart Pannenberg. Pannenberg contends that "through the cross of Jesus, the Jewish legal tradition as a whole has been set aside in its claim to contain the eternal will of God in its final formulation."[28] The "law" is consummated and fulfilled in Jesus. For support, Pannenberg calls upon Jesus' resurrection: Jesus came into basic conflict "with the law itself, that is with the positive Israelite legal tradition which had become calcified as 'the law' after the exile." But through the resurrection "the emancipation from this law" takes place. Jesus' claim to authority, in replacement of the "law" and through which he put himself in God's place, "has been visibly and unambiguously confirmed by the God of Israel..." In a word, the resurrection of Jesus Christ serves to abolish Judaism.[29]

---

[27]   John Frederick Jansen, *The Resurrection of Jesus Christ in New Testament Theology* (Philadelphia: Westminster Press, 1980), pp. 22, 84-85, 89, 92, 91.

[28]   Pannenberg here misrepresents the Jewish claim. The majority, ongoing point of view of Jewish scholars and rabbis is that the legal tradition must be continually rethought and reformulated.

[29]   Wolfhart Pannenberg, *Jesus—God and Man*, trans. Lewis L. Wilkins and Duane A. Priebe (Philadelphia: Westminster Press, 1968), pp. 67, 257, 258. The second English edition differs from the 1968 English-language edition only in the inclusion of an eleven-page afterword taking note of Pannenberg's critics. His strictures against Judaism and "the Jewish law" remain.

Pannenberg's exposition points up the way in which the teaching of an achieved resurrection can lie at the center of Christian opposition and hostility to Judaism and the Jewish people. For only with that teaching does Christian triumphalism reach fulfillment. Only here are the various human and divine-human claims making up the church's dogmatic structure furnished with the capstone of an event that is said to be exclusively God's and that in this way vindicates every other claim. The representative of this ideology declares, in effect: "It is not the Christian theologian to whom you Jews are to listen. The theologian is, after all, a fallible and sinful human being. Rather, let us have God decide the matter. But God's decision proves to be on the Christian side, not yours. *God* raised Jesus from the dead. Thus is the Christian shown to be right and you are shown to be wrong. In the resurrection God himself *confirms* the Christian gospel, the Christian cause."[30]

Those who affirm the resurrection of Jesus but who oppose Wolfhart Pannenberg's assimilation of that event to Christian imperialism are challenged to make clear how, if at all, their own affirmation avoids supersession.[31]

In our joint work, *Long Night's Journey Into Day*, first published in 1982 and revised for publication in 1988, Alice L. Eckardt and I included an intensive critique of Christian supersessionist elitism. The integrity of the Christian faith was avowed, but it was also characterized as problematic: "Through the continuous and contemporaneous asserted truth that in Jesus Christ the eschatological domain entered into human history in definitive, salvational form, Christianity has legitimized historically-theologically its supersessionism and triumphalism over Judaism and the Jewish people, as well as its exclusivism toward other faiths." If Rosemary Ruether is right that "the Christian historicizing of eschatological reality is the foundation of Christian antisemitism, and if we are correct that the center and proof of Christianity is the event of the

---

[30]   Eckardt, "Christians and Jews," pp. 106-108. Other writings of mine in this period that bear upon the issue of a supersessionist or triumphalist resurrection include "*Ha'Shoah* as Christian Revolution: Toward the Liberation of the Divine Righteousness," *Quarterly Review* 2 (1982): 52-67; "Contemporary Christian Theology and a Protestant Witness for the *Shoah*," *Union Seminary Quarterly Review* 38 (1983): 139-145; and "Antisemitism is the Heart," *Theology Today* 41 (1984): 301-308.

[31]   Eckardt, *For Righteousness' Sake*, p. 305.

resurrection, then any continued advocacy of the resurrection appears to represent in clear and authoritative form the fateful, culpable union of the Christian message and the murder camps."[32]

To conclude this review of my antithetical stage, during that period (in 1986) I referred in at least two places to the hope that a nontriumphalist apprehension of the resurrection might yet gain a place in Christian teaching.[33] These references may be received as a kind of transition to stage three of my thinking.

III. Synthesis: Antitriumphalist Affirmation

To recall to mind a point made early in this essay: A synthesis beyond both the thesis of pedestrian acknowledgment and the antithesis of critical questioning upon moral grounds need not abandon or wholly repudiate the other alternatives. The synthesis may gather up, assimilate, but also subject to critical judgment the thesis and the antithesis.

I have come at least tentatively to the view that a moral-theological remedy for Christian resurrectionist supersessionism, elitism, and triumphalism is to apprehend the resurrection of Jesus in the frame of reference "Spirit of God" (to apply the terminology of Marcus J. Borg[34]) within the special and continuing history of Judaism and the Jewish people. It is within the reality of Israel that the all-decisive meeting place or convergence of religious faith and historical event takes place. Once Christian confessions are deideologized,[35] i.e., monotheized, they may be enabled to become the spiritual implementation of what might be called "Jesus-historicity." A primary Christian challenge in the

---

32 Alice L. Eckardt and A. Roy Eckardt, *Long Night's Journey Into Day: A Revised Retrospective on the Holocaust*, revised and enlarged (Detroit: Wayne State University Press; Oxford: Pergamon Press, 1988), pp. 136, 139, 140 (slightly emended).

33 A. Roy Eckardt, "Is There a Way Out of the Christian Crime?: The Philosophic Question of the Holocaust," *Holocaust and Genocide Studies* 1 (1986): 121-126; *Jews and Christians: The Contemporary Meeting* (Bloomington: Indiana University Press, 1986), p. 156.

34 Marcus J. Borg, *Jesus: A New Vision* (San Francisco: Harper & Row, 1987); "A Renaissance in Jesus Studies," *Theology Today* 45 (1988): 280, 292.

35 If Christian ideology is resource to certain ideas and idea-systems in the service of collective self-interest, deideologization is the struggle against ideology.

shadow of the *Shoah* is not just to demythologize the Christian tradition but to deideologize it, viz., to wage war upon its supersessionist elitism.

The above "remedy" is no mere pragmatic or political move calculated to make the Jewish people or other people happy. Its character as a responsible position derives from its grounding in historical experience. The resurrection, part and parcel of the nascent world of Christian faith, is yet continuous with, even integral to, the social world of Judaism—or, in theological phrasing and following Paul van Buren, to the Covenant with Israel. Accordingly, against John Frederick Jansen's conclusion that "Israel's future is bound up with the future of Christ," we may propose that Christ's future is bound up with the future of Israel.

A few current illustrations may be adduced. Each of these can be treated as tacitly rejecting the triumphalist views of such analysts as Jansen and Pannenberg.

If only to get it out of the way I reproduce first my own somewhat mischievous midrash upon a spiritual (Spirit of God) rendering of the resurrection, the date 1987:

> We are given to understand that the Sadducees insisted that there is no resurrection (e.g., Matt.22:23)—contra Pharisee teaching. To introduce a light note (and perhaps therefore an especially serious one): We are advised that the One who sits in the heavens is not above laughing certain parties to scorn (Ps.2:4). What would be a better joke on those reactionary Sadducees than for God to raise her own Pharisee-liberal Son from the dead! She would be having a go at one of her dearest truths, and would also be giving at least a few of her people a foretaste of the things that are to come. Maybe best of all, she would be reminding the Sadducees exactly what she thought of them, meanwhile assuring her good friends the Pharisees that she was on their side.[36]

The Dutch Protestant theologian Jacobus Schoneveld provides broader and deeper conceptualization:

---

[36] Eckardt, *For Righteousness' Sake*, p. 310.

The resurrection means the vindication of Jesus as a Jew, as a person who was faithful to the Torah, as a martyr who participated in Jewish martyrdom for the sanctification of God's name. What else can this mean than the validation of Torah and vindication of the Jewish people as God's beloved people? The resurrection of Jesus confirms God's promises as well as God's commandments to the people Israel...I see the Jewish people's survival throughout the centuries in the light of what the resurrection means: the affirmation of the Torah, of the people of Israel, and of Jewish existence...

It is not true that the church has replaced Israel or taken over its vocation. Both Israel and the church await the fulfillment of the Torah, when the image of God will be visible in the whole of humanity. The Jews await this final Day incorporated in the people of Israel, the Christians incorporated in the body of Christ...Jews have expressed their faithfulness in a "no" to Jesus as his church tried to take the Torah away from them. Christians may express their faithfulness in their "yes" to Jesus who embodies the Torah, and therefore also in a "yes" to his brothers and sisters, the Jewish people.[37]

From a point of view such as that of Schoneveld, the resurrection may be legitimately and morally restored to Christianity once the poison of victimization is drained from it.

Paul M. van Buren is at one with Schoneveld in construing the resurrection (and perforce each and every authentic Christological attestation) as indigenous to God's unbroken (unbreakable?) Covenant with Israel. In this connection van Buren works to counteract (at least upon a theoretical level) the linkage between Christian resurrection doctrine and anti-Jewishness:

The fact of Easter that matters absolutely for the church is that Jesus once more proved effective in standing for God and God's cause, that, in the cause in and for which he had lived before, he was alive again... [This] claim of Easter faith cannot be itself the root of the church's anti-Judaism. [I should want to qualify this: cannot be allowed to remain the

---

[37] Jacobus (Coos) Schoneveld, "The Jewish 'No' to Jesus and the Christian 'Yes' to Jews," *Quarterly Review* 4 (Winter 1984): 60, 63 (slightly emended).

root...] That root we have seen to consist of the subtle and not-so-subtle transformation of the original witness to Jesus as a Jew committed to the renewal of his people in their covenant with God, into a witness to an anti-Judaic Jesus in deepest conflict with his people. If Easter faith concerns this one who, as Paul wrote, became a servant of the Jewish people (Rom. 15:8), if the event of Easter is preached, as Paul claimed he had both learned and practiced, "in accordance with the Scriptures" (I Cor.15:3-4), then it undercuts the anti-Judaism that developed in the church...Indeed, the Resurrection only stands in the way of anti-Judaism, since it underscores the continuity of the risen one with the Jew from Nazareth.[38]

With acknowledgment to Paul van Buren and others, I rather think now that a refusal to entertain the option of an extrabodily or spiritual resurrection of Jesus, together with a failure to insist upon the Jewishness of the resurrection (as in the original edition of *Long Night's Journey into Day*[39]), are overdrawn and probably not right. Furthermore, I now recognize a substantive discrepancy between triumphalist resurrectionism and nontriumphalist or antitriumphalist resurrectionism. Can the Christian church achieve the latter? I believe so. Or at least I hope so.[40]

I submit a concluding comment upon the resurrection in its place as an ongoing challenge but also an enigma to Christians.

We know that among the earliest followers of Jesus, as represented in the Apostolic Writings, doubt of his resurrection was present. "The resurrection is impossible"—Is not that the shattering conclusion to which especially rationalistic and/or burdensomely despairing moments sometimes drive the Christian? The rationalist and the cynic join hands in propagating the grim proposition that within the rules with which this world is "run," dead people do

---

[38]   Van Buren, *Christ in Context*, p. 110.

[39]   Cf. Eckardt and Eckardt, *Long Night's Journey Into Day*, rev. ed., pp. 142, 143. The effort is made in the original edition of that book to limit the possibilities to either a fully somatic resurrection or no resurrection at all. In the revised edition the possibility of other alternatives is raised (pp. 140-141).

[40]   There are criticisms by me still applicable to my new position on the resurrection—written, of course, before my shift— in *For Righteousness' Sake*, pp. 313-315.

not become living people. Against such a conclusion, advocates of a strictly or minimally somatic resurrection continue to array themselves. John 20:27 is among their proof texts: "Then he [the risen Jesus] said to Thomas, 'Reach your finger here; see my hands. Reach your hand here and put it into my side. Be unbelieving no longer, but believe.'" Yet we moderns tend to turn aside from somaticist explications of the resurrection. The Christology of many Christians also has problems with them, but at the same time many such persons are not happy with modernist reductionism, which restricts the resurrection to the moral and religious influence of a "great teacher" as continuing on in the world. A new and increasingly widespread Christology appears to be seeking out a resurrectionist position that navigates between and thence beyond both the Scylla of somaticism and the Charybdis of modernism. Thus does Paul van Buren proffer a synergist-covenantal viewpoint that involves a living parallel between the resurrection and the event of Sinai. To some, the resurrection

was a pure act of God; the recipients of the act were purely recipients. Or, on the contrary, it has seemed to others that the appearances were the subjective experience of believers, so that it could be said that Jesus rose into the *kerygma*, the preached faith of the disciples. Each of these conclusions misses the covenantal character of Easter: it was at once an act of God and an act of the disciples, of the nascent church. Without a doubt the witness to Easter, consistent with the witness to Sinai, insisted on the priority of God's initiative but, as in the case of Sinai, the action of those who bore witness to it was [also] constitutive to the event.[41]

To return to a distinction made at the beginning: From van Buren's standpoint the resurrection partakes of both objectiveness and subjectiveness.[42] In the vocabulary of our own day, the expression "resurrection of Jesus" may become, if you will, a spiritual—*not* "spiritualized"—metaphor or a transcending metaphor that presents us with a particularly epochal renewal of God's Covenant

---

[41] Van Buren, *Christ in Context*, p. 111; see also Tom F. Driver, *Christ in a Changing World* (New York: Crossroad, 1981), p. 8.

[42] A response of subjectiveness to the resurrection is still, in a sense, an objective datum of human history.

with Israel. I suggest that van Buren's proposal may be buttressed through the Pauline persuasion of a transformed risen body (I Cor. 15:35-44), since in that case the historically discrete aspect of the resurrection is retained as at the same time literalist-somaticist difficulties are avoided. For to separate the resurrected one from all somatic identity would be to divorce the risen Christ from Jesus of Nazareth.

The sum and substance of this position of synthesis is that the imperialization of the resurrection is definitely fightable from within the Christian community by those Christians who, just because they will to live and die in historical-moral solidarity with the Jewish people to whom the resurrection in the first instance belongs, are thereby allowed to witness to the resurrection themselves.

At the last, there is the assurance that if the God of Israel has defeated death in her son Jesus, she may well do the same again and again—for Christians, in and through the Body of Christ; for others, in and through her Spirit as it blows wherever she wills (John 3:8). In either case, the question to Mary of Magdala and the other women—the first Christian believers were evidently women—is fitting: "Why do you search among the dead?" (Luke 24:5). For is not Jesus, the Jewish *hasid* from the town of Nazareth, loose (again) in the social world, amidst all the anguish and all the joy of human events?

Comic Visions, Comic Truths
(1993)

It happened that a fire broke out in a theater. The clown came out
to inform the public. They thought it was a jest and applauded. He
repeated his warning, they shouted even louder. So I think the world
will come to an end amid general applause from all the wits, who
believe that it is a joke.

—Søren Kierkegaard[1]

Compassion is that power which survives to resist tragic suffering.

—Wendy Farley[2]

Hope has two beautiful daughters. Their names are anger and courage;
anger at the way things are, and courage to see that they do not remain
the way they are.

—Augustine[3]

In this exposition I offer the rudiments of a trialectic of God/Devil/Comedy,
employing the third of the three variables as the primary working tool.[4] The
practical reason keeps plugging away. It may be useful to recall Henri Bergson's
finding that a comic situation arises if it belongs at once to two series of events
that are independent of each other, and is capable of being assigned two entirely

---

[1]   Søren Kierkegaard, *Parables of Kierkegaard*, ed. Thomas C. Oden (Princeton:
Princeton University Press), p. 3 (taken from *Either/Or*, II).

[2]   Wendy Farley, *Tragic Vision and Divine Compassion* (Louisville: Westminster/John
Knox Press, 1990), p. 29.

[3]   Augustine, as quoted by Robert McAfee Brown, "What Keeps You Going?,"
Christianity and Crisis 51 (1991): 381.

[4]   Under the title, "A Stop Along the Road to Hear Three Jokes: Comedy and the
Campesino," this essay is in substance found in my forthcoming study, *How to Tell God from
the Devil: On the Way to Comedy*.

different meanings at one and the same time.[5] Yet surely human reactions to the incongruous, the contradictory, the absurd vary greatly. As one who stands upon the threshold of being a geriatric case—well, maybe not quite that—I am more and more leaning toward risibility, a comic treatment of the absurd, a celebration of the absurd almost in spite of itself.

I

Blameworthiness for radical evil and radical suffering[6] is carried ultimately, if not proximately, by God. God is the first and final sinner. We are the subjects of *thrownness*, consequent upon God's evident decision to make a world.

Such judgments can be tendered only by the religious believer; humanists and atheists may rest content, if their views do manage to content them, with human beings and/or natural forces as exclusive culprits for all the world's ills. The question of evil is thus viewed quite differently within a nontheological frame of reference. The theological view may be said to take evil much more seriously and poignantly than do humanist or atheist representations, since nothing could be more serious or poignant than associating evil with God. If there is to be any reconciliation between God's culpability and God's goodness, it has to come from beyond theodicy. Only from a dimension beyond argument could the Enemy ever be enabled to emerge as Friend, only under the aegis of the divine praxis, word-become-action. Otherwise we are left hanging in our anguish. Promises are of no avail. The eventuality of divine action enters in whether we speak of Judaism, Christianity, or Islam. Expressions of redemption in such traditions as these are made possible by, and thereby limited by, the language of events, historical events, the dimension of history.

How do history, faith, and comedy relate to each other? Alternately put: How, if at all, is the Absolute to break through into human life? Put yet a third way: What does God do, if God does anything, before the fact of incongruity

---

[5]   Henri Bergson, "Laughter," as referred to in Harvey Cox, *The Feast of Fools* (Cambridge: Harvard University Press, 1969), p. 144.

[6]   Wendy Farley uses the phrase "radical suffering" for "suffering that has the power to dehumanize and degrade human beings...and that cannot be traced to punishment or desert" (*Tragic Vision*, p. 12.)

in ultimate form? For that matter, what does the Devil do, if anything, before the fact of such incongruity? (Phenomenologically and morally speaking, any question we fabricate respecting God can be duplicated respecting the Devil.)

This essay centers in my concept of Realized Incongruity, a form of incongruity-in-action that does battle with the absurdities of life, particularly those tied to radical evil and radical suffering.

Reinhold Niebuhr declares that it is impossible to resolve with the aid of humor the contradiction between divine mercy and divine judgment, because "the divine judgment is ultimate judgment."[7] Sometimes Niebuhr's avowal is cited that "to laugh at life in the ultimate sense means to scorn it." I should think that everything depends upon the object of the laughter. If "life in the ultimate sense" refers to the divine life, Niebuhr cannot be questioned. Ultimately to laugh at God is sacrilege. But if "life in the ultimate sense" extends to the life of the Devil, father of radical evil, the scorn that is present is suffused with goodness. Here is a further aspect of the quest to tell God from the Devil: There is unrightful scorn and there is rightful scorn.

I suggest that humor and faith contain, along with so many of life's dualities, e.g., freedom and fate, elements of a dialectical relation, with each side driving toward the opposite side. Humor and the comic dimension are incapable in themselves of any final victory over evil, suffering, and the many vicissitudes of life. But such challenges are met or lived with in and through some kind of faith—unless they are reacted to in and through despair. And among the byproducts of faith is a comic vision that can accept even life's incongruities under the rubric of a certain nonchalance, an accompaniment of grace. Within the Christian outlook, the comedy of God is, as we shall emphasize, capable of providing a certain Joy. By virtue of the grace of God, the Devil is laughed to scorn. The comic vision is fulfilled in the divine comedy.

Reinhold Niebuhr's claim is also cited that were we to continue to laugh after recognizing the depth of our evil and sin, our laughter would become an instrument of irresponsibility. Niebuhr is talking about human laughter; he does not sufficiently distinguish between humor as human and humor as divine. Is it or is it not the case that the test of the very legitimacy of God—in God's own eyes, not to mention ours—is righteousness? The ultimate judgment of God has

---

7   Reinhold Niebuhr, "Humour and Faith," in *Discerning the Signs of the Times* (New York: Scribner, 1946), p. 118.

to be tempered by humor; otherwise, it is God who becomes irresponsible. For humankind remains utterly blameless for its creation and as well for the devilishness of temptation. Thus are we entitled to turn to the phenomenon of the laughter of God—not the idea of laughter but laughter as God's act. The question may be posed of the moral indispensability of God's mercy—for which Niebuhr himself pleads—not only for our sake but for the sake of God's own integrity. We humans laugh *at* ourselves and *with* God: God is required to laugh *at* Godself and *with* us. To Niebuhr, God's vicarious suffering, as reconciling mercy and judgment, is "far removed from laughter."[8] Even were we to agree that the same applies respecting the laughter of human beings, it is definitely not the case either with regard to the divine laughter or to the suffering of human beings. Precisely because the divine judgment is ultimate, the divine mercy must be ultimate. For we never asked to be born! It is the norm of the divine righteousness itself that demands the comedy of God.

II

One means for exploring the relationship among history, faith, and comedy is to consider continuities and discontinuities between Jewishness and Christianness. (For parsimony's sake and as a special tribute to me as ignoramus, I omit Muslimness.)

"Tragedy knows of tears and of death alone; comedy knows not only of tears and death, but of song, dance, and resurrection. The Comic Vision is Sarah's; it ends in birth and it ends in laughter. 'And Sarah laughed' (Gen. 18:12)."[9]

We consider first whether there is a peculiarly Jewish comedy. Four interpreters are called upon.

(1) In Lionel Blue's study, *To Heaven With Scribes and Pharisees*, we read that "the most typical weapon of Jewish spirituality is humor."[10] This is a

---

[8]   Ibid., p. 119.

[9]   Maria Harris, "Religious Educators and the Comic Vision," *Religious Education* 75 (1980): 431.

[10]   Lionel Blue, *To Heaven With Scribes and Pharisees* (New York: Oxford University Press, 1976), p. 75.

piquant line, although later I assay to emend it. The rabbi's aphorism opens up intriguing, even delectable, questions, such as, Where does this leave *other* weapons of Jewish spirituality? Where does Blue's finding leave *Christian* spirituality? At a minimum the rabbi is reminding us that comedy is a uniquely and terribly serious business—much more vital (life-affirming, life-sustaining) than its twin, tragedy.

(2) In *The Jewish Way*, his study of the holidays, Irving Greenberg attests that "ultimately, laughter is a unique reflection of Judaism's conception of life and reality. One of the Torah's central, positive teachings is that there is no other God.[11] If one believes in the infinite One God, then everything else is relative. No other value source, no other power has the right to claim absolute status...The presumptuousness of the demand for absolute loyalty on the part of human systems is best undermined by mockery and laughter, which puncture pretensions without giving weight to the pretender."[12] The parents of comedy are nonabsoluteness and the struggle against idolatry.

Greenberg's rendering of Jewish humor centers upon the "quintessential Jewish holiday" of Purim, with its unmatched "fun and games, masquerade and mummers, drinking, partying, and gift-giving." The rabbis speak of Esther as "the book of the hiding God. God's name is not mentioned; the redemption is brought about by flawed human effort...As one scholar [Elliot Yagod] put it, 'Wear masks, get drunk, for meaning is hidden beneath the visible.'"[13] The

---

[11] "In order to protect the oneness of God from every multiplication, watering down, or amalgamation with the rites of the surrounding world, the people of Israel chose for itself that verse of the Bible to be its credo which to this very day not only belongs to the daily liturgy of the synagogue but also is impressed as the first sentence of instruction upon the five-year-old schoolchild.

This is the confession which Jesus acknowledged as the 'most important of all the commandments,' and which is spoken by every child of Israel as a final word in the hour of death: 'Hear, O Israel! The Lord our God is One' (Deut 6:4)" (Pinchas Lapide, in Lapide and Jürgen Moltmann, *Jewish Monotheism and Christian Trinitarian Doctrine*, trans. Leonard Swidler [Philadelphia: Fortress Press, 1981], p. 27).

[12] Irving Greenberg, *The Jewish Way* (New York: Summit Books, 1988), pp. 254, 255.

[13] Ibid., pp. 227, 224, 235. There is a kind of overwhelmingness in the fact that Elie Wiesel's play, *The Trial of God*, should be set upon the Feast of Purim (New York: Random House, 1979).

celebration of Purim grows out of a wise acceptance of vulnerability...
Health, success, children can be snatched away overnight. The sweet-
ness of life should be savored today, for that is all one really has for
sure...[Purim's] dialectical resolution of the tension between dream and
reality is to celebrate the victory while poking fun at it... The way to
deal with reversals is to *play* with them; humor can be the key to sanity.
It is the only healthy way to combine affirmation with ongoing doubt...

...[The] tradition satirizes its own pretensions, affirming yet
recognizing the contradictions to its own fundamentals...

...If people insist on having extraterrestrial redeemers, they will
perceive themselves as living in a world abandoned by God, when in
fact God is the Divine Redeeming Presence encountered in the partial,
flawed actions of humans. The truth of this salvation eludes both those
who explain everything away as coincidence or random occurrence and
those who insist on "out of this world" revelation...

...Humor expresses transcendence of unredeemed reality, and it
takes sanctity itself with a sense of limits...The unchecked tendency to
respect religion all too often leads to deifying the ritual and the outward
form of God...

...One can only respond with laughter and mockery and put-on,
satirizing God and the bitter joke this world threatens to become...But
as the hilarity reaches its climax, Jews move beyond bitterness to
humor... Through the humor, Jews project themselves into future
redeemed reality that transcends the moment. Thus, hope is kept alive
and the Messiah remains possible...

Purim is the balance to Passover, it is the humor that admits that the
Shabbat is still a dream. To act as if Shabbat and the final redemption
are fact would be insane; but not to affirm the totality of hope would be
a sellout. Purim offers an alternative humorous affirmation. Thus,
Purim's laughter preserves integrity and sanity together. This is Purim's
remarkable role in Jewish history.[14]

---

[14] Greenberg, *Jewish Way*, pp. 236, 237, 246, 251, 254, 257.

One Talmudic midrash "tells us that in Messianic times, all the holidays will pass. Purim alone will endure and be celebrated (Talmud Yerushalmi Megillah 1:5)." We may comment that there could never be a Purim celebration of the Devil, because the Devil takes life too seriously and is thereby prohibited from joining in the fun.

There follows, in summary form, Irving Greenberg's viewpoint upon the foundation of Jewish humor. "In poking fun, we affirm the presence of contradiction. We speak with ultimate seriousness, but with a tentativeness that admits the alternatives. It is the way we testify in a world that appears to contradict our hope."[15]

(3) I turn to two elements within the thinking of Emil L. Fackenheim that are pertinent to the comic vision. (a) The initial entry in Michael Morgan's collection of Fackenheim's writings is the older but prevenient essay, "Our Position toward Halacha" (1938). Once Halacha, Commandment, is accepted as representative of the Absolute, the truth is equally clear that "Halacha confronts the [Jew] of today as a system with fixed content, with commandments that contain small, infinitely detailed minutiae that, vis-à-vis no less than Divinity, must necessarily appear as a totally incongruous *Kleinigkeitskrämerei* (pettifoggery)."[16]

Apart from the clear connection between humor and lengthy German words, we note *incongruous* as the most jussive term here, for does not the soul of comedy live (at least when theologically construed) amidst a dialectical incongruity between the Absolute (Nonpettifoggeriness, as we may put it with a little smile) and the "minutiae" of our very small planet? Thus is the (unbelievable?) point to be made that, in principle, the Absolute will "break through" into human life under the aegis of "totally incongruous" triflings—or *seeming* triflings.

From this perspective, we may be impressed anew with the force of Rabbi Blue's aphorism, "the most typical weapon of Jewish spirituality is humor."

---

15   Irving Greenberg, *Guide to Purim* (New York: CLAL, National Jewish Conference Center, 1979), pp. 20, 17.

16   Emil L. Fackenheim, "Our Position toward Halacha," in *The Jewish Thought of Emil Fackenheim: A Reader*, ed. Michael L. Morgan (Detroit: Wayne State University Press, 1987), p. 22.

(b) In his much more recent study *What Is Judaism?* (1987), Professor Fackenheim alludes to a Talmudic ambiguity upon the hiding of God. "Does [God] hide in wrath against or punishment of His people? God forbid that He should do so at such a time [as ours]! Does He hide for reasons unknown? God forbid that He should, in this of all times, be a *deus absconditus!* Then why does He hide?" It is his weeping that he hides. "He hides His weeping in the inner chamber, for just as God is infinite *so His pain is infinite, and this, were it to touch the world would destroy it... God so loved the world that He hid the infinity of His pain from it lest it be destroyed...*"[17]

If the laughter of God in the Psalms is a laughter of derision, it makes moral sense to indicate weeping as the fitting human response. But insofar as God Godself engages in the act of weeping, insofar as the pettifoggery of tears becomes the Way of the Absolute, in embodiment of the divine love, then is the human response reversed. Laughter bursts into laughter.

(4) Mark Shechner addresses directly the question of the nature of Jewish humor, but strictly within the American milieu. (I submit that reflection upon Jewish humor in its relation to American culture ought to begin with a singular datum: While Jews constitute only 2.7 percent of the population of the United States, yet no less than 80 percent of all people at work in various aspects of the comic enterprise are Jewish. [Comment by the Devil, Chief Antisemite: "Everybody knows, stupid, that the Jews control all our entertainment."])

Professor Shechner proposes the paradoxical phrase "ghetto cosmopolitanism," which describes a condition that "arose out of the striking conjunctions of oppression and spirituality in the ghettos and *shtetls* of Ashkenazic Jewry." The ghetto cosmopolitan "combines a parochialism bred of poverty and confinement with a universal consciousness bred of study and intellectual ambition. In him, vulgarity and sensibility go hand in hand, his coarseness of manner is not inconsistent with a high degree of intellectual and aesthetic discrimination."

In and through the concept of ghetto cosmopolitanism we are aided in apprehending the two worlds that combine to educe Jewish comedy: an exalted (transcending), spiritual world, blessed as it is with its very own language of Hebrew, and a lowly (immanent) world of ordinariness, also blessed with a language of its own: Yiddish. Professor Shechner observes that "a mind

---

[17]   Emil L. Fackenheim, *What Is Judaism?* (New York: Summit Books, 1987), p. 291.

nurtured upon a higher and a lower language" is "accustomed to shuffling between the transcendent and the worldly and defining its relationship to reality in terms of the ironies generated by such travel."[18]

As I have written elsewhere,

> instances of humor that live upon the unique incongruities generated by the two worlds of Jewry are legion. Mrs. Fishbein answers the telephone to hear a cultured voice, "'Can you and your husband come to a tea for Lady Windemere?" Mrs. Fishbein breaks in, "Oy, have *you* got a wrong number!" Dahn Ben-Amotz asks, "What if the people of Israel hadn't been elected the Chosen People?," and replies, "Some other people would have got it in the neck." An elderly Jewish lady art collector is apprised of a chance to secure another Picasso. She responds, "With Picassos I'm up to my ass already." And Woody Allen can agree that there is an intelligence to the universe all right—save for "certain parts of New Jersey." As Shechner points out, it was the "juxtaposition of higher and lower worlds within the mental economy of the Jewish people that established the terms for a *comedy of deflation*, whose basic trope was a sudden thrusting downward from the exalted to the workaday. From Sholom Aleichem to Woody Allen, this comedy of internal juxtaposition has been fundamental."[19]

In our other source from Mark Shechner he verifies the relation between Jewish comedy and the religion of Judaism: Comedy is Judaism's "inversion, its negative, its shadow. The reversal of figure and ground. Where both comedy and religion acknowledge the interdependence of two worlds, a higher and a lower, each gives primacy to a different world. Religion...translates upwards,

---

[18] Mark Shechner, "Dear Mr. Einstein: Jewish Comedy and the Contradictions of Culture," in Sarah Blacher Cohen, ed., *Jewish Wry* (Bloomington: Indiana University Press, 1989), pp. 142-146.

[19] A. Roy Eckardt, "Is There a Christian Laughter?," *Encounter* (Indianapolis) 53 (1992): 111. The quotation here included from Mark Shechner is from Shechner, "Comedy, Jewish," in Glenda Abramson, ed., *The Blackwell Companion to Jewish Culture* (Oxford: Basil Blackwell, 1989), italics added.

while comedy undercuts the transcendent, criticizes it, subordinates it to the common. The one, in effect, Hebraizes, the other Yiddishizes."[20]

To review the identity of the two Jewish worlds: We have respectively, via Irving Greenberg's conceptualization, the infinite One God vis-à-vis the realm of relativity and vulnerability, and under Emil Fackenheim's conceptualization, and again respectively, the Absolute vis-à-vis minutiae. Jewish comedy/humor is actualized in and through the tension between God/Absoluteness and relativity/pettifoggery.

Wherein lies the integrity of the bond between the Absolute and comedy as such? What is it that enables the comic vision to sustain itself—or, better, to be sustained by resources beyond itself, contra, say, a tragic vision?

I cite Emil L. Fackenheim's application of the "commanding Presence"—his morphology of human freedom—in *God's Presence in History*: "As *sole* Power, the divine commanding Presence *destroys* human freedom: as *gracious* Power, it *restores* that freedom, and indeed *exalts* it, for human freedom is made part of a covenant with Divinity itself. And the human astonishment, which is *terror* at a Presence at once divine and commanding, turns into a *second* astonishment, which is *joy*, at a Grace which restores and exalts human freedom by its commanding Presence."[21]

Human freedom is here apprehended as neither autonomous (master of its fate, captain of its soul) nor heteronomous (subject to dictates alien to itself),[22] but as, ideally, theonomous (consonant with the proper thrust of the *imago dei*). And we can then be grasped by the "second astonishment": Joy, *verbum ipsissimum* for, the *essentia* of, comedy/humor/laughter.

Jewish thinking and experience have, of course, always been cognizant of tragic elements within the human world. We are reminded, for instance, that the very ground of Sholom Aleichem's humor was the persuasion that "the prevailing social conditions oppressed and crippled...[the Jew] until he became

---

[20]   Shechner, "Dear Mr. Einstein," pp. 154-155.

[21]   Emil L. Fackenheim, *God's Presence in History* (New York: New York University Press, 1970), pp. 15-16.

[22]   Emil L. Fackenheim, *Quest for Past and Future* (Boston: Beacon Press, 1970), pp. 219-220.

not only miserable but ridiculous."[23] Nevertheless, Jewry never allows ultimacy to tragedy. For within the *Weltanschauung* of tragedy, human structures (also divine structures) must fall prey to an impersonal, remorseless Fate (*moira*), which boasts as well the power of inexorable suffering and the power of Nemesis, retribution. It is no accident that Judaism and the Jewish heritage forever refuse to exalt the "tragic hero." Again, Sigmund Freud was being a good Jew in testifying that in view of its repudiation of suffering, humor must be numbered among the great and historic foes of the human compulsion to suffer. In humor is found a nonvindictive liberation from the wounds of life.[24] The eventuality of Jewishness ever remains the eventuality of comedy, never of tragedy. Against the entire dimension of Fate, the Jewish ethos is affirming an open present and an open future. It is often said that Jews are a most historical people. To turn Jewish life into tears alone would be to subject that life to Fate. (It is possible to argue, although I do not pursue the matter here, that a central reason for the gradual eclipse of the Devil in the development of Judaism and Jewish life is the triumph of freedom over Fate.) Even the fatefulness of German Nazi demonry was to be overpowered and was overpowered. And since that evil time, the act of perpetual remembering (*zachor*) carries forward the struggle. In tragedy, things must be what they have been, are, and will be; in comedy, the future explodes into openness, into the spontaneity of play and dance. In Frederick Buechner's aphorism (from the Christian side), the tragic is the inevitable, the comic is the unforseeable. But Buechner goes even farther and suspects that from the divine perspective, "it is the tragic that is seen as not inevitable whereas it is the comic that is bound to happen."[25] (I may insert that the "freedom" of the Devil and his minions is held prisoner to tragedy or necessity, the fate of having to do radical evil.) Where there is hope there is comedy; where there is comedy there is hope. As Peter Berger writes, while

---

23   Meyer Wiener, "On Sholom Aleichem's Humor," in Cohen, ed., *Jewish Wry*, p. 50.

24   Sigmund Freud, "Humor," in John Morreall, ed., *The Philosophy of Laughter and Humor* (Albany: State University of New York Press, 1987), p. 113.

25   Frederick Buechner, *Telling the Truth* (San Francisco: Harper & Row, 1977), pp. 57, 72.

tragedy may imbue a sense of human courage, only comedy can foster a sense of hope.[26]

The opportunity ever remains of choice, of decision. Humanness is freedom, freedom is humanness. Freedom means: responsibility (obligation *and* culpability), creativity, a transcending response to incongruity, life as in the end eligible for redemption, for final wholeness. Correspondingly, as Sharon Weinstein observes, Jewish humor embodies "a prevailing optimism that this too, no matter how horrible, shall pass, and that Jews as a people will endure."[27]

III

We come to the eventuality of peculiarly Christian comedy/humor/laughter.

The Jewish teaching upon the *Anknüpfungspunkt* (meeting-place, point of confrontation) of history and the transhistorical, of immanence and transcendence, is embodied in the "giving of the Torah," the major Jewish event of Realized Incongruity, the divine implementation of, or action upon, incongruity as such, a cosmic, deliberate juxtaposing of categories.[28] The Torah makes for joy: "The law [teaching] of the Lord" is Israel's delight (Ps. 1:2). Christian comedy, never in violation of the Jewish envisionment, keeps that affirmation going under the aegis of additional, crucial, and unique historical events. Continuity is thereby shown, yet also discontinuity, as between Jewish comedy and Christian comedy. In and through divine acts of Realized Incongruity, the dimension of incongruity is fully recognized but is then pitted against itself, thus making possible the way to laughter and joy.

---

[26] Peter L. Berger, *The Precarious Vision* (Garden City: Doubleday, 1961), p. 273. Cf. Harvey Cox: "When tragedy fails you still have pathos. When comedy fails it becomes ridiculous. When tragedy succeeds it reveals to us a vision of the relentless wholeness of life. When comedy succeeds it shakes us into a new stance, it prepares us for new experiences" (*Feast of Fools*, p. 137).

[27] Sharon Weinstein, "Jewish Humor: Comedy and Continuity," *American Humor: An Interdisciplinary Newsletter* 3 (Fall 1976): 1. On the question of Jewish humor in the context of other kinds of humor, consult Christie Davies, *Ethnic Humor Around the World* (Bloomington: Indiana University Press, 1990).

[28] In Islam we have the Realized Incongruity of the Qur'ān as Word of Allah.

Christian humor is grounded, of course, in the two-world symbiosis of Jewishness. This is exemplified in the church's appropriation of Torah as "Word of God." However, while in the Christian comedy the transcendent is subordinated to the common all right, nevertheless and by way of contrast, it is faith itself that "translates" downwards. This difference obtains because of the essential fact that while Jewishness is comprised of the dual elements of religion and people (*laos*),[29] Christianness is limited to a faith. Out of its *continuity* with Jewishness, the church has kept viable the higher and lower worlds that compound into the distinctiveness of Jewish comedy. But out of its *discontinuity* with Jewishness, and while attesting to *some* kind of comedy of deflation, the church has yet seen fit to alter the juxtaposition into a translation downwards that, although it does not undercut the transcendent, does radically transform it. In the Christian schema, the ordinary is peculiarly assimilated to sacredness, to the story of salvation (*Heilsgeschichte*)—or, more carefully, certain selected elements of the ordinary are thus assimilated (since Judaism too assimilates the ordinary to sacredness). In a word, Christian comedy could never be embodied in the Marx Brothers whereas Jewish humor could.

---

[29] Insofar as the event of the restoration of the State of Israel in 1948 (after some nineteen hundred years) is to be looked at within the purview, not only of Jewish faith but also of Jewish peopleness (*laos*), it is possible to argue that the conceptualization being applied here to the understanding of Jewish humor can be applied to Israel. The reasoning might begin something like this: With Eretz Israel, we witness a uniquely unique case of the transcendent being translated downward into the immanent. Israel is the contemporary Jewish community's special joke—a joke upon all antisemites and Nazis, upon the rest of humankind, perhaps also upon itself, perhaps even upon God Godself (whose own holy language has now been pettifogged into a worldly *lingua franca*). Thus, in the measure that the event of the new Israel goes beyond the reality of Judaism as such (while of course sustaining Judaism) and falls within Jewish two-world incongruity, it becomes eligible as a joke. But, further, since Israel may also be regarded as an earnest of redemption—sometimes Israel receives a place in Jewish life comparable to the one Jesus Christ occupies in Christian life—we may be driven beyond "joke" to "Joke." But cf. Arthur Waskow's alternative rendering of the divine comedy, "God's Joke: The Land Twice Promised." To Waskow, God promised the land twice: to Isaac and his children (Israel and Jews) and to Ishmael and his children (the Palestinians). This, Waskow argues, is God's real joke (in Otto Maduro, ed., *Judaism, Christianity, and Liberation* [Maryknoll, NY: Orbis Books, 1991], pp. 73-80). We may in addition take note of an interesting literary sequence of events in Luke 2. Herod's slaughter of the infants is said to fulfill Jeremiah's word that tells of Rachel weeping for her children. But then, once Herod is dead, Joseph in Egypt is told in a dream to take the infant Jesus and go up to Eretz Israel (vss. 16-21). The eventuality of a convergence of Jewish comedy and Christian comedy can here be glimpsed.

Quite expectably, therefore, Jewish comedy can be primarily and properly directed toward secularity while Christian comedy is perforce thrust toward religious faith. (That the Feast of Purim is not free of religious elements, or at least of religious application, reminds us that the differentiation here is relative in character, a matter of emphasis, though of a distinctive and noteworthy sort.) More precisely, the Christian community has taken onto itself, or has been assigned, the propagating of no less than three Basic Incongruities. That is to say, in and through three claimed events—Incarnation, Crucifixion, Resurrection —the transcendent is linked redemptively to the immanent.

Professor Shechner points out that within the Jewish outlook "religion translates upwards," whereas comedy subordinates the transcendent "to the common." Christians are enabled to lift out this latter subordination and utilize it to confess, in some contrast to Judaism, that *in essence* the Christian faith is in and of itself, *kiveyachol*, a uniquely unique (= transcendingly unique) Joke.

The sentence just above requires at least two midrashim, before we proceed further. (a) I call attention to Heinz Moshe Graupe's identification of the Hebrew term *kiveyachol*, as just used. The concept is an appropriate one in Hebrew literature to convey religious content "that almost seems blasphemous." It is variously translated as "so to speak," "as if it were possible," and "as one might be allowed to say."[30]   I should want to tie this conceptualization substantively and decisively to my relating of *myth* and *the comic* near the beginning of my study *How To Tell God From the Devil: On the Way to Comedy*, both of which categories are viewed therein as alternate ways of reckoning with the dialectic of transcendence/immanence, ways that try to mediate between the mystery of fact and the mystery of interpretation. The concept *kiveyachol* serves to do the same thing, if in modest and simple syntactical fashion.

(b) The word "Joke" to signify one or another basic Christian event may sound offensive or demeaning to some readers, whereas the phrases "Christian comedy" and "divine comedy" probably do not. There is etymological support for such a negative reaction. *The Oxford Universal Dictionary* defines "joke" as "something said or done to excite laughter or amusement," and then adds:

---

[30]   Heinz Moshe Graupe, *The Rise of Modern Judaism: An Intellectual History of German Jewry 1650-1942*, trans. John Robinson (Huntington, NY: Robert E. Krieger, 1978), p. 249.

"a ridiculous circumstance." "Ridiculous" is defined as "exciting ridicule or derisive laughter: absurd, preposterous, comical, laughable;" also (a second meaning) "outrageous." I certainly do not mean "Joke" in such superficial or even trivial ways. Christian sacred acts or events are far from being amusing. The constructive purpose of the expression "Christian Jokes"—"Joke" and "Jokes" must always be capitalized, otherwise the point is lost before we have started—is threefold: (i) The usage points up the objectively incongruous character of the events involved (as Christian doctrine has always acknowledged and insisted upon). (ii) More crucially, the usage accentuates the *active* quality of the Christian mysteries. To joke is to do something, whereas "to be comical" is to remain in a state or condition. According to the Christian *Anschauung,* God *acts* to be incarnate, God *acts* in the death of the Crucifixion, God *acts* in the Resurrection of Jesus Christ—just as God *acts* in the giving of Torah. The Christian comedy is a set of *doings* (in direct opposition to such philosophical speculation as tries to "think God's thoughts after" God). (iii) All in all, a Christian Joke, an act of Realized Incongruity, is most serious business. The Joke is not simply a joke. Yet the pure comedy of "jokes" is itself far away from triviality. Our stand-up and sit-down performers are telling the truth about themselves, and us, and life. Humor worth its salt is always a moral creation, with moral lessons to teach. To repeat a marvelous line from Carl Reiner, a most elegant comic, "The funniest joke of all is the absolute truth stated simply and gracefully." The world of "jokes" and the world of "Joke" are bound together. The world of "jokes" is the world of God's Creation; the world of "Jokes" is a pointer toward redemption. In a word: "Christian Joke" is a means of communicating with a secularized culture that is considerably devoted to comedy.

We must, accordingly, keep in mind the essential dichotomy, referred to above, of Jewishness as entailing a *laos* (people) and Christianness as delimiting itself to a faith. As we have noted, Jewish comedy arises out of the juxtaposing of spirituality and ordinariness, God and relativity, the Absolute and pettifoggery. This is where the Jewish view locates the incongruity that is the ground of its humor. Thus is there a formidable difficulty in identifying Judaism (as a faith) under the rubric of Joke (Essential Incongruity). In the general frame of reference of Jewishness (a context broader than Judaism as such), we have a comedy of deflation: the humor is directed downward, "a sudden thrusting downward from the exalted to the workaday." All this suggests that Rabbi Blue's aphorism, "the most typical weapon of Jewish spirituality is humor," might better read, "the most typical weapon of the Jewish *double world* is humor"—whereas, in contrast, the most typical weapon of *Christian spirituality* is seen to be, *kiveyachol*: a Joke. For, on the Christian side, it is the faith itself that is so much more the Joke, because now the juxtaposition of spirituality and ordinariness is channeled and remains wholly inside that faith. Now, as previously indicated, it is the faith itself that "translates" downwards. In consequence, the faith itself remains at the center of the comedy. Christian comedy is, in essence, religious comedy. Nothing less than the domain of the transcendent is transformed in the process.

We are a little more prepared now to epitomize the Christology of comedy, deriving as that Christology does from three Jokes:

(1) *The Birth.* God hides Godself and lives singularly in *this* baby (John 1:14: 3:16).

This affirmation is not incongruent with the persuasion that God hides Godself in Torah, the holy in the profane, a *kenosis* (emptying) of Eternity into Time (cf. the Zen Buddhist teaching of *Sunyata*, emptiness).[31] While it is often insisted that Judaism and Christianity are wholly disparate when it comes to the teaching of incarnation, the truth is that the disjunction is not total and may not even be essential. Here are three citations from Jewish scholars. Lionel Blue declares: "God has no human form in Jewish theology but He reveals a very human psyche in Jewish jokes. There He enters into the suffering and paradoxes of the world, and experiences the human condition. There He is immanent, if not incarnate, and a gossamer bridge of laughter stretches over the void, linking creatures of flesh and blood to the endlessness of the *Ein Sof*, and the paralysing power of the Lord of hosts."[32] Norman Lamm writes: "God is especially immanent in Torah, and the study of Torah is therefore a means of achieving an encounter with the divine presence... Torah, as such, is far more than a

---

[31]   Consult John B. Cobb, Jr. and Christopher Ives, eds., *The Emptying God: A Buddhist-Jewish-Christian Conversation* (Maryknoll, NY: Orbis Books, 1990).

[32]   Blue, *To Heaven*, p. 78.

document of the divine legislation: it is in itself, mystically, an aspect of God."[33] And Michael Wyschogrod states: If man "is to have a relation to Hashem [The Name]...then Hashem must be near man wherever he is. And not only near man but in man, or more specifically, in the people of Israel."[34]

Nevertheless, Judaism, of course, does not accept *this* Incarnation, the Christian one.

(2) *The Life and the Death.* With the clown, everything seems but a jest.[35] With the *campesino* Jesus, there can be true Christian comedy. It is *el dios pobre* who, in and through the *campesino,* goes to every length to embody the divine compassion and the divine forgiveness. Here is found the Joy of the Incarnation. For the *campesino* and *el dios pobre* are one (John 10:30). And the *campesino* will lay down his life for the sheep, including the many sheep that "do not belong to this fold" (John 10:15-16). Christian comedy is triadic. It is the comedy of *el campesino nazareno,* of *el dios pobre* but also of *Nuestra Señora de Guadalupe,* of these who suffer yet laugh, laugh yet suffer. "*The Christian God had hands laid upon him.*"[36]

---

[33] Norman Lamm, as cited in David Birnbaum, *God and Evil* (Hoboken: Ktav Publishing House, 1989), p. 243.

[34] Michael Wyschogrod, *The Body of Faith* (San Francisco: Harper & Row, 1989), p. 101.

[35] I should be the last to denigrate the jester's role, for it is irreplaceable. Leszek Kolakowski writes: "Although an habitué of good society, [the jester] does not belong to it and makes it the object of his inquisitive impertinence; he...questions what appears to be self-evident. The jester could not do this if he himself were part of the good society, for then he would be, at the most a drawing room wit. A jester must remain an outsider; he must observe 'good society' from the sidelines, for only then can he detect the non-obvious behind the obvious and the non-final behind what appears to be final. At the same time he must frequent good society so as to know what it deems holy, and to be able to indulge in his impertinence" ("The Priest and the Jester," *Dissent* 9 [1962]: 233). I am indebted to Harvey Cox for this reference. Were Kolakowski willing or able to substitute "she" and "her" for "he" and "him," he would have it made.

[36] Frederick Sontag, *The God of Evil* (New York: Harper & Row, 1970), p. 96, italics added.

A final laugh (= judgment), upon the antisemite, Christian and other, is that the incarnational Joke, the Joke of the cross, should consist of the minutia of a poor Jewish woodworker from the town of Nazareth.[37]

Christianity is able to manifest a certain foolishness that does not obtain on the Jewish side. True, the discontinuity is not total. For when Paul declares that the message of the cross is foolishness, he can readily cite the prophet Isaiah, "I will destroy the wisdom of the wise" (Isa. 29:14; I Cor. 1:18-19). Yet the cross remains not only "foolishness to Gentiles" but "a stumbling block to Jews"—the latter with very good justification: Jesus as alleged Messiah failed to realize the hope that links Messiah to objective peaceableness and justice in the world. By contrast, it was the cross that led Paul to discern, with joyousness, that his God of Israel is at once a fool and a weakling: "God's foolishness is wiser than human wisdom, and God's weakness is stronger than human strength" (I Cor. 1:25).

However, we must go back for a moment to the concept of *kenosis*. In *Religion in the Secular City* Harvey Cox agrees that Christ "gives up the power and privilege associated with deity and becomes poor in order to reveal the love of God." But Cox alerts us to a danger in that teaching as stressed amongst today's liberation thinkers, especially by women theologians "aware of the subtle forms of domination that persist in many time-honored ideas." The danger is the perpetuating of "a concept of condescension in which all the inherent dignity is on the divine side and none on the human side. God stoops to the essentially worthless human condition to bring salvation; but the idea of an inherent human powerlessness and dependency remains." Women theologians are rightly insisting "that what they and other dominated peoples need to hear are not further assurances that deliverance will come from an outside source; rather, they need to hear that God can strengthen and undergird their own struggle, that they are not devoid of power or potential—as the sexist culture tells them they are—but are capable of standing up. God is not the St. George who saves the hapless maiden by slaying the dragon, but the One who supports and inspires her to slay it herself." Further, as far as Jesus is concerned, his

---

[37] For a treatment of the life and death of Jesus as a parable and analogy for interpreting the present, see H. Richard Niebuhr, *The Meaning of Revelation* (New York: Macmillan, 1941), pp. 124-125.

choice "was not to lower himself to an inferior station but to become a defender and representative of people with whom he already had close ties."[38]

The powerful and the powerful interests are ever and again on the lookout to utilize ideological fabrications to keep the powerless and downtrodden "in their place." Divine *kenosis* is an earnest and sign of redemption all right, but human *kenosis* can easily compound and prolong oppression. To bring together theological affirmation and moral insistence: Forgiveness never forgets that wrongness is not good. On the contrary, acts of forgiveness only point up sin in the starkness of its evil. But then these acts go beyond and against evil by judging judgment through the power of mercy. Thus is evil put to shame and the door is opened to freedom and comedy.

(3) *The Resurrection.*[39] In the presence of death, human comedy is powerless. It dies, along with everything else.[40] But what of the Comedy of God?

Is God Enemy or is God Friend? It is told that once upon a time, the *campesino* was brought out of death, *este campesino, this* peasant. Some of us still believe that, somehow, *el dios pobre* was there, and indeed brought the whole thing off. (It seems, *kiveyachol,* that God couldn't stop laughing, and this turned out to be something of a drag. This explains why things were delayed for nigh on to three whole days. But we humans can sympathize here; once in a while we too have a spell where we just can't stop laughing, try as we might.)

To return to a statement I have submitted more than once: We never did ask to be born. Neither do we now ask to be subjected to Death, the final insult and

---

[38] Harvey Cox, *Religion in the Secular City* (New York: Simon & Schuster, 1984), pp. 141-143.

[39] It is essential to their professional health and professional ethics that scholars keep up to date upon the work of other scholars in their field and do not misrepresent them by reproducing earlier viewpoints rather than later and perhaps changed ones as definitive. Darrell J. Fasching refers to my 1978 and 1982 position upon Jesus' resurrection as though it comprises my final say on the matter, all the while ignoring the diametrically opposite position I came to and published repeatedly in more than adequate time for him to use in his book, *Narrative Theology After Auschwitz* (Minneapolis: Fortress, 1992), pp. 26-27. Consult the following: A. Roy Eckardt, *Jews and Christians* (Bloomington: Indiana University Press, 1986), pp. 85-87; *For Righteousness' Sake* (Bloomington: Indiana University Press, 1989), pp. 310-312; and, a most explicit attestation to Jesus' resurrection, "Why Do You Search Among the Dead?," *Encounter* (Indianapolis) 51 (1990): 1-17.

[40] Cf. Ernest Becker, *The Denial of Death* (New York: Free Press, 1973).

final evil vis-à-vis Life. William Hazlitt calls it, fittingly, the "ugly Customer." The responsibility, at both places, our birth and our death, has, ultimately speaking, nothing to do with us. It lies wholly elsewhere. To many persons, here is grievous cause for pessimism, for emptiness, for despair, indeed for the hatred of God, even for a kind of avenging flirtation with the Devil. Yet to others, the door stays open, if only barely ajar, to a salvation wrought by God, perhaps as recompense, in a dominant respect, for our travail in the life we did not seek and for the specter of death we find so hard to endure.

One means that righteousness utilizes in order to vindicate God (Isa. 5:16) is the resurrection. Here is "theodicy" wholly beyond theodicy. In this Friend, friendship comes to completion and to rest. And here is how, at an ultimate level of reckoning, we tell God from the Devil. In other language, a provisional dualism of Enemy versus Friend is replaced by a modified monism that is finally able to assimilate Enemy to Friend.

The triumph of God over the Devil, the Shadow of God, and the triumph over God as Enemy is the Christian parallel to the Persian victory of Ahura Mazda over Angra Mainyu. Yet the promise of the resurrection also remains eschatological (as does the Zoroastrian hope). In the Final Joke the evil of death is itself subjected to death, but only in principle and proleptically. In the words of Harvey Cox, "merely to reconcile theology to existing reality is to forget the crucial eschatological factor, the one that reminds us that existing reality is provisional, is part of 'this passing age,' and therefore cannot be taken with ultimate seriousness."[41] And Wendy Farley declares, "It is in history that we live, struggle, think, act, and suffer. Without denying the legitimacy of eschatological hopes, theology must seek a historical response to evil. Otherwise, consolation and hope may degenerate into excuses for remaining passive or indifferent in the face of radical suffering and injustice."[42]

The all-decisive reason why we are made to insist that redemption is "not yet" lies in the fact that radical evil continues to afflict the life of God as well as the lives of human beings. We are not out on some utopia-trip. For the saving incongruities/congruities of God can themselves be subjected to incon-

---

[41]   Cox, *Feast of Fools*, p. 135.

[42]   Farley, *Tragic Vision*, p. 22.

gruities that are nothing less than diabolic. I adduce one example from a domain earlier referred to, today's feminist revolution.

Divine incarnation tied to a male human could turn into a Bigger Joke than God Godself, and certainly we, may comprehend or master. Many women rightly want to know how "redemption" could ever be possible in the form of a male. At least two related questions are involved here: (a) Is God's Joke of Realized Incongruity itself subject to a comic, cosmic veto?: "You thought you were redeeming us, and all you sent was a *son*! What a joke!" (b) How is it possible to perform an act of authentic Realized Incongruity when the prejudices and sins of human beings infect the subject matter of the act with their own incongruity of immorality?

About the best I can say is that a Bigger Joke does not actually drive us out of the comic realm, although it does remind us that comedy is never exempt from tragedy and it does tell us that the comic act is a most difficult thing to pull off, even for God. Put differently but pertinently: The Devil is the expert *par excellence* in fouling up things—so expert that he may even be tempting us (God too?) to downplay our own blameworthiness and responsibility. All in all, the three Jokes that comprise the Christian faith are not immune to contamination by radical evil.

Our effort here does not pretend to do something substantive to vanquish the Devil. We seek simply to distinguish Devil and God, and thereby, perhaps, to help us a little in our own battles against evil, particularly the evils of repression.

Withal, the resurrection does abide as a present reality. This is seen in at least three ways. First, the resurrection-event remains as a norm respecting various kinds of Christian affirmation—for example, the authority of the New Testament. As Clark M. Williamson writes, "It is the living Christ who explains the New Testament, not the New Testament that explains the living Christ."[43] Second, to bring H. Richard Niebuhr back into our company, "a universal teleology of resurrection," contra "a universal teleology of entombment," means that an ethic of death is countered by an ethic of life, and an ethic of life bespeaks an open future, an open society. We may add to this that an open future at once points up and reenforces the solidarity of faith and comedy.

---

[43] Clark M. Williamson, *A Guest in the House of Israel* (Louisville: Westminster/John Knox Press, 1993), (forthcoming).

Third, and still with H. Richard Niebuhr, if the resurrection reconciles us to God the erstwhile Enemy, after "enemies are reconciled, they no longer [have to] ask why it was that the animosity had developed in the past."[44]

"A curious custom in the Greek Orthodox tradition gathers believers on Easter Monday for the purpose of trading jokes. Since the most extravagant 'joke' of all took place on Easter Sunday—the victory, against all odds, of Jesus over death—the community of the faithful enters into the spirit of the season by sharing stories with unexpected endings, surprise flourishes, and a sense of humor. A similar practice occurs among the Slavs, who recognize in the resurrection of Jesus of Nazareth a joy that it is Jesus who has the last laugh"—thus does Doris Donnelly begin her essay on "Divine Folly."[45] William H. Willimon provides a counterpart of the same point: At Duke University Chapel "we do it [Easter] for no better purpose than the sheer fun of it."[46] Yet the Christian as Christian is not engaged—to borrow phrasing from today's academic humor studies—in "funny ha-ha" jokes but rather in "funny strange" or "funny peculiar" Jokes. They are in no way conducive to light laughter; their closest relatives are awe and penitence (cf. Rudolf Otto's concept of "the numinous"[47]).

And the Devil? Where does he come in? Well, some hope is being sounded here that he may be on the way out. Here is the way my mentor Jeffrey Burton Russell closes his study *Mephistopheles:*

> I look tonight from my winter window and name the stars, Procyon, Sirius and Mirzam, Aldebaran, and here in the warm south Canopus in Carina, low on the rim of the sea. I name them, but I know them not by naming but only by loving, for love is the stuff of their being and

---

[44] H. Richard Niebuhr, *The Responsible Self* (San Francisco: Harper & Row, 1978), p. 143. See also H. Richard Niebuhr, *Faith on Earth*, ed. Richard R. Niebuhr (New Haven-London: Yale University Press, 1989), especially chap. 6 - "The Reconstruction of Faith" and chap. 7 - "The Community of Faith."

[45] Doris Donnelly, "Divine Folly: Being Religious and the Exercise of Humor," *Theology Today* 48 (1992): 385-398.

[46] William H. Willimon, comp., *Last Laugh* (Nashville: Abingdon Press, 1991), p. 16.

[47] Rudolph Otto, *The Idea of the Holy* (New York: Oxford University Press, 1958).

mine. O blue blazinq Rigel, O long twins with burning heads, O stars grape-clustered in the vineyards of the night. For knowledge pauses when the blood stops beating to the brain, but love never ceases, because it is the true stuff of reality that moves the sun and the other stars. *Che move il sole e l'altre stelle.* And that is why the Devil...in whatever way he exists, is negation negated, denial denied, meaninglessness exploded into galaxies of meaning blooming bright in the darkness with the light of love.[48]

The Devil is ugly, and will not endure. Beauty must win, and, laughing, She will win.

IV

In summary: To respond to the divine action, which liberates people from their "theoretical reason," is to move over to the domain of the "practical reason," which entails fresh forms of behavior: freedom to contend for justice, a life in which meaningfulness fights off despair, a kind of nonchalance and playfulness, and the whole undergirded by hope. "Blessed are you who are poor, for yours is the kingdom of God...Blessed are you who weep now, for you will laugh" (Luke 6:20, 21). If good is nothing more than an aspect of evil, the fate of hopefulness is bleak. But if evil somehow falls under the authority of good, hope can persist.[49]

To attest to Incarnation-Crucifixion-Resurrection is to remain at home, but also to be transfixed, wholly within the Hebraic province. Thus does the *restaurazione*, the *rinnovamento* of *this* Jewish person embody and vindicate afresh the life-struggle against Necessity. The revolution contra Fate moves forward and outward. The struggle is successively—not supersessionistically—

---

[48]   Jeffrey Burton Russell, *Mephistopheles* (Ithaca: Cornell University Press, 1990), p. 301.

[49]   According to the theory of panentheism (not to be confused with pantheism), all things exist somehow "inside" the being of God, although God continues to transcend them. From this perspective, suffering and evil are not beyond the reality of God, and hence are not entirely meaningless or dispurposive. I remand this comment to a footnote because panentheist reflection falls primarily under the theoretical reason as against the practical reason, although it certainly has practical, existential import.

joined by the Christian community of faith. The reason our matriarch Sarah laughed was the birth of her son Yitzhak, the one who also laughs, the one who will laugh (Gen. 18:12: 21:1-7). *El campesino* Yeshua ("God saves") revitalizes the memory of Yitzhak, when he says to the few persons before him, "You have pain now," but one day "your hearts will rejoice, and no one will take your joy from you" (John 16:22).

We have listened to Emil Fackenheim's words, "God so loved the world that He hid the infinity of His pain from it lest it be destroyed." The dialectic of Continuity/Discontinuity fairly shouts at us: "God so loved the world that he gave his only Son..." (John 3:16). Yet it is continuity that must win the day. For it is the love of God that is heard from the opposable sides of the Grand Canyon: In the giving of God, God's love is hidden (the witness of the church). In the hiding of God, God's love is given (the witness of Israel). A bridge is built. In love is found a strange symbiosis of righteousness and forgiveness. Tragedy is countervailed by Comedy—by what Frederick Buechner calls "confession and tears and great laughter":

> [George Buttrick was preaching] that unlike Elizabeth's coronation in the Abbey, this coronation of Jesus in the believer's heart took place among confession—and I thought, yes, yes, confession—and tears, he said—and I thought tears, yes, perfectly plausible that the coronation of Jesus in the believing heart should take place among confession and tears. And then with his head bobbing up and down so that his glasses glittered, he said in his odd, sandy voice, the voice of an old nurse, that the coronation of Jesus took place among confession and tears and then, as God was and is my witness, *great laughter*, he said. Jesus is crowned among confession and tears and great laughter, and at the phrase *great laughter*, for reasons that I have never satisfactorily understood, the great wall of China crumbled and Atlantis rose up out of the sea, and on Madison Avenue, at 73rd Street, tears leapt from my eyes as though I had been struck across the face.[50]

---

[50] Frederick Buechner, *The Alphabet of Grace* (San Francisco: Harper-San Francisco, 1989), p. 44.

The laughters that burst forth from the two opposable sides of the canyon are not triumphalist or arrogant. Together they spread upon their winds the blossoms of grace—the "amazing grace" that brings into being the "second astonishment": Joy.

9

Tidying Up: In Which, Not Incidentally,
There is Struggle With "The Final Heresy"

John Updike says that to write is "to taste the black emboldening blood of print." As I look back over almost a half century of professional writing, I find a lot to criticize in what I have said (though something less in how I have said it). On the other side, that the kind of writing I do is largely self-taught can have an intoxicating effect; the only requisite training instruments are a great deal of reading, a great deal of thinking, and a great deal of practice. On balance, I am today more gratified than ungratified. That is to say, I am glad I was sent into this business rather than into some other kind—with only one real exception: I would rather have been a (lefthanded) first baseman[1] on the Brooklyn Dodgers the year (1955) they won the World Series. However, in that case I would probably not have been able to relish the "infatuation-with-the-sound-of-one's-own-words" phenomenon publicized by *The New Yorker*. You lose some, you win some.

I have learned that the engine of my effort as a whole, not always known or comprehended by me, and certainly never brought to ideal working order,

---

[1]   The increasing presence of righthanded first basemen, of artificial "grass," and of indoor ball "parks" all go to show that baseball has indeed come upon sacrilegious times.

has four cylinders: faith, reason, art, and play, with now one and now another making most of the noise.

I should estimate that my published writings approximate 2,000,000 words—hardly sufficient to ring up the Guinness people. Counting rewrites and throwaways, I should guess that the handwritten figure came near 20,000,000 words—again, anything but a record. Nevertheless, I wanted to be sure to report these attainments, lest I be judged un-American.

As a man and as a Christian, I sometimes ask myself: Were all those words necessary?

"Tidying Up," the title of this last chapter, is not meant to promise any resolution of all my unresolved problems or all my hangups; I merely hope to bring things to a close in tolerably good order. This will entail a final look at my ideas, their presuppositions, and their concerns. To that end, the section immediately to follow will "sound religious," while the two sections after that will not, for the most part, do that.

I

James Thurber said: "It is remarkable how many people are up and around." I never cease to marvel that so many human beings don't give up. It is almost as though each one, in her or his own way, were getting ready for something—some kind of deliverance, some kind of reckoning, some kind of reconciliation, some kind of Messiah. Otherwise, whence all the courage to keep going? "That things are not so ill with you and me as they might have been is half owing to the number who lived faithfully a hidden life, and rest in unvisited tombs"—thus George Eliot ended her sixth novel *Middlemarch*.

A few reviewers and other critics of the work of Alice and Roy Eckardt have cast us in the role of wreckers of the Christian faith.[2] I think it may be

---

[2]   David A. Rausch writes that in the face of the horrors of the Holocaust "some Christians have discarded their faith...Note A. Roy Eckardt and Alice L. Eckardt, *Long Night's Journey Into Day...*" (*A Legacy of Hatred* [Chicago: Moody Press 1984], p. 3n.). The issue here is one of how the Christian faith is to be identified. Professor Rausch's "faith" is of a "fundamentalist-evangelical" sort (ibid., p. 103) and is, from the standpoint of my Christian point of view, highly objectionable, because it is so far removed from a normatively biblical position, my own standing-ground. (Cf. James A. Sanders: One reason why "fundamentalism is abhorrent to many Christians is its dogmatic dishonesty. Nothing called Christian should require dishonesty at the very heart of what it professes" ["The Bible as

rather more accurate to say that we have sought to counteract certain historically influential and (for us) heretical and immoral versions of Christianity. (There are some people today who try to live along the cutting edge of Christian thought and life.) Certain of our views have impressed others as being "radical." I am not sure that our position will seem all that "radical" a hundred years from now. Tomorrow, yesterday's "radicals" may very well be received as conservatives and even reactionaries. Everything will depend, obviously, upon the directions that today's Christianity manages to take as the years and centuries pass. Across such times, various world faiths have moved far away from their original quiddity (e.g., Mahayana Buddhism is worlds apart from original Buddhism). For the Christianity of the year 500,000 and beyond, the year 2,000 will be no more than part of the early church. Today's conflicts of dogma and morality may then be construed and treated as amongst the first efforts of the Christian community to come to terms with its God and with itself. Living as we today are in the initial years of the church, we have the task to contribute responsibly to the future. With Emil Fackenheim, I propose that our singular norm, ultimately speaking, ought to be the prohibition against blasphemy.[3] "Thou shalt have no other gods before me." Sacrilege is *the* sin.

In light of my lifelong effort, on the one hand, to prosper the essentially Judaic foundation, virtue, and meaning of Christianity, and, on the other hand,

---

Canon," *The Christian Century* 98 (1981): 1250-1255]). Here are parts of a letter I wrote to Rausch in response to his charge against my wife and me: "A fundamental distinction must always be honored between wholly objective, descriptive statements and statements that proceed as though they were being objective but that are, in fact, the opposite of that because they are only made possible by a certain prior point of view. Your allegation that the Eckardts have 'discarded their faith' is an instance of the second kind of statement. I should maintain that from the standpoint of the first kind of statement, what you ought to have said was the very opposite of what you wrote, viz., 'The Eckardts have *not* discarded their Christian faith.' The very most that, in fact and morally, you may be entitled to say is: 'From the standpoint of my interpretation of the Christian faith, the Eckardts have discarded *that* version—not that they ever held it.' And even this kind of restatement is very questionable, simply because your own rendering of the Christian faith may well turn out to be wrong. The trouble with you is your narrow, exclusivist, imperialist apprehension of the meaning of the Christian faith—exactly the sort of thing that made the *Shoah* inevitable. In objective truth, you have no monopoly upon a proper or valid or post-*Shoah* understanding of the Christian faith" (8 April 1987). The other side of this matter is that, unlike so many, including friends, Professor Rausch has spelled the name Eckardt correctly and has, at this point, been justified by his actions, and merits consideration for membership in the kingdom of truth.

3   Emil L. Fackenheim, *The Jewish Return Into History: Reflections in the Age of Auschwitz and a New Jerusalem* (New York: Schocken Books, 1978), p. xii.

to honor the faith that Jesus held,[4] I think it would not be inaccurate—for all my sympathy with Christian liberalism—to identify my own viewpoint as *conservative Christian* or perhaps *orthodox*[5] *Christian*, or even *catholic Christian*. All this stands in contrast to the persuasions of many contemporary people, for whom faith in the biblical God is just no longer possible. Since Jesus was himself Jewish and adhered to the Jewish faith, conceivably one could contend that his followers may be identified as in a certain sense Jewish. But any such contention appears to be ruled out morally/historically by the norm of respect for those people who have preserved strictly Jewish reality and who identify themselves as Jews.[6] In any event, I believe that the Christian church of today is summoned to return to its roots in the Jewish person Jesus of Nazareth—not alone for its own sake, and not alone for the sake of the Jewish people, but for the sake of the world and the world's future. (To "go to the root" is the origin of the word "radical.") Had the church not cut itself off from those roots, there would have been no Christian contribution to the *Shoah*, probably no *Shoah* at all. In a word, the trouble with the majority Christian church as it has developed is its theory and practice of heresy: its betrayal of a conservative-orthodox-catholic-radical integrity—in a word, its fall into sectarianism. Michael McGarry tellingly and rightly identifies Christian supersessionism as a Christian heresy.[7]

---

[4] From this standpoint the group "Jews for Jesus" would do better to call themselves "Jews against Jesus." These people, along with many Christians, betray the life and conviction of Jesus, who was a faithful Jew.

[5] The root of "orthodox" is "to have the right opinion." I should here qualify or relativize this to read "to have *a* right opinion," since "right opinions" are legion in our pluralist world.

[6] However, according to a talmudic dictum, "he who rejects idolatry is to be called a Jew."

[7] Michael McGarry, "Emil Fackenheim and Christianity After the Holocaust," *American Journal of Theology & Philosophy* 9 (Jan.-May 1988): 131. But strangely and ironically McGarry does not always pay attention to his own words, e.g., "at the very least the Holocaust calls traditional Christianity into question" (p. 124). These words of his could be a bridge to the work of today's prophetic Christian theologians—were McGarry prepared to follow out the implications of such words.

II

Now I move on to what does not "sound religious." In doing so, I come at last to the second of this book's four epigraphs. (The third, from Cynthia Ozick, and the fourth, from Edward L. Galligan, speak for themselves.) Emil L. Fackenheim attests in the passage I have chosen that "the final heresy" is to put the decision of faith upon the same level as other decisions, thereby making God's sovereignty and existence "depend on man's belief in, or acceptance of, Him." Against such heretical posturing, "the distinctive nature of the decision of faith is that it is at the same time no decision at all, because in accepting God's sovereignty man realizes that he accepts that to which he is subject regardless of his decision."[8]

Available and rightful means for struggling to escape "the final heresy" are doubtless legion; my own poor technique (*téchnē*, art) here is to observe that the "nonreligious" is religious—if I am at all apprehending Fackenheim's meaning. For if, as in Judaism and Christianity, God is the ultimate Reckoner of creation as of final redemption, it follows that the "nonreligious" lives, as much as anything else does, in the presence of, and with the permission of, God. If it is so that the most sacred is enabled to appear under the aspect of the most profane, so it is also the case that the most profane cannot escape the most sacred.

However, I must repeat the word "struggle" of this chapter's subtitle, because I simply have no way to show or to establish that *my* profane is *the* sacred.

To the multiple ends of furthering the above-mentioned struggle, of returning to a more philosophic stance, and of affording some structure to this closing chapter, I offer a modest variation upon the theme of a Platonist dialectic of the Good/the True/the Beautiful (see Figure One). I have stolen and adapted the schema from an old picturization of the Christian Trinity. I proceed this way, not as a claimed contributor to apprehending or penetrating the three transcendent Ideas, but only for the sake of paying tribute to them.

---

8   *The Jewish Thought of Emil Fackenheim: A Reader*, ed. Michael L. Morgan (Detroit: Wayne State University Press, 1987), p. 53 (original source: Fackenheim, *Quest for Past and Future*). I take it that were my friend Fackenheim writing these words (of 1968) today, he would wish to expunge the sexist wording.

Figure One. A Dialectic of "the Ideas"

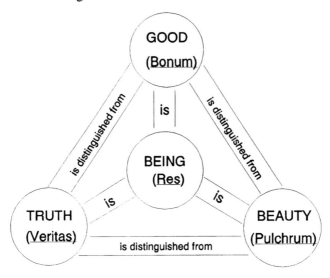

In the Platonist *Anschauung* (vision), the Ideas of Good/Truth/Beauty are inseparable, though in Plato's *Republic* the Good appears as the most noble. Certain it is that each Idea requires both of the others, further that each one nurtures the other Ideas. And, of course, all three participate in Being or Reality (*Res*), as per my little diagram. Thus, it was only to be expected that my mother would find despicable not just injustice (as I have told in chapter one) but also lying and hypocrisy. She knew that there is no justice apart from the truth. My mother was very proud of having been enabled to graduate from eighth grade (before being sent to work) in contrast to her many brothers and sisters. She was a rather brilliant person. It has been said of Phillis Wheatley that in more than her biological life is her mother's signature made clear. Had my own mother been given the chance, much of what I have sought to say and write over the years could easily have been said and written by her, or excelled by her—with many corrections and disagreements, I am sure. Furthermore, life with my mother, as with my father and brother, somehow managed to wrench out a certain beauty, despite great stretches of poverty and much travail, including my brother's eventual death and my mother's chronic illness.

For the sake of the Good. Intended tribute to the Good has been conspicuous enough throughout the stated chapters of this retrospective—perhaps over-bearingly so or sometimes even boringly so.

By way of summation, I tell one story and offer a few aphorisms.

In 1985 at the Oxford Centre for Postgraduate Hebrew Studies, Yosef Ben Shlomo, a kindly and self-effacing but dogged and perceptive Israeli philosopher from Tel Aviv University, put it to my wife and me: "How can you say such negative and revisionist things about Christianity? You are countervailing the entire Christian teaching." Were theology the primary point at issue, our colleague would have been essentially correct. Theology never completely escapes apologetics. However, the real issue is: What is the right thing to do? The challenge is how to be human, how to be responsible, and not whether to be labeled Christian, or non-Christian, in the sense of certain doctrines.

A small collection of aphorisms may also serve as reminders of a striving for the Good: "All morality begins with self-preservation" (Eugene B. Borowitz). "The purpose of literature is to correct injustice" (Elie Wiesel). No human idea or creation is exempt from the test of its moral consequences. Theology that is not welded to morality is itself immoral. Justice is indispensable to love (*agape*). Love is smashed by dishonesty.

The proposition last-listed already puts in motion the limitless quest for Truth.

For the sake of Truth. As I review the many historical chapters of this book, I am somewhat less dissatisfied by efforts therein to serve the Good than I am with efforts to serve the Truth. The issue of truthfulness/untruthfulness is perhaps the single largest problematic within *Collecting Myself* as a whole. Therefore, I take a little extra space upon this aspect of the threefold dialectic.

Cynthia Ozick may help open the way: "Though the imagination does lead to the making of images, twist it up higher, require more of the imagination, put more pressure on it—and then and only then can you have monotheism. Because monotheism requires the highest possible imagination—in order to imagine that which no image can be made of, that which you cannot see, smell, touch. To imagine the unimaginable requires the hugest possible imagination."[9]

---

[9] Cynthia Ozick, as cited in Mervyn Rothstein, "Cynthia Ozick's Rabbinical Approach to Literature," *The New York Times*, 25 March 1987.

I suggest that monotheism is, or can be, the mark, the criterion, and the motivation of an authentic devotion to the Truth. Accordingly, when in a monotheist frame of reference we speak of the pursuit of Truth, we have surmounted Benjamin Jowett's reputed claim as master of Balliol College, Oxford. Perhaps you know the jingle about him:

> This is Balliol, I am Jowett,
> All there is to know, I know it.
> What I don't know isn't knowledge:
> I am Master of this College.

Within the blessed purview of monotheism, a shift takes place from subjectivist protestations and arrogance to objectivist affirmations of the-way-things-are (*Res*).

Perhaps a comment is in order upon the probity of *experience*. Today's philosophy of liberation is candidly and insistently experientialist. Thus may the feminist emphasize that the male knows nothing of what it means to live and to die *as a woman*. (Indeed, the non-feminist woman may not know either.) As the black liberationist James H. Cone declares in *For My People*, "there is no truth outside or beyond the concrete historical events in which persons are engaged as agents." Yet the even more essential point is, as Bernard Lonergan notes, that experience is integral to all human understanding and judgment. It appears to me that the most intendedly anti-experiential philosophy, theology, or ethic does no more than range one mass of human experience against other such masses.[10] Wouldn't it be nice if the Barthians and their relatives, and especially the fundamentalists amongst Christians and Jews, could receive the grace to concede this?

I venture to commend two guidelines for basic application under the Idea of Truth. The first rests upon John Locke's distinction in the *Essay Concerning Human Understanding* respecting propositions according to reason, propositions above reason, and propositions contrary to reason. The first two types receive

---

[10] James H. Cone, *For My People: Black Theology and the Black Church* (Maryknoll, NY: Orbis Books, 1984), p. 148; Frederick E. Crowe, *The Lonergan Enterprise* (Cambridge, MA: Cowley, 1980), p. 114; A. Roy Eckardt, *Black-Woman-Jew: Three Wars for Human Liberation* (Bloomington: Indiana University Press, 1989), p. 7.

my assent, correctly or incorrectly; the third type is excluded. A second guideline comes from James Parkes: "True theology cannot be grounded upon false history."

How may such guidelines as these be applied, with respect to the question of Truth? This issue could be reckoned with in an abstract way but I shall try to avoid that. In the interests of concreteness, we may return a final time to what has become almost an *idée fixe* of this book, the question of the resurrection-event (resurrection of Jesus). This event, or presumed event, will do as well as any, or perhaps better than another one, since reader and writer have already experienced together much of the conflict that is involved (primarily under the rubric of "for the sake of goodness," i.e., morality).

To put the matter nomothetically, we are met by a disjunction between events that are capable of happening and/or do happen, and events that are incapable of happening and/or do not happen. Idiographically speaking, we encounter the argument over a specific resurrection-event that does take (has taken)/does not take (has not taken) place. It is the case that once we entertain the image of a Platonic-style dialectic as set forth in Figure One, the problematic of the goodness/evil of the teaching of a consummated resurrection cannot be separated from the problematic of its truth/falsity. However, I suggest that the *primordial reason* (under the rubric of truth) why some people may be led to conclude that the resurrection-event has not (yet) occurred has nothing to do with historical-moral considerations (such as those marshaled in earlier pages). Instead, it has to do, in the first instance, with a challenge to the Truth. The resurrection-event may be said by some not to have taken place because there is no way, within the bounds with which this world appears to be "run," for a dead person to become a living person. (This is in no way to question the clear fact that untold numbers of human beings have *experienced* in one way or another what they believe to be the resurrection-event and hence the truth of that event. Nor is it to question or obviate the faith or hope that such a "resurrection-event" may/will "one day" happen.) There are events that can and do occur (e.g., a given individual is first young and then old) and there are events that cannot and do not occur (e.g., a given individual is first old and then young).

Tributes to the Truth (e.g., the impossibility of the resurrection) and the obligations of morality (e.g., the value of anti-supersessionism) converge through a common testimony against the resurrection. The two orientations also converge at the point of human consequences as such. For to declare the resurrection-event a consummated "truth" is to drive a wedge within the Christian self, splitting it (psychologically-spiritually-ontologically) between a self that "knows" various things and a self that "believes" certain things. Such a split must bring great harm to the self as to humankind. Against such a split, we may honor the Lockean choice of propositions in accordance with reason and propositions above reason, but not propositions in contradiction of reason. Exemplifying as it does the third choice, belief in the consummated resurrection-event becomes, in a word, bad for the soul.[11]

Having disposed rather conclusively (from one point of view) of the Christian resurrection-teaching, I am still left wondering, as I look over the last several chapters, whether it may yet be possible to reinstate that teaching in ways that are (a) free of the irrationality and the personality split elucidated just above; (b) non-supersessionist; and (c) not incoherent with the New Testament history and witness. I explore this threefold possibility in *Reclaiming the Jesus of History*, and emerge with the persuasion that the resurrection may be affirmed.

---

[11] While a plurality of *interpretations* of the character, meaning, and significance of any given event is always possible (this is the level of human phenomenology), the level of human logic as such is different. For with respect to the *occurrence* of a particular event, *however the event be interpreted*, we are logically afforded just two possibilities: *Either* it happens/has happened/will happen, *or* it does not happen/has not happened/will not happen. At this place human logic is aided by mathematics as perhaps by metaphysics. Correspondingly, within the bounds of biblical historicalness—in contrast to one or another form of spiritualization—the alternatives respecting the first Easter Sunday appear to be two: the (somatic) resurrection of Jesus, and the non-resurrection of Jesus. (John Frederick Jansen points out that "body" [*sōma*] can mean either "physical body" or "spiritual body" [*The Resurrection of Jesus Christ in New Testament Theology* (Philadelphia: Westminster Press, 1980), p. 87]. In *The Random House Dictionary of the English Language* the third meaning of "somatic" is "of the body; bodily; physical." I here employ "somatic" strictly according to this latter definition.) Emphasis falls upon the brute happenedness or non-happenedness of an event as such, where in the nature of the case any third possibility beyond the two (happenedness, non-happenedness) is not possible. The observation that a presumed event either occurs or does not occur has nothing to do with adherence to, or sympathy for, such a position as "logical positivism." Such an observation is readily forthcoming from persons who have never heard of logical positivism or, for that matter, have no interest in philosophic disputes. The elementary proposition that any reputed event either happens or does not happen falls within ordinary or universal common sense, and is, in this one respect, pre-philosophic. It is a question of truth-as-such. Cf. Jacques Maritain on the primordial (pre-philosophic) intuition of existence, with its implication of the potential nothingness of *our* existence (*Approaches to God*, trans. Peter O'Reilly [New York: Collier Books, 1962], pp. 17-20).

III

For the sake of Beauty. As I begin this section, I have my father particularly in mind. (I think as well of E. B. White, who, some years back, got up and went away, leaving us deprived and dejected.) My father's place in my life, though of course contributory to goodness and to truth, was in the first instance a matter of beauty. (He could not finish grade school because he had to go to work.) In the first place, he loved great music and *objets d'art*. Second, his sense of humor was "something else"—as singular as it was redeeming. He was loved by every child he met. Third, he had an extraordinary gift of working with his hands in unique and imaginative ways. And fourth, as a foreman-electrician my father was responsible for much of the lighting of several of the great buildings (the Chrysler Building, among others) in the greatest city: New York, New York. Every time I catch sight of his lights against the night sky, I think of him and honor him. These are his epitaphs.

Ours is a world in which one beautiful animal devours another beautiful animal, in which beautiful birds crash fatally against beautiful tall buildings (some eighty million such fatalities of birds per year occur in our country alone). *Therefore*, we ought to do what we can to redeem beauty, to make beauty live. But how are we to go about that?

At this moment, as for the past seventy or so years, I've been trying to puzzle through my identity, and now with you, gentle readers, as observers. I think the best I can do for now is this: I *write*—that's who I am—or that's what I *do* (the two are *one*, are they not?). One of my heroines, Alice Walker, says, "I was brought up to try to see what was wrong and right it. Since I am a writer, writing is how I right it." Another heroine of mine, Doris Grumbach, puts the matter this way: "I think writing is an act of healing. It's an exorcism of sorts, to put into words and symbols [an] almost inexpressible anguish. That was why I started, to try and alleviate the despair."

I've never really looked upon myself as much else than a writer. Whether I do fiction or nonfiction, or both, I'm not entirely sure. Some novels impress me as nonfiction—Elie Wiesel's, for example. Some ostensible nonfiction is fiction—the Fourth Gospel, for instance, where it lies about the culpability of "the Jews" for Jesus' death. No one ever said that the Fourth Gospel isn't beautiful. Yet beauty must answer to goodness and to truth, as they in turn must, at other levels, answer to beauty.

Let me develop this third category a little further. Some of you probably remember the film "That's Dancing," a compilation of choreographic routines from the history of cinema. Fred Astaire, Ruby Keeler, Ray Bolger, Eleanor Powell, Gene Kelly, Ginger Rogers, Liza Minelli, the Nicholas Brothers, and others—they are all on hand. What can these people possibly be doing? They stand up, the music strikes, and they proceed to put themselves through all sorts of incredible movements. (My wife and I saw this particular film six miles over the Atlantic at 600 miles an hour, which made the whole thing even more unbelievable.) What does it mean? What is the dancer doing?—not excluding dancing aircraft.

The dancer is being beautiful. And what is it that another company of people does in order to redeem or rescue the beautiful, to incarnate the beautiful? Instead of putting their feet together and apart, these other people put written words together and apart. They compose sentences, then paragraphs, then pages, then chapters, then whole books. Beauty, for them, is primarily the aesthetic of words. And like dancing, it's a kind of impossibility, a kind of mystery. *How do all those letters and words ever come to get arranged this way?* It's impossible. The universe is overdetermined—we noted that way back in chapter two. Yet the miracle does happen—there are truths above reason. Could it be because Holy Being, Holy Reality is hiddenly operative here?

Nevertheless, Beauty remains forever on trial, forever having to fight its way (with Goodness and Truth) against very great odds. A certain lady, blessed with one of the most beautiful voices in the world, says that still today when she sings it's like she's *auditioning*—and as well she suffers terribly from stage fright. (She is also from Brooklyn.) For a lifetime now, I've been concocting all these articles and books and stuff—some of them rather good, to be sure—yet at this very moment I'm still auditioning. We are all in the one business really: the stand-up comic, the candidate for office, the country music artist, the sculptor, the batter at the plate, the teacher, the writer, the bandit. We're all doing and saying the one thing: Here I am, look at me, listen to me, watch me, help me count a little before all the lights go out and the dark comes! (Here is one reason I am sometimes annoyed when people run down commercial television. They don't always realize that on that small screen the historical fate of the performers is being decided.)

I am not proposing that the *content* of one's aesthetic creations does not count. But I am saying that the expression, the form, counts equally and sometimes more—the *beauty qua beauty* is a pearl of great price—which means, to be sure, that the *idolatry of form* stays around as an ever-present menace.

Another observation: The aesthetic performer is never allowed to stay in the one place. That's what puts writing so close to dancing.[12] One is forbidden to keep writing the same thing, for one's fate then is boredom and rejection—by oneself and from others. To keep changing, to keep developing, is closely reflective of moral responsibility. If it is the case that "new occasions teach new duties," so too the writer must ever fashion creations that are new and different, just as must the painter or sculptor—otherwise she or he is obligated to stop writing. To move out along the aesthetic frontier is at once to move out along the moral and intellectual frontiers. In fact, aesthetic changeability and dynamism can sometimes serve as a judge against the stagnation and lethargy that can beset *bonum* and *veritas*. This suggests that the writer who does not offend anyone has already failed.

Lastly, since beauty is no one's private property, the story of words is a constantly transcending one that drives us beyond ownership. Just as once upon a time each of us made the astounding discovery that we were alive, that the gift of life was ours, so too we discern that we are no more than the stewards of language. We don't create language, it comes to us as a gift, and then we go to work upon it, and finally we surrender it back to our sisters and brothers. Once we release it to the world, it stands over against us. It is no longer under our jurisdiction, our hegemony. In *The Human Province* Elias Canetti declares that once others touch a person's work, it is not his. "It changes under their eyes and fingers. The released work is fair game." And it's wholly possible that much in the writer's work is not comprehended by the writer, or for that matter is not even *bearable* by the writer. The writer may not grasp the wider and deeper power or meaning or consequences of the words. All of this serves to place *laughter* at the very heart of writing. For what could be more comical

---

12   The most memorable compliment I was ever paid was by an English churchperson— a retired bishop no less—who told me that the words I had just used in an address had danced.

than trying to master and control letters and words that are not one's own invention or possession?[13]

A primary accompaniment of such laughter is weeping—as when we are impelled to cast words aside. I recall Elie Wiesel regretting to my wife and me a certain arithmetical tragedy: For every word he sees through the printing process, he must put ten words to death. We who write must abandon many more words than we can ever boast. This is the final sadness of being a writer—as it is a final sadness of being human. Yet if the laughter produces weeping, the weeping is as well mother/father of the laughter.

These are amongst the things we learn when we write. Remember Alice Walker: "I think if you write long enough, you will be a healthy person."

IV

Because I write, the least I can do, at the end, is to insert a little something on how to write. You only have to have four things in your possession: a pen (the one authentic word processor; other machines never quite make it); paper in a looseleaf book (essential for changing everything and shifting everything around); a subject title; and a closing sentence. The third and fourth items simplify matters enormously. (I have always done the closing sentence first before the title; it is ever good to know where one is going. The final sentence is the culmination, even the epitome, of an author's entire purpose for a particular book. For within that one sentence may be found the *esse* of the writer's living or current outlook upon things.)

Once you have assembled these four elements, the worst of the task is over. All that's left is to fill in the interstices. And the primary way the filling in is done is by thinking. I have found that the proportion of thinking to words is roughly one to ten: One hour of thinking can usually be counted upon to supply a minimum of ten words.

So that's all there is to it. It's good—because it's beautiful. And—who knows?—it may even turn out to be truthful.

---

[13]   Cf. my study *Sitting in the Earth and Laughing: A Handbook of Humor* (New Brunswick-London: Transaction Publishers, Rutgers - State University of New Jersey, 1992).

V

This is my little story then, such as it is. The Good, the Truthful, the Beautiful—each judges the others, each is blessed by the others. What is involved, in sum, is a journey toward humanization. I am pursued by Emil Fackenheim's question: *Can there be an existential philosophy of the hidden God?*[14] That is to say: If one is to live responsibly and authentically, is it always *necessary*, morally and psychoanalytically speaking, to be unexceptionally assured that one is accepted by God and in sure relations with God? On the first day of January 1993 (today's date) I think not. On the second day of January, I may think yes. (Irving Greenberg, following Martin Buber, calls this oscillatory phenomenon "moment faith.") In my particular case, a viable yes is continually aided and abetted through my survival of a heart attack in 1974, of being laid low by a speeding, skidding automobile in 1983, and of a cancer in one kidney in 1992. Yet I remain fearful that to thank God for these survivals is ever to run the risk of putting oneself ahead of the many poor souls who do not survive such things or have no food to eat. In part for this reason, and in spite of all, the chance of a religionless Christianity appears to maintain itself as a salient, persisting motivation in what I do, insofar as I understand what I'm doing. Perhaps the peculiar thing about my effort is the dual way in which I have come to travel the path toward humanization—*outwardly*, along a frontier of newness, of fighting against saying the same things over again (e.g., on the resurrection): here, primarily, is the aesthetic drive[15]; and *inwardly*, a Christianity that lives in turn upon the foundation of a faith that stands for and yearns for love and justice. Yet in principle, my journey, long as it has been, has done little more than to take me back to where I started out as a small boy, when my mother and my father and my brother not only kindled for me a wish to pay tribute to the Good, the True, the Beautiful, but also helped turn me to the One who stands hidden behind and beneath every book, every research project, every conversation, every birth, every malady, every death.

---

[14] Emil L. Fackenheim, *To Mend the World: Foundations of Future Jewish Thought* (New York: Schocken Books, 1982).

[15] I once heard Laurie Borowsky say that the main thing an artist must have is discontent.

If it is so that to die is to run out of memories, the opposite of death is the One who ever lives to remember.

Philosophy and Ethics in the Thought of A. Roy Eckardt

Michael L. Morgan[1]

Roy Eckardt speaks of himself as a writer, and the quantity and quality of his literary output surely testifies to that designation. I think that Eckardt likes the term for its simplicity, its understatedness, its scope, and its nobility. But the word tells us too little about him. He is a writer to be sure, but he is a special kind of one—a Christian theologian, a polemicist, and an impassioned moral voice.

Eckardt's work is deeply embedded in a particular discourse. He can write about matters of great abstractness and conceptual subtlety, but his writing is best when it is not abstract but rather concrete, when it is agitated and urgent, provoked and almost angry. Articles like "Again, Silence in the Churches" and "The Devil and Yom Kippur" are classics because they reflect his literary and intellectual strengths, his use of examples, episodes, and particular illustrations, coupled with novel insights and disciplined organization, all charged with a sense of moral urgency and a polemical spirit. Roy Eckardt is a writer whose pen is mightier than a sword and whose moral courage is the engine of his theological reflection. If you have read through this volume or are familiar with his articles and books, you know this. And if you know Roy Eckardt, you know too that these are not only writer's characteristics; they are also among his personal features. He is a man of moral passion and intellectual genius, of sensitivity, wit, and humor.

Moreover, Eckardt is a philosopher who writes about moral and theological matters. But his way of doing these things is distinctive, and it is that distinctive combination of philosophical, theological, and moral interests which I would like to discuss.

---

[1] Michael L. Morgan is Professor of Philosophy and Jewish Studies at Indiana University in Bloomington. He is the author of *Platonic Piety: Philosophy and Ritual in Fourth Century Athens* (Yale University Press, 1990), and *Dilemmas in Modern Jewish Thought* (Indiana University Press, 1992), and the editor of *The Jewish Thought of Emil Fackenheim* (Wayne State University Press, 1987) and *Classics of Moral and Political Theory* (Hackett, 1992).

I have already suggested that many of Eckardt's writings are topical, concrete, and polemical, and this is important to remember. Eckardt does not stray far from the world of actual events and experiences; he is moved by a keen sense of reality. Particular events, comments, actions resonate in him; he responds to them, hoards them, refers to them, and navigates in terms of them. In this sense, Eckardt is a very empirical thinker, not because he holds any particular views about knowledge, inquiry, and thought that we would call "empiricist" but rather because his real interests, in thinking at all, concern the world and our experience, our conduct, and our lives. Reality has an intense attraction for him.

At the same time that Eckardt is world-oriented and a realist, he is deeply theological. Indeed, his primary idiom, his determinative mode of discourse, is dominated by Christian theological terms, ideas, motifs, and models. Christian theology, in short, is the way that Eckardt talks. To be sure, he appropriates bits and pieces from the social sciences, from Jewish tradition, and from philosophy, but these bits and pieces are not his literary framework. Rather that framework comes from the tradition of Christian theology, from Reinhold Niebuhr and H. Richard Niebuhr and from his other teachers. Terms like sin, suffering, guilt, faith, salvation, and righteousness dot his writings, and their meanings emerge as versions of traditional theological senses, tuned to new contexts and needs. To be sure, the idiom of Christian theology is no mere instrument for Eckardt; he uses it because it articulates what he believes and how he thinks. The world that takes shape out of this language is Eckardt's world. This is not artifice, far from it; it is the way he talks and also the way he lives. But it is not to be ignored, for the centrality of the theological in Eckardt's writing and thinking does have important implications.

One implication concerns point of view. There are many thinkers who do philosophical theology. They address various questions about God, providence, miracles, evil, and such matters and engage in detailed philosophical analysis about them. That is, such thinkers, at different moments in their enterprise, think of themselves as advocates or believers, on the one hand, and as detached, rational inquirers or investigators, on the other. They shift back and forth from the theological to the philosophical point of view, using different terms and strategies, making distinct connections, and even employing diverse intellectual tactics. Eckardt does not do this. Generally, his distinctions, reasoning, and clarifications come from one point of view, and that point of view has about it a kind of existential unity. It is an eclectic and comprehensive point of view, for it is the unified yet complex vantage of Eckardt's selfhood. It is he, using ideas and arguments as they make sense and seem compelling to him. When Eckardt engages in what he thinks of as philosophical analysis, then, it is not like the philosophical analysis of these other philosophical theologians, nor is it like what other contemporary philosophers do. It is philosophical in another way, in some sense like philosophical thinking and in some ways not.

Early in his career, for example, Eckardt took some time to study philosophical work on the nature and methods in the social sciences, on causal laws, generality and particularity, explanation, and the relations among various types of scientific inquiry.[2] He then used the relevant concepts and distinctions in a variety of contexts later on in his career, in trying to clarify, for example, how the Holocaust is unique.[3] Both originally, when he first explored these issues, and later, when he utilized them, Eckardt's thinking had philosophical features. It attempted to grasp and clarify important ideas and distinctions, and it was orderly and organized. But at the same time Eckardt was largely appreciating the significance of a conceptual distinction and employing it in precise contexts rather than exploring it for its own sake. There is a sense in which Eckardt's study of these matters and use of these concepts was philosophical, but there is a sense in which it was very much colored by his theological, existential interests and strategies.

It is hardly surprising that Eckardt could appreciate and do philosophical work. He was after all trained as a philosopher at Brooklyn College and Columbia University. What is important to notice, however, is that Eckardt's philosophical work is generally embedded in theological, religious and moral contexts, that the philosophical vocabulary he uses is regularly found alongside the idiom of Christian theology, and that it is difficult—if at all possible—to isolate what is philosophical about his thinking at any given moment.

---

[2] See Eckardt's comments in chap. 3 above, on Windelband's distinction between nomothetic and idiographic modes of thinking; also "A Note on Theological Procedure" (*Journal of Bible and Religion*, 1961).

[3] See "The Holocaust and the Enigma of Uniqueness," *Annals of the American Academy of Political and Social Sciences* (1980), and *Long Night's Journey Into Day*.

Often Eckardt calls himself a philosopher or refers to his thinking as philosophical. What exactly does he mean? Surely he does not mean that his work is like that of other contemporary philosophers. First of all, it is not like theirs, neither in vocabulary, style, method of analysis, nor even problem. Secondly, he shows little sign of having read contemporary philosophers such as Alasdair MacIntyre, Bernard Williams, Charles Taylor, Thomas Nagel, Ronald Dworkin, Derek Parfit, or John Rawls, or, if he has read them, of thinking their work relevant or important for his own. In *For Righteousness' Sake*, his most developed and most systematic work and one that is subtitled *Contemporary Moral Philosophies*, none of these philosophers is discussed or even mentioned. Yet they are among the foremost, most widely discussed and read moral philosophers of the past two decades. Rather the figures he does discuss or refer to are theologians, Jewish and Christian, such as Reinhold Niebuhr, H. Richard Niebuhr, David Tracy, James Parkes, Emil Fackenheim, and Eliezer Berkovits. In short, Eckardt is not and does not see himself as being a member of the contemporary philosophical world. In what sense then is he a philosopher?

There is a hint of an answer to this question in a remark that I heard Eckardt make about ten years ago. Referring to some of his recent work at that time, especially to his treatment of the doctrine of the resurrection, he said that his thinking was in a more philosophical and less theological stage. This was a time when, in the shadow of the Holocaust, Eckardt was radically challenging Christian imperialism by criticizing any viable Christian belief in the resurrection and when he was arguing, as he put it, that after the Holocaust the only acceptable Christian theology was Jewish theology. I recall this episode not because Eckardt is still committed to what he said then about the resurrection and Christian theology. It is clear from his retrospective in this volume and from other writings that he is not.[4] I recall it for another reason, because Eckardt then felt it appropriate to call such thinking "philosophical" rather than theological. Why? What about this critical, heterodox analysis of the doctrine of resurrection was philosophical?

First, Eckardt no doubt sees himself as a participant in the philosophical tradition of Hegel, Kant, Leibniz, Locke, Spinoza, and beyond, a tradition of

---

[4] See above in chap. 8; also, chap. 11 of *Reclaiming the Jesus of History*, and "Why Do You Search Among the Dead?" (*Encounter*, 1990).

rigorous, critical, systematic reflection on all that is important to human existence and human experience. But recently this tradition has been subject to revision. In the twentieth century, and increasingly after the rise of analytic philosophy, philosophy has come to treat certain themes and topics as either pseudo-themes and wholly inappropriate for philosophical investigation and attention or relatively peripheral, insignificant, and even soft issues. Recently, since the late seventies, the philosophical world has been changing, to be sure, but this exclusivist, narrow view was certainly dominant in postwar America through the sixties and seventies. It has its heirs and its impact today, but its hold on the philosophical imagination and the philosophical tradition is loosening. Eckardt was not trained in this analytic, exclusivist style, nor does he have much sympathy for it. His philosophical and theological mentors lived in a more traditional philosophical world, one in which the discussion of topics such as divine providence, revelation, and the incarnation were not peripheral at all. In part, then, Eckardt sees himself to be philosophical in the sense that philosophy is this rich historical tradition of reflection on God, nature, and humankind. In his introduction to Chapter 1 above, he puts it this way:

> I do tend to think in philosophical ways. I construe philosophy as the general existential-critical effort to make sense of things...I see philosophy as the general, existential quest for truth and meaning...a quest, that is, accordingly, tempered and balanced by historical experience.

But there is more to philosophy than its breadth of themes. There is too what we might call the philosophical attitude, a posture of openness, of a realistic seeking after truth, of a sense of receptivity to all that is reasonable and persuasive. It is a rejection of dogmatism and a kind of intellectual tolerance for all that can pass the bar of reasonable argument. Some associate this attitude with Socrates, who died, as Plato reminds us in the *Crito*, a martyr to the conviction that one should listen not to persons but to the truth. I do not recall Eckardt citing Socrates as a model, but clearly at crucial times, he commits himself to the Socratic principle, to the relentless, undogmatic, orderly pursuit of the truth. He claims, that is, to follow reason and argument, "tempered and balanced by historical experience," wherever they lead, even if that means the abandonment of familiar and comfortable beliefs, of central Christian commitments—like the doctrine of missionizing among the Jews or the belief in a new covenant that supersedes the old or the doctrine of a realized redemption confirmed through the resurrection. I believe that often, when Eckardt refers to himself as a philosopher, this is what he means. He will think hard, reason with rigor, and let no dogma stand between himself and the truth. He will go wherever the road leads; no theological or religious conviction is immune to reasonable evaluation and even refutation. Philosophy involves rationality, coherence, structure, and order, but it also requires a commitment to the truth that is as morally compelling as it is intellectually attractive.

Such an attitude, however, may make a thinker and writer unpopular; people may even think him or her mad. Plato saw this in the *Republic* and *Phaedrus*. Doubtless many of Socrates' fellow Athenians thought that he was eccentric, peculiar, and even crazy. But there are times, and ours may be one of them, when madness is noble. In our time, truth and integrity may be the provinces of madness, especially when going on at all, while living with the most horrific memories and a deep sense of responsibility, may require a certain kind of madness, or at least when speaking the truth may seem to others utterly mad.

When Eckardt calls himself a philosopher, then, he is expressing his relentless commitment to rational argument and the relentless pursuit of the truth; he may also be admitting that perhaps he is a bit mad. He, like all who have come to take the Holocaust and the death camps seriously, has learned from Elie Wiesel that after Auschwitz madness may be appropriate, if not somehow necessary. But in Eckardt's case, the madness has a special, three-fold contour. It is the madness of the relentless lover of truth who follows thinking wherever it takes him; it is the madness of trying to face Auschwitz responsibly and go on; and it is also the madness of challenging and even indicting one's own faith and one's own community, of calling for responsibility and for active response, when others would reject both. In Eckardt's case, that is, it is both the madness of philosophical conviction and the madness of moral polemic, and this brings us to our second question: what role does ethics play in Eckardt's thinking and writing?

Some people are moral activists; some are moral thinkers and writers. Some are both, and in some very special cases, moral writing is itself a mode of moral activism. There are, that is, literary prophets, and Eckardt is one of these people. Often, he writes about moral issues, philosophically and theologically, but what is distinctive about his entire literary career is that his work—on antisemitism, on Jews and Christians, on the Shoah, on women's liberation, and on rational questions and liberation thinking—is deeply motivated by and grounded in a sense of moral rightness. "The real issue," he says,"is: what is the right thing to do? The challenge is how to be human, how to be responsible, and not whether to be labeled Christian or non-Christian."[5] It is all about what God demands, what history demands, and human responsibility. Whatever its origins and its stimulation—in his parents and their character, in the early death of his brother, in his understanding of the Christian message, and in his teachers—this sense of moral urgency, of integrity, of passion about how one ought to live, runs through all of Eckardt's work. In this sense, he is what he says he is, "a kind of theological ethicist or political theologian."[6]

Very much in the spirit of these past two decades, Eckardt's sense of moral urgency has focussed on the relation of the Christian to the *other*—first to the Jewish other, then to the female other and finally to the racial other. But if this general theme, one's moral relationships to the other, has become popular, Eckardt's work has hardly been fashionable or followed the course of fashion. Only recently—if at all—has it been popular to call attention to the Christian responsibility for anti-Jewish persecutions, for the subordination of women, and for the oppression of the poor among Blacks, Latin American peoples, and others. Following in the steps of James Parkes and Reinhold Niebuhr, Eckardt's early attack on antisemitism was pathbreaking. It led him to a study of Judaism, an appreciation for it in its own right, and an understanding of the Jewish roots of Christianity, that has few peers. Then, in the late sixties and early seventies, it led Eckardt and his wife Alice to an encounter with the horrors of the Shoah and to the most relentless, challenging, and morally responsible confrontation with that event to be found among those Christian theologians who have been moved to do so. All along he has been motivated by the conviction that Christianity must face up to its historical impact and accept responsibility for what it has done, to Jews, women, Blacks, and the poor. Then, after such

---

[5] In chap. 9 above.

[6] In chap. 1 above.

honest self-assessment, the church must change itself, reunderstanding its central mission and reestablishing its commitment to that mission.

Eckardt's moral or political theology is grounded in an understanding of the Biblical text and what it articulates as God's demands upon the church and the Christian community. Christian ethics is about decision-making, however complex and conflicted the situation, and the guiding principles for such decision-making arise out of an understanding of both the Christian message and the complexities of the historical moment. That message is embedded in the life and story of Jesus and its meaning as it has been grasped historically. The relation between that meaning and history is dialectical; each influences the other. Eckardt explores this dialectic best in *For Righteousness' Sake*, and in various articles he aims at articulating the content of Christian responsibility in specific situations. That is, there are many ways of engaging in moral thinking and even in doing moral theory. On the one hand, Eckardt's method is very concrete. He tries to use traditional sources and a detailed grasp of contemporary problems to understand what a Christian is obligated to do. This is a kind of normative, concrete moral thinking. Recalling the wisdom of Reinhold Niebuhr, Eckardt reminds his readers that moral irresponsibility is a worse sin than idolatry. The core of his work, then, is a commitment to Christian action; at one level, Eckardt is a moral-political-theological agitator. On the other hand, however, Eckardt has been concerned about theory and the more general question, how is Christian faith related to the world and to history. This has been a life-long interest, but it is most systematically explored in *For Righteousness' Sake*.

In a sense, the inquiry in *For Righteousness' Sake* focuses on a point where Eckardt's empiricism, his sense of moral urgency about episodes of crisis, and his attempt to understand the relation of faith and history, all converge. Like Hegel, Heidegger, Gadamer, and others, Eckardt is here interested in the abstract and the concrete, the universal and the particular, thought and life. In the case of each of these pairs, which pole dominates? Which is determinative? Which directs or orients the other? And Eckardt's conclusion, the result of a careful examination of eight models or alternatives, is that while in our day we should fully appreciate the influence of history on faith, the relation is dialectical.[7] This he calls the eighth position, "history transforming faith." We live at a time when faith must expose itself to history and allow itself to be transformed by it. Contemporary understanding of the content of faith, of the New Testament message as it developed the Biblical teaching, shapes the Christian perception of the world. But, at the same time, events and experiences force the church to rethink and reevaluate that tradition in order to determine its mandate, its purpose, and its responsibility. This Eckardt calls a "Christian theocentric historicism,"[8] a post-liberal, post-modern encounter between traditional faith and the problems of today.[9] "Each new generation," he puts it, "is called to develop new sacred and secular expressions of the reign of God."[10] The call arises out of the momentous events—the Shoah, the emergence of the Jewish state, the rise of religious pluralism—that leave everything changed and transformed. To locate and enact a new historical Christian responsibility is the core of Christian morality. It arises out of history in order to act within history, pivoting on decision and will.[11] Moral theology is an attempt to "recapture meaning and nurture responsibility,"[12] and this two-fold task is radical because it involves a returning to the roots of Christianity in Judaism, a return to Israel. Eckardt finds this challenge confirmed in life as well as in theory; he calls attention, for example, to the existence of Nes Ammin, a cooperative settlement of Dutch Protestants who live in Israel and who support and thrive on their tie to the Jewish state.[13]

In form, then, Eckardt's moral thinking is grounded in a conception of how faith and history are related dialectically. On the one hand, he seeks to avoid absolutism and irrelevance; on the other, he shuns relativism and irresponsibility. In substance, moreover, this position leads him to feature the Christian

---

[7] See *For Righteousness' Sake*, p. 227.

[8] FRS, p. 225.

[9] See FRS, pp. 271-72, especially the reference to David Tracy.

[10] FRS, p. 234.

[11] See FRS, p. xi.

[12] FRS, p. 272.

[13] FRS, pp. 273-75, and above in chap. 9.

complicity in the Holocaust, the long tradition of Christian anti-Jewishness, the need to recover Christianity's rootedness in Judaism, and the responsibilities attendant upon a revised interpretation of Christian faith.[14] In this way, citing Emil Fackenheim, Eckardt recognizes that "the Shoah ruptures history but does not destroy it."[15] This moral thinking also leads him to a clarified sense of the Christian responsibility for the State of Israel, for Jewish self-determination, a way between false liberal criticisms of Israeli nationalism and right wing evangelical Zionism. Then, from these starting points, he turns to the contemporary expressions of pluralism—feminism, liberation movements in the Third World, and such—and develops an account of responsibility for oppressed groups, a "solidarity-for-justice". There is, as he often says, a need to "take sides" that is rooted in the Christian message and shaped by a sense of responsibility to the original object of Christian oppression, the Jewish people.[16]

It is possible that a serious and open exposure of Christian faith to recent history would threaten Christianity to its core. It is possible, that is, that history—the Holocaust preeminently—will lead to a trial and conviction of God, so that hope would no longer exist, so that the covenant, the promise, and the confidence would be consumed in the flames that burned infants and faith itself. To confront and engage these possibilities is the subject of "Trial of Faith, Trial of God," the final chapter of *For Righteousness' Sake.*[17] "Are there any ways to restore faith, once history has shattered faith, by continuing to struggle with

---

[14] FRS, p. 283.

[15] FRS,p. 283.

[16] FRS, pp. 291-93. One of the features of Eckardt's thinking about Christian moral responsibility and the liberation movements is the priority that he gives to the Christian persecutions of the Jews. In chap. 8 above, for example, he says: "The gathering revolution in Christian theology occasioned by the *Shoah*, the reemergence of the State of Israel, and the church's reappropriation of its Jewish roots may neither be separated from nor exalted above other revolutionary trends within contemporary Christianity: the development of liberation theology coupled with the struggle to end the oppression of the world's masses; the growth of the women's movement, including opposition to a male chauvinist sacerdotalism; and the struggle against a white racist church." Nonetheless, he continues, it is necessary to distinguish first from second things and to recognize that the separation from Judaism is what enabled the church to fall into other sins.

[17] FRS, pp. 301-325.

and against history, upon the stage of history itself?"[18] What this challenge means for Eckardt concerns whether Christianity can endure without its "imperialism, exclusivism, and supersessionism," and this means ultimately without its traditional doctrine of the resurrection.[19] Why? Because "the focal Christian teachings of Incarnation-Crucifixion-Resurrection comprise the building blocks of anti-Judaism and antisemitism."[20] When history challenges Christian faith, the problem ultimately becomes Easter and the Resurrection, the belief in Jesus' miraculous continuance and God's confirmation of hope, a belief without which early Christianity would not have developed in so radical a divergence from its Jewish roots. A wholly honest and morally responsible exposure to Auschwitz requires a hermeneutics of suspicion, as David Tracy following Paul Riceour would put it, directed at even this central belief. It requires "go[ing] behind and beyond everything that is true and beautiful and good, to seek out, with a broken heart, its falsity, ugliness, and evil."[21]

This is not the place to follow Eckardt as he carries out this task. Those who wish to do so should turn to the last chapter of *For Righteousness' Sake* and other essays, including "Why Do You Search Among the Dead?"[22] They should also follow him beyond this point, as he portrays a trial of God that reaches a more radical stage than this trial of Christian faith. Like his comrades in arms—Elie Wiesel, Emil Fackenheim, and Irving Greenberg—Eckardt asks about the indictment against God from the side of the Jewish people and then carries forward his own reflections about that trial.[23] In the end, he affirms that God cannot be forgiven, that he loves God nonetheless, that the best response may be a bizarre prayer and an eerie laughter, all an expression of a kind of disorientation, a kind of madness.

And this response, sad and bitter, amazed and conflicted, mad and sober and realistic, returns us to our earlier suggestion, that philosophical inquiry, as a

---

[18] FRS, p. 302.

[19] FRS, p. 303.

[20] FRS, p. 303.

[21] FRS, p. 304.

[22] FRS, pp. 304-315.

[23] FRS, pp. 315-325.

relentless, undogmatic pursuit of the truth, can also seem mad. An honest and serious encounter with Auschwitz is a central feature of Eckardt's thinking, and it has led him to question and revise the most central features of Christian faith. There is madness in this, just as there is perhaps in his totally committed pursuit of truth, no matter where that pursuit may lead. Eckardt's moral courage and his philosophical integrity converge, then, on what many will take to be unpopular, if not completely mad.

For Eckardt, who is a theologian, a moral thinker, and a philosopher, these personae overlap in another, the humorist who struggles to smile and laugh at a time when unqualified seriousness is both necessary and impossible. There is always a glint in Eckardt's eye, a sign of the comic effort to mitigate the sternness and the burden of the quest for the true and the good. Eckardt has a lively sense of humor, even in the midst of his polemical attack on his enemies. But it is not a gratuitous sense of the comic. Rather it enlivens his intellectual and literary work, which threatens to be too serious, a moral act that some respect as courageous and honorable, while others think a bit mad. Both readers are right, for his philosophical tenacity and his moral passion have generated a set of books and articles that are as unsettling as they are unsettled. For all that, they are good and noble works, the literary outpourings of a powerful and fine voice, for which we can all be deeply grateful.

The Place of Christian-Jewish Relations
in A. Roy Eckardt's Work

Joann Spillman[1]

This essay will celebrate A. Roy Eckardt's role as a pioneer in the Jewish-
Christian dialogue, will honor some of his major contributions to that dialogue
and will identify some dimensions of his theology which might benefit from
further refinement. I will not limit my response to *Collecting Myself* but will
consider other works as well, works which Eckardt discusses but does not
reproduce here. I will give special attention to *Christianity and the Children of
Israel*, *Elder and Younger Brothers*, *Your People, My People* and *Jews and
Christians*—four works devoted to Jewish-Christian issues—as well as relevant
sections of *For Righteousness' Sake*. At the end of this Afterword, I will narrow
my focus to *Collecting Myself* and note some contributions that this volume
makes to the understanding of Eckardt's work.[2]

In selecting Eckardt's contributions for commendation and in identifying
particular themes as needing refinement, I have tried to limit my consideration
to important issues; I have also made a special effort to focus on issues which
have not received a great deal of critical attention. However, my selection is
idiosyncratic—perhaps at times arbitrary—and certainly reflects my own
concerns. It may therefore be helpful for the reader to know something of my
background. I come to the study of Eckardt from a distance. We are of different
generations (he started writing before my birth). My general theological
orientation and denominational background are different from his. My philo-

---

[1] Joann Spillman (Ph.D., Temple University) is Associate Professor of Theology and
Religious Studies at Rockhurst College, Kansas City, Missouri. She spent the Spring 1991
semester at the Ecumenical Institute for Theological Research at Tantur. She is a member of
the Christian Scholars Group on Judaism and the Jewish People, and active in the dialogue
in the Midwest.

[2] Because it would be cumbersome to repeat A. Roy Eckardt's full name throughout
this essay, "Eckardt" is used to refer to him. References to Alice L. Eckardt include her first
name. I regret the confusion this may cause. I do not mean to slight the work of Alice
Eckardt whose contribution Roy Eckardt celebrates in this volume.

sophical training is in analytic philosophy—worlds apart from his orientation. Analytic philosophy has imbued me with a concern for precision which will lead me to call repeatedly upon Eckardt to clarify further various points. I hope that my distance from Eckardt will contribute to a helpful critical distance, but I fear it may also lead me to misunderstand his work on occasion. My greatest difficulty with his work arises from the differences in our philosophical and not our theological backgrounds. All in all, I come to the task of writing this response as an admirer of Eckardt's work—albeit an admirer with some questions and concerns.

Eckardt has been a pioneer among Christian theologians seeking better relations between Jews and Christians largely on the basis of a revised Christian theology on which that improvement could be based. He published his first book on the subject (largely reproducing his dissertation) in 1948 and another full volume in 1967. From the perspective of the 1990s, it is difficult to imagine how little had been written on this topic as late as 1967, much less in 1948. In the 1940s and even later in the 1950s and 1960s, much of the dialogue movement was little more than an attempt to provide Christians and Jews with basic information about each other's religious heritage in order to foster tolerance. From the 1940s through the 1960s, several Christian theologians did focus their attention on efforts to improve Jewish-Christian relations and did at least begin to face the enormity of Christian anti-Judaism and to call for selected reforms in Christian teaching. However, some of these early theologians of the dialogue underestimated the extent of the reform needed because they thought that Christian anti-Judaism was an aberration at the periphery of the Christian message. Also in this period, some excellent historical studies of Christian anti-Judaism were written. By the mid-1960s, a handful of very prominent theologians (including H. Richard Niebuhr, Reinhold Niebuhr, Paul Tillich and—to a lesser extent—Karl Barth) had begun to probe seriously some of the theological issues involved in Christian anti-Judaism. Yet their impact was lessened either because they discussed these issues in brief segments of larger works or because they wrote occasional papers on Jewish-Christian matters which attracted little attention. So when Eckardt wrote in 1948 and 1967, he wrote largely without models or guides.[3] It is instructive to recall that Paul van Buren, writing as late as 1983, could still lament his lack of models: "I feel acutely the lack of teachers in this enterprise."[4]. If van Buren was a trailblazer in the 1980's (and he was), how much more pioneering was Eckardt's much earlier work.

Not only did Eckardt lack models but his early work sometimes met with indifference and even derision. *Christianity and the Children of Israel* received very little attention, a fate not entirely unexpected for a book based on a dissertation. However, even *Elder and Younger Brothers* received a relatively small number of mixed reviews. Some reviews simply dismissed the book. A contributor in *The Review of Religious Research* seemed surprised—perhaps affronted?—that "Eckardt poses what is in essence a new theology for Christendom." The reviewer went on to quote a part of the conclusion of the book and added, "Most Christian theologians will dismiss the author's proposal as incompatible and impractical if not heretical."[5] The reviewer does not attempt to build a case for this judgment, presumably finding it almost self-evident.

Eckardt was not only a pioneer in Christian theology attempting to appreciate the role of Judaism but also a major contributor to it. One purpose

---

[3] Consider what had been published by these dates: By 1948 H. Richard Niebuhr, Reinhold Niebuhr, and Paul Tillich had published a few discussions; Jacques Maritain had written a book on the "Jewish Question" and James Parkes had written several important studies, mostly historical. A few articles on Jewish-Christian relations had appeared in various journals of Christian theology. By 1967 Gregory Baum's *The Jews and the Gospel*, Edward Flannery's *The Anguish of the Jews*, Franklin Littell's *The Crucifixion of the Jews*, Friedrich Heer's *God's First Love*, and Hans Joachim Schoeps's *The Jewish-Christian Argument* had been published, as well as an article by Rosemary Radford Ruether anticipating her analysis of Christology in *Faith and Fratricide*. Helpful material had appeared in collections edited by George Knight and Philip Scharper and in *The Bridge: A Yearbook of Judeo-Christian Studies*. Parkes had published several more works by 1967, much of it still historical. By 1967 articles on Jewish-Christian relations were appearing more regularly than in previous years and in a wider variety of journals of Christian theology; occasionally journals devoted entire issues to these matters (as *Lutheran World* did in 1963 and 1964). The debate over *Nostra Aetate* was widely discussed.

[4] Paul M. van Buren, *A Christian Theology of the People Israel* (New York: Seabury Press, 1983), pp. xv-xvi.

[5] Ronald L. Johnstone, review of *Elder and Younger Brothers*, *Review of Religious Research*, XI (Fall, 1969), p. 98.

of this essay is to honor some of his contributions. It will focus on eight areas for commendation, none of which has received the attention it deserves. The list is my own and is in no way exhaustive.

First, Eckardt earns the gratitude of all Christian theologians concerned about Jewish-Christian relations because he has consistently shown that Christianity's view of and relationship to Judaism are not isolated issues but rather are interrelated with all areas of Christian theology. He has demonstrated in his own writings that the discussion of Jewish-Christian issues impacts on and is impacted by doctrines of God, revelation, redemption, grace, sin, anthropology, Christology, ecclesiology, mission, etc. An examination of *Christianity and the Children of Israel, Elder and Younger Brothers, Your People, My People* and *Jews and Christians* shows that Eckardt takes up each of the issues just mentioned, usually in more than one of the books. He treats some in detail. Eckardt's recognition of Jewish-Christian issues as part of the big picture began with his dissertation (largely reproduced in *Christianity and the Children of Israel*). It has continued throughout his writing career, both in his books on Jewish-Christian matters and in other works as well. Perhaps the best illustration of his understanding of the central role of Jewish-Christian relations in Christian theology is *For Righteousness' Sake*, the book which Eckardt considers his chief work. *For Righteousness' Sake* is a comprehensive reflection on the relationship between faith and history. It has the broad sweep of H. Richard Niebuhr's classic, *Christ and Culture*; in it, Eckardt builds on *Christ and Culture* by adapting, enlarging and seeking to correct Niebuhr's five categories. *For Righteousness' Sake* does not initially focus on Jewish-Christian issues, but in the end these issues emerge as central to Eckardt's vision of "history transforming faith." By showing that Jewish-Christian issues are themselves among the "big issues" in Christian theology and are also intimately related to other "big issues" of theology, Eckardt rebuts critics of Christian theology of the dialogue who dismiss it as "single issue" theology, focused on minor matters.

Second, Eckardt's works on Jewish-Christian matters make reference to Christian theologians of various denominations and various theological schools. As a result, while his work is grounded in neo-Reformation theology, it is accessible to a wide variety of readers who can find familiar vocabulary and references to familiar authors and issues. This is a significant contribution because many theologians of the Jewish-Christian dialogue direct their message primarily to readers of their own particular denomination and/or theological orientation and are not readily understood by readers who do not share their vocabulary and premises. There is an especially large gap at times between Catholic and Protestant theologians, so much so that I sometimes wonder whether we ought to talk about a Jewish-Catholic dialogue and a Jewish-Protestant dialogue rather than a Jewish-Christian dialogue. This fragmentation tends to blunt the impact of the dialogue on Christianity as a whole and makes it easy for critics of the movement to dismiss specific works as applicable only to a single school of theology or to a single denomination and not of concern to a wider Christian audience. Eckardt helps to begin to bridge these gaps.

Third, Eckardt identifies and highlights an aspect of the Jewish-Christian dialogue which is often overlooked: Jews are a people. Individual Jews are part of that people, whether or not they are religiously committed: an atheistic Jew or a religiously indifferent Jew is still a Jew. In contrast, Christians are such by virtue of their adherence to their religion. Because Christians come to the dialogue as members of a particular religion, they can easily forget that Jews do so as members of a people. When theologians, whether Christian or Jewish, engage in *theological* dialogue, they of necessity focus on *theological* concerns; that is, they focus primarily on matters of religious belief and practice—matters of interest primarily to religious Jews. As a result, the Jewish-Christian dialogue focuses on similarities and differences, agreement and disagreement, continuity and discontinuity between the beliefs and practices of Christians and their counterparts among the Jewish people: religiously committed Jews. Failure to consider Jews as a people can cause Christian theologians to misrepresent the nature of the Jewish people and to misunderstand the role of peoplehood in Jewish thought. Whenever Christians attempt to define "Jews" in terms of religious belief and observance, they misunderstand the word; they effectively ignore the Jewish people as a whole and reduce the "Jews" to a subgroup, namely religious Jews. To use Neusner's helpful categories, Christians thus tend to reduce the community of Jews to the community of Judaists.[6] This confusion obfuscates many Christian theologians' reflections on the role of the Jews in God's plan of revelation and salvation. Do theologians who tend to confuse Jews

---

[6] See Jacob Neusner, *The Way of Torah: An Introduction to Judaism*, 3rd ed. (North Scituate, Massachusetts: Duxbury Press, 1979) pp. 24-26.

and Judaists intend such reflections to refer to all Jews or only to religiously committed Jews? When, for example, Christian theologians write of Jews and Christians sharing a single covenant or as being constituted by two parallel covenants, do they envision atheistic Jews to be part of the covenant? If yes, what does that mean and how might a Christian theologian respond to an atheistic Jew who rejects such a description? If no, how do they justify excluding non-religious Jews from the Jewish covenant, a covenant which religious Jews understand to involve the whole Jewish people? Frankly, few Christian theologians appear ready to address these questions. Eckardt has made a significant contribution to the dialogue by avoiding confusion concerning the meaning of the term "Jews" and thereby providing a model for other Christian theologians to emulate.

Fourth, Eckardt is to be commended for using the imagery of covenant in order to envision the relationship between Judaism and Christianity. Because this is a Biblical image, it is familiar to Jews and Christians alike. Because it is an image, a model (at root a metaphor), "covenant" carries with it a rich set of multi-leveled meanings and associations, which are highly elastic and thus open to further development. Although the word is used regularly in the Jewish and Christian Scriptures, in Jewish and Christian prayers, and in Jewish and Christian theological reflection (especially in Christian theology), it has retained elasticity. It has not become a technical term and thus acquired a precisely defined meaning, in either religious tradition. This flexibility provides an excellent medium for expressing new understandings of Judaism and Christianity as they emerge from the ongoing Jewish-Christian dialogue. The use of a familiar image—indeed, one from the Bible—significantly contributes to the credibility of Eckardt's discussion of Jewish-Christian issues. It is especially important that Eckardt and theologians who share his commitment to recognizing the role of Judaism use the covenant image because their opponents who champion the tradition of supersessionism use it, typically claiming that the "New" (Christian) Covenant replaces the "Old" (Jewish) Covenant, which has been revoked. Therefore it is almost mandatory for Eckardt to use the image of covenant in order to counter effectively the opposing view. Moreover he is to be commended for preserving the use of this image despite recent calls to abandon or at least downplay it.[7]

Throughout most of his writings, Eckardt has not only employed the general image of covenant but has used the more specific image of one covenant in his efforts to envision the relationship between Judaism and Christianity. While he has consistently used the one-covenant image, Eckardt's view is neither simple nor static. "The covenantal idea", he has written, "demands revolutionary rethinking."[8] He has repeatedly insisted that this image and all else in Christian theology be understood in light of the Holocaust, and he has grounded the Christian role within the one covenant in moral responsibility toward the Jewish people. In these and other ways, Eckardt has elaborated on, qualified, and explained the one-covenant image, so much so that Pawlikowski described him as early as 1980 as beginning to "hedge" in his use of it.[9] Yet Eckardt has retained this image in most of his writings on Jewish-Christian relations, and it provides a very clear and simple vehicle for rejecting any form of Christian supersessionism. If Christians claim that Judaism and Christianity share one covenant, then they cannot claim that the Jewish covenant has been revoked. To do so would imply that the Christian covenant had also been revoked. (Of course one could also reject supersessionism by using a two-covenant image in which the Jewish and the Christian covenants are seen as partners.)

The familiarity and richness of the one-covenant image, its flexibility, and its effectiveness in countering supersessionism are all solid reasons for adopting

---

[7]   Eugene Fisher has called for a reexamination of the use of "covenant" and a moratorium on the discussion of the one-covenant/two-covenant distinction in "Covenant Theology and the Jewish-Christian Dialogue," *American Journal of Theology and Philosophy*, vol. 9, (Jan.- May, 1988), p. 31. John T. Pawlikowski expresses dissatisfaction with the one-covenant/two-covenant discussion in *Jesus and the Theology of Israel* (Wilmington, Delaware: Michael Glazier, Inc., 1989), p. 12. Monika Hellwig calls the dispute between proponents of the one-covenant and two-covenant models a "blind alley" in "Bible Interpretation: Has Anything Changed?" in Lawrence Boadt, *et al*, eds., *Biblical Studies: Meeting Ground of Jews and Christians* (New York: Paulist Press, 1980), p. 185, but does not go so far as to call for abandoning the distinction. Indeed, both Pawlikowski and Hellwig continue to use the distinction.

[8] *Elder and Younger Brothers* (New York: Scribners, 1967), p. 243.

[9] John T. Pawlikowski, *What Are They Saying About Christian-Jewish Relations?* (New York: Paulist Press, 1980), p. 39.

it. Eckardt has made very effective use of the model and thus enriched Christian reflection on the relationship between Judaism and Christianity. Still the matter is complex, and there are good reasons for considering the use of the two-covenant model, as we shall see later.

The fifth and sixth points concern Eckardt's interpretation of the Bible. Eckardt has devoted many pages of his books and articles on Jewish-Christian relations to the interpretation of relevant Biblical texts, including passages from both Christian Testaments. There is only enough space here to identify two especially commendable features of his interpretation.

Fifth, Eckardt clearly identifies the key Biblical foundation for a Christian acknowledgment of the enduring election of the Jewish people: the Hebrew Scripture. Once Christians accept the Hebrew Scripture as canonical, they implicitly acknowledge the permanent role of Judaism in revelation and salvation. God's enduring commitment to the Jews is at the very heart of the Hebrew Scripture, which is, for Christians, the fully canonical First Testament. Eckardt's approach is refreshingly direct and straightforward; it is also, in my judgment, correct. I have never understood the emphasis that many Christians place on a relatively few passages in the New Testament dealing with Judaism while at the same time largely ignoring the body of the Hebrew Scripture, which is, after all, focused on Judaism.

Sixth, Eckardt is also candid and courageous in dealing with those Biblical passages unfriendly to his cause. He repeatedly acknowledges that there is anti-Judaism in the New Testament and makes no attempt to evade this unpleasant fact. I am particularly impressed with his treatment of Romans 9-11. Romans has been interpreted in two quite different ways: a) as affirming the continuing role of Judaism in God's plan of salvation (Paul does affirm that God has *not* rejected His people), an interpretation quite congenial to the Jewish-Christian dialogue, and b) as teaching a kind of supersessionism which, while recognizing the election of the Jewish people, sees that election as for all practical purposes non-functioning, a reading which is uncongenial to theology of the dialogue. There are solid scholars on both sides, including E. P. Sanders and Krister Stendahl. Eckardt is convinced (and has been since the late 1960's) that the second interpretation is—unfortunately—the correct reading of Paul. While he disagrees with Paul on this point, Eckardt acknowledges that Paul teaches a kind of supersessionism. Sanders confirms Eckardt's judgment.

I applaud his acceptance of the unfriendly interpretation of Romans 9-11. All too often theologians of the dialogue eagerly embrace all available friendly interpretations of New Testament passages and ignore the uncongenial ones. This strategy evades the hard challenge of dealing with anti-Jewish themes in the New Testament. Eckardt could have done this in interpreting Rom. 9-11. He is well aware of Stendahl's more congenial reading of Romans, according to which Paul is not teaching supersession. However, Eckardt adheres to his interpretation. Theologians who depend on friendly interpretations of Romans and other problem passages have no effective response to critics who successfully challenge the congenial interpretations.

The seventh comment on Eckardt's contributions takes the form of a personal note. While I do not agree with all he has written concerning Israel, I am most grateful for his repeated insistence on the centrality of the State of Israel in the Jewish-Christian dialogue. In years past, I sometimes tried to segregate discussion of Israel from considerations of Jewish-Christian relations. I was motivated in part by a desire to respect the integrity of both politics and theology. In my own way I was trying to avoid what Eckardt calls the "twin dangers: the theologizing of politics and the politicizing of theology." I suspect that I was also motivated by a desire to make the dialogue easier and less stressful by avoiding the troubling questions which surround Israeli politics. Two factors led me to see the folly of my efforts: first, my own experience that whenever I tried to exclude Israel from the dialogue, I could find very few Jewish partners for dialogue, and second, the repeated insistence of Roy Eckardt, Alice Eckardt, and others active in dialogue that the question of Israel is central. By this insistence, Eckardt has done great service to Christians concerned about relations between Christians and Jews.

The eighth point is a commendation for Eckardt's recent and on-going reassessment of his approach to the resurrection of Jesus. This will reassure many cautious and conservative Christians who found his earlier position too radical.

In these eight areas and in many others, Eckardt has made very valuable contributions to the Jewish-Christian dialogue. I regret that space does not permit me to continue my tribute to his work. Eckardt has taken his treatment of Jewish-Christian matters far; now I will identify some areas where he and other theologians concerned about Jewish-Christian relations may want to go still farther. Much of what I will offer here consists simply of a list of questions for further clarification and a list of aspects of Eckardt's reflections which might benefit from further refinement or, in one case, simply updating. Of the six areas proposed for further consideration, two are closely related and concern Eckardt's treatment of the State of Israel. I begin with these two.

The first suggestion is simply a call for an updating of his work on Israel. Roy Eckardt, alone and with Alice Eckardt, has written a great deal about life in modern Israel, including discussions of Israeli society, religion, politics, law and foreign relations. His comments are made in a variety of books, articles and reviews. By far his longest single piece on Israel (in actuality a book co-authored with his wife Alice Eckardt) is *Encounter with Israel*. However, much of what he has written in this area was published during the late 1960s and the 1970s. He has written much less on the specifics of Israeli life since then. Much of what Eckardt wrote about Israel is now outdated. I was struck when I reread *Encounter with Israel* while in Israel in the spring of 1991 that the Eckardts were describing a significantly different country than the one I was observing. I could only speculate on how recent events, especially on the West Bank, might have affected their perspective. Surely *Encounter with Israel* would be a very different book, if written in the 1990s. Perhaps another theologian concerned about Jewish-Christian relations will write a book of the scope of *Encounter with Israel* about Israel today.

The second comment also concerns Eckardt's writings on Israel, specifically the question of the fairness and appearance of fairness in his treatment of the Palestinian issues. Eckardt has worked hard to understand Palestinian perspectives and to be fair to both Israelis and Palestinians. Here, in chapter 5, sections II and III, he describes his preparation and that of his co-author Alice Eckardt for writing *Encounter with Israel* including the care they took to consult with Palestinians. Still, despite his efforts to learn of Palestinian concerns and to be fair to them, Eckardt has actually written very little about the Palestinians. Based on my own examination of *Encounter with Israel*, relevant sections of *Black-Woman-Jew*, and a sample of his articles on Israel, I would estimate that approximately 15% of his discussion of Israel is actually devoted to the Palestinians. Even allowing for the fact that the Palestinians were not his focus, his efforts to be fair are undermined by the rhetorical weight of allocating so little space to Palestinian issues. The problem which I identify here is not so much what he said (although I do have problems with some of it) but rather how little he said. Compounding the problem is the fact that the small portion of his writings devoted to the Palestinians says very little about the Palestinian perspective on the Palestinian-Israeli conflict. Compounding the problem still further, much of what he does say about Palestinian rights is very general. It is hard to determine what a general recognition of Palestinian rights really entails. As analytic philosophers are fond of asking, just what is the cash value of such generalities? Palestinian issues deserve more attention from theologians involved in the Jewish-Christian dialogue, including attention to the specifics of their concerns.

Eckardt's treatment of Israel is not the only element of his work that could benefit from further attention. My third area of concern is his use of the one-covenant image. In raising this question I am in no way withdrawing my comments earlier in this essay concerning the use of the image of covenant *per se* (in either the one-covenant or two-covenant form). I still advocate that Eckardt and other Christian theologians of the dialogue use the covenant image, and I still recognize that there are specific advantages to the use of the one-covenant image, as an extremely effective tool against all forms of supersessionism. The problem arises not from what the one-covenant image denies but rather with discovering what it affirms.

What do Judaism and Christianity share that would justify its use? These are very different religious traditions, with many dissimilar beliefs and practices and very dissimilar histories. Neusner does not overstate the contrast between Judaism and Christianity when he entitles the first chapter of his *Jews and Christians*, "Different People Talking about Different Things to Different People."[10] Indeed, one need only examine the term "covenant" to illustrate the disparity of Jewish and Christian beliefs. Among religious Jews, the concept of covenant is linked with the Torah, *halakhah*, peoplehood and Land, associations which are not present in Christian talk of "covenant." Another good way to illustrate the sharp differences between Judaism and Christianity is through their histories. After a brief period at the beginning of Christianity in which Judaism and Christianity were rather closely tied, they took different paths. Select any period of the common history of Judaism and Christianity after the first few

---

[10] Jacob Neusner, *Jews and Christians: The Myth of A Common Tradition* (Philadelphia: Trinity Press International, 1991).

years and compare the writings, religious speculation, leadership, patterns of worship, geographic location and extension, social and political status, and lifestyle of the Jews and Christians of the time selected. During almost any part of their 2,000 year common era, virtually all of these items will be radically different.[11]

Eckardt and other one-covenant theologians are as aware of this difference as anyone. The critical question is whether the differences between the two religions are so great and involve such central matters of belief and practice that they tend to support the two-covenant image and weigh against the one-covenant model. These considerations lead me to suggest that Eckardt and other theologians who use the one-covenant image may want to examine the alternative two-covenant image.

The fourth suggestion concerns Eckardt's use of the Holocaust as the basis for evaluating Christian theology. The Holocaust has been a major concern for Eckardt throughout his career. His earliest book, *Christianity and the Children of Israel*, contains *"Shoah* (Holocaust) theology groping in the night, before there was any such thing as *Shoah* theology."* Since then he has written a series of remarkably profound and disturbing reflections on the Holocaust, and it has been the goal of much of his work to force Christian theology to confront the Holocaust. Following Metz's example, Eckardt demands that Christian theology —all Christian theology— respond to and be changed by the Holocaust and he fashions this demand into a criterion for evaluating theology.

This criterion leads me to seek further guidance. Does it apply to all or most Christian doctrines? I can readily see how the Holocaust might demonstrate the falsity of many Christian beliefs and that certain expressions of Christian belief about God and His role in history, about divine providence, about the redemption Christ brings, etc. are not tenable in its light. However, I can also think of other doctrines which do not have an obvious link to the Holocaust. Must I relate all of them to it? Why and how shall I do so? How can I recognize when I have made appropriate changes in doctrine in light of the Holocaust? Surely not all alterations of doctrine which I might make in response to the Holocaust are appropriate. What changes are and are not demanded? These questions deserve a fuller answer than Eckardt and Metz have given thus far.

---

[11] My thanks to Dr. Stephen Atkinson (English Department, University of Missouri-Kansas City) for this illustration and for assistance in editing this essay.

The fifth question concerns two sentences in chapter 4 of *Collecting Myself*, which are part of his criticism of *Elder and Younger Brothers*. After lamenting the "chutzpah" of Christian attempts to define Jewish identity (including his own in *Elder and Younger Brothers*), Eckardt writes: "The role or roles that Jewish faith and the Jewish people may have *for* the life and faith of the Christian church is another matter [other than the illegitimate attempt to define Jews and Judaism]. Christians have both the right and the obligation to respect and proclaim that Jewish place."

My question in response to this intriguing comment is simple: Just what sort of Christian theological reflection on Jews and Judaism does Eckardt thus permit, indeed require? This question addresses not only these two sentences but also a central feature of Eckardt's whole approach to Jewish-Christian matters. For years Eckardt has repeatedly warned against Christian attempts (including his own—especially his own!) to define the nature of Jews and Judaism. Indeed, at various times he has condemned Christian attempts to specify the nature of Jewishness, of Jewish peoplehood, of the role or "function" of Jews—even the suggestion of a special Jewish "function"—and all similar efforts to impose Christian theological categories on Jews and Judaism. At various times, he calls such theology antisemitic, anti-Jewish, triumphalistic, imperialistic. His condemnation of such efforts is unremitting, even when it is done with the best of intentions—to praise the role of Judaism. In *Jews and Christians* he charges: "For all its good intentions, a positive Christian theologizing of Jews cannot escape imperialism. There can be no 'Christian theology of the people Israel.'"[12] He directs this criticism specifically against works by Mussner, Thoma, and especially van Buren (the final words of the preceding passage which Eckardt places in quotation marks are the title of one of Paul van Buren's books). The importance which Eckardt attaches to this matter is reflected in his treatment of it here in this volume, where a major theme is Eckardt's efforts to overcome his own addiction to the "Christian habit of passing judgment on things Jewish." It is, he notes wistfully, his "ambition to kick the habit entirely."

How does one distinguish the illegitimate (indeed, in Eckardt's own words, antisemitic, triumphalistic, imperialistic) Christian theologizing of Jews and

---

[12] *Jews and Christians: The Contemporary Meeting* (Bloomington, Indiana: Indiana University Press, 1986), p.143.

Judaism from the legitimate (indeed, according to Eckardt obligatory) theologiz-ing of the role(s) of Jewish faith and the Jewish people *for* the life and faith of Christians? Part of the answer lies, no doubt, in the fact that legitimate theology considers the role(s) "that Jewish faith and the Jewish people may have *for* the life and faith of the Christian church," rather than attempting to define these roles for Jews. However, that alone is not enough to distinguish legitimate from illegitimate theology. After all, much of the traditional, anti-Jewish, Christian theology of replacement specified that its view of Judaism was a Christian perspective. Certainly theologians of the Jewish-Christian dialogue, such as Mussner, Thoma, and van Buren are well aware that they are writing Christian theology. For example, in his *A Christian Theology of the People Israel*, Paul van Buren repeatedly and explicitly states that his theology is a *Christian theological reflection* on Jews and Judaism, written for the *Christian Church*.[13] Van Buren does not expect that his Christian understanding of Jews and Judaism will match Jewish self-understanding, nor does he think it should. Yet, despite his avowed goal of doing Christian theology, van Buren's work is, for Eckardt, an example of wrongful theological reflection on Jews and Judaism. So I must ask Eckardt: Just what sort of Christian theological reflection on Jews and Judaism is legitimate? What makes van Buren's efforts illegitimate? This requires a fuller explanation than Eckardt has given thus far in order to assist others in continuing his work.

The sixth and final comment points out an aspect of Eckardt's theology which can be easily misunderstood, especially by readers with a different philosophical orientation than Eckardt: his call for a morally responsible theology. Eckardt advocates that theologians consider the behavior which their theology might provoke. Responsible theologians recognize, for example, that many Christian doctrines are anti-Jewish or lead to anti-Jewish beliefs and that such theology helped pave the way for the Holocaust. Morally responsible theologians should couple their faith with moral reason and accept their moral duty to eradicate anti-Jewish doctrines. As Eckardt says, ideas—even those that speak of revelation—"are not spared judgment at the hands of their human consequences."

---

[13] *A Theology of the Jewish Christian Reality*, 3 volumes (New York: Seabury and Harper & Row, 1980, 1983, 1988), *passim*.

Unfortunately, Eckardt does not provide enough explanation of how he sees the relationship between questions of truth and falsity and questions of right and wrong. At times he seems to conflate and even confuse them. Of course, I am certain that Eckardt does not, in fact, confuse the two and I am not accusing him of doing so. He knows that a statement may be true and yet may give impetus to evil acts. However, I do caution Eckardt that he can easily be misread because he does at times appear to confuse morality and truth. Chapter 9 of *Collecting Myself* addresses this matter as part of a broad metaphysical discussion of truth, goodness and beauty. Perhaps my study of analytical philosophy has ruined me for the study of metaphysics, but I did not find Chapter 9 helpful.

Thus far, this afterword has been a response to a variety of Eckardt's writings on Jewish-Christian relations. Now my focus narrows to *Collecting Myself*. The collection is more than a convenient anthology of Eckardt's work, as so many collections like this are. It is an important guide and supplement to Eckardt's other work, which will prove an indispensable guide to serious study. The autobiographical introductions to each section provide valuable and hitherto unavailable information about the context, sources, influences, and development of Eckardt's thought. These notes also describe the extent of the collaboration between Roy and Alice Eckardt.

I found the chronicle of Eckardt's reassessment of his approach to the resurrection of Jesus and his explanation of why he regards *For Righteousness' Sake* his major work especially helpful. I hope that his comments on *For Righteousness' Sake* will draw attention to that book, which has received little critical notice. Indeed I hope that *Collecting Myself* encourages attention to all of Eckardt's work. I further hope that his work and that of others concerned about Jewish-Christian relations will inspire a revolution in Christian theology. Nothing less than a revolution is sufficient.

Reflections on A. Roy Eckardt's Theological Writings

Walter Harrelson[1]

A. Roy Eckardt has made his way through dangerous and troubled waters on many occasions during a long and complex career as teacher, lecturer, scholar, and writer. Now he has quite deliberately embarked upon another journey of great peril: to review his writings over a period of fifty or more years, select from these the ones that should appear again, and introduce them with his own evaluation of their place in the world that first received them, plus some words about their possible value for our time. Writers often collect their essays and give them a fresh introduction. Eckardt has done more than this; he has reviewed his entire corpus of written works, selecting some for republication, relating these to other works not included in the collection, and assessing the whole as to its probity, moral weight, and fitness of expression. A brave endeavor indeed!

What can we say about the theological status of such an effort? Should the project be judged the fruit of hubris of the most flagrant sort and greeted with pained politeness? That would be a great mistake. Roy Eckardt *does* think of himself as a good writer, one not well enough recognized and widely enough read. He *does* think that the public needs to hear and ponder the fruit of his intellectual and literary labors over these fifty-plus years. No doubt, hubris is present—and Eckardt, a student and longtime associate of Reinhold Niebuhr, readily acknowledges its presence. Also present, however, is a reasoned and wholesome sense of the value of his work and of the need for many of his ideas and perspectives to have a further hearing. In addition, this work also includes fresh ideas, judgments, intuitions, plus new literary creations. It is in fact a new

---

[1] Walter Harrelson is Professor Emeritus of Hebrew Bible at Vanderbilt University and Director of its Lilly Ministry Project. He served for two terms as Rector of the Ecumenical Institute for Theological Research at Tantur, Israel (1977-78 and January-June 1979). He wrote *Jews and Christians: A Troubled Family* (Abingdon, 1990) with Rabbi Randall M. Falk. He is a longtime member of the Christian Scholars Group on Judaism and the Jewish People.

work, produced with the aid of many earlier writings, but presented for our own times and in a new and appealing dress.

Like all writers, Eckardt has great confidence in the power and worthwhileness of words—words fitly written, words that capture the cogency of good thought, words that may serve the triad with which the book closes—truth, beauty, goodness. Here too, Reinhold Niebuhr's reminder of the ways by which human beings deceive themselves belongs in the picture. What Eckardt has written, as he readily acknowledges, has sometimes not served the mentioned triad as well as he would have liked. The very process of collecting and reissuing some of one's writings may do a disservice to truth or goodness or beauty or to more than one of these. To my mind, it might have been better to have excluded any writings that single out individuals by name and reproach them for their words and ideas. Perhaps if they had opportunity, as Eckardt does here, they would retract their words, or modify them.

Has Roy Eckardt estimated the value of his work too highly and treated its faults and failings too charitably? The format of the book is designed to help the author overcome such a temptation. Each section of the book has its critical introduction in which Eckardt attempts to evaluate not only the essays included but also other works belonging to the period in question. It may be that he takes a bit of an advantage of us readers by disarming our criticisms with his own. But surely we would understand much less well what we read if we had been offered his assessment only after we had formed our own, and had done so without the benefit of his "contextualization."

Many readers will wish that Eckardt had been more forthcoming about the chief events of his life during the eight epochs. Even so, it is probably more true of him than of many teachers and scholars and writers that his writings *were* the very substance of his life. The lack of personal detail has been somewhat compensated for by the fact that, in recent months, he has turned to humor, to comedy, to the place of laughter in human life. Here, unmistakably, person and thought appear together and we are treated to more than critical thought aptly presented.

I do not, in fact, regret the singlemindedness of this work. It does have a certain relentlessness, even occasional ruthlessness about it. Almost from first to last, Roy Eckardt has set out to show, with a careful use of logic, with fine turns of phrase, and with a passion that now and again boils over into rage, how the Christian community has affirmed its faith in a form that was persistently and wrongheadedly damaging to the very life of the Jewish people and of Judaism. Small wonder that some of Eckardt's critics have thought of him as a foe of true Christianity. But the opposite is clearly the case: The Christian community would never have survived the centuries without its devoted critics, and Eckardt rightly understands himself to be a defender and advocate of Christian faith.

I

As a Christian philosopher and theologian, Eckardt has addressed a number of issues other than the relations of Judaism and Christianity. Even so, that subject has clearly dominated his life and work. And indeed, within the issue of the relations of Jewish and Christian life and thought, he has concentrated upon a relatively small number of issues. Many Christian laborers in this vineyard spend much time accounting for the apostle Paul's presentation of Law and Grace, either insisting that the apostle simply got that relationship wrong or offering an interpretation that draws some distance between Law (Greek *nomos*) and divine Instruction (Hebrew *Torah*). Eckardt does not ignore the subject, but it does not, I believe, loom large in his work. Many biblical scholars concerned about the relations of Judaism and Christianity spend much of their energies dealing with the social world of Judaism and Christianity during the period shortly before and after Jesus' birth. Their efforts may be designed to show the similarities of Judaism and Christianity or to account for the differences between the two faiths. Again, Eckardt has not neglected this subject, not at all. But his energies have been focused elsewhere.

Since Roy Eckardt is a philosopher and theologian rather than a historian or specialist in biblical textual study, one can readily understand his decision not to concentrate on the issues just enumerated. But that is only a partial answer, I believe, since he is not at all averse to embarking upon studies in which a specialist's knowledge might be thought to be essential (compare, for example, his remarkably fine study of Jesus, *Reclaiming the Jesus of History*). No, these subjects do not loom as large as some might think they should because he is convinced that they are not at the center of the problem for the Christian community. The problems that stand out above all, and have therefore claimed his time and energies over this half-century, are basically four, which might in fact be reduced to three. They are the following: (1) Christian triumphalism, or the Christian understanding that since the coming of Jesus as the Messiah of Israel, any meaningful religious vocation for the Jewish people has been eliminated. (2) Closely related to this first point is the question of Jesus' resurrection, which is for Eckardt the touchstone of Christian faith but also one of the grounds of Christian exclusivism. How can there be a significant religious witness by Jews or any other group if in fact the work of God for the universe finds its unique culmination and truth in Jesus as the resurrected Christ? (3) What did Christian faith and practice, the teaching of contempt for the Jewish people through the centuries, contribute to the National Socialist attack upon the Jewish people and the ensuing Holocaust (the *Shoah*)? And (4) what is the abiding significance, for the Christian community, of the creation and the continued existence of the State of Israel?

II

This is not the place for a review of each of these major emphases in Eckardt's work. His own summary does that job clearly, fairly, and with candid acknowledgment of his perceived limitations in some of the earlier perspectives. Since others have addressed the last two points directly, I will offer a few remarks on the first two matters—on the issue of Christian triumphalism and on Jesus' resurrection.

Christian triumphalism probably has met its match at last. In many parts of the world, at least, Christians today are acquainted with persons of devout faith, strong moral commitments, and wholesome attitudes toward life and the world— persons who are not Christians and see no need to be Christians. Many Christians simply cannot with good conscience insist that such persons—Jews, Muslims, Buddhists, or adherents of another faith—should abandon their faith and become Christians.

There are, of course, many Christians who still insist on the unique truth of Christian faith, the one true faith that is to be offered to all the world. Roy Eckardt is not one of them. While for many years he affirmed the uniqueness and finality of the revelation of God in Jesus as the Christ, he never wavered in his recognition that Jews and Christians together worshiped the one God. A Christian mission to the Jews was therefore out of the question.

Today the issue is clearer. While there are close connections between Judaism and Christianity, and somewhat less close relations to Islam, the other monotheistic faith, it is no longer possible to speak of Judaism and Christianity (and Islam) against the pagan world. Our greater knowledge and experience of other forms of religious faith and practice make it impossible for many today to deny that revelatory power, truth, and divine presence are to be found in the other religious communities of earth. The confrontation with this rich pluralism has pressed upon Judaism and Christianity an urgent necessity to affirm the truth and power of their revealed religions without denying truth and power and divine presence to other religious communities. How is that to be done?

That question is not dealt with head on in the essays that Eckardt has brought together, but the lineaments of an answer do appear. The first element is the author's longtime recognition of the fallibility of all human knowledge, reasoning, willing, choosing. The human self is indeed claimed by what I like to speak of as sheer Glory, and that claiming is recognized to be a divine claiming and therefore ultimate. But every affirmation of such Glory is limited, partial, as are cultic acts designed to frame it, depictions in whatever form, and the like. In particular, not Christian Scripture, not Christian cult, not Christian creeds and confessions, not Christian moral codes, and not even the authoritative teaching of the community of faith can be called absolute in the sense that this claiming by Glory is absolute. Persons may of course submit to authority— the authority of Scripture or Church or magisterium as though absolute, but the point still stands that Christian (and Jewish) monotheism insists that the deity is One and One alone. This means that any absolute claim made for Jesus as the Christ has to be made as a claim in the name of the one God. Thus, Christianity has urgent need of the doctrine of the Holy Trinity, in some form or other, if it is to remain faithful to the affirmation of monotheism.

If the Christian community can be content to acknowledge the limitedness of its own knowledge of the one God, allowing for the truth of its revelation without claiming exclusive knowledge and understanding of that revelation, then a believing community can affirm its faith with utter confidence without insisting that it alone is entitled to such utter confidence. We can be absolutists with regard to faith while being relativists with regard to knowledge of the faith.

Such a view is compatible with Roy Eckardt's call for the Christian community to give up its absolutist claims and recognize that there is truth in other religions, and certainly truth in Judaism, the faith of the "elder brother" or "elder sister." Such a view is also compatible with Eckardt's recent reflections on the truth of comedy, the Joke that is Christian faith. For there in particular does he address the limitations of knowledge in the ordinary sense of the term. His remarkably rich study of humor in recent years has amplified his whole outlook on Christian faith, I believe.

On the other hand, this stress upon the comic dimensions of existence does not accord well with the continuing "mischievous" (his word) playing with the notion of the Devil. I find that conception quite unhelpful. Again, monotheism requires that we dispense with devil or angels in any sense other than as creatures of God with certain distinctive functions that differentiate them from human beings. And Eckardt's resort to the Devil to account for certain diabolic features of human life seems to me unnecessary and misleading. He points out that resort to comedy is tricky; so also is resort to mischievousness. Play is fine, but notions of Devil and deviltry are really not at all humorous, and they may not even be instructive in fact.

III

We now come to our last subject—Eckardt's dealing with the resurrection. It is a remarkable thing to see the central place occupied by this Christian theme. Two late forms of an affirmation of the resurrection came to appeal to him, but neither of them has full explanation in the writings here presented. A fuller presentation is found in *Reclaiming the Jesus of History* and in some other writings as well. The two forms of affirming resurrection faith are, first, by reference to the consummation that still awaits, and secondly, by reference to the notion of spirit or Spirit. Both of these points are of value and do offer worthwhile ways of addressing Jesus' resurrection. The second of these clearly rests upon Paul's own speculations as found in I Corinthians 15, and it is akin to notions found within the Dead Sea Scrolls' liturgical and spiritual literature.

The first notion is, in my judgment, the more valuable. The early Christians are confronted by their once-dead master, now raised from death by God. The best way to express the resurrection faith, I believe, is to speak of an experience of the early Christians, an experience that the general resurrection, in which many Jews believed, was already beginning to happen, in that God had raised Jesus from death. Put differently, this meant that these believers were experiencing the consummation of the work of God promised for the Last Days. The consummation of God's purposes and promises was beginning to occur—not all at once, and not all of the things promised by the prophets of Israel. One reality was transpiring, these Christians affirmed, a reality occurring especially in connection with their sacred meals: the one who died faithful to Torah, faithful to the will of God, living in covenant with God as representative of his people Israel, this one had been raised by God. The outcome of such a belief seems to have been largely to confirm the truth of what Jesus taught, to confirm a style of life in which hierarchical distinctions were largely swept away and mutual and selfgiving love loomed large, and to confirm a hope in the nearness of the consummation of all God's purposed deeds for Israel and for the world.

I believe, therefore, that Roy Eckardt's resort to belief in an eschatological resurrection is directly on target. Such an understanding well accords with the best of the Social Gospel teaching of his youth, for that faith in the possibility of building on earth the Kingdom of God itself grew out of a form of Christian eschatology not to be despised, unsatisfactory though it was with its confidence in human social possibilities. As I see it, Christian faith is eschatological faith through and through, just as Israel's prophetic faith was and is. To have confidence in the coming triumph of the divine purpose for the whole of the creation is to live constantly under the judgment of divine righteousness (see Eckardt's book *For Righteousness' Sake*, his favorite work). If God is guiding the world toward a day of consummation marked by peace with righteousness for all, then how severe is the divine wrath against our present world, so sharply at cross purposes with the age that is surely coming.

But to have confidence in this coming consummation is also to have a hope in *God*, not in mortals, that is finally indestructible. It will come to pass that the nations of earth will flow up to Zion, as once the waters of Eden flowed out to water the entire earth, and peace with righteousness will spread, through divine and also through human agency. Moreover, this faith in the coming triumph of God's purposes is a faith potentially uniting Jew and Christian. Both communities are, together, pulled and drawn toward that consummation, lured toward the glory of God's consummating work, entranced by its beauty, deeply touched and satisfied by its righteousness, and confident that God's promises are sure, for God does not lie. Goodness, beauty, and truth all belong together in this eschatological faith.

Wherein do Jewish and Christian eschatological faith differ? Surely, in the extent to which the one or the other community claims that this consummation has already burst in upon the world to claim the people of God and all who will see and hear and respond. Both communities are drawn toward the consummation, the one soberly but still joyously savoring the signs and reality of consummation already claimed in faith while still working and looking, with the other community, toward the awaited consummation.

IV

My closing word must be one of profound gratitude to Roy Eckardt and his colleague in life and in work, Alice L. Eckardt. Roy Eckardt has provided rich fare for his readers once more. I was particularly grateful for the piece on punishment and the beautiful tribute to Reinhold Niebuhr, my teacher too. My opening words raised the question whether such a collection of a writer's essays, re-introduced and re-presented to the public, could fail to suggest unseemly authorial pride. As I look back over the collection, and as I look back over the years of Roy Eckardt's engagement with his subjects, I would say that there is an enormous lot for him to take pleasure in. His has been a fervent and persistent and utterly lucid testimony to the truth and power and splendor of Christian faith. And this testimony has not been at the expense of the testimony borne by others. Rather, it has drawn deeply from Jewish faith and has, I believe, contributed copiously to the life, thought, and faith of many Jews and many Christians. And the contributions continue.

AUTHOR CHRONOLOGY

1918 Born 8 August, Brooklyn, New York, to Anna Fitts Eckardt and Frederick William Eckardt. Brother, Robert F. W. Eckardt (b. 1915)

1934 Graduate, Samuel J. Tilden High School, Brooklyn, New York

1939-1940 President, New York East Conference of Methodist Youth

1942 Brooklyn College, B.A., *magna cum laude* in philosophy

1944 Yale University, M.Div. (originally B.D.)

1944 Ordained clergyperson, United Methodist Church

1944 Married to Alice Eliza Lyons, 2 September. Children: Paula Jean (b. 1948); Stephen Robert (b. 1952)

1946-1947 Assistant professor of philosophy and religion, Hamline University

1947 Columbia University, Ph.D. in philosophy

1947-1950 Assistant professor of religion, Lawrence College (now Lawrence University)

1950-1951 Assistant professor of religion, Duke University

1951-1956 Associate professor of religion and department chairperson, Lehigh University

1955-1956 Fellow, Department of Social Relations, Harvard University (Fund for the Advancement of Education, Ford Foundation)

1955-1956 President, American Academy of Religion (founded in 1909 as National Association of Biblical Instructors; name changed in 1964)

1956-1980 Professor of religion and department chairperson, Lehigh University

1961-1969 Editor-in-chief, *Journal of the American Academy of Religion*

1963 Distinguished Alumnus Award, Brooklyn College

1963-1964 Lilly Endowment Fellow, University of Cambridge (Peterhouse) and Parkes Library

1968-1969 Fellow, National Foundation for Jewish Culture

1969 L.H.D., *honoris causa*, Hebrew Union College-Jewish Institute of Religion

1973 Visiting professor, Department of Jewish Studies, City University of New York

1975-1976 Rockefeller Humanities Fellow, University of Tübingen and The
           Hebrew University of Jerusalem
1979   Special Consultant to The President's Commission on the Holocaust
1980—   Emeritus professor of religion, Lehigh University
1980   Jabotinsky Centennial Medal
1980   Election to Phi Beta Kappa
1980-1981 Fellow, Memorial Foundation for Jewish Culture
1981-1982 Special adviser to chairperson, U.S. Holocaust Memorial Council
1982, 1985 Visiting scholar, Centre for Postgraduate Hebrew Studies at
           University of Oxford
1985   Eternal Flame Award, Anne Frank Institute
1989-1990 Maxwell Fellow in the Study and Teaching of the Holocaust, Centre
           for Postgraduate Hebrew Studies at University of Oxford
1990—   Appointed Senior Associate Fellow, Centre for Postgraduate
           Hebrew Studies at University of Oxford

AUTHOR WRITINGS

The listing that follows is correlated with chapters two-eight of the book. Not included are unpublished materials of the writer. In a number of instances there is joint authorship with Alice L. Eckardt; these instances are indicated in the listing.

1945-1950 (chapter 2) — Early Times

Review of Oswald T. Allis, *Prophecy and the Church*, in *Review of Religion* 10, (1946): 211-212.

"A Theology for the Jewish Question," *Christianity and Society* 11 (1946): 24-27.

Christianity and the Children of Israel (New York: King's Crown Press, Columbia University, 1948).

"The Real Catholic-Protestant Conflict," *Christianity and Society* 13 (1948): 21-23.

Review of Vernon Holloway, *Christians and the World of Nations*, in *Christianity and Society* 13 (1948): 28-29.

"The End of a World and the Beginning of a New One," *Christianity and Crisis* 9 (1949): 35-37.

Review-article of Jean-Paul Sartre, *Anti-Semite and Jew*, in *Review of Religion* 14 (1950): 311-318.

"Attack Upon Religion," *Christianity and Crisis* 10 (1950): 20-22. Based upon a sermon at Lawrence College (now Lawrence University).

"Theological Presuppositions for an Introductory Course in Religion," *The Journal of Bible and Religion* 18 (1950): 172-177.

"Christian Faith and the Jews," *The Journal of Religion* 30 (1950): 235-245.

Review of James Parkes, *Judaism and Christianity*, in *The Journal of Religion* 30 (1950): 272.

Review of Paul Tillich, *The Protestant Era*, in *The Journal of Bible and Religion* 18 (1950): 261-262.

1951-1962 (chapter 3) — Intellectual/Moral Concerns

Review of Morris Goldstein, *Jesus in the Jewish Tradition*, in *Review of Religion* 16 (1951): 90-91.

Review of Max Picard, *The Flight From God*, in *The Journal of Bible and Religion* 20 (1952): 205-206.

Review of Alfred J. Marrow, *Living Without Hate*, in *Jewish Social Studies* 14 (1952): 374-375.

Review of Will Herberg, *Judaism and Modern Man*, in *The Journal of Bible and Religion* 20 (1952): 291-292.

Reviews of Henry E. Kagan, *Changing the Attitude of Christian Toward Jew*, in *Journal of Religion* 32 (1952): 292-293; *Review of Religion* 17 (1953): 203.

Review of Allan D. Galloway, *The Cosmic Christ*, in *The Journal of Bible and Religion* 21 (1953): 39-40.

Review of M. J. Gruesser, *Categorical Valuations of Jews Among Catholic School Children*, in *Jewish Social Studies* 15 (1953): 188-189.

Review of James Parkes, *God at Work*, in *Journal of Religion* 33 (1953): 158.

"The Catholic Dilemma," *The Christian Century* 70 (1953): 713-715.

"Two Marginal Notes on the Prophetic View of History," *Christianity and Society* 18 (1953): 15-19.

Review of Charles H. Patterson, *The Philosophy of the Old Testament*, in *The Christian Scholar* 36 (1953): 228-231.

Review of Roger L. Shinn, *Christianity and the Problem of History*, in *Religion in Life* 22 (1953): 619-621.

"The Christian and Secular Answer to the Dilemma of Freedom and Order," *Christianity and Crisis* 13 (1953): 172-175.

"The Christ Child and Bishop Sheen," *The Christian Century* 71 (1954): 78-80.

Review of Martin Buber, *Good and Evil*, in *The Journal of Bible and Religion* 22 (1954): 46-48.

"Land of Promise and City of God," *Theology Today* 10 (1954): 482-491. Based on a sermon in the Lehigh University Chapel.

"Christian Scholarship and Christian Hope," *The Christian Scholar* 37 (1954): 126-136.

"Racial Prejudice and Discrimination: Civil and Christian Approaches," *Theology Today* 11 (1954): 354-367.

"The New Look in American Piety," *The Christian Century* 71 (1954): 1395-1397; reprinted in *Lehigh Alumni Bulletin* 42 (1955): 7-9; republished in J. Milton Yinger, *Religion, Society and the Individual* (New York: Macmillan, 1957), 408-414; also in Harold E. Fey and Margaret Frakes, eds., *The Christian Century Reader* (New York: Association Press, 1962), 53-58.

Review of Edwin E. Aubrey, *Secularism a Myth,* in *The Journal of Bible and Religion* 23 (1955): 55-56.

Review of Nicolas Berdyaev, *Truth and Revelation,* in *The Journal of Bible and Religion* 23 (1955): 60-62.

"Kenosis 1955" (verse), *The Christian Century* 72 (1955): 267.

"Down with the New Religion," *Youth* (1955): 3-6; reprinted in *Baptist Student* 35 (1956): 18-20, 37.

"Faces" (verse), *The Christian Century* 72 (1955): 752.

"Compassion" (verse), *The Christian Century* 72 (1955): 1328.

Review of James Parkes, *End of An Exile,* in *Jewish Social Studies* 18 (1956): 67.

Review-article (co-author Alexander Miller) on Will Herberg, *Protestant-Catholic-Jew,* in *The Christian Scholar* 39 (1956): 306-311.

"Between Christmas and Good Friday" (verse), *The Christian Century* 74 (1957): 128.

"The Strangeness of Religion in the University Curriculum," *The Journal of Bible and Religion* 25 (1957): 3-12; reprinted (abridged) in *Lehigh Alumni Bulletin* 44 (1957): 8-13.

Review of Hendrik Kraemer, *The Communication of the Christian Faith*, in *The Journal of Bible and Religion* 25 (1957): 264.

Review of W. Norman Pittenger, *Tomorrow's Faith Today,* in *The Journal of Bible and Religion* 25 (1957): 264-265.

Review of Benson Y. Landis, ed., *A Rauschenbusch Reader,* in *The Journal of Bible and Religion* 25 (1957): 344.

Review of Douglas V. Steere, *Work and Contemplation,* in *The Journal of Bible and Religion* 25 (1957): 340-341.

The Surge of Piety in America: An Appraisal (New York: Association Press, 1958).

Review of F. Ernest Johnson, ed., *Patterns of Faith in America Today,* in *The Journal of Bible and Religion* 26 (1958): 163-164.

"The Pulsation of Religion," *The Christian Century* 75 (1958): 1458-1460.

Review of Isaac Husik, *A History of Mediaeval Jewish Philosophy,* in *The Journal of Bible and Religion* 27 (1959): 80.

"Brotherhood" (sermon), *The Pulpit* 30 (1959): 9-11. Originally delivered in Lehigh University Chapel.

Review of Walter G. Muelder, *Foundations of the Responsible Society,* in *The Christian Century* 76 (1959): 423.

"Pre-Seminary Preparation and Study in Religion" (A.R.E. and others), *The Journal of Bible and Religion* 27 (1959): 139-142; reprinted in *JBR* 34 (1966): 166-170.

"The Conquest of Futility" (sermon), *Pulpit Digest* 39 (1959): 55-59.

"The Rise and Fall of Popular Religion," *Religion in Life* 28 (1959): 587-594.

Review of William G. McLoughlin, Jr., *Modern Revivalism,* in *Theology Today* 16 (1959): 409-411.

"The Ethical Motivation of the Christian," *Theology and Life* 3 (1960): 32-43.

Review of Richard Kroner, *Speculation and Revelation in the Age* of Christian Philosophy, in *The Journal of Bible and Religion* 28 (1960): 363-365.

"When Is Faith Not Faith?," *The Christian Century* 77 (1960): 1050-1052.

Review of Jakob Jocz, *A Theology of Election,* in *Judaism* 9 (1960): 376-378.

"Science and Man's Uniqueness" (editorial), *The Journal of Bible and Religion* 29 (1961): 1-2.

Review of Morris Keaton, *Values Men Live By,* in *The Journal of Bible and Religion* 29 (1961): 80-83.

"The Contribution of *Nomothesis* in the Science of Man," *American Scientist* 49 (1961): 76-87.

"Our Public Image" (editorial), *The Journal of Bible and Religion* 29 (1961): 91-92.

"The Mystery of the Jews' Rejection of Christ," *Theology Today* 18 (1961): 51-59.

"The End of the Science-Religion Dialogue" (editorial), *The Journal of Bible and Religion* 29 (1961): 191-192.

Review of Walter Kloetzli, *The City Church—Death or Renewal* in *The Christian Century* 78 (1961): 853.

"A Note on Theological Procedure," *The Journal of Bible and Religion* 29 (1961): 313-316.

"The Religious Possibility and the Generic Fallacy" (editorial), *The Journal of Bible and Religion* 30 (1962): 91-92.

"In Defense of Religion in General" (editorial), *The Journal of Bible and Religion* 30 (1962): 185-186.

Review of Émile Durkheim, *The Elementary Forms of the Religious Life,* and of William James, *The Varieties of Religious Experience*, in *The Journal of Bible and Religion* 30 (1962): 262.

"The Theology of Antisemitism," *Religion in Life* 31 (1962): 552-562.

"Ventures of the Post-Freudian Conscience," review-article on O. Hobart Mowrer, *The Crisis in Psychiatry and Religion*; Simon Doniger, ed., *The Nature of Man in Theological and Psychological Perspective*; and W. Earl Biddle, *Integration of Religion and Psychiatry,* in *The Journal of Bible and Religion* 30 (1962): 302-307.

"Religion, Faith and the Future," *Judaism* 11 (1962): 56-62.

1963-1967 (chapter 4) — Return to the Covenant

"'Theology' versus 'Religion'" (editorial), *The Journal of Bible and Religion* 31 (1963): 95-97.

Review of Arthur A. Cohen, *The Natural and the Supernatural Jew,* in *The Journal of Bible and Religion* 31 (1963): 240-242.

Review of David O. Moberg, *The Church as a Social Institution,* in *The Journal of Bible and Religion* 31 (1963): 267-268.

"The Protestant Christian and the Jews, " *The Ecumenist* 1 (1963): 96-98; reprinted in Gregory Baum, ed., *Ecumenical Theology Today* (Glen Rock, N.J.: Paulist, 1964), 237-244.

"Aspects of Contemporary American Religious Life," *Common Ground* (London) 18 (1964): 15-17.

Review of John M. Oesterreicher, ed., *The Bridge,* Vol. IV, in *Jewish Social Studies* 26 (1964): 248-250.

"Anti-Semitism," in George A. F. Knight, ed., *Jews and Christians: Preparation for Dialogue* (Philadelphia: Westminster, 1965), 151-164.

"An Identity Explored" (editorial), *The Journal of Bible and Religion* 33 (1965): 3-4.

"On the Reported Death of Deicide" (verse), *The Christian Century* 82 (1965): 199.

"The Jewish-Christian Dialogue: Recent Christian Efforts in Europe," *Conservative Judaism* 19 (1965): 12-21.

"Pre-Seminary Education and the Undergraduate Department of Religion," *Theological Education* 1 (1965): 149-153.

"Can There Be a Jewish-Christian Relationship?," *The Journal of Bible and Religion* 33 (1965): 122-130; reprinted in *Christian Friends* 22 (1965): 7-14.

"The Jewish-Christian *Gegenüber:* Some Recent Christian Efforts in Europe," *The Journal of Bible and Religion* 33 (1965): 149-155.

"We Pay Our Own Way" (editorial), *The Journal of Bible and Religion* 33 (1965): 211-212.

"The Irony of 'JBR'" (editorial), *The Journal of Bible and Religion* 33 (1965): 291.

"On Independence in Undergraduate Study" (editorial), *The Journal of Bible and Religion* 33 (1965): 291-292.

"Morphological Reflections" (editorial), *The Journal of Bible and Religion* 34 (1966): 3.

Review of Ernest B. Koenker, *Secular Salvations,* in *The Christian Century* 83 (1966): 210.

"End to the Christian-Jewish Dialogue," *The Christian Century* 83 (1966): 360-363; 393-395; part two reprinted in *Dimension* 1 (1967): 36-38.

"The Lilly Study" (editorial), *The Journal of Bible and Religion* 34 (1966): 95-96.

"Is the Study of Religion Peculiar?" (editorial), *The Journal of Bible and Religion* 34 (1966): 96-97.

"Pre-Seminary Education and the Study of Religion" (bibliography), *The Journal of Bible and Religion* 34 (1966): 174-175.

Review of Edward H. Flannery, *The Anguish of the Jews,* in *Jewish Social Studies* 18 (1966): 172-174.

"Is There Anything Religious in Religion?" (editorial), *The Journal of Bible and Religion* 34 (1966): 303.

Elder and Younger Brothers: The Encounter of Jews and Christians (New York: Charles Scribner's Sons, 1967; paperbound edition, New York: Schocken Books, 1973).

"Toward a Theology for the Christian-Jewish Encounter," in Gerald H. Anderson, ed., *Christian Mission in Theological Perspective: An Inquiry By Methodists* (New York: Abingdon, 1967), 125-146.

Review of Jakob Jocz, *Christians and Jews*, in *The Christian Century* 84 (1967): 84.

Review of Augustin Cardinal Bea, *The Church and the Jewish People*, in *Midstream* 13 (1967): 63-66.

"If a Man Die, Is This a Death of God?," *The Pulpit* 38 (1967): 4-6. Sermon delivered at Pennsylvania State University.

Review of Heinz David Leuner, *When Compassion Was a Crime*, in *The Christian Century* 84 (1967): 408.

"Christian Guilt," *Christian News From Israel* (Jerusalem) 13 (1967): 44-48.

"Again, Silence in the Churches," (co-author Alice L. Eckardt), *The Christian Century* 84 (1967): 970-973; 992-995; part one reprinted in *National Jewish Monthly* (Oct. 1967), 11-12, 44; part two reprinted in *Midstream* 13 (1967): 27-32, and in Spanish under title "Silencio en las Iglesias," *Maj'Shavot* (Buenos Aires) 7 (1968): 5-11.

1968-1974 (chapter 5) —
Ventures Theological-Political-Ethical

The Theologian at Work: A Common Search for Understanding (editor) (New York: Harper & Row, 1968; London: SCM, 1968).

Review of Ben Zion Bokser, *Judaism and the Christian Predicament*, in *Journal of Religion* 48 (1968): 107.

"Christians and Jews: Disrupted Dialogue," *Lehigh Alumni Bulletin* 55 (1968): 19-22.

"Notes on the Protestant Bible," *Sidic* (Rome) (Feb. 1968): 6-7.

"Eretz Israel: A Christian's Affirmation," *Midstream* 14 (1968): 9-12.

"What Is Truth?," review-article on Jean Daniélou and André Chouraqui, *The Jews*; and Ben Zion Bokser, *Judaism and the Christian Predicament*, in *The Jewish Spectator* 33 (1968): 13-17.

"Die gegenwärtige Situation der christlich-jüdischen Begegnung in Nord-Amerika," *Emuna* (Cologne) 3 (1968): 39-49; 121-130.

"The Jewish-Christian Encounter: Six Guidelines for a New Relationship," *Central Conference of American Rabbis Journal* 15 (1968): 22-30. Revision of Goldman Lecture, Northwestern University.

Review of James Daane, *The Anatomy of Anti-Semitism*, in *Jewish Social Studies* 30 (1968): 207.

Introduction to Arnold Foster, *Report From Israel* (New York: Anti-Defamation League, 1969), v-vi.

"The Reaction of the Churches," in *The Anatomy of Peace in the Middle East*, Proceedings of the Annual Conference of the American Academic Association for Peace in the Middle East (New York, 1969), 69-91.

"The Tragic Unity of Enemies: A Report from the Middle East," (co-author Alice L. Eckardt), *The Christian Century* 86 (1969): 73-76.

Review of Hannah Vogt, *The Jews: A Chronicle for Christian Conscience*, in *Jewish Social Studies* 31 (1969): 51-52.

Review of Abraham Joshua Heschel, *Israel: An Echo of Eternity*, in *Conservative Judaism* 23 (1969): 70-73.

Encounter With Israel: A Challenge to Conscience (co-author Alice L. Eckardt) (New York: Association Press, 1970).

"Rosenzweig Despite Rosenstock," review-article on E. Rosenstock-Huessy, ed., *Judaism Despite Christianity*, in *The Jewish Spectator* 35 (1970): 18-21.

Review of Michael Selzer, *Zionism Reconsidered*, in *The Christian Century* 87 (1970): 871-872.

Review of Johan M. Snoek, *The Grey Book*, in *Journal of Ecumenical Studies* 7 (1970): 815-816.

Review of Milton Rokeach, *Beliefs, Attitudes and Values*, in *Journal for the Scientific Study of Religion* 9 (1970): 268-269.

"Jerusalem's History," *The American Hebrew Christian* 55 (1970): 16. Reprint of letter in *The New York Times*.

"The Claims of the Palestinian Arabs" (co-author Alice L. Eckardt), *American Zionist* 61 (1970): 7-9. Reprint from book *Encounter With Israel*, 236-240.

Review of Alan T. Davies, *Anti-Semitism and the Christian Mind*, in *Journal of the American Academy of Religion* 38 (1970): 439-441.

Christianity in Israel (editor) (New York: American Academic Association for Peace in the Middle East, 1971).

"The Crisis in Punishment," in Harold H. Hart, ed., *Punishment* (New York: Hart Publishing Co., 1971), 164-189.

Review of Friedrich Heer, *God's First Love*, in *Commentary* 51 (1971): 91-98.

"The Nemesis of Christian Antisemitism," *Journal of Church and State* 13 (1971) 227-244; reprinted in James E. Wood, ed., *Jewish-Christian Relations in Today's World* (Waco: Baylor University Press, 1971), 45-62; also in Wood, ed., *Readings on Church and State* (Waco: Baylor University Press, 1989), 265-280.

"Toward An Authentic Jewish-Christian Relationship," *Journal of Church and State* 13 (1971): 271-282; reprinted in first Wood volume (see previous entry), 93-104; also reprinted in Jack Nusan Porter, ed., *The Sociology of American Jews* (Washington: University Press of America, 1978), 230-241.

"A Tribute to Reinhold Niebuhr (1892-1971)," *Midstream* 17 (1971): 11-18.

"Anti-Israelism, Anti-Semitism and the Quakers," *Christianity and Crisis* 31 (1971): 180-186; reprinted in *Christian Attitudes on Jews and Judaism* (London) 21 (1971): 8-11. Had also been published in *CCI Notebook* 3 (1971): 1-4, under title "Anti-Israelism, Anti-Semitism, and the Friends."

Review of John M. Oesterreicher, ed., *The Bridge*, Vol. V, in *Journal of Ecumenical Studies* 8 (1971): 885-887.

Review of Carlo Falconi, *The Silence of Pius XII*, in *Judaism* 20 (1971): 502-505.

Review of Saul Friedländer, *Kurt Gerstein: The Ambiguity of Good*, in *Women's American ORT Reporter* 22 (1971): 7, 14.

"More on the Middle East," *Christianity and Crisis* 31 (1971): 206-208.

"The Fantasy of Reconciliation in the Middle East," *The Christian Century* 88 (1971): 1198-1202.

"Theological Approaches to Anti-Semitism," *Jewish Social Studies* 33 (1971): 272-284.

"Dr. Eckardt Replies," *Christianity and Crisis* 31 (1972): 297-298.

"Politics, Morals and the Question of Israel," *Congress Bi-Weekly* 39 (1972): 10-13.

"On History's Greatest Perversion of Justice," review-article on Haim Cohn, *The Trial and Death of Jesus*, in *Midstream* 18 (1972): 72-80.

"The Holocaust and the Church," *Lehigh Research Review* 3 (1972): 5-6.

"Death in the Judaic and Christian Traditions," *Social Research* 39 (1972): 489-514; reprinted in Arien Mack, ed., *Death in American Experience* (New York: Schocken Books, 1973), 123-148.

"Christian Perspectives on Israel," *Midstream* 18 (1972): 40-50.

Review of Fred Gladstone Bratton, *The Crime of Christendom*, in *Journal of Church and State* 14 (1972): 128-131.

"Christendom as a Source of European Nihilism," in Abraham I. Katsh, *Colloquium on the Holocaust* (Philadelphia: Dropsie University-Villanova University, 1973), 19-30.

"De gevaren van Biblicistisch-moralistisch politiek denken: Commentaar op de Handreiking voor ein theologische bezinning," *In de Waagschaal* (Utrecht) 7 (1973): 17-21.

"A Response to Rabbi Olan," *Religion in Life* 42 (1973): 401-412.

Your People, My People: The Meeting of Jews and Christians (New York: Quadrangle/New York Times Book Co., 1974).

"Theological Implications of the State of Israel: The Protestant View," in *1974 Yearbook of the Encyclopaedia Judaica* (Jerusalem: Keter Publishing House, 1974), 158-166.

"A Political Approach to the Middle East Conflict," *Friday Forum* (supplement to *Jewish Exponent*) 23 (1974): 57, 64.

"The Devil and Yom Kippur," *Midstream* 20 (1974): 67-75; reprinted in Frank Ephraim Talmage, ed., *Disputation and Dialogue* (New York: Ktav, 1975), 229-239.

"Is the Holocaust Unique?," *Worldview* 17 (1974): 31-35.

"The Jewish Right to Life" (co-author Alice L. Eckardt), review-article on Hertzel Fishman, *American Protestantism and a Jewish State*, in *The Jewish Spectator* 39 (Fall 1974): 31-34.

"The Closed Doors" (co-author Alice L. Eckardt), review-article on Saul S. Friedman, *No Haven For the Oppressed*, in *The Jewish Spectator* 39 (Winter 1974): 31-33.

1975-1982 (chapter 6) — Shoah

Review of Arnold Forster and Benjamin R. Epstein, *The New Anti-Semitism*, in *Theology Today* 31 (1975): 373-377.

"How German Thinkers View the Holocaust" (co-author Alice L. Eckardt), *The Christian Century* 93 (1976): 249-252; reprinted in Harry James Cargas, ed., *When God and Man Failed: Non-Jewish Views of the Holocaust* (New York: Macmillan, 1981), 202-211.

"Consider the Animals," *Reflection* (Yale University Divinity School), 73 (1976): 13-14.

"Christentum und Judentum: Die theologische und moralische Problematik der Vernichtung des europäischen Judentums" (co-author Alice L. Eckardt), *Evangelische Theologie* (Munich) 36 (1976): 406-426; English-language version "The Theological and Moral Implications of the Holocaust," *Christian Attitudes on Jews and Judaism* (London) 52 (Feb. 1977): 1-7; 53 (April 1977): 7-12.

"Jürgen Moltmann, the Jewish People, and the Holocaust, " *Journal of the American Academy of Religion* 44 (1976): 675-691.

"Covenant-Resurrection-Holocaust," in Josephine Knopp, ed., *Humanizing America: A Post-Holocaust Imperative*. Proceedings of the 2nd Philadelphia Conference on the Holocaust (Feb. 16-18, 1977): 39-45.

Review of Irving Howe, *World of Our Fathers*, in *Theology Today* 34 (1977): 228-229.

"The Shadow of the Death Camps," *Theology Today* 34 (1977): 285-290.

"The Recantation of the Covenant?," in Alvin H. Rosenfeld and Irving Greenberg, eds., *Confronting the Holocaust: The Impact of Elie Wiesel* (Bloomington: Indiana University Press, 1978), 159-168.

"Remembering the Holocaust: A Psycho-Moral Question," *Martyrdom and Resistance* 4 (1978); 4, 9.

"Studying the Holocaust's Impact Today: Some Dilemmas of Language and Method" (co-author Alice L. Eckardt), *Judaism* 27 (1978): 222-232; reprinted in Alan Rosenberg and Gerald E. Myers, eds., *Echoes From the Holocaust: Philosophical Reflections on a Dark Time* (Philadelphia: Temple University Press, 1988), 432-442.

"Christian Responses to the *Endlösung*," *Religion in Life* 47 (1978): 33-45.

"The Achievements and Trials of Interfaith," in Symposium on "Interfaith at Fifty" (co-author Alice L. Eckardt), *Judaism* 27 (1978): 318-323.

"Can Christians Confront the Holocaust?," *Newsletter, National Jewish Conference Center* 2 (1978): 6-7.

Review of Charlotte Klein, *Anti-Judaism in Christian Theology*, in *Religion in Life* 47 (1978): 515-516.

"Christians and Jews: Along a Theological Frontier," *Encounter* 40 (1979): 89-127. Hugh Th. Miller Lectures, Christian Theological Seminary, Indianapolis. First half of article reprinted in Richard W. Rousseau, ed., *Christianity and Judaism: The Deepening Dialogue* (Montrose, Pa.: Ridge Row Press, 1983), 27-48.

"Panel Response," on "The Role of Religion in Promoting Peace in the Middle East," *The Dialogue* (National Conference of Christians and Jews) (1979): 2-3.

"Toward A Secular Theology of Israel," *Religion in Life* 48 (1979): 462-473; reprinted in *Christian Jewish Relations* (London) 72 (1980): 8-20.

Review of Roland B. Gittelsohn, *The Modern Meaning of Judaism,* in *Religion in Life* 48 (1979): 509-510.

"Contemporary Christian Theology and a Protestant Witness for the *Shoah*," *Shoah* 2 (1980): 1-13; substantially reproduced in *Union Seminary Quarterly Review* 38 (1983): 139-145.

"The Holocaust and the Enigma of Uniqueness: A Philosophic Effort at Practical Clarification" (co-author Alice L. Eckardt), *Annals of the American Academy of Political and Social Science* 450 (1980): 165-178.

Review of Paul M. van Buren, *Discerning the Way,* in *The Christian Century* 97 (1980): 922-924.

"Recent Literature in Christian-Jewish Relations," *Jewish Book Annual* 38 (1980-1981): 47-61; also in *Journal of the American Academy of Religion* 49 (1981): 99-111.

"Travail of A Presidential Commission: Confronting the Enigma of the Holocaust" (co-author Alice L. Eckardt), *Encounter* 42 (1981): 103-114.

Review of Clemens Thoma, *A Christian Theology of Judaism,* in *Theology Today* 38 (1981): 109-110.

Contribution to "Symposium: Germans and Jews Today," in *Midstream* 27 (1981): 27-29.

Review of Arthur A. Cohen, *The Tremendum,* in *The Christian Century* 98 (1981): 1000-1001.

Review of Eugene B. Borowitz, *Contemporary Christologies: A Jewish Response,* in *The Christian Century* 98 (1981): 1136-1138.

Long Night's Journey Into Day: Life and Faith After the Holocaust (co-author Alice L. Eckardt) (Detroit: Wayne State University Press, 1982). For information on revised edition, see below under 1988.

"After the Holocaust: Some Christian Considerations" (co-author Alice L. Eckardt), in Norma H. Thompson and Bruce K. Cole, eds., *The Future of Jewish-Christian Relations* (Schenectady: Character Research Press, 1982), 111-125.

"In Memoriam James Parkes 1896-1981," *Sidic* (Rome) 15 (1982): 21-24; also in *Journal of Ecumenical Studies* 19 (1982): 97-104; *Christian Jewish Relations* (London) 15 (1982): 44-52; and as appendix to James Parkes, *End of An Exile* (Marblehead, Mass.: Micah Publications, 1982), 260-267.

"*HaShoah* as Christian Revolution: Toward the Liberation of the Divine Righteousness," *Quarterly Review* 2 (1982): 52-67.

1983-1986 (chapter 7) — A Continuing Encounter

Review of Patricia Treece, *A Man for Others: Maximilian Kolbe, Saint of Auschwitz, in the Words of Those Who Knew Him,* in *Theology Today* 40 (1983): 249.

"The Holocaust and (*Kiveyachol*) the Liberation of the Divine Righteousness," in Israel W. Charny, ed., *Toward the Understanding and Prevention of Genocide: Proceedings of the International Conference on the Holocaust and Genocide, 1982,* in Tel Aviv (Boulder/London: Westview Press, 1984), 255-264.

"Was the Holocaust Unique?," contribution to a symposium of responses to Pierre Papazian (co-author Alice L. Eckardt), *Midstream* 30 (1984): 20-21.

"Anti-Semitism is the Heart," *Theology Today* 41 (1984): 301-308; also in *Christian Jewish Relations* (London) 17 (1984): 43-51.

Consulting editor, special number on "Focus on Jewish-Christian Relations," *Quarterly Review* 4 (1984).

Editorial, "Requiem for a Dream," *The Christian Century* 101 (1984): 1140.

Jews and Christians: The Contemporary Meeting (Bloomington: Indiana University Press, 1986).

"The Christian World Goes to Bitburg," in Geoffrey H. Hartman, ed., *Bitburg in Moral and Political Perspective* (Bloomington: Indiana University Press,

1986), 80-89; also published as an appendix to *Long Night's Journey Into Day*, rev. ed.

Foreword to Stuart E. Rosenberg, *The Christian Problem: A Jewish View* (New York: Hippocrene Books, 1986).

"Is There a Way Out of the Christian Crime? The Philosophic Question of the Holocaust," *Holocaust and Genocide Studies* (Oxford) 1 (1986): 121-126.

"Christians, Jews, and the Women's Movement," *Christian Jewish Relations* (London) 19 (1986): 13-22.

"An American Looks at *Kairos*," *Theology Today* 43 (1986): 217-228.

"Who Killed Jesus and Why?," contribution to a symposium in *Manna* (London): 12 (1986): 5.

1987ff. (chapter 8) — Later Times

For Righteousness' Sake: Contemporary Moral Philosophies (Bloomington: Indiana University Press, 1987).

"One *Ruse de Guerre* on the Devil," in Richard Libowitz, ed., *Faith and Freedom: A Tribute to Franklin H. Littell* (Oxford: Pergamon Press, 1987), 17-23.

"Post-Holocaust Theology and the Christian-Jewish Dialogue," lecture in booklet form (Storrs, Conn.: Center for Judaic Studies and Contemporary Jewish Life, University of Connecticut, 1987).

"Hilberg's Silence: Replies to Jeffrey Moussaieff Masson," contribution to a symposium of responses (co-author Alice L. Eckardt), *Midstream* 33 (1987): 50-51.

Review of Jacob Neusner, *Death and Rebirth of Judaism,* in *The Christian Century* 104 (1987): 666-667.

Review of Ilya Levkov, ed., *Bitburg and Beyond: Encounters in American, German and Jewish History,* in *The Christian Century* 104 (1987): 1008-1009.

"Beyond Zero-Sum Thinking in the Arab-Israeli Struggle," *The Christian Century* 104 (1987): 1143-1145; also in *Christian Jewish Relations* (London) 21 (Spring 1988): 52-59.

Long Night's Journey Into Day: A Revised Retrospective on the Holocaust (co-author Alice L. Eckardt) (Detroit: Wayne State University Press; Oxford:

Pergamon Press, 1988). Revised and expanded by Alice L. Eckardt from original edition of 1982.

Black-Woman-Jew: Three Wars for Human Liberation (Bloomington: Indiana University Press, 1989).

"For the Sake of Rachel and For the Sake of Sarah," in *Remembering for the Future: Working Papers and Addenda*, Vol. III: "The Impact of the Holocaust and Genocide on Jews and Christians" (Oxford: Pergamon Press, 1989), 3074-3083. Plenary address before the conference, "Remembering for the Future," Oxford UK, 10-13 July 1988.

"Salient Christian-Jewish Issues of Today: A Christian Exploration," in James H. Charlesworth, ed., *Jews and Christians: Exploring the Past, Present, and Future* (New York: Crossroad, 1990), 151-177.

"Comedy Versus Tragedy: Post-Shoah Reflections" (Oxford: Centre for Postgraduate Hebrew Studies, 1990) (booklet). First Maxwell Lecture on the Study and Teaching of the Holocaust, 24 April 1990.

"A Reply to Michael McGarry" (co-author Alice L. Eckardt), *American Journal of Theology & Philosophy* 11 (1990): 153-155.

"Why Do the Ruethers Imagine a Vain Thing?: Personal Rejoinders" (co-author Alice L. Eckardt), *Continuum* 1 (1990): 128-130.

"'Why Do You Search Among the Dead?,'" *Encounter* 51 (1990): 1-17; also published under the title "The *Shoah* and the Affirmation of the Resurrection of Jesus: A Revisionist Marginal Note," in Alan A. Berger, ed., *Bearing Witness to the Holocaust 1939-1989* (Lewiston, NY: Edwin Mellen Press, 1991), 313-331.

"Women and Jesus," *Bridges: An Interdisciplinary Journal of Theology, Philosophy, History, and Science* 3, 1/2 (1991): 33-39.

Reclaiming the Jesus of History: Christology Today (Minneapolis: Fortress Press, 1992).

Sitting in the Earth and Laughing: A Handbook of Humor (New Brunswick-London: Transaction Publishers, Rutgers-The State University of New Jersey, 1992).

"Divine Incongruity: Comedy and Tragedy in a Post-Holocaust World," *Theology Today* 48 (1992): 399-412.

"Is There a Christian Laughter?," *Encounter* 53 (1992): 109-117.

"Is There a Mission to Jews?," in Clark M. Williamson, ed., *A Mutual Witness: Toward Critical Solidarity Between Jews and Christians* (St. Louis: Chalice Press, 1992), 65-82.

Review of David Novak, *Jewish-Christian Dialogue: A Jewish Justification,* in *Studies in Contemporary Jewry* (Oxford-Jerusalem) 8 (1992): 342-344.

"The Heirs of Itzhak," *Society* 29, 4 (1992): 34-42. Republication of *Sitting in the Earth and Laughing,* chapter 11.

"The Place of the Jewish State in Christian-Jewish Relations" (co-author Alice L. Eckardt), *European Judaism* (London) 25 (Spring 1992): 3-14.

Collecting Myself: A Writer's Retrospective, ed. Alice L. Eckardt with Norman Girardot and Harriet Parmet; Afterwords by Michael L. Morgan, Joann Spillman, Walter Harrelson (Atlanta: Scholars Press, 1993).

"The Content of Jewish Education and Its Responsibility Within the Jewish-Christian Encounter" (co-author Alice L. Eckardt), in Glenda Abramson, ed., *The Jewish Academy* (Reading, U.K.: Gordon and Breach Science Publishers/Harwood Academic Publishers, 1993).

No Longer Aliens, No Longer Strangers: Christian Faith and Ethics for Today (forthcoming).

"Jews, Christians, and the Comic Vision: A Few Midrashim on the Philosophy of Emil L. Fackenheim" (forthcoming).

How To Tell God From the Devil: On the Way to Comedy (forthcoming).

On the Way to Death: Essays Toward a Comic Vision (forthcoming).

"God-Language, Victorian Silences, and a Comic Vision" (forthcoming).

"From Shadow to Shekinah: A Comic Journey" (forthcoming).

"The Ugliest Customer: A Life History of Death" (forthcoming).

Index

486

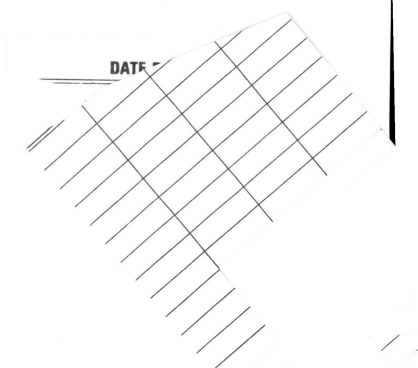

DATE

DEMCO 38-297